CW01022528

English Hospitals 1660–1948

The Middlesex Hospital, London, detail of main elevation. The photograph was taken not long after the completion of the new main hospital block in 1935.
[Photograph in an album held in the Middlesex Hospital Archives]

ROYAL COMMISSION ON THE HISTORICAL MONUMENTS OF ENGLAND

English Hospitals 1660–1948

A Survey of their Architecture and Design

edited by

Harriet Richardson

contributors

Ian Goodall

Kathryn Morrison

Ian Pattison

Harriet Richardson

Robert Taylor

Colin Thom

ROYAL COMMISSION ON THE HISTORICAL MONUMENTS OF ENGLAND

Published by the Royal Commission on the Historical Monuments of
England at the National Monuments Record Centre, Kemble Drive,
Swindon SN2 2GZ

© Crown copyright 1998

Applications for reproduction should be made to the RCHME

First published 1998

ISBN 1 873592 29 9

British Library Cataloguing in Publication Data
A CIP catalogue record for this book is available from the British Library

All rights reserved
No part of this publication may be reproduced or transmitted in any form
or by any means, electronic or mechanical, including photocopying,
recording or any information storage and retrieval system, without
permission in writing from the publisher.

Designed by Chuck Goodwin, 27 Artesian Road, London W2 5DA

Printed in Great Britain by BPC Wheatons Ltd, Exeter

Contents

Commissioners

CHAIRMAN

The Right Honourable Lord Faringdon

VICE CHAIRMAN

Anne Riches

Peter Addyman

Malcolm Airs

Amanda Arrowsmith

Richard Bradley

Eric Fernie CBE

Michael Fulford

Richard Gem

Derek Keene

Trevor Longman

Helen Maclagan

Marilyn Palmer

Wendy Sudbury

Robert Yorke

SECRETARY

Tom Hassall

Chairman's Foreword

In the last ten years the National Health Service has witnessed profound changes in medical practice and health-care policy. As a result, England's vast stock of largely 19th-century hospitals is becoming redundant and an entire building type is beginning to disappear from the landscape. As the inevitable process of closure and redevelopment gathered momentum throughout the country, the Royal Commission on the Historical Monuments of England (RCHME) responded to the threat by conducting a national survey of English hospitals of the period 1660–1948. The methodology and aims of this project are described in the Introduction.

This book draws on the results of the survey and presents an analysis of the evolution of English hospital design during a period of enormous change in English society and of important discoveries and developments in medical science. Over the last two hundred years hospitals have evolved from a handful of infirmaries which served a minority of the population into a network of institutions which are central to the health and welfare of the entire country. Yet, for buildings which occupy such an important place at the very heart of our society, they remain little understood, and much of their story endures only in the surviving fabric. It is intended that this study, and the archive on which it is based, will help to enhance the understanding of hospital architecture. Such an understanding is particularly important at a time of major change, providing the basis for discussions and decisions on the future of the buildings, and assisting those addressing this complex subject in the future.

Commissioners are grateful to all the administrators, staff and, in some cases, new owners, of the hospitals visited for allowing access to the buildings in their care. Commissioners also wish to acknowledge the work of all the RCHME staff involved in the survey, especially Ian Goodall, Kathryn Morrison, Ian Pattison, Harriet Richardson, Robert Taylor and Colin Thom, who investigated the buildings and contributed the text for this volume. Particular tribute should be paid here to the late David Black, who was responsible for the original project design and the inception of the recording programme. The many other staff who assisted with the project and the production of this book are credited in the Acknowledgements.

FARINGDON

Acknowledgements

A national study of hospitals was largely the idea of David Black, the former Head of Architectural Survey within the Royal Commission (RCHME), who, sadly, died in April 1991 before work was fully under way. Commissioners maintained a keen interest in the project, but particular thanks are due to Malcolm Airs, Derek Keene and Ann Riches, who read the complete text and made valuable comments. The help of John Bold, John Greenacombe, Kate Owen, Stephen Porter, Hugh Richmond, Robin Taylor and Robin Thornes, who also read and commented upon the text, is greatly appreciated. Thanks are also due to Jacqueline Hall, who assisted with documentary research and some fieldwork, Sid Barker, Alun Bull, Steve Cole, Derek Kendall, Pat Payne, Tony Perry, Mike Hesketh-Roberts, Bob Skingle, Dank Silva and Peter Williams, who took the archive and publication photographs, Roger Featherstone, who supervised aerial photography, and Tony Berry and Nick Hammond, who prepared the survey drawings for the archive and publication. Davina Turner provided clerical support and assisted with editing the text, and Simon Taylor assisted with editing the gazetteer. Advice on editorial, design and publication issues was provided by Kate Owen, Robin Taylor and Diane Williams. Susie Whimster copy-edited the text and the index was compiled by Ann Hudson.

Many thanks are due to the administrators and staff at all the hospitals visited and recorded by RCHME staff. Buildings formerly used as hospitals were also visited, and the owners and occupiers of these properties deserve thanks for their co-operation.

Documentary research for the project was facilitated by the assistance the RCHME received from the staff of record offices and libraries throughout England, in particular the Wellcome Institute for the History of Medicine, the Public Record Office, the Greater London Record Office (now London Metropolitan Archives), Cambridge University Library, Cambridge University School of Architecture and The King's Manor, York. Individual historians and scholars very generously made their knowledge and experience available, including David Brady, Elain Harwood, M Emrys-Roberts and Jeremy Taylor. Thanks are also due to Mr and Mrs P Clifford who helped with fieldwork in Devon.

Illustration Credits

Unless otherwise specified below, illustrations are the copyright of the RCHME. The negative numbers are given in brackets at the end of the captions to assist reference and the ordering of prints from the National Monuments Record.

The RCHME gratefully acknowledges permission from the following institutions and individuals to reproduce illustrations:

James Bettley: Fig 118; Blackburn, Hyndburn and Ribble Valley Health Care NHS Trust: Fig 22; British Library: Figs 5, 160, 161 163; British Architectural Library/Royal Institute of British Architects: Fig 32; the Duke of Buccleuch and Queensberry: Fig 144; the Syndics of Cambridge University Library: Figs 52, 53, 54, 75; Elizabeth Garrett Anderson Hospital, UCLH NHS Trust: Figs 106, 108; Gloucestershire Record Office: Fig 18; Greater London Record Office (now London Metropolitan Archives): Figs 138, 139, 145, 174; Guildhall Library, Corporation of London: Fig 134; G G Halliday: Fig 17; the Trustees of the Imperial War Museum: Fig 101; Lancashire County Library, Burnley Division: Fig 7; Middlesex Hospital: frontispiece, Fig 33; copyright J Millar: Fig 73; Rochester upon Medway Studies Centre: Fig 84; Royal National Hospital for Rheumatic Diseases, Bath (gift of the late Dr G D Kersley): Fig 123; Archives Department, St Bartholomew's Hospital, The Royal Hospitals NHS Trust: Fig 13; University of St Andrews Library: Fig 165; Wellcome Institute Library, London: Figs 1, 2, 4, 10, 11, 12, 100, 104, 125, 156, 157, 183; Westminster Archives Centre: Fig 51; Yorkshire Regional Health Authority: Fig 70.

Every effort has been made to trace copyright holders; the RCHME wishes to apologise to any who may have been inadvertently omitted from the above list.

Introduction

This study is based on a survey of English hospitals carried out by RCHME staff between 1991 and 1994. The survey was prompted by recent changes in the pattern of health-care delivery by the health service and the consequent closure of many hospital buildings, and by the need to understand more about this substantial but little-studied building type.

The project set out to create a representative archive of all types of purpose-built hospitals of the period 1660–1948, that is from the earliest purpose-built post-medieval hospital in England, Bethlem Hospital in London, to the inauguration of the National Health Service. It covered the entire range of hospital types: general hospitals, mental hospitals, isolation hospitals, and those devoted to specific diseases. Hospitals attached to workhouses were also included because they served the community and often became general hospitals, but those attached to institutions such as schools and orphanages had a limited range of functions and were excluded. The hospital buildings of the armed forces were included because they formed a substantial and readily identifiable group of buildings that was at risk.

Fieldwork was undertaken by three teams of two investigators based at the RCHME offices at York, Cambridge and London. Each site has been entered on to a database, and a file created which generally contains a brief report, Ordnance Survey maps, available documentation (including information from *The Builder*, *Building News*, and Kelly's *Directories*), and 35mm photographs. More detailed records were made for selected sites. Professional ground photography was undertaken for a proportion of sites, and extensive use was made of aerial photography for the large and complex sites – notably mental hospitals. Additionally, files were created for important demolished sites, such as the original St Thomas's Hospital and Bethlem Hospital in London, which set the pattern for later hospitals.

The project is an example of the thematic surveys, such as those recently published by the RCHME on textile mills in Yorkshire and Cheshire. It differs from all previous RCHME surveys in covering almost all of England, and in having been undertaken simultaneously from three separate offices.

The archive comprises information on some 2,000 hospital sites, and a county-by-county list of these is given in an appendix to this book. The archive material is publicly accessible in the National Monuments Record Centre at the Royal Commission's head quarters at Kemble Drive, Swindon, SN2 2GZ (telephone 01793 414600). Files for sites in the Greater London area are held in the Commission's Public Search Room at 55, Blandford Street, London, W1H 3AF (telephone 0171 208 8200).

Only a selection of hospitals has been discussed in this book, each having been chosen to demonstrate an aspect of the evolution of hospital design. Whilst a wide variety of both the typical and the atypical find their place in the ensuing chapters, many fine examples inevitably are absent. However, information concerning many of these can be found in the archive reports. Chapter 1 is a general introduction that sets the buildings in their historical context, each of the following chapters then describes a particular hospital type and analyses its development. Illustrations range from historic images and original plans and elevations, to newly commissioned photographs and drawings. Imperial measurements are used throughout the text, but plans drawn by the RCHME's draughtsmen have scales in feet and metres.

Conversion Table

1 in = 25.4 mm
1 ft (12 ins.) = 304.8 mm
1 mile = 1.6 km
1 acre = 0.4 ha
1 cu ft = 0.0283 cu m

1
Historical Context

A hospital, in the modern sense of the word, signifies an establishment primarily dedicated to the care of the sick. Yet most of the thousand or so hospitals existing in England prior to the Dissolution of the Monasteries in 1536–40 served a broader purpose, such as lodgings for pilgrims and travellers, almshouses, or schools. Those which did care for the sick are first noted in the years following the Norman Conquest and were usually to be found in the largest towns. Many evolved their nursing and medical role from the need to care for sick pilgrims, whether for those who had set out in search of a cure or for those who fell ill in the course of their travels.[1] Three London hospitals for the sick effectively survived the Dissolution: St Mary of Bethlehem, which had become increasingly secularised since coming under the jurisdiction of the City of London in 1346; and St Bartholomew's and St Thomas's, refounded in 1546 and 1551 respectively. These three remained the principal and, for a long time, the only hospitals in the country, until the emergence of the 'voluntary hospital' movement in the 18th century.

About 250 voluntary hospitals, financed by charitable endowments and donations, had been established by the middle decades of the 19th century, when the only health care provided by central or local authorities was for paupers, either in workhouses or county lunatic asylums. Increasingly wide-ranging public health legislation gradually changed the proportion of charitable hospitals, until, by the outbreak of the Second World War, two-thirds of the 3,000 hospitals in England and Wales were local-authority establishments, providing four-fifths of the available beds. State concern with, and intervention in health care culminated in the inauguration of the National Health Service on 5 July 1948, which absorbed nearly all the existing hospitals. Only about 200 retained their independence and these were mostly small, run by religious communities, or catered for a particular section of society. One of the largest to remain in private hands was the Royal Masonic Hospital in London, which treated Freemasons, their wives and children over the age of 12.[2]

Hospitals in their present form are the product of a long evolution, which from the beginning was characterised by an element of specialisation. The diversity of patients generated a need to tailor accommodation to suit particular conditions. Medieval hospitals for the sick usually comprised a large aisled hall with a chapel to the east. But from the 12th century, as leprosy began to spread throughout the country, special hospitals were established for its victims, who were considered to be highly infectious and aroused great fear. Excluded from towns, lepers were accommodated in secluded communities of separate cottages with detached chapels.

Most of the 345 leper hospitals, or 'lazar houses', known to have existed were founded between the late 11th and the early 13th centuries, but after 1350 the incidence of leprosy declined and by the mid 15th century few leper hospitals remained. Over 100 hospitals were established which provided care for the non-leprous sick, although only about 20 of them were exclusively for this purpose. The hospital of St Bartholomew at Gloucester was one of the largest of these, with accommodation for ninety sick men and women by the early 14th century. From this time, however, such hospitals began to decline, principally as a result of the general late-medieval economic malaise and the decrease in population in the wake of the Black Death.[3]

By 1535 more than half the medieval hospitals for the sick poor either were admitting far fewer patients, or had been converted into more lucrative schools, secular colleges or fee-demanding almshouses. The remainder were shut down at the Dissolution, the buildings of St Bartholomew's and St Thomas's standing empty until the hospitals were refounded. The small hospital of St Mary of Bethlehem, which cared for lunatics, escaped suppression, and was granted a royal charter by Henry VIII collectively with St Bartholomew's.

Lunatics, many of whom were in good physical health, required rather different accommodation and care, and so were excluded from general hospitals such as St Bartholomew's and

Figure 1
St Bartholomew's
Hospital, London,
showing the medieval
buildings that existed
before the major
rebuilding scheme
carried out in the 18th
century. The church and
the gateway (erected in
1702) were retained and
survive today. To either
side of the gateway can
be seen houses and shops
facing Smithfield.
[Stow 1720 I, 184
(Wellcome Institute Library,
London, V13002)]

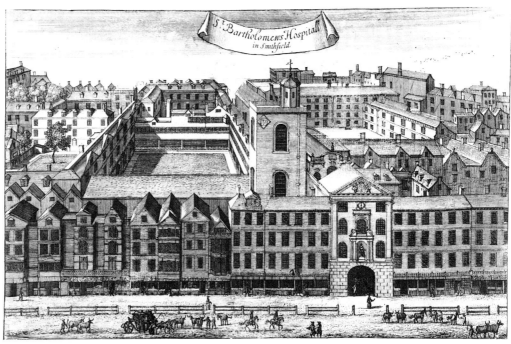

St Thomas's, which otherwise admitted a variety of cases. St Bartholomew's (Fig 1), with its medieval arrangement of buildings, courtyards, cloisters and gardens, had special wards for 'Cutting', 'Diet' and 'Sweat' cases by the late 16th century. St Thomas's had provided a lying-in ward for unmarried mothers by the mid 15th century and wards for patients suffering from venereal disease by the late 16th century. Accident cases were also admitted, as were sick and wounded soldiers and sailors. During the Civil War casualties were taken to the London hospitals, many of the wounded having to be transported over great distances to receive treatment. St Bartholomew's alone took in over 1,000 'maimed soldiers and other diseased persons' in 1644.[4]

The first attempts by the state to provide some form of public health care were prompted by the devastating effects of infectious diseases. After leprosy, plague was the first to cause widespread alarm. There had been intermittent outbreaks of plague since at least the 6th century, but by the time the Black Death reached London in 1348, earlier onslaughts had been long forgotten. The Black Death was the first of a series of major epidemics, the last of which in England was the Great Plague of 1665–6 (the last instance of plague elsewhere in western Europe occurred in Marseilles in the 1720s). The upper ranks of society could escape the disease, which was rife in the overcrowded homes of the poor, by abandoning the city and taking up residence in the countryside until the epidemic subsided. But there was no avoiding the disruption it caused or the pervasive fear of

the disease. Various public precautions against the plague were taken in cities on the Continent, notably in Italy, where, in the 1340s, officials had been appointed to deal with the Black Death soon after its first appearance. Permanent boards of health were established in Florence and Venice in the 15th century and some hospitals were built to quarantine victims. No such steps were taken in England before 1518. In that year Henry VIII issued a proclamation which aimed to make plague victims identifiable by requiring them to hang bundles of straw from their windows for forty days, and carry a white stick when they were away from home (similar measures had been introduced in Paris in 1510). The first plague hospitals in England were established from *c* 1537 in the form of small, temporary pesthouses, and by the end of the century funding was provided through general taxation for the relief of the sick. But England still lagged behind its European neighbours, such as France, where, in 1607, Henri IV founded the Hôpital Saint Louis in Paris for plague victims as part of his ambitious scheme to embellish the city. No comparable grand royal or civil hospital was erected in London.[5]

The same *ad hoc* system of temporary pesthouses operated during the early smallpox epidemics. Smallpox had been endemic since at least the 15th century, and it became the most feared disease once the plague had died out. It was highly contagious and less socially discriminating than the plague, claiming the life of Queen Mary in 1694. Whereas no medical means of allaying the ravages of plague could be found, medicine was used successfully for the first time

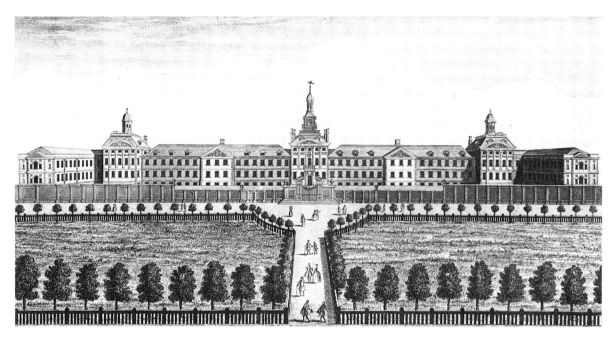

in the prevention of disease with inoculation and vaccination against smallpox. Inoculation was introduced to England in the 1720s by Lady Mary Wortley Montagu, who had herself been disfigured by the disease. She had become aware of the process and its benefits while staying in Turkey with her husband Edward, the British Ambassador, between 1716 and 1718. Inoculation was undertaken with considerable success in England before vaccination was discovered by Edward Jenner at the end of the 18th century. Vaccination steadily gained acceptance and was given official sanction when the Vaccination Act of 1853 made it compulsory for infants.[6]

From 1831, cholera became the new scourge, the first devastating epidemic claiming some 22,000 lives.[7] Despite the alarm which it caused, there was scant progress in providing hospitals for victims of this disease, although many cases may have been admitted to the existing pesthouses or the few fever hospitals which had been erected from the early years of the 19th century. Paupers were cared for in the more numerous fever blocks erected at workhouses. As with the plague, the first measure taken against cholera was to isolate its victims, but this had only a limited effect, as the cause of the disease was misunderstood. During the 18th century doctors had developed the theory that disease was the result of bad air or miasma. This was based largely on the observation that many infectious diseases were more prevalent in areas of poor housing than in wealthier districts. Such ideas were promoted by Dr (later Sir) John Pringle, a Scottish physician, whose distinguished career culminated in his appointment as head of the

Army Medical Service. His *Observations on the Diseases of the Army*, published in 1752, suggested that disease was caused by 'a corruption of the air, pent up and deprived of its elastic parts by the respiration of a multitude', and that infection was derived from 'the poisonous effluvia of sores, mortifications, dysentric and other putrid excrements'.[8] More prosaically and more pervasively, cholera is actually transmitted through the water supply, and it was only after this fact was established in the late 1840s that there was any hope of preventing future epidemics. Even so, many leading figures clung to the miasma theory long after it had been disproved, including such influential reformers as Sir Edwin Chadwick and Florence Nightingale.

The slow progress in providing isolation hospitals contrasted with the rapid expansion of the voluntary hospitals movement, which, from somewhat hesitant beginnings in the early 18th century, had become firmly established by the mid 19th century. The earliest new hospital buildings erected after the Reformation, however, were for St Mary of Bethlehem (or Bethlem) and St Thomas's. The new Bethlem Hospital (Fig 2) of 1675–6 was designed by the eminent scientist Robert Hooke, who, as one of the surveyors for the rebuilding of London after the Great Fire, also achieved some distinction as an architect. Stylistically, this palatial building demonstrated Hooke's awareness of architectural developments in Europe, particularly in France and Holland, and set new standards for large public buildings in England. Its plan was carefully adapted to the accommodation of lunatics, confinement being the governing principle, and

Figure 2
Bethlem Hospital, Moorfields, London. This engraving shows Robert Hooke's building of 1675–6 with the wings added at either end in the 18th century. The hospital was superseded by a new building in St George's Fields (now the Imperial War Museum) in the early 19th century, and Hooke's palatial edifice was subsequently demolished.
[Wellcome Institute Library, London, V13180]

its combination of long corridors and rows of cells provided the model for later asylums.

Apart from substantial rebuilding at St Thomas's Hospital between 1693 and 1709, no further hospitals were erected until the 1720s. From that time there was a steady increase in the number of new hospitals which, like St Thomas's and St Bartholomew's, were intended to provide free care for the poor. People with a sufficient income procured what medical attendance they could afford in their own homes. Private physicians and surgeons attended the rich, and apothecaries served the middle ranks of society, while itinerant quacks attended whoever their skills could attract.

Perhaps surprisingly, members of the medical profession did not take the lead in establishing hospitals. The majority owed their existence to lay philanthropists, such as Thomas Guy, who amassed a considerable fortune selling South Sea stock, and served as a governor of St Thomas's Hospital. He was so distressed at the plight of incurable patients refused admission to St Thomas's that he resolved to found a new

institution which would exclude neither the incurable nor lunatics. In 1722 Thomas Dance was commissioned to prepare a design for the new hospital, and the double courtyard plan which he devised echoed the basic forms of St Bartholomew's and St Thomas's, as well as collegiate buildings. As with Hooke's Bethlem, the building had a formal and imposing appearance, although the grand pedimented entrance front was a later refinement added in the 1770s by Richard Jupp (Fig 3).

Guy's Hospital was intended to provide accommodation for 400 patients, a far greater number than most of the voluntary institutions established in the 18th and early 19th centuries. Smaller hospitals, such as the original Manchester Infirmary erected in the mid 1750s, often bore a superficial resemblance to domestic villas or country houses, but a discernible air of formality, or a degree of austerity, distinguished them as public buildings. They were a visible expression of pride in the foundation as well as an encouragement to potential subscribers.

The internal arrangements of hospitals were subject to periodic alteration, the uses of rooms changing as demands on hospital accommodation varied. The principal component of a hospital, the ward, had no strict form or size until the second half of the 19th century, as opinions shifted between a preference for them to be large or small. In addition, there was a need for other patient areas, such as operating theatres, as well as administrative offices and staff accommodation. Inevitably, the grandest apartment tended to be the boardroom or committee-room, where the hospital governors held their meetings. Since it was not in continual use for committee purposes, this room often doubled as a chapel, thus catering for the spiritual as well as the temporal needs of the patients, staff and visitors. During the 19th century it became more common for a separate chapel to be provided and at many hospitals the chapel is the finest architectural feature. The importance attached to the chapel was often an indication of the proportion of ambulant patients. Asylums and workhouses invariably made some provision for worship, and from the mid 19th century onwards chapels at asylums were usually prominent detached buildings.

The efficacy of the voluntary hospital system remained unquestioned throughout the 18th century. It operated on a subscription basis, subscribers acquiring the right to nominate patients and, for a certain sum, the status of governor. The system was endorsed by social reformers, who perceived the benefits of improving the health of the working classes, but

Figure 3
This detail of the main elevation of Guy's Hospital, London, shows the new entrance front added by Richard Jupp in the 1770s. The statues in the niches on the piano nobile *were executed by John Bacon, RA (1740–99).*
[NMR CC38/538]

4

it was not without flaws. Although accident cases were admitted without question, all other admissions required a subscriber's letter. This shortcoming was recognised by Dr William Marsden, who in 1828 founded the London General Institution for the Gratuitous Care of Malignant Diseases. Despite its alarming nomenclature, this hospital fulfilled a pressing need for free treatment without letters of recommendation. A great success, the Institution attracted the patronage of the new queen in 1837, becoming the Royal Free Hospital.

Further impetus for change was provided by the growing corpus of literature on hospitals. From the late 18th century, a number of critical accounts drew attention to the appalling conditions that existed in many institutions. Indeed, during the 18th century and the first half of the 19th century a stay in hospital could in itself be fatal. Mortality rates, particularly after surgery, were so high that hospitals were seen as death traps. One of the most powerful critiques of contemporary hospitals was produced by John Howard, the philanthropist and prison reformer, whose *Account of the Principal Lazarettos in Europe* was first published in 1789. Throughout his extensive travels he was aware of the personal dangers to which he was exposed. He stated his basic, if enigmatic, precautions as being 'never [to] enter an hospital or prison before breakfast, and in an offensive room I seldom draw my breath deeply'. In setting out 'the many disorders that ought to be rectified', Howard provided an authoritative body of evidence and inspiration for future reformers.[9]

Other major surveys of hospitals were undertaken in the 19th century. Dr John Bristowe and Timothy Holmes, for example, visited hospitals in Britain at the behest of the Privy Council, and their report, published in 1864, included analytical descriptions and many ground plans. An even wider study was written by (Sir) Henry Burdett, whose prodigious *Hospitals and Asylums of the World* was published in four volumes in 1891 and 1893. Burdett wrote extensively, and not merely on the subject of hospitals – he was also associated with the London Stock Exchange and amongst his other works were *National Debts of the World, A Practical Scheme for Old Age Pensions* and *Dwellings of the Middle Classes*. Burdett devised a classification system for hospital plan types which included pavilion, block, corridor, and irregular (or 'heap of buildings'). An invaluable portfolio of plans accompanied the volumes, prepared with the expert assistance of one of the foremost architectural practices in hospital design, Keith Young & Henry Hall.

Not all publications were so comprehensive. Many dealt with discrete areas of hospital design or management, usually drawing on personal experience, as is the case with Samuel Tuke's description of The Retreat, near York, published in 1813. Founded by Tuke's grandfather, The Retreat was arguably the most influential early lunatic asylum in terms of the treatment of the patients there, and this publication aimed to improve conditions in asylums throughout the country. Similarly, in 1847, John Conolly, the medical superintendent of the Middlesex Lunatic Asylum, published *The Construction and Government of Lunatic Asylums and Hospitals for the Insane*, which served as a pattern-book for asylum designers. It provided guidelines on every aspect of planning, including furnishings and fittings, even to the extent of suggesting that green-coloured blinds should be fitted to sunny windows to shade the patients.

The best-known writer and reformer was Florence Nightingale, whose name became synonymous with hospital ward design. Her experience of nursing, particularly in the Crimea, made her an avid and informed campaigner and led to the reorganisation of both the military medical services and the nursing profession. She achieved success through her own persistence and a circle of powerful friends, playing a key part in the introduction of the pavilion plan to hospital design in the years following the Crimean War. This can be seen as the single most important development in hospital planning, significantly improving patients' chances of successful treatment and recovery by creating an environment which was both sanitary for the patient and convenient for the nurse. The pavilion plan is characterised by a greater degree of separation and segregation than earlier designs, featuring wards (commonly called Nightingale wards) in long, rectangular pavilions, cross-ventilated by opposing windows. Nightingale, however, was only one of a group of people, including John Roberton, a Manchester surgeon, and George Godwin, editor of the weekly architectural journal *The Builder*, to whom credit must be given for the introduction of this plan to England in the mid 19th century.

The pavilion plan was developed in France, although, ironically perhaps, it was inspired by an English precedent. When a fire destroyed much of the Hôtel Dieu, the principal hospital in Paris, in 1772, several ambitious proposals were made for its replacement. The design which eventually won official approval was drawn up by Jacques Tenon, an eminent medical practitioner, and the architect Bernard

Key
A Women's entrance
B Gallery
C Iron grille
D Men's section of
   main gallery
E Men's entrance
F Main stair
G Men's ward
H Lying-in ward
I Women's ward
K Hall
L Pavilions
M Stair
N Semicircular rooms
   with operating
   theatres over
O Hall
P Porter's lodge
Q Visitors' room
R Gallery
S Lying-in ward
T Covered walk
U Open court
V Open court
X Open court
Y Gentle ramps
Z Covered walk

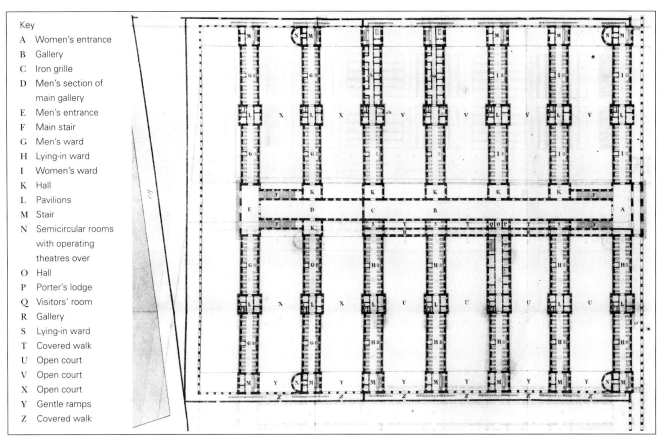

Figure 4
Proposed design for the Hôtel Dieu, Paris, by Jacques Tenon and Bernard Poyet, and published in 1788.
[From M Tenon, Mémoires sur les hôpitaux de Paris, *1788 (Wellcome Institute Library, London, L0025476800)]*

Poyet (Fig 4). It comprised two parallel rows of seven pavilions, linked by an open colonnade, on either side of a gallery. The pavilions were rectangular, with opposed windows, and contained large wards with the beds placed in pairs, their heads against the window piers. All other departments, such as kitchens and administrative offices, were located in separate blocks. The inspiration for this design was provided by the Royal Naval Hospital at Plymouth of 1758–62 (a plan of which was published by John Howard in 1784), with its series of detached ward blocks, although the internal arrangements were quite different (Fig 5).[10]

Work on the new Hôtel Dieu was delayed, and with the outbreak of the French Revolution Tenon and Poyet's designs came to nothing. But in the period between 1820 and 1850 their ideas were realised in a number of large new hospitals, including St Andrew's Hospital in Bordeaux, and the Beaujon and the Lariboisière hospitals in Paris (see Figure 21). No hospital was built to such a plan in England before the late 1850s, although, in a few buildings, certain aspects of pavilion planning are evident, notably the large, cross-ventilated wards erected at the military hospital at Fort Pitt in Chatham in the 1820s, and the new ward wings added to St Thomas's Hospital in London in the 1830s and 1840s.

The pavilion plan was first publicly advocated in England by John Roberton in a paper presented to the Manchester Statistical Society in March 1856. Such societies provided an important forum for the discussion and promotion of social reform in the mid 19th century. Roberton criticised the unhealthy state of many hospitals, laying the blame squarely on inadequate ventilation and poor planning, while extolling the virtues of the Continental pavilion plan, which was 'at once ingenious and perfectly successful' in preventing the formation of an 'injurious hospital atmosphere'.[11] He was convinced that plentiful fresh air and separation would rid the hospital environment of the fatal miasmas responsible for disease (even though the miasma theory was already being questioned by this date).

Roberton's criticisms of contemporary hospital design found a focus when plans for a new army hospital at Netley, near Portsmouth, were revealed in 1856. Designed as a general military hospital, it had been planned with an arrangement of small wards opening off corridors, following the prevailing hospital plan type during the first half of the 19th century. But it appeared at the very moment when public opinion was roused by the appalling

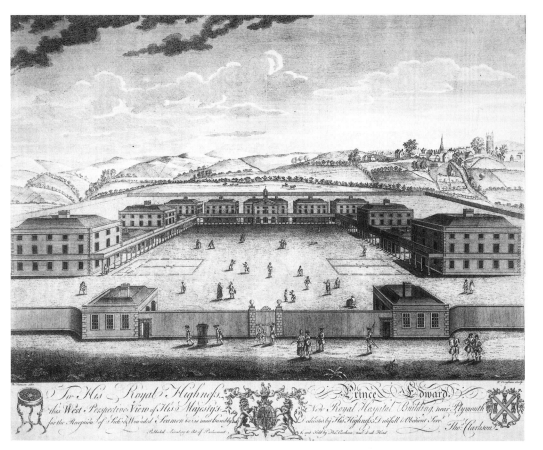

Figure 5
Royal Naval Hospital,
Plymouth, erected in
1758–62. The design is
attributed to Alexander
Rovehead. This perspec-
tive view shows the
detached blocks on three
sides of the square; the
fourth side has the
ground plans in place of
the actual buildings.
This device not only
allows for a clearer view
of the layout of the
hospital but illustrates
the internal arrangement
of the ward blocks, with
their principal wards
placed back to back.
[Engraved by W Tringham,
after a drawing by Thomas
Clarkson, c 1762 (British
Library, Kings Top XI)]

conditions that had existed in the Crimea, where more soldiers perished from fevers contracted in hospitals than from battle wounds. A fierce controversy raged over hospital planning, and the national, medical and architectural press united in a campaign against Netley Hospital in particular. George Godwin's impassioned editorials in *The Builder* helped to change the way in which architects approached hospital planning, and Florence Nightingale was able to bring considerable political pressure to bear. As a result, the government ordered an inquiry into the design of Netley Hospital and a Sanitary Commission was appointed to carry out a full investigation into conditions in military hospitals. The report of this Commission, published in 1858, gave official sanction to the pavilion plan,[12] and the latter was also publicised by Nightingale in her *Notes on Hospitals*, first published in 1859, which included three articles reproduced from *The Builder* on siting and construction.

In 1858 the first two pavilion-plan hospitals in England were commenced: Blackburn Infirmary and the Royal Marine Barracks Hospital at Woolwich. The plan was soon adopted, with modifications, to accommodate all types of patients, though it was of limited value for the mentally ill, being suitable only for the most manageable cases, requiring less confinement or supervision. The principles of pavilion planning were employed by architects in most types of institutional building; separation was the key, and 'cross-ventilation' became the watchword of architects well into the 20th century.

The two most important early pavilion-plan hospitals, if only because of their sheer size, expense and the publicity which they received, were the Herbert Hospital at Woolwich, commenced in 1861 (see page 95 and Figures 93 and 94), and the new St Thomas's Hospital, begun in 1868 on a prominent site across the Thames from the Houses of Parliament (see Figures 25 and 26). Fashionably Italianate, their ranks of elegant pavilions rhythmically asserted the confidence upon which they were founded. At the outer ends of the pavilions were twin towers resembling *campanili*, their architectural 'fancy dress' disguising their true purpose, which was to house the sanitary facilities. However, this was altogether consistent with the spirit of near-veneration in which sanitation was held in the second half of the 19th century, when it seemed to provide the means of improving public health.

The swift and widespread adoption throughout the country of the pavilion plan was aided by its adaptability, it could be dressed in almost any architectural style – apart from the early Italianate examples, Gothic was enduringly popular, with architectural embellishment usually concentrated on the administration block containing the main entrance. Alternatively, it could be cheaply functional, a seductive advantage, particularly to parsimonious Poor Law guardians, anxious to mollify their ever-vigilant ratepayers. There was no limit to size, although a maximum of two storeys was recommended for pavilions, and there had to be sufficient space between them to provide good light and a free circulation of air. In addition, pavilion ward blocks could be added to existing hospitals with ease.

Early refinements to the pavilion plan concerned the arrangement of the beds and of the sanitary facilities. At first, beds were placed in pairs between the windows, as advocated by Tenon and Poyet, but this layout soon gave way to the more familiar arrangement with only one bed occupying the window pier. As for the sanitary facilities – baths, sinks and water closets – these became more and more separated from the ward itself. The comparative plans in Figure 6 demonstrate this development and show how sanitary towers became such distinctive architectural features of hospitals. Sadly, in many cases, the exuberant caps to these towers have been lopped off in the cause of economic maintenance, but there are still pleasing examples of Gothic spikes, Tudor turrets and ogee cupolas scattered about the country.

The pervasive rectangular pavilion ward was challenged in the later 19th century by a circular version, which, enthusiastically promoted by Godwin, enjoyed a brief vogue in the 1880s. The first hospital to be built with circular wards was in Antwerp, where work began in 1878, but at the same time John Marshall, a renowned anatomist and surgeon, was advocating the benefits of such a plan to an English audience. In his view, the prime advantage of the circular ward was that 'having no blank ends like an oblong ward, its uniformly rounded exterior, receding from all adjacent buildings, would receive light, air, and wind from every direction'.[13] This echoed one of the chief preoccupations of hospital designers, who, from the 18th century, grappled with the complexities of ventilation, heating and sanitation. Aesthetically, too, these circular ward-towers had an undoubted attraction (Fig 7).

Marshall's ideas were published in *The Builder* and taken up by such notable hospital architects as Young & Hall and Henry Saxon Snell. Although many schemes for hospitals with circular wards were proposed, relatively few

Figure 6 Comparative plans (1:500) of sanitary facilities showing their increasing detachment from the main body of the ward. The last two examples, with their cross-ventilated lobbies, remained the favoured form throughout the later 19th century and into the 20th century.

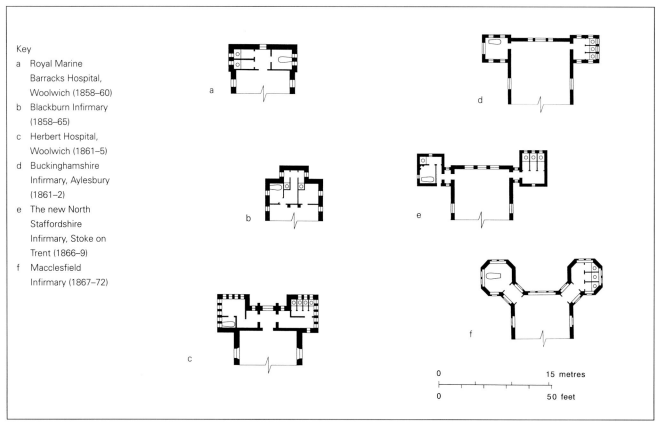

Key
a Royal Marine Barracks Hospital, Woolwich (1858–60)
b Blackburn Infirmary (1858–65)
c Herbert Hospital, Woolwich (1861–5)
d Buckinghamshire Infirmary, Aylesbury (1861–2)
e The new North Staffordshire Infirmary, Stoke on Trent (1866–9)
f Macclesfield Infirmary (1867–72)

0   15 metres
0   50 feet

were actually built, and they tended to be erected only where ward accommodation was required on tight and restricted sites. As early as 1885 Snell, for one, had lost his early enthusiasm for them and no more were built after about 1910.[14]

The advent of pavilion planning coincided with the beginning of a general decline in mortality rates in hospitals. As a result, demand for admission increased, and the pressure on space forced the so-called general hospitals to become more exclusive, refusing admission to patients who were considered obnoxious, whose presence was not deemed suitable, or whose stay was likely to be protracted, such as chronic or incurable cases. This exclusion led to the establishment of specialist hospitals, which proliferated during the later 19th century, eventually forcing general hospitals to offer their own specialist departments. At about the same time beds for paying patients were introduced and a few hospitals were established specifically for the middle classes, who could afford a modest fee in return for their care.

However, even the introduction of the pavilion plan, with all its supposed merits, did not stop the seemingly endless flow of articles, pamphlets and substantial books on ventilation, heating and sanitation. The persistent belief that disease was caused by foul air led many to stress the importance of thorough ventilation, although opinions were divided on the relative merits of artificial and natural systems. In the mid 18th century Sir John Pringle had recommended that windows should be kept open and warmth provided by open fires, which would also improve the circulation of air. John Howard, too, was an early champion of cross-ventilation. In the 19th century a great variety of systems was available, such as Boyle's or Howorth's revolving ventilators, and Tobin's Tubes.[15] Complex systems of artificial heating and ventilation were installed in a number of institutions – not merely hospitals. The ventilation system selected for the Derby County Asylum had been tried and tested at the Kent County Asylum, Bath Gaol, Derby Gaol and the Model Prison at Pentonville.[16] An early example,

Figure 7
For the Victoria Hospital at Burnley, the local firm of William Waddington & Son used circular ward-towers to striking visual effect. Their idiosyncratic design comprised no less than seven single-storey ward-towers surrounding the central administration block. The hospital was erected between 1884 and 1886, but only two of the towers were actually built.
[Engraving of 1886, Lancashire County Library, Burnley Division, Q12]

devised *c* 1815 by the Marquis de Chabannes, a French *emigré* and technological speculator, was installed in John Nash's Ophthalmic Hospital in London. Chabannes' system for 'conducting air by forced ventilation' centred on his patented *Calorifère Fumivore* Furnace, from which warm air was piped to one end of the wards, ventilation tubes extracting vitiated air at the other.[17] The system was also installed at the Covent Garden and Olympic theatres, the House of Commons and Fort Clarence at Chatham.

Apart from good ventilation, cleanliness and fire-prevention also had a direct bearing on hospital design. In 1730 James Gibbs designed the new buildings for St Bartholomew's as four detached blocks so as to lessen the risk of the spread of fire, noting that the Capitol in Rome, having burnt down three times, was rebuilt by Michelangelo as three blocks detached from each other for this reason.[18] By the early 19th century, fireproofing, chiefly associated with industrial buildings, had become equally important in hospitals where patients were confined to bed, and particularly in the early asylums, where fires frequently broke out. One of the earliest documented examples of the use of iron for fireproof construction in a hospital was at Brislington House, near Bristol, a private lunatic asylum established by Dr Edward Fox *c* 1804.[19]

In general, however, traditional building materials were used for hospitals and locally available brick or stone was commonly chosen for the exterior facing. Special requirements for the internal surfaces, which needed to be non-absorbent and easily cleaned, led to a preference for glazed bricks, tiles, hard plaster, Parian cement, and scrubbed deal or terrazzo floors. These were all perceived as vital weapons in the fight against infection. Indeed, cleanliness became all but an obsession; even wallpaper was shunned, because it might be pervious to foul air, and angles were rounded to avoid nooks and crannies where dirt and disease could lodge.

Until the later 19th century, governments had interfered little with the steady development of a hospital system throughout the country. However, the lack of resources and facilities to cope with widespread epidemics of infectious disease forced the state to take action. From the early 1800s national boards of health were instituted from time to time in the hope of devising ways of preventing or containing epidemics, but they were dissolved once the epidemic had subsided. These boards appointed local medical officers for health, many of whom became key figures in the improvement of regional health care. In the second half of the 19th century the pace of reform quickened, with a series of inquiries into the state of the nation's health and welfare, carried out initially by the Privy Council and later by the Local Government Board, which resulted in a succession of public health Acts.

In London, the problems posed by epidemics were exacerbated by the overcrowded conditions in the metropolitan workhouses, which led, in 1867, to the establishment of the Metropolitan Asylums Board. This provided hospital accommodation for London's paupers suffering from fever, smallpox or mental handicap, and as such constituted a significant step towards the provision of a municipal health service. Indeed, it resulted in the erection of the first state hospitals in the country. The earliest was a temporary smallpox hospital in Hampstead, a complex of hastily erected iron-and-timber huts designed by Pennington & Bridgen, which aroused fierce local opposition from the affluent residents alarmed by the proximity of this repellent disease.

It was also from the mid 19th century that new developments in medicine began to transform hospital treatment. In the early 19th century, patients were equally likely (or unlikely) to survive an operation carried out on the kitchen table of a private house as in a hospital operating theatre. However, the discovery of the anaesthetic properties of ether and chloroform in the 1840s opened up new possibilities for surgeons, and the number of operations increased rapidly. Although anaesthetics freed patients from pain, at first their chances of survival were little improved because of the risk of infection, or sepsis, after the operation. Joseph Lister made the first successful attempt to combat sepsis by using carbolic acid, and by the 1870s a steam-powered carbolic spray was in common use during orthopaedic and accident surgery. This was superseded by the practice of sterilisation, which provided the required antiseptic conditions.

These were developments which architects had to take into account when planning hospitals. The design of operating theatres became more complex, and, as a result of safer and more successful surgery, their numbers increased, as did the ratio of surgical wards to medical wards. Theatres usually faced north and were often top-lit to provide the required even lighting. A single theatre was considered sufficient, even for the largest hospital, until the early 20th century; from then on, in response to advances in medical knowledge and techniques, a general hospital might have a suite of operating theatres served by ancillary rooms for anaesthetising, sterilising, storing instruments, washing and changing. In teaching hospitals, theatres were also provided with tiered stands or seating from which students could observe the proceedings.

Wilhelm Konrad Röntgen's discovery of X-rays in 1895 provided a new avenue for diagnosis and treatment. Electrical and X-ray departments proliferated as the equipment was refined and by the 1920s they had become an established part of hospitals. As with operating theatres, an electrical department had to be designed to provide a variety of spaces. Rooms were required for therapy and diagnosis, the X-ray equipment itself, a generating plant and darkroom.

During the 19th century, if not earlier, it was clearly recognised by medical practitioners and architects alike that the form of a hospital could have a direct influence on the condition of the patients. A close association between the medical and architectural professions, therefore, might be expected. Yet documented examples of such collaboration are relatively rare. For the most part architects looked for inspiration and guidance to other recently erected hospitals, although the increasing complexity of hospital planning led to the emergence of specialist 'hospital architects' in the 19th century. At the same time, county asylums and, from the late 19th century, isolation hospitals, tended to be designed by architects, surveyors or engineers employed or retained by local authorities, who usually would have been experienced in the planning of public or institutional buildings.

Architects who made their names designing hospitals or asylums often sought to widen their renown by publishing their achievements. In asylum design, William Stark was one of the earliest to venture into print, publishing a pamphlet on the construction of asylums in 1810.[20] Nearly a century later the demand for such publications was undiminished. One of many articles on hospital design to appear in the early 20th century was a survey of asylums and asylum planning written by George T Hine, whose practice was almost entirely dependent on hospital commissions.[21]

Henry Saxon Snell was another prolific hospital architect: his practice flourished in the later 19th century and his two sons, Alfred and Harry, followed him into the profession. In the 1880s, not only was he responsible for a publication on *Charitable and Parochial Establishments*, but he collaborated with a medical practitioner, Frederick J Mouat, to produce a volume on *Hospital Construction and Management*. Snell was an influential figure who, on several occasions, was requested to judge competitions for the design of hospitals; he also achieved international status when he secured the commission for the Royal Victoria Infirmary in Montreal.

Hospital design grew increasingly complex from the late 19th century, particularly after the First World War when departments for specialised treatment multiplied rapidly. The use of specialist architectural firms became more common. Practices such as Young & Hall, Adams Holden & Pearson, and Burnet, Tait & Lorne, dominated hospital design in the early 20th century, building up considerable expertise from which important innovations were forthcoming. Keith Young seems to have been the first to recognise that the sanitary tower or annexe was no longer a necessity. In 1913 he asserted that:

In the old days, when sanitary plumbing was a lost art, or, rather, had not been developed ... it no doubt was necessary to interpose a ventilated lobby between the sanitary offices and the ward; but now, with the almost perfection that sanitary work has got to, I see no real necessity for it ... it would be an immense help in planning if we could get rid of the projecting towers.[22]

In 1914–16 Young's design for the women's hospital at Chelsea incorporated the sanitary facilities within the main building, and, during the First World War, temporary military hospitals were built without sanitary annexes with no injurious effect on the health of the patients. In the inter-war period, sanitary facilities were finally subsumed within the main body of the hospital. This development was possible not only as a result of improvements in engineering and construction, but also because the nature of disease was understood more clearly, germs or bacteria being accepted as the primary cause. More importantly, the separation provided by pavilion-plan hospitals was no longer regarded as essential.

The architectural press remained an important platform from which to launch innovations in design. In the early 1930s Charles Ernest Elcock publicised what he described as 'veranda wards', where one wall of a ward was formed solely of windows which could be peeled back to let in sunshine and air. A dependence upon abundant air and sunlight was first evident in the design of sanatoria at the beginning of the 20th century and remained a hallmark of hospitals for both pulmonary and non-pulmonary tuberculosis. But, from at least the 1930s, open-air and sunlight treatments were adopted in a number of other hospitals, if only at the basic level of providing large opening windows and verandas on to which beds could be wheeled. New methods of construction provided the means for a more sophisticated application of this type of treatment: the introduction of reinforced-concrete and steel framing allowed vast areas of wall space to be glazed, and this was well exploited in hospital buildings of the inter-war years, a period when the beneficial effects of fresh air and sunshine were applied almost universally.

From this background of social reform, medical advances and architectural developments, a number of distinctive types of hospital

Figure 8
One of the cubicle
isolation blocks added in
1937 to the South West
Middlesex Hospital,
Twickenham, in the
London Borough of
Hounslow. The building
was derelict when visited
in 1991 and the site
later cleared to make way
for a supermarket.
[NMR CC47/854]

had emerged by the end of the 19th century. Distinctive either in form or function, or both, though with certain aspects of planning in common, these hospitals can be classified as general, cottage, workhouse, military, specialist, isolation, mental and convalescent. Their chief characteristics are briefly outlined below, and the development of each type is analysed in greater depth in the succeeding chapters.

General hospitals, on the lines of St Thomas's and St Bartholomew's, were established in cities and large towns throughout the country from the early 18th century. Their services were free, funding being supplied by subscription. The buildings that were erected combined an air of economy – they were, after all, intended to serve 'the poor' – with the dignity befitting both the worthiness of the cause and the subscribers. During the first half of the 19th century there was a steady rise in the number of new hospitals being founded, and between 1861 and 1911 their numbers increased fourfold. The almost universal adoption of the pavilion plan by general hospitals throughout the country inevitably produced a similarity in their appearance.

Cottage hospitals, which were in effect small general hospitals, were a phenomenon of the mid to late 19th century, and were set up to serve patients from rural communities, unwilling, or unable, to make the journey to a larger town hospital. By charging modest fees cottage hospitals catered for a slightly higher class of society than most general hospitals and often sought to set themselves apart by creating a deliberately domestic appearance.

At the bottom end of the social scale, paupers were provided with medical care in workhouse infirmaries. Here domesticity was shunned and the infirmaries were almost invariably of a utilitarian appearance. As funding was provided from the poor rate, the comfort of the ratepayer was often given greater consideration than that of the patient.

As far as possible, the Army and Navy maintained their own hospitals and staff, and kept aloof from civilian medical provision. There was a long tradition in the armed forces of caring not only for sick but also disabled or aged soldiers and sailors. The architectural distinction of the royal hospitals at Chelsea and Greenwich, both founded in the late 17th century, is a testimony to the status of the armed forces. War, or the threat of war, was the catalyst for establishing military and naval hospitals to deal with casualties both at home and close to the scene of battle. In addition, wars have consistently proved to be a stimulus to the development of surgical techniques, devised to cope with injuries inflicted by increasingly sophisticated weaponry. Despite their exclusivity, some of these hospitals have been highly influential architecturally, principally in the development of the pavilion plan.

The variety of hospitals catering for particular diseases, parts of the body or classes of patients can be considered together under the generic term 'specialist hospital'. This disparate group includes some of the earliest and latest hospital types to occur. The majority were founded by members of the medical profession, frustrated by gaps in the existing hospital system, which excluded a great many cases from admission, and prevented them from practising their preferred specialisation. Within the profession, establishing a specialist hospital was quickly recognised as a potential route to fame and fortune. Whilst a great many of these new institutions resembled the general hospitals of the day, with only minor adaptations to suit particular needs, certain types of illness produced a distinctive architectural response. Chronic or incurable cases required a lengthy stay in hospital and a great emphasis was placed on creating homely and pleasant surroundings. Similarly, for sea-bathing or mineral-water hospitals, the site was obviously crucial and a complex arrangement for piping the health-giving waters or providing indoor bathing-pools placed unusual demands on the architects' resourcefulness.

Two distinct types of isolation hospital developed, those for consumptives and those for the treatment of other infectious diseases. The design of early isolation or fever hospitals demonstrates the lack of understanding of diseases and the means by which they were spread, but in the later 19th century, as medical knowledge improved, the buildings became more distinctive. The pavilion plan was adapted to provide an even greater degree of separation, with the ward pavilions either completely detached or linked only by a covered way. In the early 20th century the cubicle isolation block was devised, which made provision for the accommodation of each patient in a separate cubicle, thus allowing a variety of cases to be housed within one building. The ingenuity of architects led to some highly individual designs where a strictly functional form was given powerful architectural expression. At the South West Middlesex Hospital in Twickenham, two cubicle blocks were built on a 'half-butterfly' plan. The cubicles were lit by a continuous band of glazing and the windows were set on runners to allow them to be folded back, providing the ultimate in through ventilation (Fig 8).

Consumption, or tuberculosis, was only identified as an infectious disease in the late 19th century, and thus the hospitals and sanatoria designed for its treatment evolved quite separately. The number of sanatoria rose swiftly in the early decades of the 20th century. They were designed most commonly with a sun-trapping butterfly (or half-butterfly) plan, treatment principally consisting of the patient spending as much time as possible in the open air. For this reason the site and the planting of the grounds were considered equally as important as the design of the building. Patients were provided with south-facing rooms flooded with light from large windows which gave access to a balcony or veranda.

Of all the hospital types, lunatic asylums were usually the largest. With the exception of the very earliest, they tended to be built on secluded country sites and formed self-sufficient communities. After the rebuilding of Bethlem Hospital in 1675–6, no further hospitals for lunatics were established before the 18th century. From that time there was a steady rise in the number of new asylums and a growing 'trade in lunacy' which centred on private madhouses where handsome fortunes were made by unscrupulous owners.[23]

Legislation in the 1840s made the provision of county pauper asylums compulsory, resulting in a rapid increase in both the number erected and their size. Their design was, inevitably, quite different from that of hospitals for the physically ill. The need to secure patients led to the development of a corridor plan, inspired by Bethlem, comprising a series of single cells reached from a broad corridor or gallery which served as the patients' day-room. As with the majority of hospitals, economy, with perhaps a nod to the currently fashionable style, dictated appearance.

Figure 9
Claybury Hospital, Woodford, in the London Borough
of Redbridge. This huge asylum was built in 1889–93
to designs by the prolific hospital architect, G T Hine.
The aerial photograph clearly shows the arrangement of
the patients' blocks en échelon, *and the long, straight*
corridors that linked the various buildings. In the
centre, the main water tower can be seen, and, next to it,
the recreation hall, with the sun glinting on its roof.
[NMR AP 4724/68]

As the understanding of mental illness improved, the classification of patients became more sophisticated and more complex plans were devised. In the late 19th century an 'échelon' plan was developed and widely adopted throughout the country. Claybury Hospital (Fig 9), in north-east London, was one of the earliest built on a large scale, with the distinctive arrangement of patients' blocks *en échelon*, and the communal service and administrative buildings in the centre. Around the turn of the century the 'colony system' began to gain precedence, where patients were housed in detached villas. This was particularly favoured for new institutions established in the inter-war period to care for the mentally handicapped.

Convalescent homes provided little medical care but offered patients a place in which to recover their strength through rest and good diet. They were established in increasing numbers from the mid 19th century, when there was a great pressure to vacate hospital beds as soon as possible. After they were discharged from hospital, many patients quickly relapsed when they returned straight home and to work. A brief stay in a convalescent home was seen to be the solution. As the patients were seldom confined to bed, recreation rooms – including smoking rooms for the men – and pleasant garden grounds were important requirements. The sites chosen, too, acknowledged the health-giving properties of country or sea air.

Hospital design has evolved from its medieval origins to a highly specialised form. From the inception of the voluntary hospital movement in the early 18th century, hospitals were erected with at least a superficial resemblance to contemporary mansions or domestic villas, but their plans were increasingly directed by the complex requirements of different treatments or of groups of patients. Continual refinements in planning were prompted by progress in medical knowledge as much as by new methods of construction. Yet, above all, specialism was the key to the development of hospital architecture, and it is only from an analysis of the different types of hospitals erected that their distinctive appearances can be understood.

2
General Hospitals

Most people's experience of a hospital, either as a patient or a visitor, is of the general hospital. It may seem surprising, therefore, that by the end of the 18th century there were only about thirty general hospitals in England, and that nearly all of the present general hospitals were established only in the last 200 years. For most of the 18th and 19th centuries, general hospitals were the resort solely of the poor, the better-off being treated in their own homes. Until well into the 20th century, the majority were funded by voluntary subscriptions and the subscribers, rather than the medical staff, controlled the admission of patients. Even then, hospital rules excluded many cases, such as chronic or incurable illnesses or infectious diseases.

The First General Hospitals and the Emergence of the Voluntary Hospital Movement

After the Dissolution of the Monasteries only two general hospitals were refounded: St Bartholomew's, situated on the fringes of the City of London, in 1546, and St Thomas's, then in Southwark, in 1551. Each occupied a motley collection of buildings, many of which had been part of the medieval hospitals. Although additions were made at both sites, no radical changes took place until the late 17th and 18th centuries, when first St Thomas's and then St Bartholomew's undertook comprehensive rebuilding schemes.

At St Thomas's the governors decided to rebuild in 1693. By that date most of the buildings were in a decayed state and required a considerable and constant outlay on repairs. The 'greatest Wards' occupied a 'lofty old building' which was 'very cold notwithstanding the greatest care taken to prevent it'.[1] Rebuilding began early in 1694, but was not completed until 1709 (Fig 10). The existing collegiate layout was retained, with the wards and offices grouped around three main courts. The new buildings, colonnaded on the ground floor, had pilastered upper storeys and pedimented centrepieces. Over 250 patients could be accommodated in wards, mostly on the upper floors, each containing from 12 to 29 beds. The various service buildings, administrative offices and staff houses faced an irregular yard at the extreme eastern edge of the site. This was also the location of four 'foul wards', for isolating patients with venereal disease. A new chapel was also provided, despite the fact that St Thomas's Church, which formed part of the site, was rebuilt at the same time. The finest room in the hospital was the governors' hall, where gold-lettered wall tablets recorded the names of subscribers, and there was a handsomely carved chimney-piece. In 1700 John Linton was paid £10 15s for 'drawing King Edward the sixths Picture' to hang in the hall, commemorating the royal re-founder of the hospital.[2]

Some of the earliest new general hospitals established in the 18th century were paid for by wealthy philanthropists. Among the first to found such hospitals were the physicians John Radcliffe of Oxford and John Addenbrooke of Cambridge. Radcliffe left bequests for both the extension of St Bartholomew's in London and the erection of the Radcliffe Infirmary in his home town. Both men died in the first decade of the 18th century, but the hospitals which they founded were not built until considerably later. In the mean time, Guy's Hospital had been erected in London in 1722–5 on a site adjacent to St Thomas's. Thomas Dance (apparently no relation to the more famous George) drew up the plans for this essentially plain building of three storeys, plus basement and attic, with a somewhat crudely applied classical frontispiece on the central entrance block (Fig 11). The hospital was intended to accommodate at least 400 patients. The wards were lit by opposed windows (a key feature of the pavilion-plan hospitals of the later 19th century), but box beds lined the walls with no regard to the fenestration, impairing the ventilation.

Where Guy's may have lacked architectural finesse, the new buildings for St Bartholomew's were by contrast stately and elegant (Fig 12). The two royal hospitals of St Bartholomew's and St Thomas's had evolved into fierce political

Figure 10
This engraving shows
St Thomas's as it was
rebuilt between 1693 and
1709 on the hospital's
original site in
Southwark, London,
looking eastwards from
Borough High Street.
The tower of St Thomas's
Church can be seen to the
right. The church and
one of the 19th-century
ward wings were all that
survived demolition after
the hospital was forced to
move in 1862 to make
way for the expansion of
the railway and the
enlarging of London
Bridge Station.
[Stow 1720 I, 189
(Wellcome Institute Library,
London, V13743)]

Figure 11
This charming engraving of Guy's Hospital, London, appeared in 1725, the year that the hospital was completed. It clearly shows the curious entrance designed by Thomas Dance, with the blank wall spaces to either side. The details surrounding the main illustration provide an invaluable and rare glimpse of the hospital's interior. Although the cartouche in the principal picture calls Guy's a 'hospital for incurables', it was, and has always remained, a general hospital.
[Engraving by Thomas Bowles, 1725 (Wellcome Institute Library, London, V13695)]

rivals,[3] and once Whig St Thomas's had completed its extensive rebuilding work it was unlikely that Tory St Bartholomew's would wait too long before embarking on an even more impressive scheme. Situated at Smithfield, Bart's had narrowly escaped the Great Fire of 1666, but by the early 18th century it had insufficient space to treat all those who applied for admission. The existing buildings, erected at various dates, formed a disparate group, and the governors complained that 'the whole has hardly so much as the outward appearance of an hospital' (see Figure 1). In 1729, therefore, they decided on reconstruction, stipulating that 'all buildings which shall be erected for the future ... shall be agreeable to one uniform Plann so that in the process of time the whole Fabrick may become regular and more usefull'.[4] The new buildings were designed by James Gibbs, one of several prominent architects who were also governors of the hospital. (The others were Lord Burlington, Nicholas Hawksmoor and the elder George Dance. There is no evidence, however, that they were asked for or submitted designs.) Gibbs's architectural response to the chaos of the existing hospital was to produce a thoroughly up-to-date design that was clear, ordered and symmetrical, with four large, three-storeyed blocks placed in a formal composition around a courtyard (Figs 12 and 13). The separation of the independent ranges enclosing the court encouraged a free passage of light and air, and

their fine Palladian façades gave a uniformity of appearance to the whole.

Three of the four ranges contained the wards, accommodating a total of 504 patients, while the fourth range, on the north-west side of the site, housed the administrative offices. Altogether there were 36 wards, set back to back, each with 14 beds. The ward entrances and staircases were in the centre of the blocks and earth closets were placed in annexes at the far end of the wards. There was no precedent for this type of design in other hospitals of the period. Gibbs's layout was praised by later hospital reformers for its innovative use of detached blocks to reduce the spread of cross-infection (the principal preoccupation of hospital designers in the late 18th and 19th centuries). However, it is unlikely that this was Gibbs's intention. The arrangement of the buildings at Bart's reflects the 18th-century beau ideal of a college court, and closely resembles Gibbs's own earlier design for King's College, Cambridge (1724). Indeed, Gibbs himself regarded the separate blocks as a practical measure to reduce the risk of the spread of fire (see page 10).

Excepting the Gibbs surrounds to the windows and urns crowning the cornices, there were no expensive embellishments, such as a portico or order of columns, and, until Ralph Allen of Bath offered to supply, at low cost, stone from his quarries at Coombe Down, it had been intended that all the buildings should be faced in brick with Portland stone dressings.[5] As

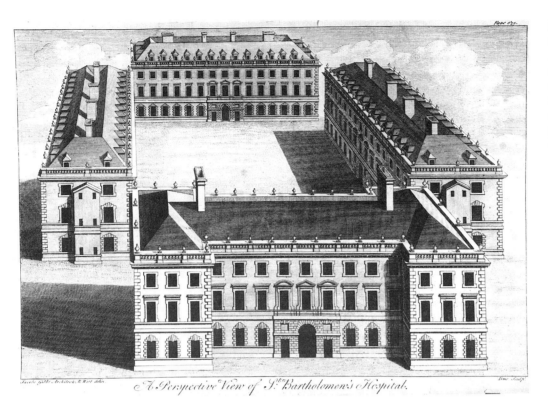

Figure 12
St Bartholomew's
Hospital, London, as
rebuilt in 1730–68 to
designs by James Gibbs,
with the administration
block in the foreground.
[Wellcome Institute Library,
London, V13001]

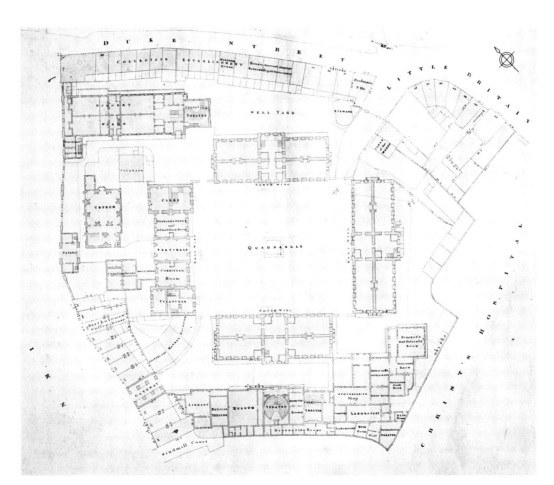

Figure 13
Ground plan of St
Bartholomew's Hospital
in 1848, showing
Gibbs's four blocks as
originally erected.
[Archives Department, St
Bartholomew's Hospital,
The Royal Hospitals NHS
Trust, HC55 Plan book
London Properties and
Hospital Site, 1848]

19

Figure 14
The governors' hall of
St Bartholomew's
Hospital, London,
designed by James Gibbs.
This fine room, situated
on the first floor and
rising through two
storeys, occupies the
whole of the central
section of the adminis-
tration block.
[NMR BB92/30691]

Figure 15 (opposite)
The governors' hall of
St Bartholomew's
Hospital (in Figure 14)
is reached from this
richly ornamented stair
hall. Hogarth's canvases
can be seen in the upper
part, set off by whimsical
trompe-l'oeil *decora-*
tion which picks up the
main decorative elements
of the building, with its
urns, scrolls, swags and
sinuous acanthus
leaves.
[NMR BB92/30681]

a result of Allen's offer, St Bartholomew's became one of the earliest buildings in London to be faced in Bath stone.[6]

The administration block was the first to be built. Completed in 1738, it contains the governors' hall, one of the grandest ceremonial halls in London (Fig 14). The walls here are adorned with panels bearing the names of benefactors, and the enriched plaster ceiling combines shells, cyphers and scrolling acanthus. Unusually for a commission of this size and importance, Gibbs did not rely on his favourite Italian *stuccatori*, Giovanni Bagutti and Giuseppe Artari, but employed instead the otherwise unknown Frenchman John Baptist St Michèle.[7] Situated on the first floor, the governors' hall is reached by an equally lavish grand staircase (Fig 15), with a decorative scheme devised by William Hogarth who, like Gibbs, was a governor of the hospital. Hogarth himself provided the two huge painted canvases which line two of the walls in the upper part of the stair hall. These depict the biblical stories of the Good Samaritan and Christ at the Pool of Bethesda, both aptly illustrating the spirit of the hospital's work. The remainder of the painted decoration in the stair hall was carried out by the obscure Mr Richards, who also executed the lettering and cartouches in the governors' hall.

While the remaining three blocks of St Bartholomew's were rising slowly in the City, the voluntary hospital movement was gradually emerging. The first general hospital to be established by voluntary subscriptions was the Westminster, which opened in 1720 in a house in Petty France. By 1724 its growing number of patients necessitated a move to a larger house in Great Chapel Street, and the hospital moved again in 1735, taking over three houses in Castle Lane, where it remained until a purpose-built hospital was erected in Broad Sanctuary in 1834 (see page 25). Domestic properties were not the only buildings to be pressed into use. The Bluecoat School at Chester was occupied as a hospital from 1755 and in the same year the Crown and Sceptre Inn provided the original home of the Gloucester Infirmary. (This was not merely an 18th-century phenomenon; as late as 1920 Minehead and District Hospital was established in the former Town Hall.)

Such humble and haphazard beginnings were typical of voluntary hospitals, which relied on the charitable inclinations and enthusiasm of the local community. The first to be established in the provinces was at Winchester, where a house in Colebrook Street opened as a general hospital in 1736. Alured Clarke, prebend of Winchester Cathedral and later Dean of Exeter, was closely involved with the foundation of the hospitals in

Figures 16 and 17
The main (north-west)
front and original plans
for the ground and
upper floors of the former
Devon and Exeter
Hospital. As built, the
hospital differed some-
what from the original
plans: the central three
bays are advanced rather
than recessed, and the
flanking ward wings
were built to just five
bays rather than nine.
The colonnade was also
omitted.
[NMR BB95/12080; plan
NMR BB92/34401 (copy-
right GG Halliday)]

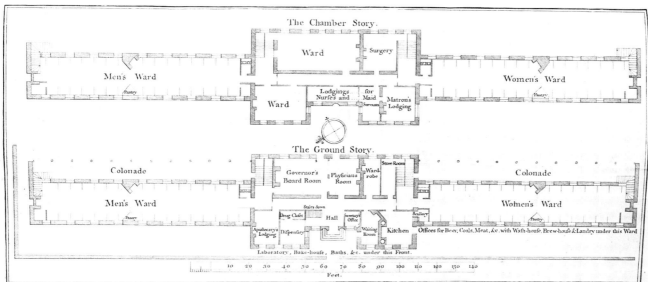

both these cities. The local nobility often contributed to new foundations, or assisted by granting a site, either free of charge or at a 'modest fee'. Early subscribers to Liverpool Infirmary in the 1740s included the 20th Earl of Derby, 'and some few Gentlemen at a distance'.[8]

Although general hospitals by their nature treated a variety of medical and surgical cases, certain patients were commonly excluded during the 18th and early 19th centuries. At Liverpool Infirmary, for example, it was stipulated that:

no Woman big with Child, no Child under seven Years of Age, except in extraordinary Cases, as Fractures, or where cutting for the Stone, or any other Operation is required; no Persons disordered in their Senses, suspected to have the Small-Pox, Itch [scabies], or other infectious Distemper, that are apprehended to be in a dying Condition or

Incurable, be admitted as In-Patients, or if inad-vertently admitted be suffered to continue.[9]

Apart from the large London hospitals of St Thomas's, St Bartholomew's and Guy's, early general hospitals rarely exceeded 100 beds, and many had fewer than 50. Extensive buildings were not, therefore, usually required and virtually all the administrative, service and medical accommodation could be brought together under one roof. As with other public buildings of the period, there was often a similarity in appearance to domestic properties, and in some cases even their plans showed little evidence of their more specialised purpose. However, the first purpose-built voluntary general hospital – the Devon and Exeter – was exceptional, its plan closely foreshadowing the pavilion-plan hospitals of the later 19th century (Figs 16 and 17).

John Richards, a local surveyor, provided the design free of charge, and the hospital was erected in 1741–3. It comprised three storeys over a basement, with a central block flanked by wings containing large wards. The basement housed most of the service rooms, including a bakehouse and brewhouse, and the central block contained the administrative offices, staff accommodation and further service rooms, as well as at least two small wards. Such a combination of large and small wards remained typical of hospitals built up to about 1780. Similarly, the arrangement whereby male patients occupied one wing and females the other became the usual practice in the smaller, symmetrical hospitals. As at Guy's, the wards in these wings had opposing windows and the original intention was that there should be a colonnade on their east side on the ground floor.

At the Liverpool Infirmary, the different functions were divided floor by floor. Services were in the basement, administrative offices on the ground floor, and, apart from one small ground-floor ward, patients' accommodation was on the first and second floors, servants residing in the attics. There was an operating theatre on the second floor, which had additional lighting from a skylight, and two wards near by for the surgeon's patients. Such 'operation wards' were commended by John Howard, the prison and hospital reformer, in the late 18th century, and became a standard feature.

Most of the hospitals built from the 1750s to the 1770s contained wards that were entered from corridors (giving rise to the term 'corridor-plan'), usually in a rectangular or H-shaped layout. For Manchester Infirmary, erected in 1754–5, the unknown architect opted for a simple rectangular plan. The infirmary was a substantial building of three storeys over a raised basement, the principal elevation with Palladian details looking deceptively like a gentleman's country mansion. This air of well-to-do domesticity was gradually eroded as the infirmary expanded with a succession of additions and alterations, and eventually obliterated altogether when the site was cleared in 1910, and the infirmary moved to its present home in Oxford Road.

Gloucester Infirmary was similarly domestic in appearance but had an H-shaped plan. It was built in 1755–61, the only known work of an obscure architect, Luke Singleton.[10] The building he designed was of two storeys over a raised basement and had a simple and dignified Classical façade, with a handsome double flight of stairs leading up to the main entrance. An engraving of the hospital published in 1764 (Fig 18) shows the extensive walled kitchen garden

to the rear with espaliered fruit trees and what were apparently 'Windsor beans' (another name for the common broad bean). Excess produce was sold for the benefit of the charity.[11] The Gloucester plan was repeated for the Radcliffe Infirmary. This is not surprising, as its 'competent but rather dull' architect, Stiff Leadbetter, had acted as Luke Singleton's builder at Gloucester.[12] It also served as a model for Anthony Keck's Worcester Infirmary of 1766–70, and was perhaps the basis for the Norfolk and Norwich Hospital of 1771–2.

Towards the end of the 18th century, a number of writers drew attention to problems associated with hospitals. The physician John Aikin lamented that every hospital had its own peculiar disease, 'the inbred pestilence of crowded receptacles for the sick', and it was widely believed that 'hospital disease' was caused by corrupt, stagnant air tainted by a variety of noxious effluvia from the patients (see Chapter 1). Improving the ventilation was seen as the principal means to counter this. The Leicester Infirmary, erected in 1768–71, had a degree of cross-ventilation in its wards, which had apertures in their corridor walls opposite the windows. This experiment was 'found to succeed', and was also adopted in the contemporary Leeds Infirmary designed by John Carr.

In an attempt to prevent the spread of disease, a number of smaller wards, rather than one or two large ones, was thought to be beneficial, as it introduced an element of separation and isolation. At the Northampton General Infirmary of 1790–3, Samuel Saxon's plan would have won the approval of both Aikin and John Howard, with its small wards for no more than ten beds, and one or two opposed windows providing a modicum of cross-ventilation. In the early 19th century some hospitals introduced artificial ventilation systems to replace stale air with fresh. The Derbyshire General, built in 1806–10, included a system which circulated warmed air through ducts from a basement furnace.

Developments in the 19th Century

Increasing urbanisation and the rapid expansion of new industrial towns in the 19th century encouraged the establishment of new general hospitals. Many developed from dispensaries, which were provided to dispense gratuitous advice, treatment and medicine to the poorer classes. The dispensary movement had originated in the later 18th century and by the mid 19th century a great many had been established which often remained independent from and

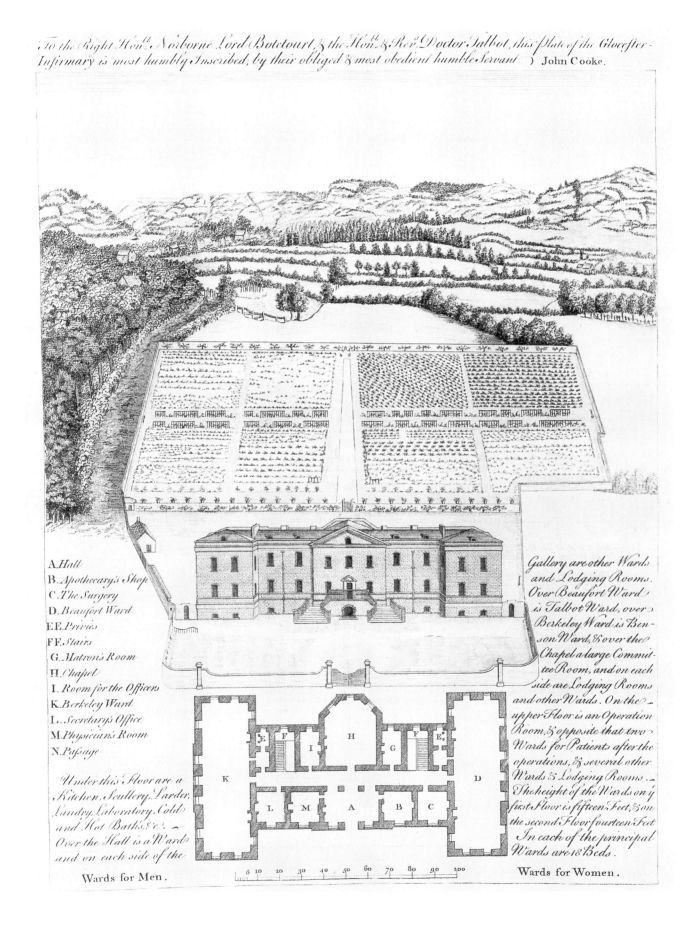

To the Right Hon.ble Norborne Lord Botetourt, & the Hon.ble & Rev.d Doctor Talbot, this plate of the Glocester Infirmary is most humbly Inscribed, by their obliged & most obedient humble Servant) John Cooke.

A. Hall
B. Apothecary's Shop
C. The Surgery
D. Beaufort Ward
E.E. Privies
F.F. Stairs
G. Matron's Room
H. Chapel
I. Room for the Officers
K. Berkeley Ward
L. Secretary's Office
M. Physician's Room
N. Passage

Under this Floor are a Kitchen, Scullery, Larder, Landry, Laboratory, Cold and Hot Baths &c. Over the Hall is a Ward, and on each side of the

Gallery are other Wards and Lodging Rooms. Over Beaufort Ward is Talbot Ward, over Berkeley Ward is Benson Ward, & over the Chapel a large Committee Room, and on each side are Lodging Rooms and other Wards. On the upper Floor is an Operation Room, & opposite that two Wards for Patients after the operations, & several other Wards & Lodging Rooms. The height of the Wards on y.e first Floor is fifteen Feet, & on the second Floor fourteen Feet. In each of the principal Wards are 18 Beds.

Wards for Men.

Wards for Women.

complementary to a general hospital in the same town or city. The North Staffordshire Infirmary at Etruria, Stoke-on-Trent, grew out of a dispensary which had been founded in 1802 and had proved so successful that the management committee was encouraged to extend its usefulness by erecting a general infirmary. This was designed by the County Surveyor, Joseph Potter, who practised as an architect and builder in Lichfield.[13] Built of stone, it was completed in 1819 and had a symmetrical front elevation, with the entrance set behind a colonnade. The wards and offices were grouped around a central stair and light-well, and included several specialist wards. On the ground floor these were for fever and accident cases, and two on the first floor were reserved for eye diseases. In addition, a 'burnt ward' was provided in a separate block on the north side, and an out-patients' department was set apart in a wing to the north west. One of the earliest improvements was the erection of a separate fever block, completed in 1829, which provided 30 beds. Further extensions were made in the 1850s, but by this time the noxious effects of local industries prompted the governors to consider erecting 'a more suitable building on a healthier site' (see pages 29–30).[14]

New general hospitals were also erected in London, where University College Hospital was built in 1822–4, a new building for St George's Hospital was erected in 1826, Charing Cross Hospital followed in 1831–4, and St Mary's, Paddington, in 1845. These were all substantial buildings, and at least two were designed by leading architects of the time. William Wilkins gained the commission for St George's and Decimus Burton that for Charing Cross. St Mary's was designed by Thomas Hopper, a significant figure amongst early 19th-century architects, though less well known today, while Alfred Ainger, a genteel City man of independent means, produced the plans for University College Hospital. The large numbers of patients gathered together made the small wards typical of provincial hospitals impracticable as they would have needed high levels of nursing staff to provide adequate supervision. Larger wards were therefore more usual. Those at University College Hospital and, in particular, in the wings added to St Thomas's in the 1830s and 1840s, closely prefigured pavilion planning in their arrangement.

University College Hospital was built on the opposite side of Gower Street from William Wilkins's imposing college building. It created a fitting complement, its tall, pedimented centre-piece aligned with the college entrance and grand portico. Ainger's plan was reminiscent of the Devon and Exeter Hospital, comprising a central entrance block with an axial corridor giving access to flanking ward wings. The wards had opposing windows and were heated by two open fireplaces. Sanitary facilities, in the form of small closets, were placed near the entrance to the wards and approached by short lobbies. A single-storey corridor at the back of the building provided access to offices on the ground floor and to a huddle of single-storey buildings in the back court housing the operating theatre, out-patients' department, mortuary and post-mortem room. In an attempt not to hamper cross-ventilation, this corridor was kept below the height of the windows of the ground-floor wards.

At St Thomas's, new wings were erected in 1833–5 and 1840–2, designed by the hospital's surveyor Samuel Robinson and his pupil James Field. An early photograph shows how these wings dwarfed the old hospital buildings (Fig 19). Each wing contained spacious and lofty wards with tall sash windows set opposite each other along the side walls (Fig 20). At the south-east end there were stairs, a Sister's room and a small kitchen, and at the north-west end, another Sister's room and the sanitary facilities. These components and their arrangement closely foreshadowed pavilion-ward blocks, but such advanced planning was not immediately recognised, and elsewhere the more traditional corridor plan or back-to-back wards remained the norm. At the new, and 'somewhat handsome' Westminster Hospital, none of the wards had opposing windows and they were all relatively small, accommodating between nine and twelve patients each.[15] A system of artificial heating and ventilation supplemented open fireplaces, and the water closets were placed in small wooden cabinets in the corners of the wards. The hospital was designed by William & Charles Inwood with a strong Gothic flavour, in keeping with its location opposite Westminster Abbey.

The sanitary facilities at the Westminster Hospital were eventually overhauled in the 1870s and at the same time an additional storey was built containing isolation wards and day-rooms for convalescent patients. In 1879 two of the wards were decorated by the Kyrle Society, which had been formed to supply 'artistic adornment for those who cannot possibly afford to indulge themselves in such a taste'.[16] William Morris supplied designs for the women's convalescent ward, and supervised the work there, while in the Bouverie ward (which was also for convalescents) the decorative painting was carried out by amateurs under the superintendence of the architect Charles Harrison Townsend, who was a member of the Society's committee. The need to accommodate convalescents had been appreciated since the late 18th

Figure 18
Gloucester Infirmary, built in 1755–61 to designs by Luke Singleton. This engraving of 1764 shows the main elevation of the hospital in its grounds, with a plan below. The hospital was demolished in the early 1980s.
[From the archives of the Gloucestershire Royal Hospital deposited in the Gloucestershire Record Office, HO 19/8/1]

Figures 19 and 20
These photographs of St Thomas's Hospital in London
were taken in 1862. The general view (above) shows in
the foreground the new wings that were added in the
1830s and 1840s, with the remaining part of the old
hospital in between, the three ranges that originally
stood nearest to Borough High Street having been
demolished. The tower of St Thomas's Church can be
seen behind the south wing (on the right of the picture),
and the building behind that is part of Guy's Hospital.
The interior view (right) shows the spartan arrange-
ment of one of the new wards, eerily devoid of patients.
[NMR BB84/2657 and NMR BB84/2658]

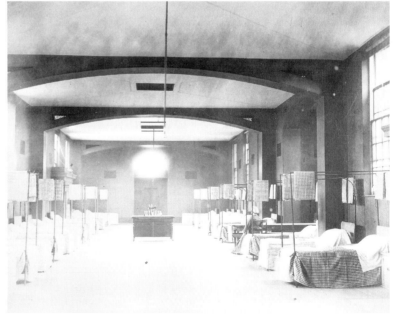

century. John Aikin felt that 'the circumstance of continuing through the day in the room where [the patients] slept' aggravated the evil of bad air. He recommended that 'large airy halls' should be provided for patients to occupy during the day, perhaps on the lines of the convalescent accommodation at Leeds Infirmary, where, in 1792, the central part of John Carr's building had been raised to provide an attic ward for this purpose.

For non-convalescent patients, back-to-back wards were still being built as late as the 1850s. They were adopted by Thomas Bellamy in his design for the new King's College Hospital, which had been founded in 1839 as a teaching hospital in connection with the college. It originally occupied the former St Clement Danes' Workhouse in Portugal Street on a 'highly objectionable' and restricted site that was nevertheless retained for the new building, constructed in two phases in 1854 and 1861.[17]

The corridor plan remained dominant throughout the first half of the 19th century. Developments in planning at that time reflected changes in the pattern of care and treatment, with the addition of convalescent wards and out-patients' departments. The number of people applying to general hospitals for treatment as out-patients rose steadily in the first half of the 19th century, and new hospitals generally included extensive out-patient departments, while older establishments found it necessary to build new ones. The Bristol General Hospital, for example, had been founded in 1832, opening in converted premises with 20 beds. When a new purpose-built hospital was erected in 1856–7, designed by the local architect William Bruce Gingell, it included an out-patients' department large enough to accommodate over 300 people. In the separate waiting-rooms for males and females, the long bench-seats were fixed upon the 'alternating principle' – that is, alternately to opposite sides of the room, creating a snaking, sitting queue – which apparently prevented confusion and pushing.[18]

Although the corridor plan continued to have its adherents, a major change took place in hospital design in the middle of the 19th century when the continental pavilion plan was promoted as a remedy to the dreaded 'hospital disease'. Within a few years, this new plan form was adopted for virtually all new general hospitals, as well as for additions to existing ones, and continued in use without serious challenge well into the 20th century (see Chapter 1).

The vast Continental models extolled by John Roberton, George Godwin and Florence Nightingale – the principal champions of pavilion planning – were adapted by architects to suit the smaller scale of the average English general hospital. On the Continent, where wards were built to accommodate up to 40 beds, and the hospitals typically housed several hundred patients, ranks of ward pavilions were set on opposite sides of a courtyard. The Lariboisière hospital was perhaps the best-known example of the pavilion plan (Fig 21). English hospitals were more likely to contain between 40 and 140 beds; the main wards in smaller hospitals might have as few as 8 beds, while those in the largest had up to 32. Two basic layouts evolved. The first, which made its début in 1857 in the competition designs for Blackburn Infirmary, was the more closely related to the Continental model, having a central three-storey administration block linked by an axial corridor to two-storey ward pavilions. The second, widely adopted for smaller hospitals, appeared for the first time in 1859 at Ashton-under-Lyne Infirmary, and harked back to the Devon and Exeter Hospital, with a central administrative block flanked by ward wings.

At Blackburn the competition for the new infirmary was won by a little-known architect, James Turnbull, whose design was hailed as a model of excellence.[19] The novel feature of Turnbull's design was his positioning of the wards on either side of a long axial corridor (Fig 22). This space-saving device enabled the architect to keep the distance between the pavilions to a minimum, without blocking light or air. A centrally placed administration block, including some small wards and an operating theatre, separated the women's wards on the south from the men's wards to the north. Building work began in 1858, but lack of funds caused delays and by 1865 only the administration block and two flanking pavilions had been completed. As the first pavilion-plan general hospital, the design and planning of Blackburn Infirmary commanded respect and it was held up as an exemplar. However, the small number of beds (just 8) in each ward was criticised, as was the lack of separate rooms for the ward nurses.

At Ashton-under-Lyne, the infirmary was also the result of an architectural competition. Some of the competitors clearly were influenced by Blackburn, but the selected design by Joseph Lindley was less elaborate. Following modifications to the plans, by John Roberton amongst others, the infirmary was erected in 1859–61. The wards were only slightly larger than those at Blackburn, with 10 instead of 8 beds, and included a nurse's room from which the ward could be kept under observation. The main inspiration for the design was the

Figure 21
Plan of the Lariboisière
Hospital, Paris, built in
1846–54 to designs by
Martin Pierre Gauthier.
The wards could only be
reached from the long
corridor that surrounded
the centre court, and
each ward pavilion had
its own separate stair,
ancillary rooms and, at
the far end, sanitary
facilities.
[Nightingale 1859a, pl 3
(NMR BB94/19968)]

recently completed military hospital at Vincennes, the plan of which was published in Florence Nightingale's influential *Notes on Hospitals* of 1859. Vincennes also served as the model for the Buckinghamshire Infirmary at Aylesbury. The original plans by David Brandon, T H Wyatt's former partner, were produced in April 1860, but following consultation with Nightingale, various amendments were made before work commenced. Completed in 1862, the infirmary was built of brick with modest stone dressings in a mildly Italianate manner (Figs 23 and 24). Square sanitary towers flanked the ends of the ward wings, one containing water closets, the other a bath and wash-hand basins. The principal wards were on the first floor only – the ground floor housed an out-patients' department and service rooms. With 22 beds, these wards were considerably larger than those at either Ashton or

Blackburn. The beds were placed in pairs between the windows, and two open fireplaces supplied the heating.

While Ashton-under-Lyne Infirmary was the first to adapt the pavilion plan into a single block, the refinements introduced at the Buckinghamshire Infirmary made it the more influential, winning the approval of Nightingale, and the Buckinghamshire plan was quickly copied across the country. Versions appeared at Rochester in Kent, where a new building was provided in 1861–3 for the medieval foundation of St Bartholomew's; at the Surrey County Hospital, Guildford, built in 1862–6; and at the Hampshire County Hospital in Winchester, erected in 1864–8. Although this simplest adaptation of the pavilion plan was closely related to earlier hospitals such as the Devon and Exeter and University College Hospital, the greater degree of separation of the different functions and the emphasis

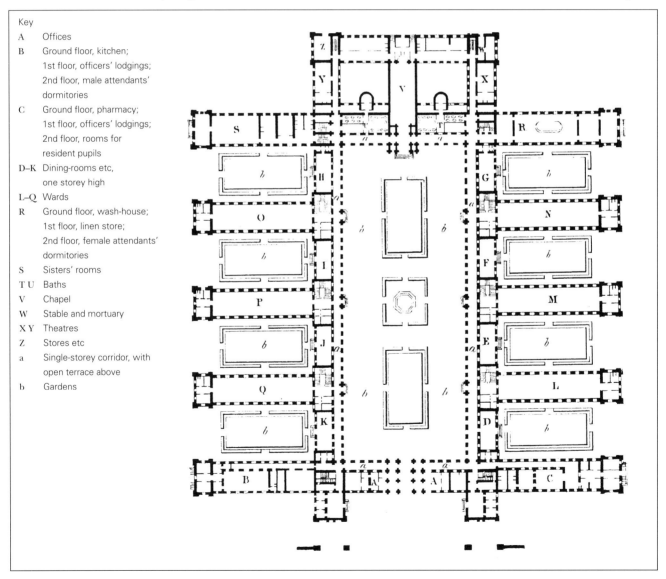

Key
A   Offices
B   Ground floor, kitchen;
     1st floor, officers' lodgings;
     2nd floor, male attendants'
     dormitories
C   Ground floor, pharmacy;
     1st floor, officers' lodgings;
     2nd floor, rooms for
     resident pupils
D–K Dining-rooms etc,
     one storey high
L–Q Wards
R   Ground floor, wash-house;
     1st floor, linen store;
     2nd floor, female attendants'
     dormitories
S   Sisters' rooms
T U Baths
V   Chapel
W   Stable and mortuary
X Y Theatres
Z   Stores etc
a   Single-storey corridor, with
     open terrace above
b   Gardens

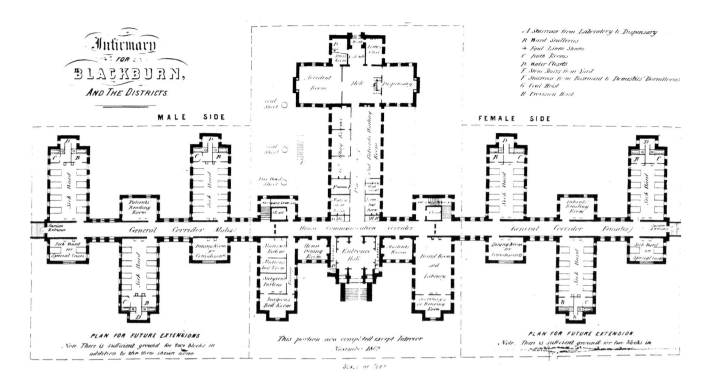

on improved sanitation were new developments. As the plan was further refined, cross-ventilated lobbies separating the sanitary facilities from the wards became a standard feature, introduced so that no harmful 'miasmas' could encroach upon the ward, and the wards themselves were healthily flushed by currents of fresh air that blasted in through one window and out through the one opposite.

The Vincennes model was later eclipsed by versions of the Blackburn type, with its axial corridor, even where only a single pair of ward pavilions was required. By the mid 1870s, most basic permutations for arranging and separating pavilion blocks in new buildings had been explored. The ward pavilions were usually set at right angles to the corridor, thus creating plans in the shape of a U or an H, with the occasional layout in the shape of a T or an E (others completely defy alphabetical categorisation). The contemporary battle of the styles is often in evidence, although financial constraints some-times produced uncompromisingly utilitarian buildings, with no discernible style whatsoever.

The largest of the early pavilion-plan general hospitals were built at Leeds, Stoke-on-Trent and in London. At both Leeds and Stoke these were closely modelled on the Lariboisière, with ward pavilions on either side of a courtyard. The Leeds General Infirmary was designed by George Gilbert Scott (by then already well experienced in the design of large institutional build-

ings) to replace Carr's earlier hospital, and was built in 1864–8 with accommodation for 296 patients. Scott employed his preferred Gothic style, complete with hood mouldings, plate tracery and a spiky skyline combining steeply pitched roofs and gables. In many respects these stylistic details prefigure those of the Midland Grand Hotel at St Pancras, commenced just as the infirmary was completed. Scott made the most of the sloping site, creating a highly complex plan. In essence, the hospital comprised a central arcaded courtyard with staff accommodation to the west and a chapel to the east, the ward pavilions extending to the north and south. The main entrance was centrally placed on the south front, sheltered by an ornate *porte-cochère*. All the services, administrative offices and the out-patients' department were on the lower ground level on this side.

At Stoke-on-Trent, the new North Staffordshire Infirmary was built at Hartshill in 1866–9, to replace the original hospital at Etruria (see page 25). The plans were drawn up jointly by G B Nichols of West Bromwich and a local architect, C Lynam, in consultation with Florence Nightingale. With 211 beds the North Staffordshire Infirmary was not so large as that at Leeds. It was largely of two storeys, built of polychrome brickwork in a pedestrian Ruskinian Gothic style, with none of the flamboyancy of Scott's building. Many of the infirmary's features remained typical of hospitals for

(see page 25)

Figure 22
Plan of Blackburn Infirmary, designed by James Turnbull and erected in 1858–65. The design shows the influence of Continental pavilion-plan hospitals such as the Lariboisière: the wards were reached from a long corridor (arranged on the north–south axis of the hospital), and included sanitary facilities at the far ends of the pavilions. [Plan scale 1:750, reproduced by permission of Blackburn, Hyndburn and Ribble Valley Health Care NHS Trust; document deposited at Lancashire Record Office (Ref: HRBK 4/1) (NMR BB94/19947)]

the next fifty years: in the wards, for example, the floors were of oak and the walls finished with Keene's cement, materials which were considered impervious and were easily cleaned. An out-patients' department was provided in one of the pavilions, with physicians' and surgeons' consulting-rooms adjacent to a large waiting-room, and day-rooms and small wards were placed in two small pavilions.[20]

In large hospitals there was a growing trend to provide each function or department with self-contained accommodation. At the North Staffordshire Infirmary there were several buildings detached from the main complex. These included a service block – containing the boiler house, laundry and mortuary – the gate lodge, stables, a fever block and the Smith

Hill Child building. This last was erected from funds provided by Sir Smith Hill Child in memory of his eldest son, and effectively functioned as a separate children's hospital. Such provision for children was exceptional. Up to the mid 19th century they were seldom admitted to hospital, and for much of the rest of the century opinions were divided over the merits of special accommodation for them (see Chapter 6).

By far the largest pavilion-plan general hospital to be erected at this time was the new St Thomas's, built in 1868–71 on a prominent Thames-side site directly opposite the Houses of Parliament. It was designed by Henry Currey, a pupil of Decimus Burton, who had been appointed as architect and surveyor to

Figures 23 and 24 Principal elevation and first-floor plan of the Buckinghamshire Infirmary, Aylesbury, designed by David Brandon and erected in 1861–2. The square sanitary towers can be seen in the foreground of the photograph, on the left. On this side of the building they have lost their pyramidal roofs. The Venetian window in the centre, between the towers, lit the end of the ward. [NMR BB92/6763; plan (1:750) Nightingale 1863, pl 3 (BB94/19961)]

30

St Thomas's in 1847. The new building provided accommodation for 600 patients, and was thus the closest in scale to the Continental pavilion hospitals yet built in England. However, the long narrow site ruled out a courtyard arrangement. Instead, Currey set six ward pavilions side by side, at right angles to the river, their paired sanitary towers facing the seat of government (Figs 25 and 26). The axial corridor, services, theatres, out-patients' department and staff accommodation were arranged on the eastern side of the site, on either side of a huge entrance hall. Above the hall was the chapel, but the main administrative offices, including the governors' hall and committee-room, were in a separate block to the north. An extensive medical school occu-

pied the southern wedge of the site, with three theatres, dissecting-room, laboratories and a museum (Fig 27). Many hospitals possessed a museum containing anatomical specimens and items of medical interest for the edification of the staff. St Thomas's medical school was dominated by a water tower in the form of a slender campanile, the finishing touch to the ostentatiously Italianate hospital. Enormous expense was lavished upon the buildings, inflated by problems with the foundations and the necessity of embanking the Thames. The completed buildings created a far more fitting prospect from the Houses of Parliament than the previous 'hideous aspect of the fore-shore, overladen ... with dank tenements, rotten wharves, and dirty boat-houses'.[21]

Figures 25 and 26 Photograph and first-floor plan of the new buildings for St Thomas's Hospital in Lambeth, London. To the far right of the picture the medical school can be seen with its distinctive water tower, and beyond this Lambeth Palace. St Thomas's was bombed during the Second World War, resulting in the demolition of the three northern ward pavilions. [NMR CC41/46; plan BB94/16116]

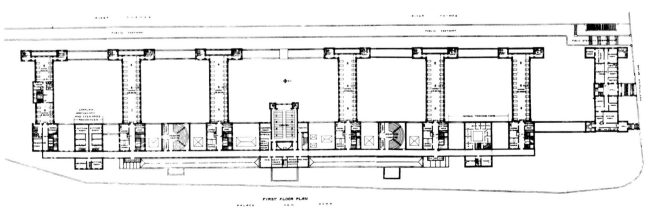

FIRST FLOOR PLAN

Figure 27
This stunning, if rather gruesome, photograph of the Medical School Museum at St Thomas's Hospital in London was taken by Country Life, *probably in the 1920s. The galleries, shelves bearing specimens and top-lighting are all typical features.*
[NMR Country Life *collection, 10263/15; © Country Life]*

Innovations in the Late 19th and Early 20th Centuries

Although pavilion planning dominated hospital design in the late 19th century, a little diversity was provided in the form of circular wards (see also pages 8–9), which made their first appearance in England at the Miller Memorial Hospital in Greenwich, where an exceedingly plain ward-tower was built in 1883–4 (Fig 28). It was designed by the well-established firm of hospital architects, Young & Hall, in response to a particularly awkward site. Although schemes were produced for hospitals with numerous circular wards, in most cases only one or two were actually incorporated on a site. When Liverpool Royal Infirmary was rebuilt in 1887–90, Alfred Waterhouse's design comprised two circular and four rectangular ward pavilions. The medical wards were provided in the larger rectangular pavilions to the south of the main axial corridor, and had balconies on their southern ends. The

pavilions to the north – including the two circular towers – were smaller and contained the surgical wards.

Not all the general hospitals built in the late 19th century slavishly followed the pavilion principle. A few smaller institutions returned to the corridor plan, with domestic-scale wards. In some cases this can be attributed to a particularly cramped or awkward site, but there may also have been a deliberate decision to create a different environment, especially where the hospital offered a particular type of treatment or served a separate section of the community. The Hahnemann Homoeopathic Hospital in Liverpool built in 1887, for example, and the French Hospital in London, erected in 1890, eschewed pavilion planning.

A different kind of accommodation was certainly required at the new private hospitals which began to emerge in the mid 19th century. The first 'pay-hospital' opened in London during the 1840s 'for persons belonging to the middle

classes', but it was a short-lived venture.[22] Pay-beds did not become common until much later in the century, after considerable controversy within the medical profession. Advances in hospital design, medical practice and treatment led to a steady improvement in the status of hospitals and attracted patients from an increasingly wide sphere, instead of being restricted to the 'deserving poor'. Private hospitals and pay-beds catered for the better-off and, unsurprisingly, usually provided patients with rather more privacy. Two of the earliest private hospitals opened in Northampton in 1879 and Fitzroy Square, London, in 1880, while the first general hospital to admit paying patients was St Thomas's, where the St Thomas's Home for Paying Patients (comprising two existing wards) opened in 1881.[23]

One of the first purpose-built private hospitals was the somewhat grandiloquently named Empire Hospital, erected in 1912 in Vincent Square, Westminster (Fig 29). Designed by Wilberforce E Hazell, a pupil of Alfred Waterhouse, it provided between 40 and 50 beds for middle-class patients. Architecturally, the building had few pretensions, although its bay windows and iron-railed balconies are still attractive features. Part of the ground floor to

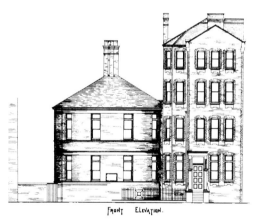

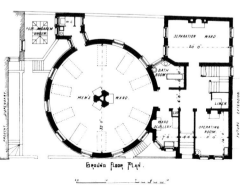

Rochester Row was designed to be let as three shops, not an uncommon feature in central London hospitals of about this date. The rest of the ground floor was taken up by waiting-rooms, offices and two bedrooms for nurses, as well as four single-bed wards overlooking the square. The main stair wound round a lift situated directly opposite the main door, and the upper floors had suites of generously sized private rooms, each with a fireplace and many with the luxury of two windows. Four of the wards on each floor overlooked a small courtyard at the rear of the building, an arrangement severely criticised for restricting the circulation of air. With its wealth of private rooms, the building was castigated for having been designed more on the lines of a hotel than a hospital (prophetically, as it had been converted into a hotel by the early 1990s).[24]

For most of the 19th century, the need for specialist medical staff and facilities to treat particular ailments or conditions had been provided by specialist hospitals. These institutions

Figure 29 (above)
The former Empire Hospital in Westminster, built in 1912 to the designs of W E Hazell. The photograph shows the principal elevation to Vincent Square and the side elevation. [NMR BB93/25081]

Figure 28 (left)
This engraving from The Builder, *23 Aug 1884 shows the circular ward-tower of the Miller Memorial Hospital at Greenwich. The hospital was established to augment the Kent Dispensary, which had been founded in 1783. [NMR BB94/16632]*

Figure 30
The nurses' home at the
Derbyshire Royal
Infirmary in Derby,
designed by Young &
Hall and built in
1892–4.
[NMR BB93/35767]

Figure 31(opposite)
Interior of the Middlesex
Hospital chapel,
London, designed by J L
Pearson in 1890, and
erected as a memorial to
Major Ross, Chairman
of the Board of
Governors. The sump-
tuous marble and
mosaic decoration was
finally completed in the
1930s by Pearson's son,
Frank.
[NMR BB91/28007]

were often regarded with distrust and hostility by staff in general hospitals, but as specialist hospitals thrived, their opponents were forced to reconsider their stance. As a result, a wide variety of specialist departments grew up in the larger general hospitals. At Young & Hall's new Derbyshire Royal Infirmary of 1891–4, these specialist departments, as well as all the other sections of the hospital, were kept apart or given a separate building. Designed in a free Jacobethan manner, with mullioned-and-transomed windows, tall chimneys and, on the administration block, a multi-gabled skyline, the architects managed to achieve 'considerable architectural effect towards the London-road'.[25] The ends of the ward pavilions were particularly ornate, with 'open loggie in stone connecting the sanitary turrets', rather in the manner of St Thomas's.[26] An important element in the infirmary complex was the substantial nurses' home, situated at the edge of the site, its gabled roofline echoing the administration block (Fig 30).

Detached nurses' homes had become more common from the 1880s onwards, when they were either added to existing hospitals or formed part of new schemes. Developments in hospital planning and design had gone hand in hand with the reform of the nursing profession, and Nightingale, for one, recognised the need to provide nurses with better accommodation within the hospital. At first, nurses' status resembled that of servants rather than professionals, and they were expected to sleep either in the wards, in rooms overlooking them, or in the garrets. The Royal Berkshire Hospital at Reading had one of the earliest nurses' homes,

a single-storey building of 1872 with eight bedrooms and a sitting-room. In later homes, the nurses were usually provided with single rooms, and servants' accommodation was often placed on the top floor. The hierarchical nature of the nursing profession was reflected in the planning, with the sisters, staff nurses and probationers carefully segregated and their accommodation suitably differentiated. Each group had its own sitting-room and the best-appointed homes included quiet or reading-rooms and a library.

It was not only the physical comfort of staff and patients that preoccupied hospital governors and architects, but also their spiritual well-being. Chapels were invariably a feature of even the smallest general hospital, although they might have to double as the committee-room. Seldom large, they were attended by staff, visitors and those few patients who were mobile. Although a chapel was usually part of all hospital plans from the outset, as a non-essential feature its construction was often deferred or made the object of a special fundraising effort or bequest. The Middlesex Hospital chapel, erected in 1890–1, is one of the most exquisite in the country. The architect selected was John Loughborough Pearson, who designed a simple rectangular nave and an apsed chancel, with a small narthex or ante-chapel at the liturgical west end. Built as a memorial to Major A H Ross, a former chairman of the governors, additional funding was provided, largely from Major Ross's family, for a lavish scheme of decoration. The stunning marble and mosaic interior combines Byzantine, medieval-Italian and Romanesque motifs (Fig 31). Although the first phase of the decoration was completed in 1897–8 the whole scheme was not finished until the 1930s, work after Pearson's death being carried out by his son, Frank.

The late 19th and early 20th centuries witnessed a resurgence in the building of large general hospitals. Those at Halifax, Birmingham, Newcastle upon Tyne and Manchester occupied extensive sites and were able to provide each department with its own building. However, when University College Hospital was rebuilt in 1897–1906, Alfred Waterhouse ingeniously reconciled the need for extensive accommodation on the restricted site with the principles of pavilion planning (Fig 32). The imposing building rises to five storeys and attics above a basement, with a dramatic skyline, in wild contrast to the former hospital and the college opposite. It was constructed of deep-red coloured brick, with copious dressings of pinkish terracotta supplied by Doulton. From first-floor level the building takes the form of a St Andrew's cross, which

Figure 32
Alfred Waterhouse's perspective, with its inset plan, captures the striking visual impact of this large hospital, which, when it was built in 1897–1906, must have jarred with the neighbouring buildings even more than it does today. Despite a few insensitive additions, this vibrantly red building, with its soaring Gothic towers and richly detailed brick and terracotta facings, still remains impressive.
[British Architectural Library/Royal Institute of British Architects]

ensured that no ward would be unduly deprived of light and air. Although symmetrical in plan, and with much of its detail and decoration derived from Classical and Northern Renaissance sources, the building gives an overall impression of verticality and sublimity that has more in common with the Gothic revival architecture of the High Victorian era. Just as its overall plan differed from that of most existing hospitals, so too did the layout of the wards. Each ward wing was in the form of a cross, with beds down each side as usual, but with an extra-large bay at either side. The wings were connected to the central tower by short bridges and at their extreme ends loomed the sanitary towers, capped by steeply pitched slated roofs, their jagged profiles echoing the spire of the central stair tower.

The importance of thorough ventilation had preoccupied hospital architects throughout the 19th century, but in the early years of the 20th century there was a growing belief in the beneficial effects of sunshine and fresh air. Open-air treatment for tuberculosis met with marked success, and exposing other patients to the beneficent elements gained increasing popularity. Verandas and balconies, sun-rooms and roof-terraces sprouted on general hospitals throughout the country, as architects rushed to

embrace the new obsession. New technology, too, had to be accommodated. Following the discovery of X-rays in 1895, X-ray equipment was eventually installed in all general hospitals, but its diagnostic capabilities made it the natural adjunct to out-patients' departments. For the new King's College Hospital, built at Denmark Hill in 1909–13, William Pite designed an extensive 'electrical department', which included a Finsen Light for artificial-sunlight treatment, and a gymnasium and massage room for physiotherapy.

Towards the National Health Service

The increasing sophistication of surgery and the march of medical progress made it ever more advantageous for the affluent to seek medical treatment in hospital rather than at home. Voluntary general hospitals began to shake off their image of charitable institutions for the poor. At the other end of the social scale a major change was ushered in by the Local Government Act of 1929,[27] which empowered local authorities to appropriate former workhouses and workhouse infirmaries. Many of these were subsequently developed as municipal general hospitals,

administered by Public Health Committees, and provided thousands of hospital beds for the general public, previously available only to paupers.

With this rise in the social status of hospitals came a great expansion in the number of pay-beds. On the whole these were added to voluntary hospitals rather than being supplied by independent private hospitals, and even former workhouse infirmaries began to admit paying-patients. At the Nottingham General Hospital and the Manchester Royal Infirmary, substantial separate buildings were constructed for private patients which functioned independently from the parent hospitals with their own operating theatres and services. The majority of paying-patients' departments, however, were less extensive than these, and used the main hospital's facilities.

Advances in medicine and new methods of building construction led to major developments in hospital design in the 1920s and 1930s. Discoveries in the field of bacteriology demonstrated that infection took place by direct contact with infected matter, and no amount of cross-ventilation could kill germs. In the light of these developments, some of the general principles on

which hospital construction had been based could at last be laid aside. Lionel G Pearson, one of the leading hospital architects of the time, acknowledged that a new era in hospital design had commenced in which compact planning, the avoidance of long corridors and the centralisation of services ruled. In these new hospitals the wards and services were more fully integrated into one vertical building, inspired by the multi-storeyed hospitals constructed in America along the lines of office buildings, hotels and apartment blocks in the years immediately following the First World War. This vertical planning contrasted with the customary English, and indeed European, predilection for the horizontal, but on restricted urban sites the only possible direction for expansion was upwards.

In 1927 an ambitious rebuilding programme was begun at the Middlesex Hospital in central London. By the 1920s James Paine's 18th-century Palladian building was in danger of falling down, and a new hospital was designed for the site by Alner W Hall (the son of Henry Hall, of Young & Hall) which was built in phases between 1927 and 1935 (Fig 33). As well as incorporating some classical motifs in homage

Figure 33
Middlesex Hospital, London, photographed during the rebuilding. The west wing, to the left, was completed in 1929, and was the first section of the new hospital to be built. It can be seen here towering over the remaining parts of the old hospital, which was pulled down in 1931–2. Work then began on the central range and east wing. The official opening, by the Duke and Duchess of York, took place in May 1935.[Photograph in an album held in the Middlesex Hospital Archives]

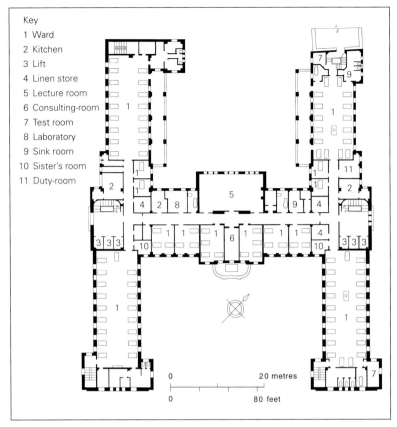

Key
1 Ward
2 Kitchen
3 Lift
4 Linen store
5 Lecture room
6 Consulting-room
7 Test room
8 Laboratory
9 Sink room
10 Sister's room
11 Duty-room

0   20 metres

0   80 feet

Figure 34
First-floor plan of
A W Hall's new
building for the
Middlesex Hospital,
London. The plan shows
the combination of old-
style pavilion wards with
smaller wards in the
centre of the building in
which the beds are placed
parallel to the windows.
[Plan (1:750) based on
Architects' Journal, *18*
Sep 1929, 413 and The
Builder, *28 Jun 1935,*
1196]

to the building it replaced, Hall followed the H-plan of the old hospital, lengthened and widened it, and shifted the whole slightly to the east, allowing the chapel to be extended (Fig 34). Built of red brick and Portland stone, the new hospital was much higher than its predecessor, comprising seven floors above ground and two below. In the entrance hall, with its teak-veneer walls and marble floor, are four large figure-paintings by Frederic Cayley-Robinson, painted in 1916–20 for the vestibule of the old building; to the north is the committee-room, panelled in pine mostly retrieved from its predecessor. Further administrative offices were provided on the ground floor of the west wing, while the east wing housed the X-ray diagnostic department. Above, the hospital was symmetrically divided with surgical wards to the west and medical wards to the east. Large open-air balconies (since filled-in) overlooked a pleasant garden to the rear. The fifth floor was devoted entirely to facilities for women, with gynaecological and maternity wards, including three labour rooms planned *en suite*, and a subsidiary corridor for quietness. Four large operating theatres were provided in the central section on the sixth floor.[28]

Although the new Middlesex Hospital employed the up-to-date method of steel-frame construction and provided modern medical facil-

ities, its appearance was a still-fashionable neo-Georgian, perhaps with a few transatlantic over-tones. The contemporary Royal Masonic Hospital at Ravenscourt Park in west London, erected in 1931–3 to a design by Sir John Burnet, Tait & Lorne, was, by contrast, a *tour de force* of the Modern Movement. A steel-frame construction was employed here to give great freedom in design, allowing the walls to be punctuated by long bands of fenestration that created a particularly light and airy interior. The administration block sets the tone for the hospital, with its imposing façade, austere in its sparing use of ornament but striking in its massing, and with an audacious use of large areas of blank wall space. A tall window over the entrance lights the full-height entrance hall, its two deep mullions soaring upwards to end in sculpted busts, representing Health and Healing, by Gilbert Bayes. Linked to the administration block is a U-shaped ward block where the wards, which contain no more than four beds, overlook a garden court containing an ornamental pool (Fig 35). The cantilevered sun-balconies at the end of each wing were among the hospital's most innovative features. Behind the ward block to the north, an annexe originally contained the boilers and service rooms as well as the main entrance for patients arriving by ambulance. The electrical and surgical block contained the operating theatres on the top floor, and the radiology and physiotherapy departments and nurses' dining-rooms on the ground floor.[29]

Even at some of the smaller hospitals, buildings erected in the inter-war years embraced technical innovations inspired by new developments abroad. In 1932–3, 'veranda wards' were built at Hertford County Hospital (Fig 36). Designed by Charles Ernest Elcock, these ward blocks, of 4-in. brick covered externally with white cement stucco, were in stark contrast to the original Victorian hospital. The window lintels, floors and flat roofs were of reinforced concrete, the roofs being finished in asphalt. Wide windows occupied as much of the wall space as possible, their sliding and folding frames permitting the entire side of a ward to be opened up in suitable weather. This allowed maximum exposure to sun and air, and rendered sun balconies unnecessary. The beds were placed parallel to the window wall instead of at right angles to it, and were in groups of two or four, separated by glazed screens. Various features were introduced for the patients' comfort: unduly strong sunlight could be excluded from the wards by large roller blinds fixed at sill level and extending upwards; heating was by continuous pipes placed beneath the windows all round the wards; and steel-and-glass screens between the groups of beds carried

separate light and wireless points to each bed.

The new Westminster Hospital of 1933–9, by Adams, Holden & Pearson, was exceptional in many respects. One of the largest general hospitals yet built, it comprised two vast new buildings, erected on the east and west sides of St John's Gardens in Westminster. The west block contained the nurses' home and medical school and the east block the hospital proper (Fig 37). A total of 400 beds was provided, including 44 for paying patients, and the block was so designed that as many wards as possible faced the gardens. In an attempt to improve access, the architects adopted the novel device of a roadway running through the centre of the hospital building. Traditional pavilion-type wards were combined with smaller wards off corridors, and single rooms for the private patients. But the hospital's most unusual aspect was the way in which it dealt with out-patients. Rather than providing one separate out-patients' department on the edge of the hospital complex, it had a general clearing-station for patients, from which they were directed to consulting-rooms and clinics placed alongside specialist departments on each floor. Each patient would then be in close contact with the particular unit of the hospital which dealt with their individual case, and with their medical history and papers. In this way it was hoped to create the 'No-Waiting Hospital'.[30] The Westminster had other claims to originality: it was the first hospital designed to be gas-proof (as a precaution against air raids), and to be 'noiseless', with shock-absorbing floors that prevented vibrations.

The Westminster set the trend for ever bigger general hospitals, with increasingly sophisticated equipment and a wider range of specialist departments. Since the 18th century, when so many cases were excluded – from pregnant women to incurable diseases such as cancer – medical treatment had changed dramatically, and in the 20th century specialist departments were set up in many general hospitals. Pooling resources and

Figure 35
View of the ward block of the Royal Masonic Hospital, London, designed by Sir John Burnet, Tait & Lorne and built in 1931–3, showing the elegantly curved, cantilevered balconies that terminate each ward wing.
[NMR BB92/30854]

Figure 36
This utilitarian-looking block, added to Hertford County Hospital in 1932–3 by C E Elcock, provided innovative 'veranda wards' on the first floor. The long windows were designed so that the central band of glazing could be folded back, like a concertina, effectively turning the whole ward into a veranda.
[NMR BB93/27092]

centralising services, so much a part of the National Health Service, began in the inter-war period, when finances were already becoming stretched in many establishments. Improved transport also played a part, enabling large general hospitals to serve wider areas, and to be built on open sites on the outskirts of towns.

Large greenfield sites gave architects more scope in the choice of design and planning. In Birmingham, a site close to the University and some two miles from the city centre was presented to the city by the Cadbury family in 1926 and an ambitious scheme was embarked upon to build a new general teaching hospital. The existing Birmingham General and Queen's Hospitals were to amalgamate, and it was hoped that other specialist hospitals in the city would move out to the new site. It was calculated that the land was sufficient to provide hospital accommodation for a total of 3,000 patients, the only proviso being that neither mental illness nor infectious fevers would be treated on the site.

A competition was held for the design for a hospitals complex in November 1928. The list of architects invited to compete included some of the best-known practices concerned with hospital planning, among them Elcock & Sutcliffe; Wallace Marchment; Pite, Son & Fairweather; Saxon Snell & Philips; and Sir Aston Webb & Son. The commission went to Lanchester & Lodge, a firm which was familiar with hospital work, and equally complex, large public buildings.

In the early stages of planning, the building committee visited hospitals in Europe and America, and debated whether to adopt the pavilion principle or the multi-storey block. It decided on a compromise, in which multi-storey pavilions were to be combined with small wards of 2 or 4 beds, after the design of the Westminster Hospital. When the first phase of the Birmingham Hospitals Centre opened in July 1938, it presented an astonishing group of vast buildings, solidly massed, with a rhythmic repetition of forms, rising to the monolithic clock tower at the heart of the complex (Fig 38). Pale buff-coloured bricks were used to face the buildings with a minimal use of stone dressings, against a backdrop of bright green lawns, dark green hedges and trees, and bright scarlet bedding plants.[31]

Emergency Medical Service Hospitals

In the month before the Birmingham Hospitals Centre was officially opened, the Ministry of Health had instituted the Emergency Medical Service (EMS). As war with Germany became more likely, arrangements were made for dealing with the anticipated large-scale casualties from enemy bombing. Vast numbers of additional hospital beds were thought to be needed, and plans were drawn up for the construction of hutted annexes at existing hospitals, or completely new hutted hospitals on fresh sites. Furthermore, hospitals which did not possess all the facilities and surgical equipment needed for a casualty hospital were to be upgraded.

In March 1939 the Office of Works was commanded to organise emergency accommodation for 52,000 patients throughout Britain. It collaborated with the Royal Institute of British Architects, amongst others, to select architects experienced in hospital design to carry out the construction of EMS hospitals in their local areas. About seventy-five architects were engaged to work on the scheme, and the first contracts were completed before the outbreak of war. Most of these schemes comprised hutted annexes attached to former workhouses, mental hospitals and sanatoria, where space was readily available, although a number of general hospitals and even a few cottage hospitals were also brought into the scheme.

A 'General Description of Ward Blocks' drawn up by the Ministry of Health and dated 3 May 1939 noted that blocks were to be spaced 30 ft apart and set on concrete bases. The blocks followed a standard arrangement with ancillary rooms (usually including a ward kitchen, store room and the sanitary facilities) at the entrance, with the ward itself beyond. The wards were heated by one or more central stoves, and often had alternating casement and french windows in the side walls and a french window at the far end. At most sites the huts were built of brick or concrete blocks; less than half were of timber construction and a few used compressed wood-wool slabs, which had good insulating properties, for external and internal walls. The huts were arranged in regular groups known as spider blocks, connected by covered ways, and air-raid shelters were distinctive features on all the sites (Fig 39).

Early in 1940, a second programme was put in hand which included further hutted annexes as well as a number of complete hospitals, among them Stoke Mandeville Hospital in Buckinghamshire, and Ronkswood Hospital in Worcester.

Figure 37
General view of the Westminster Hospital, London, built in 1933–9 to designs by Adams, Holden & Pearson, seen from St John's Gardens. On the top floor, in the centre, was the chapel, its position marked by a white Latin cross on the end wall. This hospital replaced the former premises at Broad Sanctuary, but has itself been superseded, and, along with the nurses' home and medical school on the other side of the gardens, now lies empty. [NMR BB93/36265]

Figure 38 (above) The Birmingham Hospitals Centre, now Queen Elizabeth Hospital, designed by Lanchester & Lodge and built in 1933–8. This aerial photograph was taken not long after the hospital was completed and shows the main hospital block with the nurses' home to the rear and medical faculty in front.
[NMR AA92/2076]

Figure 39 (right) Block plan of Ronkswood Hospital, Worcester (now part of Worcester Royal Infirmary), designed by Braddell, Deane & Bird and built in 1940–2.
[Based on The Builder, 6 Nov 1942, 392]

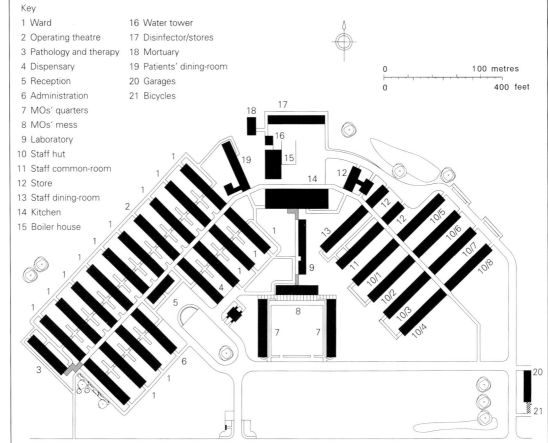

Key

1 Ward
2 Operating theatre
3 Pathology and therapy
4 Dispensary
5 Reception
6 Administration
7 MOs' quarters
8 MOs' mess
9 Laboratory
10 Staff hut
11 Staff common-room
12 Store
13 Staff dining-room
14 Kitchen
15 Boiler house
16 Water tower
17 Disinfector/stores
18 Mortuary
19 Patients' dining-room
20 Garages
21 Bicycles

0   100 metres
0   400 feet

Figure 40
A typical hutted ward
block at the Emergency
Medical Service Hospital,
Ronkswood, Worcester.
[NMR BB93/24041]

This programme coincided with the fall of France, which led to increasing difficulties in the supply of materials. The use of timber was forbidden, and a flat roof of precast units was devised which used a minimum of steel-rod reinforcement.[32] At Ronkswood, the firm of Braddell, Deane & Bird carried out the scheme which comprised a V-shaped arrangement of ward huts placed on either side of the central services. The huts were constructed of brick and had pitched, corrugated-iron roofs, supported on reinforced-concrete and asbestos trusses designed by the consulting engineer, Donald Stewart (Fig 40).

Hutted blocks of EMS hospitals were quickly erected and proved perfectly adequate for their purpose. The new hutted hospitals had been built, as far as possible, where they would be of use to civilians after the war. The majority of them, together with the annexes to existing hospitals, became part of the greatly varied building stock inherited by the National Health Service in 1948. Although by then many of the oldest hospital buildings had been replaced, the general hospitals transferred to the National Health Service nevertheless constituted a rich architectural heritage, ranging from the compact infirmaries of the Georgian era to the vast complexes of the 20th century which embraced many specialist departments in addition to the general medical and surgical wards. However, far outnumbering these, were the solidly constructed general hospitals erected by the Victorians in the second half of the 19th century, instantly recognisable by their strict adherence to the pavilion plan.

3
Cottage Hospitals

In 1859 a country doctor in Surrey, Albert Napper, opened a small hospital in a converted cottage which he named Cranleigh Village Hospital (Fig 41). This event had much more than a local significance, for the principles on which the hospital was founded and the rules by which it was run were widely copied, creating a new type of medical institution: the cottage hospital.[1]

Napper had spent nearly twenty years as a surgeon in Guildford before moving to a country medical practice, where he soon became acutely conscious of its disadvantages. He complained of the 'impossibility of rendering efficient aid in urgent cases of accident or disease, with no other accommodation than that afforded by the ... miserable abodes of the poor', when the nearest county hospital was too far away for the patient to bear the journey. In addition, relatives were often reluctant that the patient should be removed to such a distance that they would find visiting difficult.[2] These problems were exacerbated in the mid 19th century as the spreading railway network and increasing mechanisation in farming and mining produced a greater number of severe accident cases in rural areas. Amongst the earliest patients to benefit from treatment at Cranleigh Village Hospital was a 6-year-old boy whose thumb had been crushed in the cogs of a threshing machine.

Apart from having to watch the patients' sufferings with little means of ameliorating their condition, doctors were beset by other frustrations. Their careers were unlikely to flourish if the local gentry saw that they could not cope with complicated cases, which had to be sent to a town hospital. As Napper pointed out, the upper classes considered that the position of hospital physician or surgeon was 'a sufficient guarantee of high professional attainments'; by contrast the country doctors were regarded with distrust. Napper sought 'a practical remedy', and concluded that a small and inexpensive institution could be established in the countryside, on the lines of an urban general hospital but on a greatly reduced scale, which would 'alleviate many of the evils and inconveniences

so severely felt'.[3] In the eyes of his fellow medical practitioners, Napper's most seductive argument for establishing small local hospitals was the increased prestige they would gain, accompanied by fees for attending the wealthier clients, who would otherwise have sent to town for a surgeon.

Napper argued that the 'rustic labourer feels more at ease in lodgings similar to his own',[4] and both he and subsequent writers stressed that a local, village hospital should resemble the poor man's cottage. However, it was the 19th-century romantic image of a 'rustic cottage' that he envisaged. This was a vision which had been fostered by the thoughtful model cottages built by John Nash in the first decades of the century and popularised by John Claudius Loudon in the 1830s in his monumental *Encyclopaedia of Cottage, Farm, and Villa Architecture*. In the late 1850s and 1860s the aesthetic qualities of rural vernacular architecture were being exploited by such architects as Philip Webb, George Devey and Norman Shaw, and, in the last decades of the century, an appreciation of vernacular styles and building methods became central to the tenets of the Arts & Crafts Movement.

It was in these terms that Napper, and those who shared his views, perceived the type of 'cottage' which would be suitable as a hospital. What they envisaged, far from the mean and squalid dwellings of one or two rooms in which many of their prospective patients resided, was a small farmhouse, or 'a double-tenemented cottage' of considerable size, 'having on the ground-floor, a kitchen, sitting-room, scullery, and larder, and upstairs, from four to six rooms, well ventilated'.[5] For new buildings, Napper recommended the local Surrey style, of brick or stone to first-floor level and hung tiles above. This form was not only in tune with the contemporary architectural aesthetic, but had the practical benefits of being economical, durable, warm and free from damp.

Similarly, Edward Waring, writing in 1867, dwelt on the importance of retaining the 'cottage element', waxing lyrical about homeliness and the benefits to the labouring man of surroundings which would 'approximate as

nearly as possible to those of his own humble dwelling'.[6] But there was an inescapable discrepancy between the romantic imagery and reality, and Waring had to admit that the homes of the poor were, in fact, totally unsuitable for use as hospitals, consisting generally of 'small, ill-constructed, ill-lighted apartments, destitute alike of efficient means of ventilation, drainage, cleanliness, and other accessories which are universally recognised as invaluable aids towards the recovery of the sick'.[7]

Cranleigh Village Hospital itself was a two-storey building, the central entrance leading straight into a large kitchen with a sitting-room to one side and the back kitchen and pantry to the other. Above were two wards, measuring 16 ft by 11 ft and 16 ft by 12 ft, each containing 2 beds, with a small bedroom for a nurse and an operating room. The hospital was widely praised and served as the model for other small hospitals which opened in converted premises.[8] The majority of buildings chosen as suitable for conversion were domestic in origin, such as the dilapidated house, with 'no pretension to taste or design', at Wrington in Somerset, which was converted into 'a thoroughly useful and comfortable little hospital' in 1864.[9] Similarly, No. 2 Green Hedges Cottages was used in 1863 for East Grinstead Cottage Hospital. This house belonged to the local general practitioner, Dr John Henry

Rogers, whose only attempt to adapt the building to its new function was to add a large room with a bay window to the rear. The garden, 'which teems with a profusion of flowers', attracted quite as much interest as the arrangements within the hospital.[10] A few cottage hospitals occupied industrial buildings, among them Crewkerne Hospital in Somerset, which opened in premises which had formerly been part of a factory for manufacturing girth-webbing. The building was donated by the factory owner, Robert Bird, who later founded and endowed an almshouse for his retired web-weavers.[11]

As a conversion rather than a new building, Cranleigh Hospital was of greater long-term importance for its organisation than its plan. Indeed, it was in their administration that cottage hospitals differed significantly from existing general hospitals. Although both were largely funded by voluntary subscriptions or endowments, and patients were admitted on the recommendation of subscribers, at cottage hospitals all patients were required to pay a 'small weekly sum' towards their treatment and upkeep. These fees were insufficient to make the hospitals profitable, covering no more than a third of their expenditure, and in the majority of cases amounting to less than a tenth of their total income. But, as well as the increase in revenue, however minimal, charging fees

Figure 41
Cranleigh Village Hospital, Surrey, established by Albert Napper in 1859 in a picturesque house. This engraving was used by Horace Swete as the frontispiece to his Handy Book of Cottage Hospitals, *published in 1870.*
[Swete 1870, frontispiece (NMR BB94/19940)]

according to the patient's means was thought to deter the wealthy from applying for admission. This was one of the perceived abuses of general voluntary hospitals, where numerous patients were admitted who were in fact capable of paying for medical attendance in their own homes. Napper considered that such cases were granted admission 'more with a view of gratifying the subscriber than of benefiting the patient',[12] and he was convinced that even the very poor (excepting paupers) would not be excluded if fees were demanded, as 'friends, relatives, or employers are ever ready to provide the means when under the influence of anxiety and fear'.[13] Later, fee-paying was further justified as conferring dignity upon the poor patient who, by paying his way, would benefit from feelings of 'self-help and independence'.[14]

Medical attendance at cottage hospitals also differed from that at urban hospitals and was fundamental to their local character. All doctors could attend their own patients and, if an operation was required, had the option of performing it. To allow this to function smoothly, one medical practitioner was engaged to superintend the work. At most cottage hospitals the patients came from quite a narrow social group. They were principally the 'deserving poor' and anyone above or below this status tended to be excluded. Although paupers were generally sent to a workhouse infirmary, 77 of the first 100 patients treated at Cranleigh Village Hospital were, in fact, in receipt of poor relief. Of these, ten were accident cases or required an operation, for which the Board of Guardians paid £36 in fees for surgery.[15] Reflecting the practice in contemporary general hospitals, pregnant women, lunatics and those suffering from infectious diseases usually were excluded, although a few cottage hospitals did provide isolation wards or even a separate fever block.

The need to establish a cottage hospital was soon recognised in nearly all areas where transport was poor, where no general hospital existed within easy reach, and where prospective patients were unable to undertake a lengthy or arduous journey. At Tamworth in Staffordshire, the problem of transporting accident cases was the main reason for establishing a cottage hospital there in 1878. The local vicar wrote that: 'We happily live in a neighbourhood where the accidents in the coal pits are of a far less dangerous nature than in some districts, but there are nonetheless, accidents, which require a treatment different from that which can be given in an ordinary house, and the journey to Birmingham is almost as bad as a new accident'.[16]

The cottage hospital movement grew with remarkable speed. Within the first five years after Cranleigh Village Hospital was established, eight similar hospitals had opened and by 1870 the number had risen to around sixty. By 1895 there were nearly 300, and Rutland and Huntingdonshire were the only counties without them. This rapid expansion was encouraged by the numerous publications which began to appear in the 1860s, such as the pamphlet *On the Advantages Derivable by the Medical Profession and the Public from Village Hospitals*, written by Napper himself and published in 1864, Waring's *Cottage Hospitals: Their Objects, Advantages, and Management*, of 1867, and Horace Swete's *Handy Book of Cottage Hospitals*, of 1870.

Figure 42
This old photograph of St Leonard's Hospital in Sudbury, Suffolk, designed by E Salter and erected in 1867–8, shows the original appearance of the building before substantial alterations were made. The west wing was raised to two storeys in 1906 and the east wing raised in 1927–8.
[NMR BB90/9385]

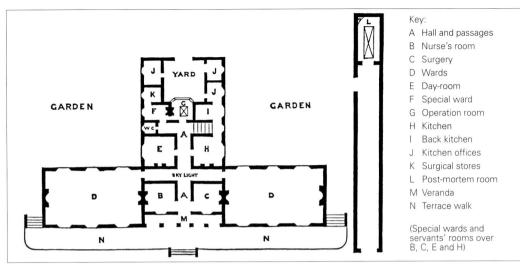

Key:
A Hall and passages
B Nurse's room
C Surgery
D Wards
E Day-room
F Special ward
G Operation room
H Kitchen
I Back kitchen
J Kitchen offices
K Surgical stores
L Post-mortem room
M Veranda
N Terrace walk

(Special wards and servants' rooms over B, C, E and H)

Figure 43
Swete's model plan of a cottage hospital to contain 12 beds, published in 1870, was closely based on the plan of St Leonard's Hospital. [Swete 1870, opp page 44 (NMR BB94/19963)]

Horace Swete, like Napper, was a doctor. His *Handy Book* explained in some detail how to proceed with founding, building, equipping and running a cottage hospital, and was the first to include plans. Also, like Napper, Swete was convinced that the domestic appearance of the hospital was an important aspect and he urged that:

> the cottage element should not be lost sight of ... all ideas of existing county or general hospitals should be laid aside, and the mind imbued with the idea that it is the cottage that is to be converted into the hospital, and not that the hospital is to be built with regular wards, sister's rooms, &c., in the outward form of a cottage.[17]

In his desire for economy and dislike of architectural pretensions Swete gave a remarkably early evocation of Arts & Crafts principles when he called for new cottage hospitals to create a unity of design by reflecting 'the usual style of building' in the area: 'A Gloucestershire stone house, with its roof of slabs of Pennant grit, would look quite out of place amidst the brick and weather-tiled cottages of Surrey.'[18] In practice, however, it was the economically picturesque brick and tile-hung cottage traditionally associated with the south of England that sprang up the length and breadth of the country during the first wave of cottage hospital building.

The architectural press, notably *The Builder*, strongly advocated cottage hospitals, as did (Sir) Henry Burdett, who produced three editions of his book on the subject, those appearing in 1880 and 1896 augmented by illustrations and descriptions of a number of examples. As ever, Burdett was comprehensive in his advice, covering every aspect of design, administration and equipment. No matter was too insignificant for his attention. He recommended fresh flowers in the wards during the summer for their cheering effect, was keen on

family prayers, and was strongly in favour of bathing the patients. Every patient should take a bath before bed on first arrival, otherwise 'it will be found impossible to keep the wards clean and free from many objectionable features, while the beds will soon become more lively than habitable'.[19]

The form of cottage hospitals was restricted by the overriding consideration that the building should be modest in size. The ideal number of beds was a point of argument, but in general half a dozen beds was considered ample in agricultural districts, and up to about twenty-five beds in mining areas, where 'village has grown upon village in quick succession, to keep pace with the growth of works, and in almost all such cases there is dense overcrowding of the population'.[20] Both the local medical practitioners and local industrialists responded to this growing need for hospitals to serve local communities of shipbuilders, ironworkers or coalminers. For example, in 1870 Charles Mark Palmer established the Palmer Memorial Hospital in Jarrow for the workers in his shipyard. The hospital was maintained by weekly contributions from the workforce and an annual subscription from the company.

Guidelines on the optimum number of beds often had to give way to other considerations, and, if the hospital was to be purpose built, current thoughts on design and sanitary provision inevitably influenced planning. St Leonard's Hospital in Sudbury, Suffolk, designed by Edward Salter and erected in 1867–8, was the first to be based on the pavilion plan (Fig 42). It particularly impressed Horace Swete, who used it as the basis for his own model plan for a 12-bed hospital (Fig 43).[21] Salter created a simple and pleasing – though unmistakably institutional – appearance with a central two-storey block flanked by single-storey wings containing the

wards. Unlike urban pavilion-plan hospitals the wards had no sanitary annexes. The provision of effective sanitation proved to be one of the greatest hurdles in rural districts, where no system of sewage or water drainage existed. For this reason, earth closets were considered preferable to water closets. Edward Waring's comment that commodes were more suitable for patients than a water closet 'which in peasants' hands soon gets out of order'[22] was, perhaps, a little extreme, but the inadequacies of the local water supply and drainage forced architects to make compromises, whilst adhering to the pavilion plan's spirit of separation as best they could.

Indeed, the pavilion plan was not as widely adopted for cottage hospitals as for other hospital types, despite the fact that its emergence and widespread acceptance in hospital design coincided with the appearance of the first cottage hospitals. It is significant, therefore, that although variations of the pavilion plan were adopted for many of these small hospitals, too close an association with what was rapidly becoming the standard hospital form was strenuously avoided. This avoidance cannot be accredited purely to defective drains; there was evidently a desire to set cottage hospitals apart from their urban counterparts and create a quite different image.

At Grantham, the architect R Adolphus Came freely adapted a basic pavilion plan to create a picturesque elevation for the cottage hospital built there in 1874–5. The wards were T-shaped, an unusual arrangement which was commended as novel, pleasing and noteworthy by Burdett, who thought that they presented a cheerful and airy appearance 'which fills the visitor with much pleasure'.[23] However, the plan did not have many imitators.

Elsewhere, architects eschewed pavilion planning altogether and aimed to achieve a closer affinity with the Cranleigh type. Stratton Cottage Hospital at Bude was erected in 1866–7 to provide 6 beds in a rectangular double-fronted building of two storeys. It was every inch the 'cottage built on purpose' that Swete advocated, and 'built as far as possible in accordance with the suggestions of Mr Napper'.[24] Similarly, the somewhat dreary main elevation of Rugeley Hospital in Staffordshire bore a closer resemblance to a suburban villa than a hospital (Fig 44). Erected in 1871 to designs by W A Bonney, the building provided 18 beds in wards on the ground and first floors.

Petersfield Cottage Hospital in Hampshire, designed by F W Hunt and erected in 1870–1, is characteristic of such hospitals built during the last decades of the 19th century (Figs 45 and 46). The hung tiles, diapered brickwork and tall chimneys evoke the vernacular revival of Norman Shaw and Nesfield, and the cluster of gables and casement windows seem a world away from most contemporary urban hospitals which instantly proclaimed themselves as public buildings by their austerity and utilitarianism. With its central two-storey section flanked by single-storey wings, the Petersfield hospital bears a superficial resemblance to the simplified pavilion plan of St Leonard's Hospital at Sudbury, but in its plan follows none of the pavilion principles. Each of the wings contained two small wards, one of which was not cross-ventilated at all, and the other barely so. Earth closets were provided, but these were not placed beyond cross-ventilated lobbies. This had an unfortunate effect later, when the difficulty of obtaining fresh earth caused 'disagreeable smells' to pervade the corridor and small wards.[25] The only concession to the principles of pavilion planning seems to have been the provision of a separate mortuary building which was attached to the wood-shed.

A compact variation of the Petersfield type was built at High Wycombe in Buckinghamshire in 1874–5 to designs by Arthur Vernon. The steeply sloping site enabled the architect to tuck the mortuary on to the back at lower-ground level. The building had an almost colonial appearance, with its deep eaves and a veranda running across the central three bays.

The earliest hospitals which followed the plan of Petersfield had between 8 and 10 beds, but at Stratford-upon-Avon Hospital of 1884, E W Mountford adapted that layout to create a

Figure 44
Rugeley Hospital, Staffordshire, designed by W A Bonney and built in 1871. The former laundry building is on the left, behind it was the mortuary, which formed part of the original hospital complex.
[NMR BB91/21994]

Figures 45 and 46
Elevation and plan of
Petersfield Cottage
Hospital, Hampshire,
built in 1870–1 to
designs by F W Hunt.
[Elevation NMR BB94/
19960; ground plan
(1:500) from Burdett 1880,
between pages 416 and 417
(NMR BB94/19959)]

Figure 47
Stratford-upon-Avon
Hospital, Warwickshire,
built in 1884 and
designed by E W
Mountford. Although
Mountford is better
known for his large
public buildings, such as
the town halls at
Sheffield and Battersea,
this was not his only
cottage hospital. In
1885 he won the compe-
tition for Whitchurch
Cottage Hospital,
Shropshire, erected in
1886.
[NMR BB92/23959]

far more substantial building which could accommodate thirty patients (Fig 47). The administrative offices occupied the centre and wards were placed to either side, with a corridor at the rear of the building providing access to the wards and sanitary annexes. Despite its large size, Mountford took care to retain a picturesque appearance with a lively skyline of tall, slender chimneys, gables, and a clock turret.

A number of cottage hospitals provided limited accommodation for convalescent patients. At the former Surbiton Cottage Hospital built in 1882 to designs by Ernest Carritt, the large bay-windowed convalescents' room with a timber veranda was a prominent feature. The admission of convalescents was condemned by Burdett, who considered it 'a Quixotic line of treatment to send the comparatively healthy convalescent, at the risk of a relapse, to share the vitiated air of a hospital ward'.[26] Nevertheless, a few institutions were established which served jointly as convalescent homes and cottage hospitals. A particularly fine example was built at Saltash in 1887–8 to designs by George H Fellowes Prynne. It comprised a single block of two and three storeys which was lent a picturesque appearance by numerous gables, tile-hanging and timber-framing. Established by a Mrs Ley in memory of her husband, the Reverend Richard Ley, the St Barnabas Cottage Hospital and Convalescent Home had a prominent chapel, an unusual feature for a cottage hospital,

where the spiritual welfare of the patients was generally attended to by a close association with the parish church. Patients were encouraged to attend Sunday services, and the rector or curate would pay regular visits to the hospital. At St Barnabas the chapel was provided at the request of its foundress, who also placed the management of the hospital under the charge of nursing sisters of St Mary's, Wantage.

In the later 19th century, as the numbers of cottage hospitals rose, an increasing proportion of them adopted variations of the pavilion plan, with miniaturised ward wings to accommodate the small number of beds. At Newbury District Hospital in Berkshire of 1885 the wings were just three bays long, containing 4 beds placed along one wall only, and the ward pavilions at the Worksop Jubilee Cottage Hospital in Nottinghamshire of 1898–1900 were exceptionally short and stubby, with octagonal sanitary annexes that appear disproportionately large. A more aesthetically pleasing solution was achieved by Henry Percy Adams for Woburn Cottage Hospital in Bedfordshire (Fig 48). It was built for the 11th Duke of Bedford in 1901–3 and Adams's design was based on a sketch plan by the Duchess. The white-painted rendering and low, sweeping roofs echo Voysey's elegant domestic works. Indeed, the striking main elevation and, in particular, the massing of the central three gables point to the involvement of Charles Holden, who had joined

Adams's practice in 1899. Here the pavilion plan is fused with the Petersfield type, the central two-storey section containing staff rooms with the kitchen in a single-storey annexe to the rear. In addition, a detached isolation block for one patient was provided.

In the 1890s a distinctive plan type emerged that divided the hospital into two distinct blocks connected by a covered way at the centre. This form is more reminiscent of hospitals for isolation than general cases. The cottage hospitals at Dartford, Wellingborough and Stanmore were all built to this design, with an administration block of one or two storeys at the front, and a ward pavilion to the rear. At Wellingborough, Sharman & Archer used the familiar combination of brick and half-timbering to suggest a 'cottage style', with the odd bay window and elongated chimney-stack thrown in. The front block contained staff rooms and the kitchen, and the ward wing had two 6-bed wards at each end with a small surgery, operating room, and a single-bed ward in the centre.

At Dartford, the hospital was founded in the 1890s as a belated memorial to David Livingstone, the Scottish missionary and traveller, who died in 1873. Designed by a local architect, G H Tait, the foundation stone was laid by Henry Morton Stanley whose mission to 'find Livingstone' in Africa had achieved famous success with the meeting at Ujiji in 1871. Many cottage hospitals were built to

commemorate national celebrities or events. Queen Victoria's Jubilees prompted a spate of 'Victoria Cottage Hospitals', and other royal events – particularly funerals and coronations – provided popular and ready-made pretexts for establishing new institutions. Other cottage hospitals asserted their local identity by serving as a memorial either to a local figure, such as a medical practitioner who had died in the line of duty, or to local people killed during the First World War, such as Brampton War Memorial Hospital in Cumbria of 1922–3. This is a modest building, with the traditional arrangement of a two-storey central block flanked by single-storey wings. It was designed by Samuel W B Jack to accommodate eight patients.

In the early 20th century a greater element of specialisation is evident, especially in larger cottage or district hospitals. Wards or complete departments for children, out-patients, and maternity cases became increasingly common, just as in contemporary general hospitals. From the outset, most cottage hospitals seem to have admitted children and one of the earliest with its own children's ward was Louth Hospital and Dispensary, which opened in 1873. Swete noted that every cottage hospital should have at least one child's cot, and recommended that the type of iron cot in use at Great Ormond Street should be installed. His description closely matches the cot seen in a late 19th-century photograph, with its sliding

Figure 48
Woburn Cottage Hospital, Bedfordshire, designed by Adams & Holden after a sketch by the Duchess of Bedford, and erected in 1901–3. The building is now occupied by Maryland College.
[NMR BB92/6894]

tray for toys or food which could be 'pushed to or from the child as required' (Fig 49):

> *I hardly know a more pleasing sight than the wards of these hospitals for children – the little ones, who are well enough, sitting up in their cots, in warm scarlet Garibaldi's [a type of blouse], and playing with their toys in the sliding tray.*[27]

As the 20th century progressed the value of a separate children's ward became more widely accepted. At Port Sunlight, the cottage hospital designed by Grayson & Ould in 1905 for the Lever brothers originally had just two ward wings for adults, but by 1916 a third had been added so that a separate children's ward could be provided.

In the design of Port Sunlight Hospital there is a fitting awareness of the growing preoccupation with the beneficent effects of fresh air and sunshine. The original pair of wards were angled southwards and verandas were added as part of the later extension which were unusually spacious, and more like sun-rooms or open-air wards in design.

Another notable feature at Port Sunlight Hospital was the small surgery and dispensary, with an equally small waiting-room for the reception of out-patients. The inclusion of out-patients' departments in cottage hospitals was a point of argument as they were seen to have become a drain on the funds of general hospitals, as well as being subject to abuse by those well able to pay. The few cottage hospitals which did offer out-patient care made it a rule only to treat 'the poor', although paupers and members of benefit clubs were excluded.[28] Unsurprisingly, cottage hospitals which evolved from dispensaries often had better-developed out-patients' departments, and a small number of more ostentatious hospitals paid for by generous local benefactors provided a combination of hospital and dispensary facilities. The Patrick Stead Hospital at Halesworth in Suffolk of 1881–2 is a good example. With just 9 beds in wards on the first floor, it had a large dispensary, consulting-room and waiting-room for out-patients on the ground floor. Patrick Stead was a maltster, whose generous legacy of £27,000 paid for a lavish building with the appearance of a Victorian country house. Henry Hall produced the design in a robust Jacobean style with ball-finialled gables, strapwork and an ogival lantern. A carved stone panel depicting Jesus healing the sick, executed by Harry Hems, was set into the central gable.

During the first half of the 20th century developments in medicine and public health legislation affected the scope of cottage hospitals. Out-patients' departments improved significantly with the inclusion of X-ray and electrical equipment, and maternity wards proliferated following the Maternity and Child Welfare Act of 1918,[29] which gave county and district councils power to provide maternity services, as well as providing some funding. Hospital services in mining areas were indirectly improved under the terms of the Mining Industry Act of 1920,[30] which established a levy on coal to create a Miners' Welfare Fund. The Fund helped equip

Figure 49
This photograph of a child in its cot was taken in the 1890s at Great Ormond Street Hospital, London, and is a poignant counterpart to Swete's description, as the child looks far from happy, clasping a toy horse and soldier, and resting his arm upon the sliding tray. Swete described the children as wearing Garibaldis; a Garibaldi was a type of ladies' blouse, originally bright red but later also of other colours.
[Bedford-Lemere photo, NMR BL 12178/1]

and extend existing hospitals and, in 1925–7, even bore the full cost of constructing the South Moor and Craghead Welfare Fund Hospital in County Durham.

Many of the cottage hospitals built in the inter-war period resembled urban general hospitals in size and in the increasingly sophisticated range of facilities that they offered. Their growing complexity is demonstrated by the Cromer and District Hospital of 1930–2. Designed by Edward Boardman & Son in a vernacular Dutch manner, with shaped gables and hipped, pantiled roofs, it provided administration, kitchen and operating departments, and public and private wards in self-contained blocks linked by corridors (Fig 50).

Whilst the Cromer and District Hospital clung to the 19th-century desideratum that a cottage hospital should be picturesque and homely, elsewhere architects incorporated innovative building methods and embraced the clean lines of the Modern Movement. Veranda wards made their first appearance in England at the cottage hospital at Warminster in Wiltshire designed by Elcock & Sutcliffe and built in 1928–9. Characterised by wide windows capable of being opened to their full width, these wards enabled patients to enjoy the benefits of fresh air and sunlight without the need for a true veranda. The new wards proved successful and in 1931–2 the same architects provided veranda wards at the Alfred Bean Hospital at Driffield in East Yorkshire.

International Modernism was used to striking effect at the new district hospitals erected to replace outgrown cottage hospitals in Surbiton and Oxted in Surrey. An open competition held in 1933 to design the new hospital at Surbiton stipulated that the building should provide accommodation for the patients on the ground floor only, and that staff accommodation should be on an upper floor. Wallace Marchment was appointed architect and he produced a sparsely Modern design with many up-to-date features, including veranda-style wards with large doors facing the garden so that beds could be wheeled outside in good weather. The hospital had an operating suite, maternity and casualty departments and the labour unit was cut off by double walls and sound-proof doors. As a final flourish, the hospital name was displayed on the porter's

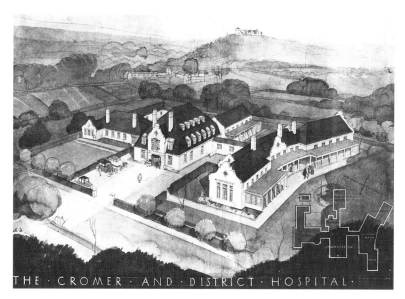

lodge and office in stainless-steel lettering, floodlit at night.

At Oxted, a cottage hospital had been established as a war memorial in 1923, but by 1938 it had extended to the limits of the site. Plans for a new hospital on the outskirts of the town were commissioned from H Edmund Mathews & E D Jefferis Mathews. An open meadow was selected as the new site, sheltered by trees to the north and sloping southwards with attractive views over the surrounding countryside. This was borne in mind in the design of the hospital, which attempted to give all the wards 'the fullest benefit to be derived from the southern aspect and view'.[31] At the same time, both the out-patients' department and the accident cases reception area were conveniently located by the main drive and close to the operating theatre and X-ray departments. The outbreak of the Second World War delayed building work and the hospital was not completed until 1947.

Oxted Hospital can be seen as the culmination of cottage hospital design prior to the inception of the National Health Service. From modest origins, the cottage hospital became an important element in the gallimaufry of health-care services that existed by the 1940s. Although such hospitals expanded almost beyond recognition, they still preserved their essentially local character, serving small communities, charging moderate fees to the patients, and relying on the services of the local general practitioners.

Figure 50 Cromer and District Hospital, Norfolk, built in 1930–2 to the designs of E Boardman & Son. [The Builder, 10 Oct 1930, after p 604 (NMR BB94/19956)]

4
Workhouse Infirmaries

Before the existence of the Welfare State, sickness could reduce a whole family to poverty, and from the mid 19th century admittance to the workhouse infirmary was the only option for vast numbers of the population, who, because of the nature of their illness and their poverty, had nowhere else to go. However, the workhouse system was not set up with a view to creating a network of infirmaries for paupers. Indeed, the first workhouses erected in the wake of the Poor Law Amendment Act of 1834[1] were designed with only minimal accommodation for the sick, such provision being solely for cases of illness or infection arising within the workhouse. Necessity and practicality soon outweighed the original intentions of the Act and an infirmary became a vital component of the workhouse complex. The earliest infirmaries were simple, utilitarian buildings, generally quite small, and placed so that there was convenient access from each division of the workhouse. As the guardians of the poor and the hard-pressed medical officers were unable to cope with the inadequacies of these measures, larger infirmaries were built and sick paupers admitted to them directly from their homes.

As they developed, workhouse infirmaries followed progress in planning and design in contemporary general hospitals, the main difference being the absence of out-patients' departments and operating theatres. They also admitted a range of cases normally excluded from voluntary general hospitals, such as unmarried pregnant women, and people suffering from venereal and incurable diseases. Before the widespread provision of isolation hospitals at the end of the 19th century, accommodation was provided for cases of infectious diseases or smallpox arising in the workhouse. Similarly, insufficient places for pauper lunatics in the county asylums, particularly for 'harmless imbeciles' and epileptics, meant that space often had to be found for such cases within the workhouses. With the exception of London, it was not until the early 20th century that separate institutions for mentally handicapped paupers began to be established.

Although workhouse infirmaries became primarily long-stay institutions caring for chronic cases, they were, nevertheless, effectively the local hospital for a large section of the population. Eventually these infirmaries became the first municipal general hospitals, and formed an important and significant element in the new National Health Service when it was inaugurated in 1948.

The Pre-1834 Workhouse Infirmary

Poor relief was administered on a parochial basis throughout England from Elizabethan times until the Poor Law Amendment Act of 1834, and generally involved supplying the needy poor with either outdoor relief in their own homes or indoor relief in a poorhouse or workhouse. Able-bodied paupers were first set to work in the late 16th century, but it was not until the 17th century that 'working-houses' were established for this purpose.[2] The parishes of Bristol united to set up a workhouse under a Local Act in 1697, and other towns rapidly followed suit. Such establishments provided shelter for 'impotent' paupers as well as employment for the able-bodied.

Two 18th-century Acts encouraged workhouse provision. Knatchbull's Act of 1722[3] empowered any parish to purchase or hire a workhouse, and Gilbert's Act of 1782[4] enabled parishes to unite to provide a large, communal poorhouse which would cater for impotent rather than able-bodied paupers. The latter would be employed by the parish outside the workhouse. Although all workhouses took in a certain number of helpless paupers, including the aged, orphans and the mentally handicapped, it was general practice for sick paupers to be given outdoor relief whenever possible.

Few workhouses set aside accommodation for sick inmates, and establishments on the scale of the 300-bed St Marylebone Parish Infirmary in London, erected on the workhouse site in 1792, were extremely rare (Fig 51).[5] This austere building had a courtyard plan with wards opening off a corridor surrounding the central yard. It was designed by John White, Surveyor to the Duke of Portland, who had been employed

from 1787 to lay out the Portland estate in Marylebone.[6] In 1799 the resident staff of the infirmary comprised an apothecary, a matron and four paid nurses in addition to a number of pauper nurses. Moreover, a physician and surgeon each received a gratuity of 100 guineas to visit regularly, and both had pupils who lodged in the workhouse. The capacity of the infirmary was increased in 1825, with the addition of a north range designed by the otherwise unknown Edward Tilbury.[7]

The St Marylebone Parish Infirmary remained an exceptional institution. In the majority of workhouses, sick inmates would have been kept in their ordinary dormitories unless their condition was regarded as infectious, in which case they would have been isolated. Many of the large 18th-century 'houses of industry' in East Anglia are known to have provided detached pesthouses for this purpose. Although none of these buildings survives, the plans and specifications for the Shipmeadow pesthouse in Suffolk, dated 1767, show it to have been a rectangular building of two storeys and an attic, with two rooms on each floor to either side of a central staircase.[8] The *raison d'être* of such buildings was to provide isolation, thereby avoiding epidemics which could sweep through the workhouse with devastating consequences.

Rising poor-rates in the years following the Napoleonic Wars, coupled with the belief that outdoor relief had become too prevalent, led a few parishes such as Bingham and Southwell in Nottinghamshire to open 'deterrent workhouses'.

By establishing the principle of 'less-eligibility', whereby conditions in the workhouse were worse than in the homes of the lowest class of independent labourer, and by proclaiming this policy to be an economic and social success, these parishes paved the way for the 'New Poor Law' of 1834.[9]

The Poor Law Report of 1834 and the Model Workhouse Plans

In 1832 a Royal Commission was appointed to investigate the Poor Laws and make proposals for new legislation. Its report of 1834 formed the basis of the Poor Law Amendment Act.[10] The Commissioners assumed that the majority of sick paupers would continue to receive outdoor medical relief, and were concerned principally with the abolition of outdoor relief to the able-bodied through a harsh workhouse system.[11] To put this policy into operation the majority of the 15,535 parishes of England and Wales were grouped into Poor Law Unions, each of which appointed a board of guardians answerable to the ratepayers on the one hand, and to the three-man Poor Law Commission in London on the other.

The first task of the guardians was to provide workhouse accommodation which would permit a strict classification of inmates. The Report of 1834 had suggested that the aged and 'impotent', children, able-bodied females and able-bodied males be accommodated in separate buildings.[12] It was thought that existing workhouses and converted dwelling-houses would suffice. The Report only

Figure 51
St Marylebone Parish Infirmary, London, built in 1792 to designs by John White. Beyond the infirmary can be seen part of the main workhouse. The infirmary later moved to a new site in north Kensington, and the old buildings have been demolished.
[Westminster Archives Centre]

Figure 52
The second floor of
Sampson Kempthorne's
'Square Plan' of a work-
house, published in
1835. The central
building is in fact
cruciform, although the
perimeter buildings
formed a square.
[PP 1835 (500), XXXV.
107, Appendix A, no. 10
(By permission of the
Syndics of Cambridge
University Library)]

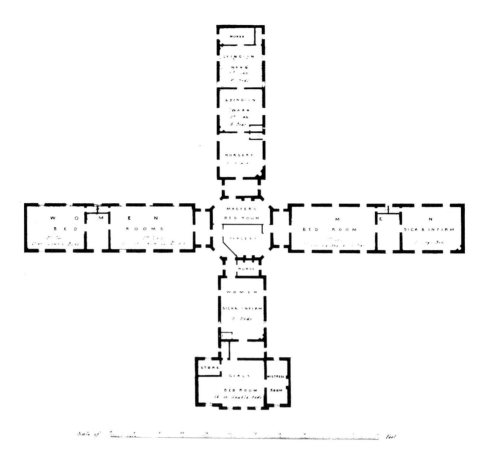

fleetingly contemplated the possibility of creating separate establishments for the sick:

> *in the workhouse of a single parish the rooms appro-*
> *priated for the reception of the sick must often be*
> *empty; in a house for the reception of the sick from a*
> *number of parishes, the absence of patients from one*
> *parish would be met by an influx from another, and*
> *a more steady average number maintained, and so*
> *with the other classes of inmate.*[13]

This idea came to nothing. Initially, some unions did attempt to distribute their paupers between several existing buildings, but usually as a temporary measure. Others adapted a single existing building as a workhouse, but by 1841 at least 320 of the 536 recently formed unions had undertaken to erect a general mixed workhouse. Only a handful of recalcitrant unions, such as Todmorden in Yorkshire, refused to provide a workhouse of any description.

The only planning guidelines available for new workhouses were five model designs for general mixed institutions to hold 200, 300 or 500 inmates, published with the first and second annual reports of the Poor Law Commissioners in 1835 and 1836.[14] In the 'rural workhouse for 500 persons' designed by Assistant Commissioner Sir Francis Bond Head, ranges surrounding a courtyard were divided into small units, inferior in size and materials to the humble cottage occupied by the 'honest hard-working independent labourer'.[15] The design was adopted by a number of unions in Kent, but it made no special provision for the sick or mentally ill, despite the implications of clause (v) of the 'Orders and Regulations to be Observed in Workhouses', issued by the Commissioners in 1835.[16] According to that rule, upon admission paupers had to be examined by the medical officer in the probationary wards, whence they would be assigned to the able-bodied ward, the sick ward or the ward for lunatics and imbeciles.

The other four model designs were all by Sampson Kempthorne, whose father's friendship with one of the Poor Law Commissioners secured his appointment as architect to the Commissioners.[17] Each of Kempthorne's designs set aside joint wards for the sick and infirm but none for lunatics and imbeciles. He categorised the designs according to their size and the basic shape of their ground plans as follows: the 'square plan of a workhouse to contain 300 paupers', the 'workhouse to contain 200 paupers', the 'hexagon plan of a workhouse to contain 300 paupers' and the 'workhouse for 200 paupers adapted for the less pauperised districts'. (Confusingly, the upper-floor plans shown in Figures 52 and 53 are shaped neither in the form of a square nor of a hexagon, but it was on these floors that the sick wards were located.)

In Kempthorne's square plan joint sick and infirm wards, each with 12 single beds, were located on the first floor, at the ends of the main male and female accommodation ranges. Stairs in the centre of both ranges separated these wards from the larger ordinary dormitories in which healthy male paupers occupied bunk beds and females shared double beds. Able-bodied and sick wards alike were lit by opposing windows and had adjoining water closets. There was more extensive accommodation for the sick on the second floor (Fig 52). This comprised two nurse's rooms, a surgery, a 12-bed men's ward, an 11-bed women's ward, a nursery and two 6-bed lying-in wards. Kempthorne's hexagon-plan workhouse contained 16-bed wards for the sick and infirm on the first and second floors, again at the ends of the main male and female accommodation ranges, with two lying-in wards and a nursery on the second floor (Fig 53). However, neither a surgery nor rooms for nurses were provided. The 200-pauper plan for less pauperised districts allowed for a higher proportion of sick and infirm inmates than the other designs. Its sick and infirm wards occupied the inner half of each of the main wings on both ground and first floors (Fig 54). A surgery and a lying-in ward were placed alongside the girls' and boys' bedrooms on the first floor of the front range.

The key features of Kempthorne's model plans, in terms of their provision for the sick,

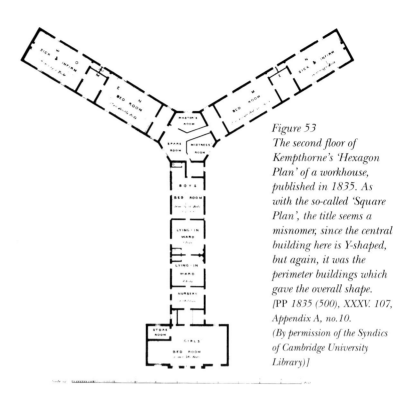

Figure 53
The second floor of Kempthorne's 'Hexagon Plan' of a workhouse, published in 1835. As with the so-called 'Square Plan', the title seems a misnomer, since the central building here is Y-shaped, but again, it was the perimeter buildings which gave the overall shape.
[PP 1835 (500), XXXV. 107, Appendix A, no.10. (By permission of the Syndics of Cambridge University Library)]

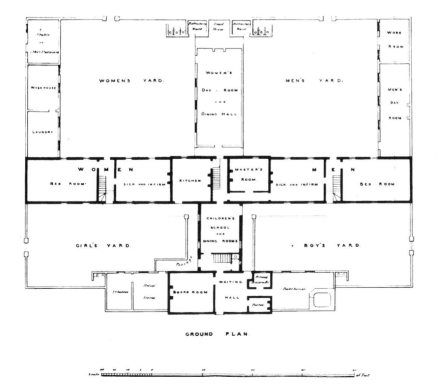

Figure 54
Ground-floor plan of Kempthorne's 'workhouse for 200 paupers' published in 1836.
[PP 1836 (595), XXIX. Appendix no.15. (By permission of the Syndics of Cambridge University Library)]

Figure 55
The infirmary block at
Chesterton Union
Workhouse (later
Chesterton Hospital),
Cambridgeshire, erected
in 1836–8 to designs by
John Smith.
[NMR BB94/8414]

were that wards were to be shared by the sick and infirm, and male and female wards were to be located at the extreme ends of the main house, rather than together within a single infirmary block. It is also worth noting that although lying-in wards and nurseries were provided, no special accommodation was set aside for the mentally ill or mentally handicapped, or for those suffering from itch (scabies), venereal disease and other 'foul' or 'offensive' complaints (gangrene, cancer, etc), which were excluded from general hospitals. Fever cases were similarly neglected.

Workhouse Infirmaries, 1835–1867

Before emigrating to New Zealand in 1841–2, Sampson Kempthorne was appointed architect of several union workhouses, among them Chertsey and Ticehurst, and he generally adopted his own hexagon plan for them. His designs were also widely copied by other architects, but usually in a modified form. In particular, modest detached or semi-detached infirmaries were added, usually tucked out of sight at the back of the workhouse. As the central authority had failed to provide guidelines for such buildings, they varied considerably in form.

The architect of the Chesterton and Cambridge union workhouses, John Smith, provided each with an infirmary. At the smaller square-plan Chesterton workhouse, built between 1836 and 1838, the infirmary occupied all three floors of a block adjoining the end of the girls' range (Fig 55). It had its own entrances and staircase, and there was access to the main building at first-floor level. On the ground floor there was a large room for the surgeon and a smaller store room, on the first floor a lying-in ward and a women's ward, and on the second floor two sick wards for men. Water closets opened off the first and second-floor landings rather than directly off the wards. The Cambridge workhouse, built in 1838, was quite different, comprising parallel entrance and accommodation ranges with a completely detached, asymmetrical, two-storeyed infirmary to the rear. On the ground floor of the infirmary were two entrances, a surgery, bathroom, nurse's room, water closet, and two men's sick wards. From the surgery there was access to a yard with a mortuary on its north side, and there was a boiler house on the east side of the infirmary. On the first floor were three small rooms, curiously identified as 'private wards', together with a women's sick ward and a lying-in ward.

The principle of separating the sexes by floor was common to both the Chesterton and Cambridge infirmaries, but it was more usual to divide men and women into wards on either side of a symmetrically planned building. At the Leicester Union Workhouse of 1838–9, designed by the well-established local architect William Flint, the infirmary had two separate entrances and staircases in the centre, with the men's ward on the left and the women's on the right.[18]

A similar arrangement was devised for the original infirmary of the Wells Union Workhouse in Somerset. The workhouse itself was built in 1837 to designs by S T Welch, a Bristol architect and inventor of revolving window shutters.[19] Designed on a T-shaped plan, the workhouse had an unusually attractive Gothic façade, but the decoration stopped abruptly away from the street front.[20] The infirmary was a single-storey, symmetrical block situated to the rear of the combined dining-hall and chapel, with which there was direct communication. It had a central hallway leading to a surgery, with two small and two large wards on either side. One of the large wards seems to have been used as a nursery. Although there were no indoor closets in the workhouse for ordinary inmates, who had to make do with privies in their exercise yards, in the infirmary, each pair of wards was served by a 'self-acting closet of simple construction', invented by the architect especially for the use of infirmary patients.[21]

Some of the most substantial workhouse infirmaries erected in this period were designed by George Gilbert Scott and William Bonython Moffatt, who, either singly or in partnership, were responsible for over forty workhouses, before their partnership ended in 1846.[22] Scott had worked briefly as Kempthorne's assistant in 1834, before setting up in practice with Moffatt and actively seeking out workhouse commissions, or 'union-hunting', as he termed it.[23] He and Moffatt soon abandoned Kempthorne's model plans, and the majority of their workhouses comprised parallel entrance and accommodation ranges with an E or U-plan infirmary. Usually the infirmary was situated at the back of the site with service buildings to either side. At Macclesfield, the stone-built infirmary had a solid, vernacular appearance, with a strong vertical emphasis in the three gabled bays (Fig 56). Scott & Moffatt's infirmaries had more separate rooms than was usual, but little evidence of their original use survives. Two unexecuted plans for Launceston Union Workhouse dating from *c* 1838, which may be attributed to Scott & Moffatt, indicate the kind of accommodation they included in addition to the usual wards, such as a nurse's day-room, a surgery, 'sick day-rooms' and infectious wards.[24]

Although many of the earliest union workhouses were not provided with purpose-built infirmaries, probably making do with sick-rooms on the Kempthorne model, by the mid 1840s a large number had added a separate infirmary to serve the sick of both sexes. Buildings such as these had not been anticipated by the model designs, by the Poor Law Report, or in earlier workhouse buildings. Economy of nursing was the obvious advantage in locating male and female sick wards together, rather than placing them at opposite ends of the main building as suggested in the model plans. Once men and women were placed in a single infirmary it must have seemed logical to locate it centrally, behind the main building, where it would be easily accessible from both divisions of the house. The majority contained a nurse's duty room or medical officer's surgery, sometimes both, but as there was no resident medical staff, staff bedrooms were not required. The provision of infirmary yards, but not day-rooms, was standard. Segregation by ailment was almost non-existent, although sometimes lying-in wards and nurseries were incorporated within the infirmary rather than the main house. From the outset Macclesfield infirmary seems to have had lunatic

Figure 56
Macclesfield Union Workhouse Infirmary, Cheshire, built in 1843–5 to designs by Scott & Moffatt. The building now forms part of West Park Hospital.
[NMR BB92/9600]

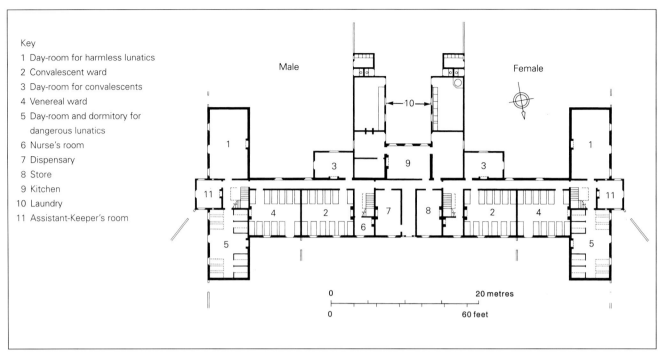

Key
1 Day-room for harmless lunatics
2 Convalescent ward
3 Day-room for convalescents
4 Venereal ward
5 Day-room and dormitory for
   dangerous lunatics
6 Nurse's room
7 Dispensary
8 Store
9 Kitchen
10 Laundry
11 Assistant-Keeper's room

Male

Female

0   20 metres
0   60 feet

Figure 57
Ground-floor plan of the infirmary built in 1843–5 at Portsea Island Union Workhouse, Hampshire, to designs by T E Owen and A Livesay.
[*Plan (1:500) based on Portsmouth City Records Office BG/WP/1A/2/1*]

wards with padded cells, and the infirmary of Bath workhouse had a section devoted to imbeciles, but few unions acknowledged a need for such specialised accommodation. Infirmaries were occasionally supplied with sanitation which was superior to that in the main workhouse building, as at Wells, but rarely with superior lighting or ventilation. Kempthorne's recommendation that wards should have opposing windows was almost universally ignored, as was his suggestion that the sick and infirm should be housed together in the same wards.[25]

From their inception the new union workhouses accommodated a higher proportion of the aged and infirm, the sick, imbeciles, and harmless lunatics than had been anticipated.[26] The small infirmaries were hopelessly inadequate to cope with such numbers, and sick inmates spilled over into ordinary workhouse dormitories. No single factor explains this phenomenon. It had been thought that the possibility of having to enter the workhouse would frighten the poor into independence, into making provision for the day when they or their dependants might become old or sick, but in reality few could afford to do so. More significantly, it could not have been foreseen that, as the industrial revolution progressed and large numbers of people shifted from country to town, fewer sick and infirm paupers could be cared for by relatives or friends at home.

Poor Law medical officers, appointed by the guardians to tend sick paupers, realised that their patients recovered more quickly in a workhouse infirmary than at home, and were there-

fore less of a burden on the ratepayers. Removing them to the workhouse also lessened the distances medical officers needed to travel to see patients. Consequently, workhouse infirmaries gradually ceased to be purely for cases of sickness arising in the workhouse, and sick paupers came to be admitted from outside directly into the infirmary or, when that was full or non-existent, into makeshift wards within the body of the workhouse itself.

The medical officer, who visited his patients in the workhouse once or twice a week, was poorly paid and had to supply drugs from his own purse. Although he had responsibility for the sick and could order special diets, he was subordinate to the master of the workhouse and was frequently frustrated in his efforts to make improvements. The daily care of the sick was in the hands of the workhouse matron and untrained, unpaid pauper nurses, habitually portrayed in the literature of the period as immoral, drunken characters. Until the late 1860s the notion that sick paupers should not receive better medical care in the workhouse than the labourer would in his squalid cottage discouraged guardians from improving their infirmary accommodation or employing trained nurses. The principle of less-eligibility ruled for the sick as for the able-bodied.

There were, however, one or two enlightened boards of guardians in the mid 19th century. In 1843–5 Portsea Island Union constructed one of the largest and most self-sufficient infirmaries to be built in the provinces during that decade. The main workhouse was a handsome Italianate

building, but, as usual, the infirmary was given more sparing embellishment. It was designed by Thomas Ellis Owen, already a prominent figure in Portsmouth, who developed Southsea with stuccoed brick terraces and Italianate villas.[27] He worked on the infirmary with Augustus Livesay of Ventnor, who was known chiefly as an estimating surveyor.[28] Originally of two storeys, staff accommodation and services were situated in the centre of the building with the wards to either side (Fig 57). There were separate wards for convalescents, venereal patients, lunatics, imbeciles and the ordinary sick of both sexes. The first-floor sick wards were the largest, with 24 beds. Lying-in wards were absent and must have been located within the main workhouse building. The small day-rooms for convalescents on the south side were an innovative feature in workhouse infirmaries. Day-rooms were also provided for dangerous and harmless lunatics, separated by stairs and a room for an assistant-keeper.

Another unusual aspect of the Portsea Island infirmary was that it had its own governor and matron, although they probably had no medical training. Indeed, the only defects of the infirmary were ineffective sanitation and ventilation, which were ubiquitous deficiencies in Poor Law infirmaries and voluntary hospitals alike. Only the sick wards had water closets; all the other occupants had to use privies and lavatories in their exercise yards. The beds were very close together and, as usual, there was no cross-ventilation, wards being

lit on one side only. By 1866, when Dr Edward Smith, the medical officer to the Poor Law Board (the successor to the Poor Law Commission), visited the infirmary, shuttered windows had been inserted into the corridor walls in an attempt to ameliorate this.[29] Dr Smith also recorded that the water closets on the upper landings had had to be removed due to poor ventilation.

The debate about hospital design which took place in the late 1850s led to the construction of large pavilion-plan general hospitals. Chorlton Union in Manchester, serving a population of 180,000, was one of the largest Poor Law authorities in the country and was the first to build an infirmary on the pavilion plan.[30] The workhouse itself had been built in 1854–5 to designs by the local firm of Hayley, Son & Hall, and was an imposing Italianate complex of buildings which included two infirmary wings. However, in 1862 the guardians took the advice of George Greaves of the Manchester Statistical Society and commissioned the notable Manchester architect Thomas Worthington to design a new infirmary on the pavilion system (Fig 58). This was erected on a site behind the workhouse between 1864 and 1866, and provided a total of 480 beds in five three-storeyed ward pavilions. Spaced 100 ft apart, the pavilions were connected at their southern end by a single-storey arcade with a flat roof or promenade. An administration block was planned to serve the infirmary, but was never built.

Figure 58
Elevation and ground-floor plan of the infirmary added to Chorlton Union Workhouse, Manchester, in 1864–6, designed by Thomas Worthington. The buildings survive as part of the present Withington Hospital. [Plan (1:500) based on The Builder, *17 Jun 1865, 430]*

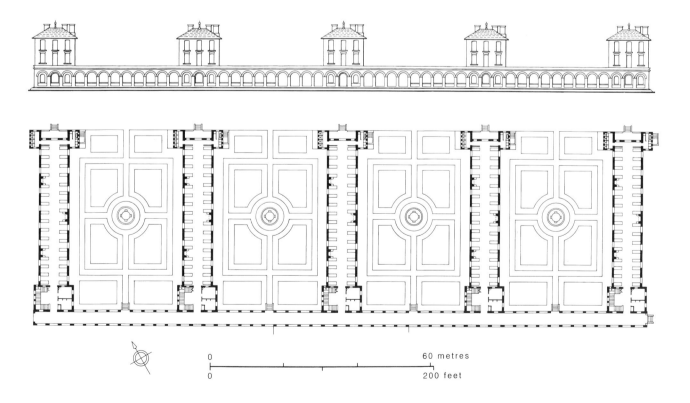

0   60 metres

0   200 feet

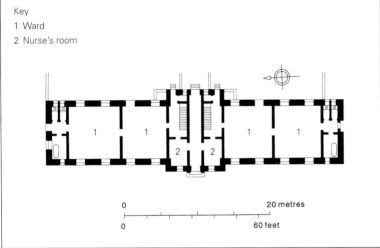

Key
1 Ward
2 Nurse's room

0   20 metres

0   60 feet

*Figures 59 and 60
East elevation and
ground-floor plan of the
infirmary built for
Southampton Incorpor-
ation Workhouse,
Hampshire, in 1865–8,
designed by T A Skelton.
The paired windows in
the end bay to the left lit
the water closets.
[NMR BB94/4738; plan
(1:500) based on OS 1:500
map Hants LXV.II.12,
1868]*

At the entrance to each pavilion there was a central hallway with a staircase on one side, and a ward kitchen and nurse's room (complete with inspection window) on the other. The wards had 32 beds and were heated by means of three fireplaces in the side walls. At the north end of each ward were balconies for convalescents, set between twin towers containing the sanitary facilities. One tower contained a lavatory and bathroom while the other contained water closets and a sink. The occupants were allowed a generous amount of space, which at 1,300–1,380 cu ft of air per patient, was more than was provided in most contemporary voluntary hospitals. It was also

vastly above the meagre allowance of 500 cu ft for workhouse infirmaries, which had been recommended since 1855 by the Poor Law Board.

The cost of the infirmary was calculated to be £60 per bed, and on learning of the project Florence Nightingale wrote to Worthington as follows:

> *If you succeed in completing the buildings for anything like the money with due regard to the simple sanitary requirements of so great a building, you will have inaugurated a new era in building. And we shall hasten to imitate you; for you will have set up a model to the whole country.*[31]

Although widely admired, the Chorlton infirmary had little immediate influence amongst guardians. Building on such a scale was expensive and most guardians feared censure from the ratepayers if they spent large sums on 'undeserving' paupers. Thus, while the pavilion plan was accepted by members of the medical profession, reformers and architects, as the only one suitable for a hospital, small workhouse infirmaries continued to be erected throughout the 1860s on non-pavilion lines.

A greater awareness of the principles of pavilion planning appeared at the new Southampton Incorporation Workhouse built in 1865–8 (Figs 59 and 60). Designed by the local architect and surveyor Thomas Alfred Skelton, the infirmary comprised a central section containing the entrance, stairs and nurses' rooms with pavilion ward wings to either side. Single-block pavilion-plan hospitals similar to this had been built recently at Aylesbury (the Buckinghamshire Infirmary, see page 28), and Hounslow (the Cavalry Barracks Hospital, see page 97). However, at Southampton, each wing contained two rooms (either a ward and a day-room or two wards), with the water closets and bathroom at the far end. These last were separated by a central lobby, lit and ventilated by a window in the end wall, but were integral to the ward wing. This was a feature of the earliest pavilion-plan hospitals such as the naval hospital built at Woolwich in the late 1850s (see pages 85–6), and the Lariboisière Hospital in Paris of 1846–54, which was so influential in England (see page 28).

The Outcry of the 1860s and the Official Response

By the mid 1860s, although a handful of new workhouse infirmaries incorporated the principles of pavilion planning, the majority were inadequate in every respect, notably in terms of ventilation and sanitation. The situation

was particularly acute in the metropolis, where most establishments had evolved out of 18th-century parish workhouses on congested central London sites.

An important crusader for reform was Louisa Twining, who began visiting workhouses in 1854, and was instrumental in establishing the Workhouse Visiting Society in 1857. From 1859 to 1865 the Society produced a journal, exposing the poor standard of nursing in workhouse infirmaries. Following on from Twining's work, the *Lancet* appointed a Commission to investigate the condition of London's workhouse infirmaries, and in 1865–6 published a general report and accounts of sick wards in seventeen of the workhouses administered by the capital's thirty-nine Poor Law authorities.[32] The *Lancet* report argued that workhouse infirmaries were 'the real hospitals of the land' and highlighted the contrast between conditions in overcrowded workhouse wards with those in the relatively spacious wards of voluntary hospitals.[33] While eighteen voluntary hospitals provided 3,738 beds for London's poor, the capital's workhouses nominally held 7,463 beds for the sick and 7,000 for the infirm.[34] Individual *Lancet* reports were particularly critical of the siting, ventilation and sanitation of infirmaries, the absence of proper segregation in wards, dependence on pauper nurses, and the working conditions of Poor Law medical officers.

Further pressure was brought to bear on the Poor Law Board by the Association for Improving London Workhouse Infirmaries, founded in February 1866.[35] The Association made specific recommendations for the future organisation of metropolitan infirmaries, suggesting that central funds be provided to replace London's existing infirmaries (each of which had an average of 160 beds), with six district hospitals, each accommodating 1,000 patients.[36] The government responded in April 1866, when Henry B Farnall, the Poor Law Inspector of Metropolitan Workhouses, and Dr Edward Smith, a Poor Law Inspector and medical officer to the Poor Law Board, were appointed to undertake separate official inquiries.[37] Their findings, published in the summer of 1866, broadly agreed with those of the *Lancet*.

Following a change of government in July 1866, Gathorne Hardy replaced Charles Villiers as President of the Poor Law Board and ordered fresh inquiries which resulted in yet another report on London workhouses.[38] In addition, a committee was appointed to consider the cubic space of metropolitan workhouses. In its report, produced in February 1867, the committee recommended 850 cu ft of air for the ordinary sick, surgical, venereal and itch cases, and 1,200 cu ft for offensive cases, who should occupy separation wards, and for lying-in cases. At the other end of the scale, chronic and infirm wards were only required to have 500 cu ft of air, and the 300 cu ft allowed to healthy adults and children was to remain unchanged.[39] The outcome of these reports was the Metropolitan Poor Law Amendment Act of 1867.[40]

Metropolitan Workhouse Infirmaries, 1867–1914

The Metropolitan Poor Act set out to remove lunatics and imbeciles from London workhouses, to provide separate accommodation for fever and smallpox cases, to combine unions into 'sick asylum' districts and to erect dispensaries for outpatients.[41] As a first step, the Metropolitan Asylums Board was established in May 1867 to set up imbecile asylums and fever hospitals (see pages 136 and 173). In 1868 six Sick Asylum Districts were formed out of seventeen unions, but for economic reasons only those of Central London and Poplar and Stepney survived for more than one year.[42] The constituent unions of the disbanded districts regrouped with a view to converting one of their existing workhouses into an infirmary, and remaining unions were to build new infirmaries, either on separate sites or adjacent to their workhouses. A strong financial incentive was provided by the newly created Common Poor Fund, which would pay for officers' salaries, medicines and medical appliances once a satisfactory infirmary was in operation. This was particularly significant in the creation of separate-site infirmaries. Where the infirmary was on the same site as the workhouse there was no difficulty in using the able-bodied inmates to work in the kitchen, laundry and wards, but when the infirmary was at some distance guardians were forced to pay for nursing and domestic staff.[43]

From the late 1860s onwards substantial building work was undertaken by boards of guardians throughout London, generally including additional infirmary accommodation. Only a few unions resisted such expense and simply redistributed their paupers. The majority of guardians extended or rebuilt their existing infirmaries, and a few of the largest authorities carried out highly ambitious building schemes, purchasing sites away from the workhouse on which to construct large-scale independent

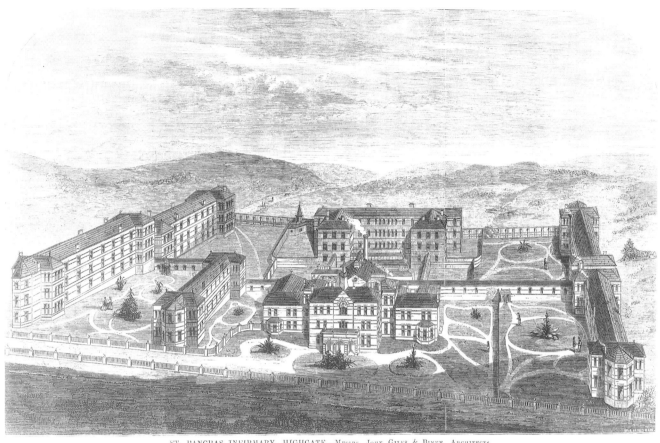

ST. PANCRAS INFIRMARY, HIGHGATE.—Messrs. John Giles & Biven, Architects.

Figures 61 and 62
The St Pancras Infirmary was built at Highgate, London, in 1868–70 to designs by John Giles & Biven. The site was close to the Smallpox Hospital of 1848, adjacent to which the Islington Workhouse Infirmary, designed by William Smith, was erected in 1898–1900. The Holborn Union Workhouse Infirmary of 1877–9 by Henry Saxon Snell was also close by. All four institutions were united under the National Health Service as the Whittington Hospital.
[Perspective, block plan and plan of ward from The Builder, *9 Jan 1869, 28–9 (NMR BB94/16637 and BB94/16636)]*

infirmaries on the pavilion plan. The first separate-site infirmaries served St Pancras (1868–70), Poplar and Stepney (1868–71), Holborn (1877–9) and St Marylebone (1879–81). Whether on a separate site or not, the new infirmaries all had a separate management from the workhouse, with a resident medical superintendent in charge of a resident medical staff.

The 524-bed St Pancras Infirmary of 1868–70 was designed by John Giles & Biven in 'the plainest style', as laid down by the rules of the competition (Figs 61 and 62).[44] John Giles was the senior partner, the firm later becoming Giles & Gough, and subsequently Giles, Gough & Trollope, workhouse and asylum commissions forming a large part of their work. At St Pancras, following the arrangement of earlier pavilion-plan hospitals, the administration block, kitchen and laundry were located centrally, with the main ward pavilions on either side. Each ward contained 32 beds and had a day-room with a broad bay window at the far end. The sanitary facilities were not separated from the wards by cross-ventilated lobbies.

Such lobbies were a recent innovation that took a while to become the standard arrangement. In other respects the St Pancras Infirmary was highly advanced, with operating theatres included for the first time in a workhouse infirmary (hitherto, surgical cases had been sent to voluntary hospitals), situated beside the main corridor, in front of the laundry. The operation wards were located in a detached block at the rear of the site, conveniently close to the 'dead house'.

It was not long before most of the refinements which were taking place in pavilion planning appeared at workhouse infirmaries. The Poplar and Stepney Sick Asylum erected in 1868–71, to designs by A & C Harston, seems to have been the earliest at which clearly defined cross-ventilated lobbies separated the sanitary facilities from the wards.[45] Bay windows at the end of the pavilions probably lit day-rooms, as at the St Pancras Infirmary, and open bridges over the main corridor allowed convalescents to take the air. The Sick Asylum was a substantial complex, providing some 572 beds, including accommodation for the aged and infirm, a class which was

ST. PANCRAS INFIRMARY, HIGHGATE.

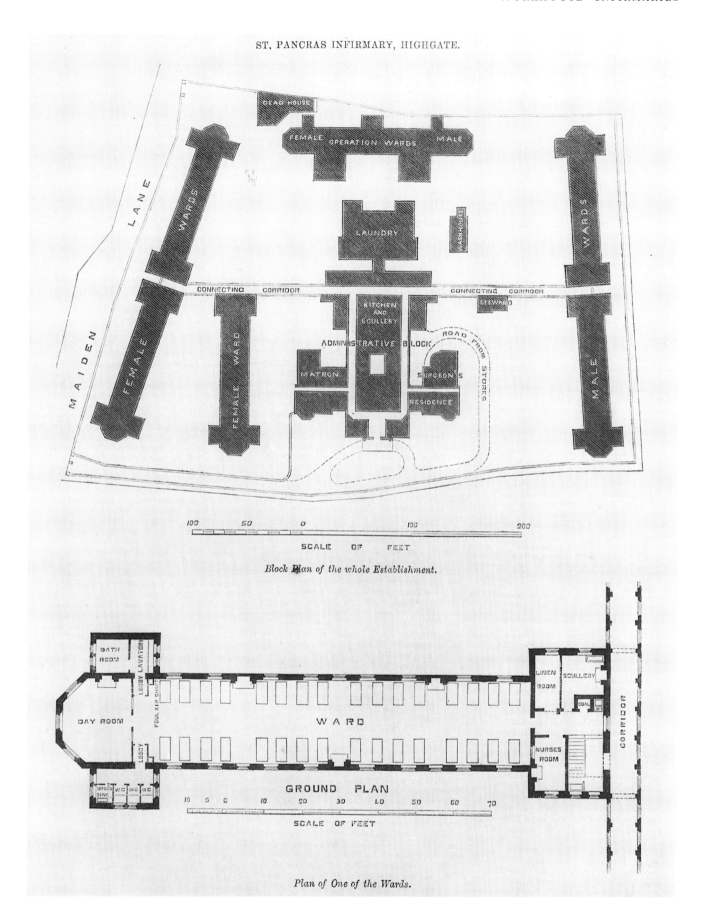

Block Plan of the whole Establishment.

Plan of One of the Wards.

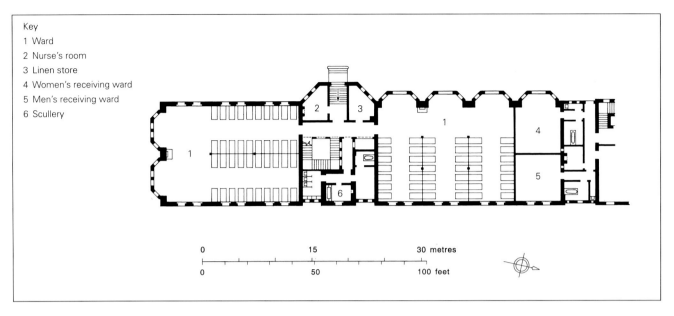

Key
1 Ward
2 Nurse's room
3 Linen store
4 Women's receiving ward
5 Men's receiving ward
6 Scullery

0   15   30 metres
0   50   100 feet

Figure 63
Ground plan of the infirm wards designed in 1870 by Henry Saxon Snell for St Luke's Workhouse, City Road, London. The plan shows Snell's innovative ward design.
[Plan (1:500) based on Snell 1881, 4]

Figure 64 (opposite)
General view of the west elevation of Holborn Union Infirmary (now the Archway Wing of the Whittington Hospital), London, built in 1877–9 to designs by Henry Saxon Snell. A similar ward arrangement to that of the infirm wards at St Luke's was used here, with the same distinctive sequence of bay windows.
[NMR BB93/11595]

usually consigned to the workhouse rather than the infirmary. They occupied back-to-back wards in the pavilions nearest to the administrative centre.

Henry Saxon Snell, one of the foremost hospital architects employed by London guardians in the 1870s and 1880s, experimented with a new ward design for aged and infirm paupers at two workhouses, St Marylebone (1867–8) and the Holborn Union Workhouse, formerly St Luke's Workhouse, City Road (1870).[46] Figure 63 illustrates the novel arrangement of beds in these large wards, those in the centre being placed on either side of partitions. The overall arrangement attempted to remove as many beds as possible from cold exterior walls, and away from draughts – conditions which were unavoidable in a pavilion ward.

The Holborn guardians were so impressed with Snell's new design that they determined to adopt it for their new infirmary at Islington, only allowing a larger cubic space per patient than at St Luke's. However, the Local Government Board, which had replaced the Poor Law Board as the central authority in 1871, objected, and a compromise was reached: part of the infirmary was erected to Snell's new plan but two pavilion ward wings were included (Fig 64). Snell's experiment at Holborn Union Infirmary was never repeated, possibly because supervisory nursing would have proved extremely difficult in its huge, 50-bed wards. Several metropolitan unions, however, continued to erect such large dormitories for aged and infirm, and sometimes able-bodied, paupers.

Snell also designed new infirmaries for the London unions of St Olave's (built in Southwark in 1873–6), St George's (erected on Fulham Road, Chelsea, in 1876–8), and St Marylebone (built well outside the parish, in north Kensington, in 1879–81). All of these buildings incorporated innovations such as a single tower at the ends of the pavilions to contain all the sanitary facilities, and, within the wards, 'thermhydric' stoves – an invention of Snell's own, manufactured by Potter & Son of South Molton Street. These stoves could stand against walls, as they did at St Marylebone, or in the centre of wards with descending flues passing under the floors to the outer walls, as at Holborn. Iron chambers containing water flanked the fire and heated radiators to either side.[47] Snell's wards, unlike those in the earlier infirmaries of St Pancras and Poplar and Stepney, had no associated day-rooms. From 1871 the Local Government Board had argued that day-rooms were unnecessary in metropolitan infirmaries, because their wards allowed patients a larger amount of cubic space than those of provincial infirmaries.[48]

The St Marylebone infirmary was generally thought to be Snell's most successful. According to *The Hospital*:

The only fault it will be possible to find is that it is too good ... the ratepayer who goes through these spacious corridors and airy wards ... is very apt to feel that parochial benevolence has been a little overdrawn, and that if guardians of the old school had too great a regard for the ratepayers' money, surely the new school has somewhat too little.[49]

Although more recently Pevsner described the building as a 'grim fortress-like pile',[50] its Gothic details and soaring clock tower contrasted with the utilitarian appearance of most Poor Law buildings and contributed to its air of extravagance.

There was a considerable range of staff accommodation at the St Marylebone infirmary, a typical feature of metropolitan infirmaries erected at this time, including those built on the same site as the workhouse. The entrance block included residences for the medical officer, matron and assistant medical officer as well as a chapel, and there was accommodation for fifty-eight trained nurses on the upper floors of the administration block. Among the papers which had been contributed to the government's committee on cubic space in workhouses of 1867 was one by Florence Nightingale addressing the problem of obtaining trained nurses for workhouse infirmaries.[51] In 1884 St Marylebone became one of the first unions to build a nurses' home for probationers, under the management of a lady superintendent. (A school of nursing at St Pancras had lasted only until 1878 and does not seem to have occupied special accommodation.) Louisa Twining had set up the Association for Promoting Trained Nursing in Workhouse Infirmaries in 1879, but for a long time it remained difficult to entice nurses into workhouse infirmaries where working conditions were relatively poor. Nevertheless, there were 936 probationer nurses in workhouse infirmaries by 1896 and 2,100 by 1901.[52] The increase in paid trained workhouse nurses during the 1890s is reflected in the number of nurses' homes added to infirmaries throughout the country at that time.

The main variation on the pavilion plan to be produced in the late 19th century was the circular ward block (see page 32), and circular wards were built or proposed for a number of workhouse infirmary sites. Henry Saxon Snell published a design for a 700-bed workhouse infirmary with circular wards in 1881,[53] in which each block was three storeys high and contained 32-bed wards with a diameter of 70 ft, and a central ventilation shaft and fireplace. A service block and a sanitary tower were attached to each block. However, Snell's plan was never carried out, and the first circular ward block to be erected on a workhouse site was designed by Charles Bell (who had trained under John Giles) for Hampstead Union, and was built in 1884–5.[54] The circular form was particularly suitable at Hampstead where the workhouse buildings occupied a cramped site, hemmed in by streets and houses (Fig 65). The tower was three storeys high, plus basement and attic, with wards 50 ft in diameter and containing 24 beds. At the Camberwell Infirmary an even taller circular ward tower, rising to four storeys, was erected in 1888 from the designs of Robert P Whellock, who is principally remembered for a handful of public buildings in south London. Other circular ward blocks were built later in the

provinces, for example at the Halifax Union Infirmary of 1897–1901 (see page 72).[55]

From the late 1880s workhouse infirmaries in London tended to follow orthodox pavilion plans. Among the largest new establishments were the 763-bed St Saviour's Infirmary in Dulwich, built in 1885–7 by Henry Jarvis & Son (Jarvis senior was District Surveyor of St Giles, Camberwell), and the 750-bed Bethnal Green Infirmary built in 1896–1900 by Giles, Gough & Trollope. After 1900 the main developments in ward design at these huge infirmaries related to the location of sanitary facilities and the provision of balconies and sun-rooms. Wandsworth Union Infirmary erected in 1910–14 to designs by James S Gibson, was a good example of these developments. Some 600 beds were provided in ward pavilions aligned east–west rather than north–south, and in keeping with the planning of voluntary hospitals the sanitary facilities were no longer beyond cross-ventilated lobbies at the far end of the ward. In addition, each pavilion had 'sunning balconies' on the south side and a fire escape to the north.[56]

Provincial Workhouse Infirmaries, 1867–1914

The *Lancet* followed up its reports on metropolitan infirmaries with a short series of reports on provincial infirmaries, published in 1867.[57] Meanwhile, Dr Edward Smith had prepared an official report on forty-seven provincial workhouse infirmaries for the Poor Law Board.[58] Acknowledging that variations existed between town and country workhouses, Dr Smith found that on average five-sixths of their inmates were classified as either aged and infirm, or sick. His various recommendations concerning the location and design of infirmaries and medical care were not followed up by legislation, as they had been in London. However, in June 1868 the Poor Law Board circulated a pamphlet entitled 'Points to be Attended to in the Construction of Workhouses', which recommended that in larger workhouses the sick should be divided into the following classes: ordinary sick, lying-in, itch, dirty and offensive, venereal, fever and smallpox, and children.[59] A smaller amount of cubic air space per inmate was permitted than in metropolitan infirmaries: 600 for the ordinary sick, itch and venereal cases, and 900 for lying-in and offensive cases.[60] Despite the fact that there was no Common Poor Fund to encourage building, hundreds of provincial infirmaries were extended or rebuilt on the pavilion plan between 1870 and 1914. In most cases infirmaries were adjacent to workhouses,

Figure 65
The circular ward block of Hampstead Union Workhouse, London, rises above the surrounding houses. It was built in 1884–5 to designs by C Bell, and was one of many additions and alterations to the workhouse which later became known as New End Hospital.
[NMR BB91/14839]

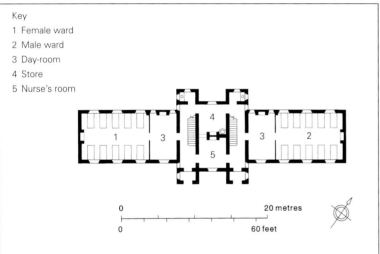

Key
1 Female ward
2 Male ward
3 Day-room
4 Store
5 Nurse's room

0   20 metres

0   60 feet

Figures 66 and 67
General view and
ground-floor plan of the
infirmary at Wells Union
Workhouse (later part of
Priory Hospital),
Somerset, built in 1871
to designs by E Hippisley.
[Photograph NMR
BB95/4843; plan (1:500)
based on Somerset Archive
and Record Service
D/G/WE/32/3]

but at the turn of the century a few were built on separate sites.

After 1870 single-block pavilion-plan infirmaries, on the lines of the Southampton Incorporation Workhouse infirmary of the 1860s, became very popular, particularly where fewer than 60 beds were required. A variant of this plan type was adopted throughout the country for infectious diseases blocks at workhouses as well as general infirmaries. Wells Union Workhouse infirmary is an early example (Figs 66 and 67). It was designed in 1871 by Edwin Hippisley, Surveyor to the Dean and Chapter of Wells Cathedral. The central block contained nurses' rooms and the staircases, with water closets in annexes at the back. On either side were the ward wings, the beds arranged in a rather haphazard manner, some directly under the windows. Day-rooms, with independent heating, were provided on the ground floor and a 2-bed lying-in ward was

created by partitioning the end bay of the women's ward on the first floor.

Not all infirmary blocks served both sexes, and it was common for a new building to house male patients while older accommodation, often still within the main workhouse, was given over to women. Single-sex infirmaries did not have to be symmetrical. The male infirmary at Daventry Union Workhouse had a ward on one side, and a day-room and nurses' rooms on the other, on each floor. The plain red-brick building of two storeys was designed by Edmund Francis Law of Northampton in 1869 for a sloping site which enabled the architect to include hearse and ambulance sheds in the basement.

The division of ward wings into two separate rooms, already seen at Southampton in 1865, continued to be favoured, and it became usual in the 1880s and 1890s to devote the outer wards to offensive, itch or venereal cases, usually with separate sanitary annexes. Alcester Union Workhouse Infirmary elaborated on this with an unusual arrangement of the sanitary facilities. The two-storeyed sanitary annexe of the ordinary wards abutted the single-storeyed annexe of the 'special' wards, and a corridor ran through the centre of both giving access from one ward to the other. The infirmary was designed by the prolific workhouse architect William Henry Ward and built in 1899–1900. It had a rare degree of architectural embellishment, with hipped and half-hipped roofs, ridge tiles, iron finials and stepped and dentilled cornices. Elsewhere, an even greater degree of separation for offensive cases was preferred, and at many workhouses in the late 19th century they occupied a separate building. At Coventry, for example, accommodation was provided in 1886 for females suffering from itch and venereal disease in a small single-storeyed building, divided into two self-contained wards.

Reigate Union Workhouse infirmary, designed by the local architects Thomas Rowland & Vincent Hooper in 1914 and completed in 1916, illustrates the changes which such infirmaries had undergone by the First World War (Fig 68).[61] The administrative centre occupied more than a third of the entire length of the building, and, in addition to the usual offices and ward services, it included bathrooms, a labour ward, and an operating suite. Canted bay windows on the ground floor lit day-rooms, and their flat roofs formed a balcony for the tuberculosis wards above. Verandas and balconies along the eastern sides of the wards allowed patients to sit in the open air.

The standard layout at provincial infirmaries with over 60 beds comprised a central, partly administrative block, linked to flanking ward

pavilions by short covered ways. Individual ward blocks were recommended to be no more than two storeys high and to hold a maximum of sixty patients each.[62] The 68-bed infirmary erected to the rear of Bromsgrove Union Workhouse in 1884 was typical (Fig 69). A central block housed a dispensary, linen room, nurse's bedroom and receiving room on the ground

floor, and a lying-in ward, labour ward, and a second nurse's bedroom upstairs. To either side were covered ways leading to the ward pavilions. As usual, the pavilions were divided up to provide day-rooms, ordinary sick wards and venereal wards. While day-rooms were increasingly common for the ordinary sick they seldom provided for venereal or 'offensive'

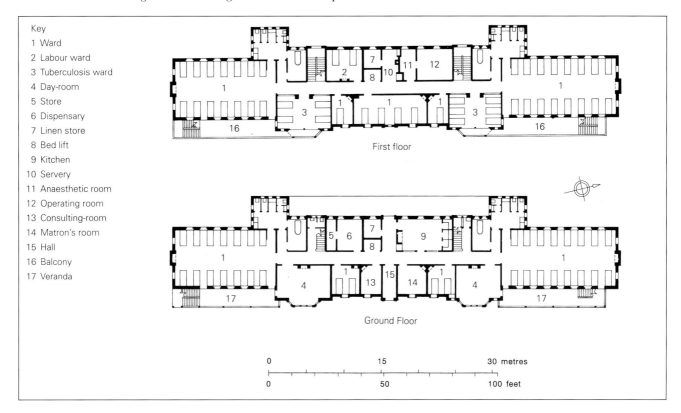

Key

1 Ward
2 Labour ward
3 Tuberculosis ward
4 Day-room
5 Store
6 Dispensary
7 Linen store
8 Bed lift
9 Kitchen
10 Servery
11 Anaesthetic room
12 Operating room
13 Consulting-room
14 Matron's room
15 Hall
16 Balcony
17 Veranda

First floor

Ground Floor

0   15   30 metres
0   50   100 feet

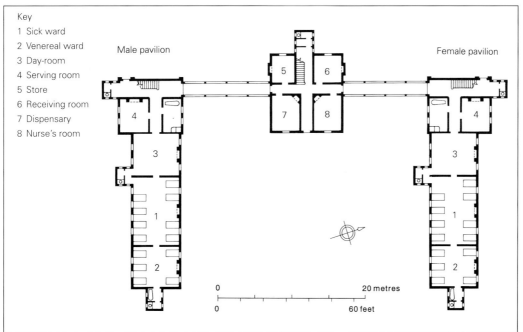

Key

1 Sick ward
2 Venereal ward
3 Day-room
4 Serving room
5 Store
6 Receiving room
7 Dispensary
8 Nurse's room

Male pavilion

Female pavilion

0   20 metres
0   60 feet

Figure 68 (above) Ground and first-floor plans of the infirmary added to Reigate Union Workhouse, Surrey, in 1914–16, designed by T Rowland & V Hooper. [Plans (1:500) based on Building News, 6 Feb 1914, 192–3]

Figure 69 (left) Ground-floor plan of the infirmary erected in 1884 at Bromsgrove Union Workhouse (later part of All Saints' Hospital), Hereford and Worcester. [Plan (1:500) based on PRO MH14/5]

patients, possibly reflecting the punitive attitude which was still maintained at that date towards 'foul' cases, although in principle a deterrent policy for the sick had ceased to operate. The original design of the Bromsgrove infirmary allowed for its future extension. This was common practice, but extensions to workhouse infirmaries rarely followed the lines of earlier plans.

Lying-in and labour wards were frequently situated on the upper floor of the central block, as at Bromsgrove, but from the 1880s onwards some single-storey or 'bungalow' maternity blocks were built, reflecting contemporary ideas on the design of maternity hospitals (see page 107). The handsome Dorking Union Workhouse infirmary of 1899–1901 designed by Henry Percy Adams, and the Exeter Incorporation Workhouse infirmary of 1904–5 by R M Challice, both included single-storey maternity blocks.[63] However, it was still fairly common at that time for lying-in wards to be located within the workhouse.

Workhouses in many provincial cities had pavilion-plan infirmaries on a scale rivalling, or even surpassing, those of London. One of the very largest was designed in 1876 for the Manchester Union Workhouse at Crumpsall by Mills & Murgatroyd, who designed a number of prominent public buildings in and around Manchester. The infirmary provided 1,400 beds in three-storeyed double pavilions: four for women

on one side of the administration block, and three for men on the other.[64] While Manchester adopted a conventional layout, an alternative was produced by the ever-resourceful W H Ward for the infirmary of Birmingham Union Workhouse in 1888. Harking back to the design of Blackburn Infirmary (see page 27), it comprised nine ward blocks set alternately to the east and west sides of the main corridor, with the administration block situated at its southern extremity. Ward repeated this alternation of blocks at his smaller Stockport Union Infirmary of 1901–5, and T Worthington & Son adopted a similar arrangement for their Prestwich Union Infirmary of 1906–10, which had a curved corridor.

One of the most impressive of the large-scale provincial infirmaries was that built at Halifax in 1897–1901 to designs by the local architect, William Clement Williams (Fig 70). It accommodated 400 patients in four rectangular and two circular ward blocks, arranged off a U-shaped corridor, with the nurses' home, administration block and kitchen on its central axis. In a vaguely free style with Jacobethan details, including strapwork and segmental-pedimented gables, tall chimneystacks and an elaborate clock tower, the infirmary forms an impressive group. It was one of a number of infirmaries erected on a site distant from the workhouse – in rapidly expanding towns, there was little likelihood of acquiring adjacent land. Two of the earliest separate-site infirmaries to

Figure 70
This aerial photograph of Halifax Union Infirmary, West Yorkshire, designed by W C Williams and erected in 1897–1901, shows the combination of standard rectangular ward pavilions, with, in the foreground, two circular ward blocks. These ward blocks are placed on either side of the administrative and service buildings.
[Yorkshire Regional Health Authority, Hunting Aerofilms Ltd, No. 54382]

Figure 71
General view of the main front of Wayland Union Infirmary at Attleborough, Norfolk, erected in 1911–12 and designed by H J Green.
[NMR BB92/31588]

be erected outside the metropolis were those of Salford (1880–2) and Croydon (1881–5); later examples included Southampton (1899–1902), Stockport (1901–5), Leicester (1903–5), and Prestwich (1906–10). On average these infirmaries accommodated between 300 and 500 patients, more than most contemporary voluntary hospitals.

Even the largest workhouse infirmaries differed in many respects from voluntary general hospitals, although by the late 19th century they invariably had a resident medical staff and treated some surgical cases. In 1893, (Sir) Henry Burdett enumerated the main differences.[65] Workhouse infirmaries never had out-patients' departments, and seldom admitted accident and emergency cases. They accepted incurable, offensive and contagious cases, and complaints 'resulting from intemperate, careless, and dissolute habits in earlier years', all of which would have been excluded from general hospitals.[66] Furthermore, they were never provided with an attached medical school, or with post-mortem facilities.

The need for smaller Poor Law infirmaries continued in the early 20th century. The only ones built on separate sites seem to have been the union infirmaries at Worksop (1901–6), and Wayland (1911–12) and Hartismere (1913–15) in East Anglia, both designed by Herbert J Green, the Diocesan Surveyor for Norwich and a former pupil of A W Blomfield. At the Hartismere infirmary the ward wings were set at an angle to create a sun-trap and verandas were provided along the south fronts. The Wayland infirmary, too, had balconies and verandas where patients could sit out and enjoy the fresh air (Fig 71).

Wayland is typical of modest hospitals built in the first decades of the 20th century. The dignified neo-Georgian façade gives it the air of a voluntary hospital rather than a Poor Law building. Nevertheless, at both of the East Anglian infirmaries, ancillary buildings included a laundry on the female side and a boiler room on the male side, retaining the labour division of the able-bodied workhouse.

In the early 20th century the guardians of numerous unions adapted some existing workhouse accommodation for tubercular patients, who had hitherto mixed freely with the other inmates.[67] Alterations to buildings were often of a rather basic nature, such as the addition of verandas or the enlargement of windows in order to practise open-air treatment. Shelters, and occasionally tents, might be erected in the grounds, and new infirmaries sometimes incorporated more specialised accommodation. Buildings erected at Reading (1909–11) and Hull (1911–14) devoted their entire top floor to tuberculosis cases: the centre of each building rose to four storeys and provided access to flat roofs and glazed shelters over the wings. Even in London, the Camberwell Board of Guardians provided top-floor wards for consumptives in the new infirmary buildings added to the site in 1903, designed in an attractive free style by Edwin T Hall (Fig 72).[68]

Only a handful of new Poor Law buildings, however, merited the name 'sanatorium'. These included a detached ward block erected on the site of Kettering Union Workhouse and one at Gateshead Union's infirmary at Shotley Bridge. Three Poor Law authorities in the Liverpool area provided a joint sanatorium on a new site, an unusual step which was also taken by Bradford.[69]

Figure 72
One of the infirmary blocks erected in 1903 as part of the expansion of the Camberwell Workhouse Infirmary (later St Giles's Hospital), London, designed by E T Hall.
[NMR BB92/23896]

Poor Law Infirmaries 1914–1929

The Royal Commission on the Poor Laws and the Relief of Distress, 1905–9, could not agree on the future administration of workhouses and produced two reports, neither of which was immediately adopted but both of which stimulated debate for the next twenty-five years.[70] The Majority Report favoured the retention of a 'Public Assistance Authority', but urged greater co-operation with voluntary authorities. The Minority Report, on the other hand, recommended the repeal of the 1834 Poor Law Amendment Act, and with it the disbandment of the 'Destitution Authority', whose power and duties would be transferred to the relevant committee of the county councils (education, health, asylums or pensions).

In the early 20th century the numbers of paupers in workhouses began to fall. Specialised institutions, such as children's homes and epileptic colonies, removed whole categories of inmates, and the introduction of non-contributory old-age pensions in 1908 saved many elderly men and women from having to face the end of their days in the workhouse. The National Insurance Act of 1911 provided health and unemployment insurance for certain workers, reducing the number of the able-bodied poor seeking relief. During the First World War the workhouse population was directly affected by the evacuation of institutions taken over by the military, and many of the able-bodied left to join the war effort. From 1917 venereal disease was treated free of charge in clinics, reducing the need for venereal wards in workhouse infirmaries, and as unemployment soared after the war the government spent huge sums on outdoor relief rather than herding the unemployed into deterrent workhouses. After the war, mental-deficiency colonies were established gradually throughout the country and by the early 1920s sanatoria set up by local authorities were treating tubercular patients who would previously have entered the workhouse. Thus, by the 1930s, Poor Law Institutions (administered since 1918 by the Ministry of Health) were almost exclusively occupied by the aged and infirm, vagrants, unmarried mothers and the sick.

The facilities and staffing of those infirmaries which had been taken over by the military between 1914 and 1918 had been greatly improved, and their staff no longer had a second-class reputation.[71] Infirmaries increasingly resembled voluntary general hospitals, although they still lacked out-patients' departments, pathology laboratories or teaching facilities. Some began to take in paying patients, accepting tuberculosis and maternity cases from voluntary hospitals at a rate of 25s to 30s a day. 'Hospital' now replaced 'infirmary' or 'sick asylum' in the name of many institutions (the Poplar and Stepney Sick Asylum, for example, became St Andrew's Hospital in 1925).

Financial constraints prevented the erection of new Poor Law buildings in the immediate aftermath of the First World War, but, in an effort to attract much-needed nurses to Poor Law infirmaries, the Ministry of Health approved expenditure on staff accommodation from *c* 1923.[72] Existing nurses' homes were extended and a number of new homes erected, such as that designed by Paine & Hobday for Dudley Union in 1925. Few large-scale infirmary projects were initiated between 1924 and 1929, possibly due as much to uncertainty surrounding the future of Poor Law administration as to economic restraint.

One of the most ambitious schemes carried out at this time was the 308-bed Davyhulme Hospital for Barton-upon-Irwell Union in Lancashire, designed by Elcock & Sutcliffe in 1924. It was hailed as 'the first instance of a distinct effort being made on a large scale to develop the Poor Law Hospital on more efficient and modern lines, in conformity with present

Figure 73
This is an early
photograph of the main
administration block
and a ward wing of
Derby City Hospital,
built in 1926–9.
[NMR BB90/6714,
copyright J Millar]

general hospital requirements'.[73] A more stream-lined appearance was achieved by abandoning sanitary towers in favour of integrating the bath-rooms, water closets and sluice rooms within the ward pavilions. As with the majority of inter-war hospitals, a great emphasis was placed on open-air and sunlight treatment. The most striking features of many new ward blocks were their capacious verandas and flat roofs. End bays of ward pavilions were sometimes partitioned off to create day-rooms or sun-rooms with access to verandas. Derby City Hospital, built in 1926–9, was typical (Fig 73); it even provided shelters on the flat roofs to allow convalescents and tubercu-losis cases to benefit from plenty of fresh air.

The range of facilities expanded greatly in the 1920s to include operating-theatre suites, X-ray equipment and a variety of specialist wards. At Derby City Hospital there was a detached maternity block and a special treatment block housing the X-ray department, an ophthalmic ward, dental room, and wards for massage and sun treatment. Similarly, at Davyhulme, the hospital included a cubicle isolation block (see page 142), and separate units for sick and healthy children, maternity cases, and ophthalmic opera-tions, as well as a building containing a labora-tory, dispensary and mortuary. Most of these departments might have been encountered in a voluntary general hospital, but the healthy chil-dren's unit with its 36 beds is a reminder that this was a Poor Law building.

The new hospital for Billericay Union in Essex combined an emphasis on lightness and airiness with a degree of specialisation. It was designed by Hugo R Bird and built in 1925–7 to provide accommodation for seventy patients. There were four separate buildings: a nurses' home, an administration block, an operating theatre and a main hospital wing. Unlike most Poor Law hospi-tals, this last was a sprawling single-storeyed building. The first consideration had been 'to place the wards so that they may obtain the maximum of sunshine and be as bright and cheerful as possible'.[74] They terminated in open verandas with glazed roofs and had flat roofs for open-air treatment. Specialist facilities within the new building included wards for maternity and cancer cases and a children's sun ward.

Chamberlain's Local Government Act of 1929[75] finally disbanded the Poor Law unions. The duties of boards of guardians were passed on to the Public Assistance and Public Health Committees of the county and county borough councils. The most up-to-date Poor Law infir-maries were taken over as municipal hospitals from 1930 onwards, and were often greatly extended. General mixed institutions continued to accommodate healthy paupers incapable of caring for themselves. The work-house system lingered on in these Public Assistance Institutions until 1948. Although few of the workhouse buildings then inherited by the National Health Service had been erected as infirmaries, many were adapted for the sick, or for the aged and infirm. Other former workhouse buildings were retained by local authorities as accommodation for the elderly, and as late as 1960 about half of such accommodation was in old workhouses.[76]

5
The Hospitals of the Armed Forces

Two of Britain's finest secular buildings are associated with hospitals for the Army and the Navy. The Royal Hospital at Chelsea was founded for the Army in 1682, and the Royal Hospital at Greenwich for the Navy in 1694. In their royal connections and the grandeur of their architecture these hospitals emulate the magnificent *Hôtel des Invalides* in Paris, founded by Louis XIV in 1670.

The Royal Hospital at Chelsea was established by Charles II and, like the *Invalides*, was intended for aged or disabled soldiers. The buildings were designed by Sir Christopher Wren, and erected in ample grounds beside the Thames, being laid out around an open courtyard, with colonnades affording shelter to pensioners wishing to take the air. The Royal Hospital at Greenwich, on an equally fine site overlooking the Thames, occupied the unfinished royal palace begun by Charles II in the 1660s, but abandoned by William and Mary in favour of Hampton Court. Like Chelsea, Greenwich was founded as a home for aged and disabled servicemen, and Wren was the first of several important architects to design new buildings there. Separate infirmary accommodation for sick inmates was provided at both Chelsea and Greenwich. Sir John Soane designed a new U-shaped infirmary for the Chelsea hospital in 1810 while the infirmary at Greenwich was designed by James 'Athenian' Stuart and erected in 1763–8 (Fig 74).

Although neither Greenwich nor Chelsea were ever hospitals in the modern sense of the word, their dignified and imposing buildings had a profound influence on both the appearance and planning of later hospitals erected for sick and wounded servicemen. These did not, of course, aspire to the same level of grandeur as the Royal Hospitals. Nevertheless, something of their stateliness and formality percolated through to these more workaday buildings, which frequently displayed an architectural distinction often lacking in their civilian counterparts. The buildings erected as hospitals for the services are closely related to other military establishments, such as dockyards, barracks and academies, with a remarkable unity of style and an unmistakably military air. This cannot be attributed solely to the use of the services' own architects and engineers: it was undoubtedly important that the sense of order, hierarchy and dignity expected of naval and military personnel should be reflected in the buildings that they occupied. As a group, these buildings have a definite cohesion that is augmented by the extraordinary survival of so many of the earliest and pioneering hospitals.

In form and plan military hospitals were closely related to civilian general hospitals. One very obvious difference, however, was the lack of provision for women and children, who were excluded from general military and naval hospitals until the 20th century, although the largest military stations did provide separate 'female' or 'families' hospitals from the mid 19th century onwards. In wartime, forces hospitals inevitably received a high proportion of surgical cases, and at all times they admitted cases which would have been excluded from voluntary general hospitals, such as itch, mental illness, venereal disease, tuberculosis and other infectious diseases.

Naval Hospitals

Before the Royal Navy established its first general hospitals in the mid 18th century, sick and wounded seamen were looked after by contracted medical staff on hospital ships, in hired houses and inns at the principal ports, and in reserved beds at the main London hospitals. These arrangements were the responsibility of the Surgeon-General during peacetime, but from 1653 a Commission for Sick and Hurt was periodically convened to administer a wartime medical service.

In the course of the first Dutch War (1652–4) it proved extremely difficult to house the large numbers of sick and wounded who were landed after actions fought off the south and east coasts. The situation was particularly acute in Portsmouth, where Dr Daniel Whistler, medical adviser to the Admiralty, suggested centralising the care of the 300 men scattered throughout

establishments in the Portsmouth and Gosport area, either by erecting a new hospital or by converting Portchester Castle.[1] The crisis abated, however, and nothing was done.

During the second Dutch War (1665–7) the need for a general naval hospital became pressing once again. John Evelyn, then serving on the Commission for Sick and Hurt, drew up plans for a hospital at Chatham with 400 or 500 beds, but no money was made available to put them into effect.[2] Then, in 1690, the physician Dr Richard Lower advised the Admiralty to convert several large buildings into naval hospitals. One of the buildings suggested by Lower for this purpose was the unfinished Royal Palace at Greenwich, and after the Battle of La Hogue in 1692, the King Charles Block was fitted up as a

temporary hospital for the sick and wounded. In 1694 this building and the surrounding lands were formally granted to the Navy by William III.[3]

However, the first permanent hospitals for the sick and wounded were established abroad, where *ad hoc* arrangements such as those in England were not always possible. A hospital was built in Jamaica in 1704, and one in Lisbon in 1706. Purpose-built hospitals were also constructed on the two Mediterranean territories ceded to Britain by the Treaty of Utrecht in 1713; that at Minorca, which the British had captured in 1708, being built in 1711. At Gibraltar three designs were prepared in 1734, but nothing was achieved there before 1741, when a 1,000-bed hospital was finally approved.[4] Completed in 1746, it was built of materials and

Figure 74
Greenwich Hospital Infirmary, London, was erected in 1763–8. It was designed by James 'Athenian' Stuart to a courtyard plan, and contained small wards opening off central corridors. The infirmary later became the Dreadnought Seamen's Hospital.
[NMR BB92/23863]

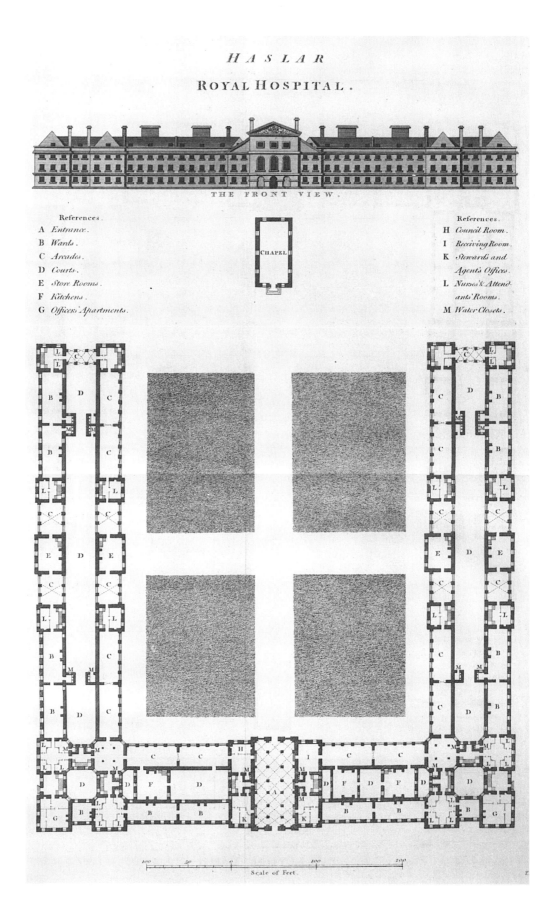

Figure 75
Elevation and ground-floor plan of the Royal Naval Hospital at Haslar, Hampshire, as erected between 1746 and 1761 to designs by Theodore Jacobsen.
[Howard 1789, pl 19 (By permission of the Syndics of Cambridge University Library)]

Notebook Architecture

A hospital that needs the best care

Marcus Binney
Architecture Correspondent

Among the grandest compositions in European architecture are the great naval and military hospitals — Greenwich and Chelsea in London, Les Invalides in Paris. With them belongs the Royal Haslar Hospital in Gosport, which has been in use for nearly two and half centuries, providing pioneering care for sick and wounded sailors.

Haslar's first physician was the celebrated James Lind, who more than anyone was responsible for raising medical standards in the Royal Navy — it was he who started bottling lemon juice in the cellars at Haslar to prevent scurvy.

Haslar has played a noble, indeed heroic, role in wars ever since, notably the Falklands. But on March 31 Haslar will cease, in official parlance, to be "a military unit" and control will pass from the Ministry of Defence to the National Health Service. Late in 2009 all services and staff are due to transfer to an enlarged Queen Alexandra Hospital at Cosham, outside Portsmouth.

The initiative for building Haslar was substantially due to the 26-year-old Earl of Sandwich, who in 1744, as newly appointed Lord Commissioner of the Admiralty, fixed on Portsmouth as the preferred site for the first naval hospital in Britain — earlier ones had been built in Minorca and Gibraltar, while Greenwich was more of an almshouse than hospital proper. The architect chosen was Theodore Jacobsen, who had provided the designs for the London's most renowned 18th-century philanthropic venture, the Foundling Hospital. Jacobsen also furnished the

Haslar has been providing care for wounded sailors since 1761

designs for the main quadrangle of Trinity College Dublin.

The chosen site at Gosport, across the harbour from Portsmouth, had the advantage of isolation — both for containing infection and reducing temptations to desert — as well as its own jetty. Jacobsen conceived Haslar as a giant quadrangle with 550ft-long (168m) sides surrounded by double ranges — though only three sides were built. Opened in 1753, it was designed to house 1,500 patients, this was increased in 1754 to 1,800 and by 1779 2,100 patients were being cared for in more than 80 wards.

The need for economy meant Haslar has little in the way of architectural adornment — but Jacobsen designed grand centrepieces for each front with one sloping pediment or gable set in another in the manner of Palladio's famous church of San Giorgio Maggiore in Venice.

Haslar is centred on a grand axis worthy of the Sun King himself — a 2,200ft straight line leading from the Gosport jetty up an avenue, across a

great forecourt through a vaulted hall with echoes of Somerset House, and continuing to a centrally placed chapel with a terrace of officers' houses that closes the composition.

In the 19th century a new accent was added in the form of tram lines leading from the jetty straight to the main entrance, providing patients with the smoothest of ambulance rides to the hospital door.

A formidable local campaign to save Haslar from closure has been running for several years. Gosport councillor Peter Edgar explains: "They said in 1998 the hospital would close in 2001 and it is still running. It is folly to close a superbly equipped, well-staffed hospital when the population will rise sharply with the building of over 80,000 new homes in the Solent area."

Councillor Edgar also challenges suggestions that the sale of the Haslar site may yield up to £50 million for new hospital buildings, including extensions to Selly Oaks to provide new rehabilitation facilities for wounded soldiers. "Even if they re-

ceive treatment there, Haslar remains ideal for recuperation. In France there are 14 military hospitals. Britain must not be left without one."

Development on the Haslar site will be constrained not only by listing, conservation area status and now inclusion on the English Heritage Register of Parks and Gardens, but also by the very large number of burials on the site.

Gosport council is also against any further residential development in the town and has designated the site for health and community use. It is clear, however, that the whole flank of the site running along the sea wall would be highly desirable for residential use. There are a number of Victorian blocks with iron balconies that would convert very well.

Haslar Hospital is far too important a site to be subject to the kind of procrastination and piecemeal carve-up that has blighted so many former mental hospitals.

At Greenwich Hospital the successful transformation to university and music school, combined with greater public access, was secured by vesting all the buildings in a charitable trust. At Haslar the need is to explore a mixed solution, including both health and community uses. One body that could undertake this is the Prince's Regeneration Trust — Kit Martin, its principal director of projects, undertook the restoration and conversion of the Royal Naval Hospital in Great Yarmouth as apartments.

Officials are fond of saying it is first too soon and then too late to consider alternatives but in this case there is no excuse for not initiating a proper constructive study of the best solution for this historic enclave.

Personals

Judge not, that ye be not judged. For with what judgment ye judge, ye shall be judged: and with what measure ye mete, it shall be measured out to you again. Matthew 7.1-2 (AV)

Births

CULLUM On 2nd March 2007, to Emily (née Harbottle) and Benjamin, a son, Talford John Wild.

LAWSON JOHNSTON On 9th March, to Sarah (née Parker) and Justin, a son, Fergus Coats, a brother for Zara and Jake.

Forthcoming Marriages

MR J.E.C. BRIDGEMAN AND MISS A.J. HARGREAVES
The engagement is announced between James, eldest son of the Hon Charles Bridgeman, of Leaton Knolls, Shropshire, and Mrs Nicola Bridgeman, of Shrewsbury, and Amy, younger daughter of Mr and Mrs Nicholas Hargreaves, of Alderley Edge, Cheshire.

MR W.D. HAMILTON AND MISS S.M. HUNT
The engagement is announced between William, son of Mr and Mrs Tim Hamilton, of Notting Hill, London, and Susanna, daughter of Dr and Mrs Peter Hunt, of Harpenden, Hertfordshire.

MR G.A.G. HUDSON AND MISS A.F. SOPER
The engagement is announced between Guy, younger son of the late Dr Gerald Hudson and of Mrs Maura Hudson, of Cambridge, and Anneke, younger daughter of Mr and Mrs Jonathan Soper, presently of Bucharest, Romania.

MR P.M. LIELL AND MRS J. BUSH
The engagement is announced between Peter Mark Liell and Jean Bush (née Brooker) both of Little Heath, Potters Bar, Hertfordshire.

MR C.D. SWALLOW AND MISS S.E.THOMPSON
The engagement is announced between Christopher, elder son of Mr and Mrs Anthony Swallow, of Prestbury, Cheshire, and Stefanie, youngest daughter of Mr and Mrs Patrick Thompson, of Rugby, Warwickshire.

Deaths

BOWLES Derek George late of Brentford, Middlesex on 11th March 2007. Son of the late Elsie and Bernard of Newport, South Wales and dear brother of the late Martin. Retired British Airways Cabin Crew. Funeral Mortlake Crematorium on Friday 23rd March at 2.30 pm. Contact Patrick Ryan & Daughter 0208 567 1664.

FLIND Christopher James, peacefully on 12th March, aged 76. Beloved husband of Jane and much loved father, grandfather and father-in-law. Funeral service at All Saints Church, Fulham, SW6 at 11.00 am on Monday 26th March. Donations, if you would like, to the British Heart Foundation c/o Cooperative Funeral Care, 799 Fulham Road, London, SW6 5HF.

LYALL Alexander William - born sleeping on January 15th 2007, beloved son of

Gifts

THE TIMES Birthdate newspaper 1847-2007 from £25 each. Freephone 0800 138 0990 www.bygonenews.com/times

Legal Notices

No 642 of 2007
IN THE HIGH COURT OF JUSTICE
CHANCERY DIVISION
COMPANIES COURT
IN THE MATTER OF LEVERSEDGE TELECOM SERVICES LIMITED
AND IN THE MATTER OF
THE COMPANIES ACT 1985
NOTICE IS HEREBY GIVEN that the Order of the High Court of Justice Chancery Division dated 14th February 2007 confirming the reduction of the share capital of the above-named company by £130,000 was registered by the Registrar of Companies on 20th February 2007
Dated this 16th day of March 2007
Batchelor Myddelton Solicitors
Brosnan House
Darkes Lane
Potters Bar
Hertfordshire
EN6 1BW
Ref: JAB/NGK/L40.1
Solicitors for the above-named company

The Insolvency Act 1986
Ash Fibre Processors Limited
Company No: 01332415
Emblem Technology
Company No: 01956143
Morgan Industrial Systems Limited
Company No: 01956136
Ormandy Stollery Electronic Components Limited
Company No: 01320141
Morganite Exports Limited
Company No: 467665
(all in Liquidation)
NOTICE IS HEREBY GIVEN that the creditors of the above named companies, which are being voluntarily wound up, are required, on or before 13 April 2007 to send in their full christian and surnames, their addresses and descriptions, full particulars of their debts or claims, and the names and addresses of their solicitors (if any), to the undersigned Andrew Philip Peters of Deloitte & Touche, 1 Woodborough Road, Nottingham, NG1 3FG, the Joint Liquidator of the said companies, and if so required by notice in writing from the said Joint Liquidators, are, personally or by their solicitors, to come in and prove their debts or claims at such time and place as shall be specified in such notice, or in default thereof they will be excluded from the benefit of any distribution made before such debts are proved.
Note: These Members' Voluntary (Solvent) Liquidations of dormant companies are being undertaken for reorganisational reasons only. All creditors have or will be paid in full.
Date: 13 March 2007
Andrew Philip Peters, Joint Liquidator

CB HOUSE PURCHASE LIMITED
Company No. SC011803
CB TRUSTEE NOMINEES LIMITED
Company No. SC013991
CLYDESDALE BANK (HEAD OFFICE) NOMINEES LIMITED
Company No. SC026263
CLYDESDALE BANK (LONDON) NOMINEES LIMITED
Company No. SC011800

No. 1791 of 2007

IN THE HIGH COURT OF JUSTICE
CHANCERY DIVISION
COMPANIES COURT
IN THE MATTER OF
SITA 2007 LIMITED
and
IN THE MATTER OF
THE COMPANIES ACT 1985
NOTICE IS HEREBY GIVEN that a Petition was on 8 March presented to Her Majesty's High Court of Justice for the confirmation of the cancellation of the share premium account of the above-named Company.
AND NOTICE IS FURTHER GIVEN that the said Petition is directed to be heard before the Companies Court Registrar at the Royal Courts of Justice, Strand, London WC2A 2LL on Wednesday the 28th day of March 2007.
Any Creditor or Shareholder of the said Company desiring to oppose the making of an Order for the confirmation of the said cancellation of share premium account should appear at the time of the Hearing in person or by Counsel for that purpose.
A copy of the said Petition will be furnished by the undermentioned Solicitors to any such person requiring the same on payment of the regulated charge for the same.
Dated the 19th day of March 2007.
Allen & Overy LLP
One Bishops Square,
London E1 6AO
Solicitors for the above-named Company

No. 1456 of 2007

IN THE HIGH COURT OF JUSTICE
CHANCERY DIVISION
COMPANIES COURT
IN THE MATTER OF SUBWAY DEVELOPMENTS (LONDON) LIMITED
AND IN THE MATTER OF
THE COMPANIES ACT 1985
NOTICE IS HEREBY GIVEN that a Petition was on Monday 26th February 2007 presented to Her Majesty's High Court of Justice seeking the reduction of the capital of the Company from £500,000 divided into 500,000 Ordinary Shares of £1 each to £54,383 divided into 54,383 Ordinary Shares of £1
AND NOTICE IS FURTHER GIVEN that the said Petition is directed to be heard before the Registrar of the Companies Court at the Royal Courts of Justice, Strand, London, WC2A 2LL. on Wednesday the 28th day of March 2007 AT 10.30am.
ANY Creditor or Shareholder of the said Company desiring to oppose the making of an Order for the confirmation of the said reduction of capital should appear at the time of the hearing in person or by Counsel for that purpose.
A copy of the said Petition will be furnished to any such person requiring the same by the undermentioned Solicitors on payment of the regulated charge for the same.
DATED this 12th day of March 2007
Sherrards Solicitors
45 Grosvenor Road
St Albans
Hertfordshire
AL1 3AW
Tel: 01727 832 830
FAX: 01727 832 833
DX: 141853, St Albans 17.
Ref: 1/A1192/5
Solicitors for the above named Company

Claim No: 13 Of 2007

IN THE HIGH COURT OF JUSTICE
CHANCERY DIVISION
COMPANIES COURT
IN THE MATTER OF INDUSTRIAL SECURITIES GROUP LIMITED
- and -
IN THE MATTER OF
THE COMPANIES ACT 1985
NOTICE IS HEREBY GIVEN that the Order of the High Court of Justice Chancery Division dated 1 March 2006 confirming the reduction of the share capital of the above-named company from £20,000,000 divided into 18,500,000 A ordinary shares of £1 each, 1,000,000 B ordinary shares of £1 each and 500,000 C ordinary shares of £1 each to £15,000,000 divided into 18,500,000 A ordinary shares of 75 pence each, 1,000,000 B ordinary shares of 75 pence each and 500,000 C ordinary shares of 75 pence was registered by the Registrar of Companies on 28 February 2007.
Dated the 9th day of March 2007
Howard Kennedy
19 Cavendish Square
London
W1A 2AW
Solicitors for the company

No. 1794 of 2007

IN THE HIGH COURT OF JUSTICE
CHANCERY DIVISION
COMPANIES COURT
IN THE MATTER OF
SITA HOLDINGS UK LIMITED
and
IN THE MATTER OF
THE COMPANIES ACT 1985
NOTICE IS HEREBY GIVEN that a Petition was on 8 March presented to Her Majesty's High Court of Justice for the confirmation of the reduction of the share capital of the above-named Company from £700,000,001 to £394,212,059.90.
AND NOTICE IS FURTHER GIVEN that the said Petition is directed to be heard before the Companies Court Registrar at the Royal Courts of Justice, Strand, London WC2A 2LL on Wednesday the 28th day of March 2007.
Any Creditor or Shareholder of the said Company desiring to oppose the making of an Order for the confirmation of the said reduction of share capital should appear at the time of the Hearing in person or by Counsel for that purpose.
A copy of the said Petition will be furnished by the undermentioned Solicitors to any such person requiring the same on payment of the regulated charge for the same.
Dated the 19th day of March 2007.
Allen & Overy LLP
One Bishops Square,
London E1 6AO
Solicitors for the above-named Company

NO. 1810 OF 2007

IN THE HIGH COURT OF JUSTICE
CHANCERY DIVISION
COMPANIES COURT
IN THE MATTER OF
HILLBOROUGH PROPERTIES LIMITED
- and -
IN THE MATTER OF
THE COMPANIES ACT 1985
NOTICE IS HEREBY GIVEN that a Petition was on 8 March 2007 presented to Her Majesty's High Court of Justice for the confirmation of the cancellation of the share premium account of the above-named Company.

by craftsmen imported from England. Although built by the Navy, both the Minorca and Gibraltar hospitals were run by contractors.

Pressure to build comparable hospitals at home reached a peak during the War of Jenkins's Ear against Spain, which broke out in 1739. From August 1739 to September 1740, 15,868 sick and wounded were landed from the fleet, the majority at Gosport and Plymouth. In March 1741 the Commission for Sick and Hurt estimated that the annual cost of caring for 1,000 men at Gosport would be reduced from £21,526 12s 8d under the existing contract system, to £13,879 6s 8d in a hospital built and run by the Navy.[5] The following October, the Admiralty proposed that 750-bed hospitals be built at Queenborough in Kent and at Plymouth, and a 1,500-bed hospital at Gosport. A plan which appears to have accompanied the proposal comprised a large courtyard surrounded by single ranges of back-to-back wards.[6] This may have been inspired by the Queen Anne Block of the Royal Hospital at Greenwich, which was completed in 1728 and included two parallel ranges of back-to-back wards. Until Stuart's detached infirmary for the Greenwich hospital was completed in 1764, these wards accommodated sick pensioners.[7]

The matter lapsed until September 1744, when the First Lord of the Admiralty, the Earl of Sandwich, suggested that if money was short £38,000 should be spent on a 1,500-bed hospital at Gosport in preference to the smaller hospitals.[8] An Order in Council followed, authorising the construction of hospitals at Gosport, Plymouth and Chatham which would be run by the Navy. It further stipulated that contractors were to be used only to supplement the system in wartime and in areas remote from naval hospitals.

An Admiralty letter dated 18 June 1745 directed that plans for a hospital at Haslar near Gosport be prepared by Sir Jacob Ackworth, the Surveyor of the Navy, together with the architect of the Foundling Hospital in London, Theodore Jacobsen, and the Commission for Sick and Hurt.[9] Their Lordships stipulated that the hospital be 'a strong, durable, plain building', and instructed their architects 'to consider attentively to the disposition, situation and dimensions of the wards for sick men, the convenience of light and air; to avoid narrowness as also crowding the beds too close together'. A letter dated 27 June 1745 shows that the Commission had consulted with the architects, but that Jacobsen did not approve of a plan drawn up by Ackworth, offering instead to prepare his own.[10] It was Jacobsen's plan that was adopted, but surviving drawings demonstrate that the design

was modified several times before work began in 1746, and that further changes were introduced before its completion. The Earl of Sandwich had estimated that the hospital would take only four or five years to finish, but it was not actually completed until 1761.

The Royal Naval Hospital at Haslar is a massive red-brick building with Portland stone dressings, comprising double ranges of wards embracing three sides of a quadrangle (Fig 75). The double ranges may have been influenced by the parallel ranges of the Queen Anne Block at Greenwich, which were also separated by a narrow courtyard. The north side of Haslar hospital was completed by 1754, and when the east and west sides were finished Haslar could boast of being not just the largest hospital in England, but also the largest brick building, the bricks being made from the local clay.[11] The projected south side, which would have incorporated a chapel, was never built, and so a detached chapel was erected in 1756. It was found necessary to close the quadrangle by railings in 1796 to deter desertion.

In accordance with Admiralty instructions, the building was largely devoid of ornamentation, apart from the Portland stone pediment crowning the administration block in the centre of the north side, which displays the Royal Arms of George II and personifications of Commerce and Navigation (Fig 76). The carving was executed in 1752 by Thomas Pearce. The administration block housed the council room, dispensary and offices of the steward and agent. Identical grand blocks were intended for the centre of the east and west sides of the quadrangle, but these were abandoned in favour of more modest central blocks of three bays, flanked at ground-floor level by open arcades. On either side were double ranges, separated by courts 34 ft wide. Kitchens and dining-rooms were to have been erected within all of these courts, but only those on the north side were completed. The wards were large, measuring 60 ft by 24 ft, and placed end to end, with access from one to the other. Nurses' rooms, officers' apartments, water closets and staircases were arranged around central light-wells at the junctures of the main ranges. From the outset, the hospital seems to have received every type of illness. It included wards for medical, surgical, fever, flux (dysentery), smallpox, consumptive, scorbutic (scurvy) and recovery cases, as well as a number of cells for lunatics.

The construction of the Royal Naval Hospital at Plymouth did not begin until 1758, two years into the Seven Years War, because some time was spent considering whether a local prison could be converted more cheaply.

Figure 76
This detail of the administration block of the Royal Naval Hospital at Haslar shows the fine carving in the pediment executed by Thomas Pearce in 1752.
[NMR BB92/29877]

The hospital was completed in 1762, providing accommodation for 1,200 patients in sixty wards. The design is attributed to the obscure Alexander Rovehead or Rouchead, who certainly supervised the construction. An early proposal, showing a courtyard surrounded by three single ranges and one double range, was undoubtedly inspired by Haslar, but the final design comprised a courtyard surrounded by detached blocks connected by a single-storey Tuscan colonnade, its flat roof serving as an ambulatory for convalescents (Fig 77, and see Figure 5).[12]

Most of the architectural embellishment was reserved for the administration block, situated centrally on the east side of the courtyard (Fig 78). Surmounted by a clock turret and lantern, its Venetian and Diocletian windows give it a dignified Palladian air. The administration block was not occupied solely by offices, but also contained a surgery, laboratory and dispensary on the ground floor, a chapel and committee-room on the first floor, and recovery wards and nurses' rooms in the attics.[13] The ten rectangular ward blocks were all three storeys high and originally contained two 20-bed wards on each floor, separated by a spine wall, together

with water closets and a nurses' room or 'cabin'.[14] In addition to the ward blocks there were four single-storeyed blocks which contained kitchens and mess rooms, but by the end of the 18th century new uses had been found for three of them, accommodating the steward's store room, smallpox wards, labourers' apartments and four cells for lunatics. An Admiralty letter of 25 August 1763 directed that the staff complement should be exactly the same as at Haslar, with the exception of a ferryman. (One was employed at Haslar at £20 a year, but Plymouth had none despite the fact that patients had to be ferried up Stonehouse Creek to the hospital jetty.)[15] Both hospitals employed female nurses who lived in small rooms or cabins.[16]

The design of the Plymouth hospital was seen to have many virtues. In 1784 John Howard explained that the ward blocks were detached 'for the purpose of admitting freer circulation of air, as also of classing the several disorders, in such manner, as may best prevent the spread of contagion'.[17] There is no evidence, however, that this had been Rovehead's intention. An unexecuted design by Wren for the Royal Hospital at Greenwich, dated between 1696 and

1702, comprised detached blocks ranged on either side of an oblong courtyard and connected by a colonnade in the manner of Plymouth, but as they were not intended to house sick wards their arrangement could hardly have been devised for the separation of diseases.[18] Similarly, the detached buildings of James Gibbs's St Bartholomew's Hospital, built 1729–68, seem to have been designed to prevent the spread of fire rather than infection (see page 10). Whatever the initial purpose of the separate blocks at Plymouth, this arrangement, together with the vast central courtyard (720 ft by 128 ft) and the cordon round the perimeter, ensured both isolation and a free circulation of air. Indeed, when Jacques Tenon and Charles-Augustin Coulomb, two representatives of the French Royal Commission appointed to investigate foreign hospitals, visited the hospital in July 1787 they reported that: 'in not one of the hospitals of France and England, we would say in the whole of Europe, except the Plymouth hospital are the individual buildings destined to receive patients as well ventilated and as completely isolated.'[19] The success of Plymouth, which had a lower mortality rate than Haslar in time of war, seemed to justify the separate ward system which French architects were advocating but had not yet put into practice.[20] As its wards lacked cross-ventilation, however, Plymouth cannot be viewed as a true precursor of the pavilion-plan hospitals of the 19th century (see page 6).

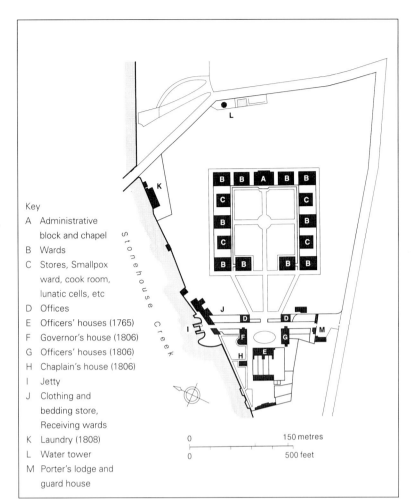

Key
A   Administrative block and chapel
B   Wards
C   Stores, Smallpox ward, cook room, lunatic cells, etc
D   Offices
E   Officers' houses (1765)
F   Governor's house (1806)
G   Officers' houses (1806)
H   Chaplain's house (1806)
I   Jetty
J   Clothing and bedding store, Receiving wards
K   Laundry (1808)
L   Water tower
M   Porter's lodge and guard house

Figure 77 (above)
Block plan of the Royal Naval Hospital, Plymouth, Devon, as it was in 1831. The hospital was originally built in 1758–62 to designs by Alexander Rovehead.
[Based on site plan by G L Taylor, drawn in 1831, at the National Maritime Museum, London]

Figure 78 (left)
*General view of the administration block of the Royal Naval Hospital, Plymouth, marked **A** on the plan above.*
[NMR BB81/3630]

Figure 79
Terraced housing built
for the governor and
lieutenants at the Royal
Naval Hospital at
Haslar, Hampshire,
designed by Samuel
Bunce and erected in
1796–8.
[NMR BB92/29858]

As the administrative staff of naval hospitals were naval personnel, it was necessary to provide them with accommodation, either on the site or close by. The Haslar and Plymouth hospitals were each administered by a physician, surgeon, agent and steward. At Haslar, two pairs of brick houses were built for them *c* 1756, and at Plymouth a four-house brick terrace was erected *c* 1765. When a governor was appointed to each hospital in 1795, larger residences were constructed for him and his lieutenants.[21] The brick residences at Haslar were designed by Samuel Bunce, Architect to the Admiralty from 1795 to 1802, and built in 1796–8 (Fig 79). They comprised a central house for the governor, linked to flanking terraces of four houses each. With their projecting and covered-in front porches, they resemble dockyard officials' houses, such as those at Chatham and Portsmouth. The new houses at Plymouth were located to either side of the earlier terrace, creating a 'square' in front of the inner hospital gates (see Figure 77). The earliest designs for these ashlar-faced houses were signed by Samuel Bentham, but by October 1804 Edward Holl had taken over the project.[22] Samuel Bentham, brother of the more famous Jeremy, was the first and only Inspector General of Naval Works, serving from 1795 to 1812. In his department were some of the first professional architects to serve the Navy, notably Samuel Bunce and Edward Holl.

In 1785 the Commission for Sick and Hurt prepared a report on 'what manner the hospitals abroad may be best conducted in future'.[23]

Figure 80 (opposite)
Detail of the Royal
Naval Hospital at Deal,
Kent, rebuilt in 1811 to
designs by Edward Holl.
[NMR BB92/31818]

It specified that hospitals should occupy open, elevated, airy sites, that wards should have windows in 'opposite directions', and that an airing ground should be provided for convalescents. As it had already recommended in 1781, the Commission laid down that each patient should have a minimum of 600 cu ft of air. Haslar and Plymouth both allowed 864, but were presented as special cases: 'these are permanent hospitals built for long duration and at great expense.' It did not matter whether the heads or sides of beds were placed against the walls, and the patient was not to be spared from the 'dying looks of his companion' by cubicles, since they obstructed the circulation of air.[24] These general precepts were followed in the 300-bed naval hospitals erected at Deal and Great Yarmouth during the French Wars.

The Royal Naval Hospital at Deal was built *c* 1795. It comprised a central administration block flanked by large wards with opposing windows, and service rooms, offices and smaller wards in end wings. After lightning caused minor damage in 1809, cross-wings were added at either end of the building.[25] The north wing housed the guard-room and accommodation for the hospital mate and steward, while the larger south wing included the laundry, officers' wards and matron's quarters. In 1811 it was decided to demolish the building of 1795, and erect a new hospital between the later wings (Fig 80).[26] The new block, designed by Edward Holl, also had wards with opposing windows, but removed the

stairs, water closets and nurses' cabins to rear projections. In 1813 staff residences and an outbuilding containing the mortuary, an extinguishing-engine house, an 'insane house' and porter's apartments were added. The insane house, heated by underfloor pipes, comprised three cells with open-barred fronts, opening off a short corridor.[27]

For the Royal Naval Hospital at Great Yarmouth, erected between 1809 and 1811, the architect William Pilkington adopted a courtyard plan, comprising four single-depth ranges linked by quadrants, with a continuous colonnade round the central court (Fig 81).[28] The north range contained the kitchen, bathroom, stores, mess room for convalescents, wards for commissioned, warrant and petty officers, and staff accommodation. The other three ranges contained four wards, measuring 47 ft by 24 ft, on each floor. Between each pair of wards was a staircase, a water closet and two nurses' rooms. Two 'necessaries' in each of the corner blocks completed the sanitary arrangements. In the centre of the west range was the chapel, in the centre of the east range the dispensary, and in the centre of the south range the north-facing operating theatre, conveniently placed next to the mortuary. Operating theatres came much later to naval hospitals than to their civilian counterparts; operations were usually carried out

in wards and it was only c1780 that Haslar could boast of the first operating theatre in the Navy.[29]

The 252-bed Royal Naval Hospital at Chatham, soon renamed the Melville Hospital, was erected in 1827–8 to replace the *Argonaut* hospital ship and the sick bay at Chatham Marine Barracks. Designed by Edward Holl's successor at the Navy Board, George Ledwell Taylor, it bore a closer resemblance to the north and south ranges of the naval hospital at Plymouth than the more recent hospitals at Deal and Great Yarmouth.[30] A broad colonnade linked three, three-storey ward blocks with single-storey kitchen blocks between them (Fig 82). On each floor of the ward blocks were two 14-bed wards (measuring 50 ft by 24 ft and placed back to back), two nurses' cabins with adjoining sculleries, and a sanitary tower projecting from the end wall. In the 1840s this hospital was highly praised by the Principal Medical Officer of the notoriously insanitary Army hospital at nearby Fort Pitt.[31]

The Melville Hospital was the last to be erected by the Navy for thirty years. As the 19th century progressed, the Royal Navy engaged in fewer conflicts off the English coast, and required less hospital accommodation on home ground. Much of the Haslar hospital was given over to accommodate naval lunatics, and the Great Yarmouth hospital had been handed over

Figure 81
The Royal Naval Hospital (later St Nicholas's Hospital), Great Yarmouth, Norfolk, designed by William Pilkington and built in 1809–11. This aerial photograph gives a clear view of the hospital's courtyard plan with its graceful colonnade. The west range, containing the chapel, is on the bottom right-hand side. The building was converted recently into private residences by Kit Martin. [NMR AP 4864/31]

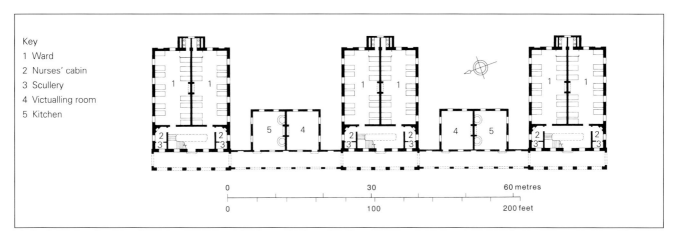

Key
1 Ward
2 Nurses' cabin
3 Scullery
4 Victualling room
5 Kitchen

0   30   60 metres
0   100   200 feet

to the Army for barracks after Waterloo. No new naval hospitals were established until after the Crimean War of 1854–6, when a hospital was erected on the site of the Royal Marine Barracks in Woolwich. Built in 1858–60, this achieved a wider significance as one of the first English experiments in pavilion planning.[32] It was designed by William Scamp, the Chief Assistant to the Admiralty Director of Engineering. By the time that he commenced work on the design, the continental pavilion plan had already been publicised by individuals such as John Roberton, George Godwin and Florence Nightingale (see Chapter 1), and had received official sanction in the report of the Sanitary Commission, published early in 1858 (see pages 94–5). No pavilion-plan hospital, however, had yet been erected in England.

Scamp's plan was novel, but it also represented a compromise (Fig 83). Of its 273 beds, 168 were in four pavilion-plan ward blocks opening off a broad corridor 320 ft in length, but at both ends of the corridor stood old-fashioned symmetrical blocks with rooms opening off internal corridors, including offices, wards for infectious diseases and officers' wards. The pavilion-ward blocks were of three storeys, standing approximately 50 ft high and 45 ft apart, a spacing criticised by some authorities who calculated that the distance between ward pavilions ought to equal twice their height.[33] The three-bay wards (60 ft by 24 ft) contained 14 beds, the usual complement in naval hospitals at that time, and provided each patient with 1,583 cu ft of air space. On either side of the entrance to each ward there was a nurses' room and a sick-room, and at the far end were a bathroom and water closets, separated by a lobby with a window in its end wall. This followed the sanitary arrangements at the much-publicised Lariboisière Hospital in Paris (see page 28, Figure 21), and was advocated in *The Builder* in 1858.[34] Despite its precocious adoption of pavilion wards, the Woolwich hospital had

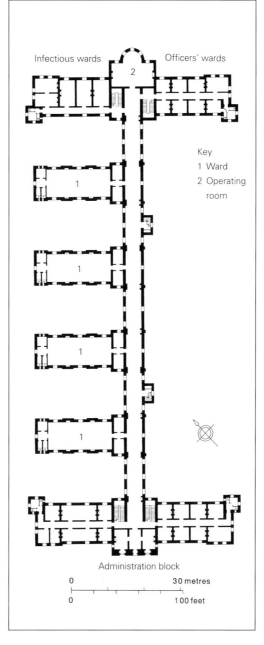

Infectious wards   Officers' wards

Key
1 Ward
2 Operating
  room

Administration block

0   30 metres
0   100 feet

Figure 82 (above)
Ground-floor plan of the Royal Naval Hospital at Chatham, Kent (later called the Melville Hospital), built in 1827–8 to designs by George Ledwell Taylor. The hospital was replaced by new premises in the late 19th century, and the old buildings were demolished.
[Plan (1:750) based on PRO ADM/140/121(1)]

Figure 83 (left)
Ground-floor plan of the hospital built for the Royal Marine Barracks at Woolwich, London, in 1858–60, and designed by William Scamp. It was one of the earliest hospitals built on the pavilion plan in Britain.
[Plan (1:1,000) based on PRO ADM 140/1169]

little direct influence. Its wards were considered too small for efficient nursing and its sanitary facilities insufficiently separated from the wards, faults which were remedied at the Army's Herbert Hospital, begun on a nearby site in 1860 (see page 95).

In the late 19th and early 20th centuries Haslar and Plymouth continued to be the most important naval hospitals in the country. They both maintained similar establishments, and carried out many additions at this time. Although Haslar had long provided the main lunatic asylum for the Navy, special accommodation for lunatics was also erected at Plymouth in 1905, and new buildings added at Haslar in 1908–10. Pavilion-plan hospitals for infectious diseases were added to the Haslar site in 1898–1902, and to Plymouth in 1900, and at about the same time buildings were added for the medical staff. In 1917 a large, almost colonial-style 'sick-berth' (nursing) staff mess was erected at Haslar with money donated by the women of Canada; equivalent accommodation at Plymouth was completed in 1926.

The naval hospital built at Chatham to replace the Melville was the last to be built on a large scale. It was erected on the pavilion plan between 1899 and 1905 to the designs of John C T Murray, who became chief architect to the Admiralty in 1905 (Fig 84).[35] Its banded stone and brick facings, copper cupola, stone domes and tall campanile have more than a hint of J F Bentley's Westminster Cathedral, but also recall the contemporary Royal Naval College at Dartmouth by Aston Webb. The main hospital

provided 468 beds, with a further 102 in the infectious division. As well as 28-bed pavilion wards, it included a wing subdivided into officers' rooms, a 16-bed ophthalmic ward and a lunatics' ward with barred windows and stoves protected by iron screens.

The Royal Naval Hospital at Portland, erected in 1901, also adopted the pavilion plan but was much smaller, providing approximately 80 beds. The training ship HMS *Ganges* at Shotley Point in Suffolk, and the Britannia Royal Naval College at Dartmouth, also had substantial sick quarters. At Dartmouth, the hospital, designed like the College by Aston Webb, was erected in 1901. The hospital at Shotley was erected in 1900–2, and enlarged in 1907 with the addition of a general ward block which had a sanitary tower to the side rather than the usual pair at one end. This reflected developments in civilian hospitals.

The Navy did not erect any new permanent hospitals to deal with casualties of the First and Second World Wars. In preparation for the Second World War, auxiliary hospitals were established at a safe distance from the south coast, where naval hospitals had traditionally been located. The majority of these establishments occupied requisitioned civilian hospital sites, especially mental hospitals, and included only one large hutted hospital, the Royal Naval Auxiliary Hospital at Sherborne, which was erected between July 1941 and February 1942.[36] After 1948, several naval hospitals passed into the hands of the National Health Service.

Figure 84
The new Royal Naval Hospital at Chatham, Kent, designed by John C T Murray, and built in 1899–1905 to replace the Melville Hospital. This contemporary view shows two of the general ward blocks with the clock tower in the background. The hospital (now known as Medway Hospital) has been absorbed by the National Health Service and the buildings considerably altered. [Rochester upon Medway Studies Centre]

Military Hospitals

BEFORE THE CRIMEAN WAR

The British Army did not erect large hospitals on home soil before the end of the 18th century. In war as in peace, regiments were served by their own small hospital establishments. Usually accommodating about forty patients, these were staffed by poorly paid surgeons and their mates, with additional nursing provided by untrained soldiers and their wives.[37] Until permanent Army barracks were erected, sick and healthy troops alike occupied hired accommodation. In 1764, an Army physician, Dr Brocklesby, noted that:

> Most commonly, the habitation hired for an infir-
> mary has for some time been altogether unoccupied,
> with the walls all damp, the boarded floors half
> rotten, and the roof, in several parts, open above. ...
> I have indeed seen such a cottage stuffed with forty,
> fifty, sixty, nay, seventy or eighty poor sick soldiers,
> all lying heel to head, so closely confined together
> within their own stinking cloaths, foul linen, etc,
> that it was enough to suffocate the patients, as well
> as others, who were obliged to approach them.[38]

One of the first purpose-built regimental hospitals was a stone building designed for the barracks in Berwick-upon-Tweed in 1745 (Fig 85). The architect was Dugal Campbell, Engineer in Ordinary to the Board of Ordnance. The new building replaced a house which had served as the hospital for the barracks since 1730, and had a similarly domestic plan incorporating one or two rooms to either side of a central hallway on all three floors. In 1863 it provided 40 beds and was described as 'a miserable place'.[39]

From the late 17th century onwards, large temporary military hospitals were commonly set up during wartime under the control of the Physician General, Surgeon General and Apothecary General of the Army Headquarters Staff. These hospitals were situated close to the front line and relieved regimental hospitals of their wounded. They were of two distinct types: transportable 'marching' or 'flying' hospitals with tents capable of accommodating several hundred sick and wounded men, and 'fixed' or 'general' hospitals, which occupied buildings at a convenient distance.[40]

During the War of the Austrian Succession (1742–8) the Physician General to His Majesty's Forces Overseas, Dr John Pringle, was responsible for improving the standard of general hospitals, which were frequently overcrowded and insanitary and consequently prone to outbreaks of fever. His ideas were to influence the Army's approach to hospital provision for the next century. Observing that the sick recovered more

quickly in small regimental hospitals than in large general hospitals, Pringle advised against concentrating large numbers of patients in restricted spaces.[41] He stressed the importance of cleanliness, and recommended that windows be kept open to improve the ventilation of wards, having noticed the beneficial effects of broken window-panes in makeshift hospitals.

In the absence of a permanent military hospital in England, sick and maimed soldiers returning from overseas suffered great hardship, although the Royal Hospital at Chelsea provided a home for many old and disabled soldiers. The first general military hospitals in England were established *c*1781, to cater for soldiers returning from the American War of Independence. They were located at Portsmouth, Chatham and at Carisbrooke on the Isle of Wight, but nothing is known about the buildings which housed them.[42] The first purpose-built general military hospitals seem to have been those erected during the French Revolutionary War at Gosport (1796), Plymouth (1797) and Walmer, near Deal (1797).[43]

The Military Hospital at Plymouth was erected on the opposite side of Stonehouse Creek to the much-admired Royal Naval

Figure 85
This solid and utilitarian building was erected in 1745 as a hospital serving the Berwick-upon-Tweed Barracks, Northumberland, and was designed by Dugal Campbell.
[NMR BB93/34488]

Hospital of 1758–62. It is an arresting stone building, set on raised ground, which emphasises its formal composition. Above a long arcade, surmounted by a balustraded terrace, rise four three-storeyed ward pavilions, between which, unseen behind the arcade, are three single-storeyed kitchen blocks (Fig 86). The ward blocks provided some 362 beds. Neither they nor the kitchen blocks were given any ornamentation, but they achieve a dignified solidity, their shallow pitched roofs hidden behind a simple parapet.[44] The composition echoed the north and south sides of the neighbouring naval hospital, which may have exerted a direct influence, but the name of the architect of this accomplished building has not come to light. The internal arrangements of the wards were very different from those of the naval hospital (Fig 87). On each floor a wide central corridor was flanked by large wards, the staircase occupied the middle of the corridor, and a rear projection housed nurses' rooms and water closets. The Walmer hospital was smaller but had an identical layout.[45]

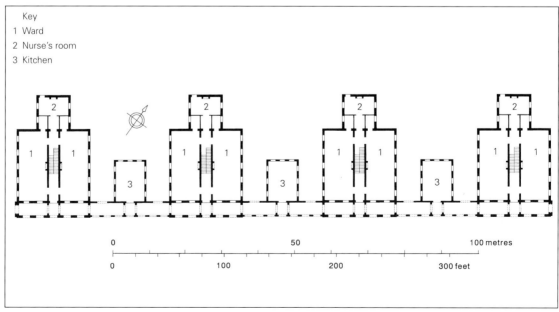

Figures 86 and 87 General view and ground-floor plan of the Military Hospital at Plymouth, Devon, built in 1797. The separate blocks linked by an arcade echo the design of the Royal Naval Hospital at Plymouth, which was situated near by, on the other side of Stonehouse Creek.
[Photograph NMR BB93/15741; plan (1:1,000) based on PP 1861 (2839), XVI. 1, 127]

Key
1 Ward
2 Nurse's room
3 Kitchen

The Army Medical Board, set up to control the medical organisation of the Army in 1793, was split over the need for general hospitals at home. Nevertheless, about a year later the York Hospital at Chelsea was established in the former Star and Garter Inn, and subsequently was extended by hutted accommodation.[46] In addition, the Depot Hospital, originally established at Chatham, moved *c* 1800 into newly erected premises at Newport on the Isle of Wight.[47] (These included a timber-framed building which now serves as the administration block of Parkhurst Prison.)[48] Further hospital accommodation was provided by a large Ophthalmic Depot which had been established at Selsey following the high incidence of 'Egyptian ophthalmia' or trachoma, encountered during the Egyptian campaign of 1801 (see page 120).[49] For economic reasons, the Inspector of Army Hospitals, Francis Knight, closed the general hospitals at Gosport, Plymouth and Walmer after 1802. They reopened in 1809 to receive the sick and wounded from the Peninsular and Walcheren campaigns, but Walmer was closed again in 1812 due to poor landing facilities.

In the mean time a new general hospital was established at Fort Pitt, Chatham, constructed between 1805 and 1819, which received wounded soldiers from 1814 onwards. At first casemates served as wards, but in 1823–4 a purpose-built hospital was provided, designed on an H-plan containing eight large wards lit by opposing windows (Fig 88).[50] The building was vehemently criticised by Dr Andrew Smith, the Principal Medical Officer at Fort Pitt, in 1843: 'There is nothing in its appearance to attract attention, and were it elsewhere, without its wooden colonnade, it would, probably, be surmised to be a merchant's warehouse'.[51] Smith contrasted Fort Pitt with the most up-to-date general hospital of the Navy – the nearby Melville Hospital (see pages 84–5) – which was of a similar size and date. He commented upon the 'magnificent appearance' of the naval hospital, and praised its 14-bed wards, all of which were served by water closets and afforded 1,340 cu ft of air to each patient. He found the 27-bed wards of Fort Pitt too large to heat effectively; their occupants had only between 640 and 690 cu ft of air each, and had to suffer defective sanitary arrangements.[52] The cubic-air space allowed to patients in Fort Pitt was actually above the minimum of 600 cu ft laid down by the Army at that time.

In 1857 Dr Sutherland of the Sanitary Commission made an adverse comparison between the military hospital on Lion Terrace in Portsmouth, erected *c* 1853, and the much older Royal Naval Hospital at Haslar.[53] Although the Portsmouth hospital provided accommodation for some 279 patients, it was, in fact, an aggregation of regimental hospitals, which maintained their separate establishments under one roof. Similar congeries of regimental hospitals existed in other towns with a large military presence, for

Figure 88
The Military Hospital at Fort Pitt, near Chatham in Kent, built in 1823–4. Traces of the former wooden colonnade can still be detected.
[NMR BB74/3487]

example at Plymouth, where the military hospital of 1797 was probably used in this manner.

Regimental hospitals formed the core of the Army medical service between the Napoleonic and Crimean Wars. Many, like the Berwick-upon-Tweed hospital of 1745, had a straightforward domestic plan. They were roundly criticised after the Crimean War, and were condemned *en masse* by *The Builder* in 1858:

> They generally resemble a small ill-planned village residence, belonging, perhaps, to the attorney or the doctor. There are usually a narrow passage, a narrow staircase, and small rooms, in which the sick are stewed up: these rooms have a window or two here and there, as if each building had been an especial victim of the window tax. Buildings of this class have not such a thing as a proper ward. They have merely little bed-rooms, and everything else upon a little scale.[54]

Few of these regimental hospitals have survived, as most were replaced in the wake of such condemnation. Not all of them, however, were 'house-hospitals' of the type described in *The Builder*. The 130-bed hospital of Winchester Barracks, built in 1855–6, is a late representative of a popular design. It had a symmetrical plan, with a central entrance and staircase and three wards on either side. Meagre sanitary facilities opened off the half-landings. Windows inserted in the corridor walls provided additional lighting and, potentially, ventilation. This was a popular feature of Army hospitals at this date, recurring, for example, at Sheffield and Ashton.[55] Hospitals with a similar corridor plan, but without internal corridor windows, included the Royal Ordnance Hospital at Woolwich,[56] the Regent's Park Barracks Hospital,[57] and the large Chatham Garrison Hospital at Brompton, which was identified in 1861 as the original model for 'recent defective hospitals'.[58]

THE CRIMEAN WAR AND ITS AFTERMATH

During the Crimean War the main Army hospitals were located at Scutari and Kuleli, occupying respectively a converted Turkish barracks and a Turkish military hospital. The mortality rate at Scutari rose to 42.7 per cent at the beginning of 1855, on account of disease rather than wounds, but dropped significantly following sanitary improvements instituted later that year.[59] In contrast to Scutari, the prefabricated hospital designed by Isambard Kingdom Brunel, shipped out to Turkey and erected near the village of Renkioi from May 1855, had a mortality rate of only 3 per cent (Fig 89).[60]

The basic unit for fifty patients at Renkioi was a wood and tin hut of the lightest, cheapest construction possible. The wood was covered by extremely thin and highly polished tin to provide insulation from heat, and every bit of woodwork not covered by tin was whitewashed inside and out. In the inner end of each hut was the orderly's bedroom, a bathroom, and a surgery. Beyond that were two wards, separated by a spine wall and heated by means of a small boiler over candles, and at the end of the wards were water closets and lavatories. For ventilation and lighting, there were apertures under the eaves along the full length of each unit and in the gable ends. Artificial ventilation was installed but never used. The ward blocks were connected by a covered way, 22 ft wide, which was boarded up in winter. At the time peace was declared, plans were being made to build a railway line along the covered way, to deposit incoming patients at the doors of their wards. Additional buildings on the site included segmentally roofed corrugated-iron kitchen huts.[61] The Renkioi wards can be contrasted with the rather basic 24-bed hospital huts employed by the Army elsewhere in the Crimea from the winter of 1855 onwards. These were framed and double-boarded huts, with six small windows in their side walls, a lobby at either end, no sanitary facilities and no orderly's room.[62]

Back in England, Fort Pitt proved inadequate for the numbers of invalid soldiers returning from the Crimea, and in January 1856 the War Department appointed a committee to prepare plans for a huge general military hospital to be built at Netley, on Southampton Water. The committee considered separate buildings which 'afford the most convenient mode of distributing the patients according to the peculiar characteristics of each disease', but opted for a single building, 'being the most convenient for the purposes of administration and attendance'.[63] The plans were drawn up by R O Mennie, Surveyor of Works to the War Department, and the foundation stone of the hospital was laid by Queen Victoria on 19 May 1856.

When *The Builder* published plans of the Netley hospital in August 1856 (Fig 90) it was uncritical, but in September a leading article, probably written by the editor George Godwin, launched a serious attack on the expensive, 1,000-bed hospital.[64] He drew heavily on the authority of the surgeon John Roberton, whose ideas on hospital ventilation and planning had been presented to the Manchester Statistical Society in March of that year.[65] Godwin pointed out that Netley ignored the basic tenets of the pavilion system. The majority of its small wards had external windows on one side only, and opened off a common corridor which was described in the *British Medical Journal* as 'a pipe to conduct the contaminated atmosphere of one ward to the comparatively pure air of its neighbour'.[66] Florence Nightingale, who had returned from the

*Figure 89 (opposite)
Site plan of Brunel's innovative prefabricated hospital erected at Renkioi in Turkey, in 1855–6. This huge hospital complex, with each ward capable of accommodating fifty patients, had a sophisticated design, typical of the renowned engineer.
[Based on plan in Parkes 1857]*

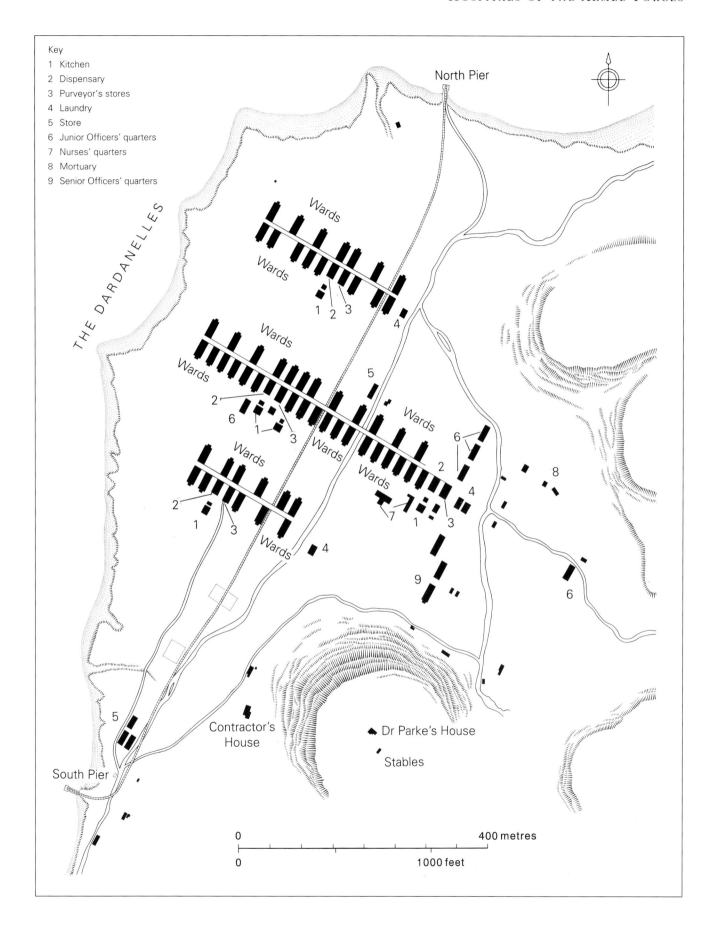

Key
1 Kitchen
2 Dispensary
3 Purveyor's stores
4 Laundry
5 Store
6 Junior Officers' quarters
7 Nurses' quarters
8 Mortuary
9 Senior Officers' quarters

THE DARDANELLES

North Pier

Wards
Wards
1 2 3
4

Wards
Wards
2
6
1
3
5
Wards
6
2
4
Wards
Wards
7 1 3
9

Wards
2
1 3
Wards
4

8

6

5

Contractor's House

Dr Parke's House

Stables

South Pier

0   400 metres
0   1000 feet

Crimea in August 1856, joined the attack on Netley two months later when she met Lord Panmure, Secretary of State for War, the man ultimately responsible for the Netley project.[67] Panmure invited Nightingale's opinion on the Netley plans, and was taken aback by her highly critical response. At Christmas 1856 she enlisted the support of the Prime Minister, Lord Palmerston, who intervened on her side. In January 1857 he wrote to Panmure:

It seems to me that at Netley all consideration of what would best tend to the comfort and recovery of the patients has been sacrificed to the vanity of the architect, whose sole object has been to make a building which should cut a dash when looked at from the Southampton river. ... Pray therefore stop all progress in the work till the matter can be duly considered.[68]

Panmure procrastinated, but a memorial presented to him in February from physicians

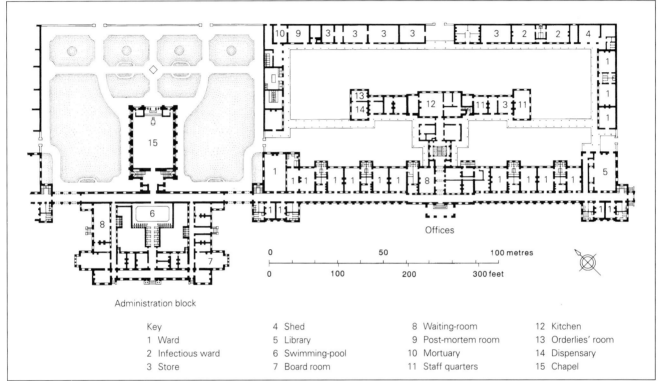

Offices

Administration block

Key			
1 Ward	4 Shed	8 Waiting-room	12 Kitchen
2 Infectious ward	5 Library	9 Post-mortem room	13 Orderlies' room
3 Store	6 Swimming-pool	10 Mortuary	14 Dispensary
	7 Board room	11 Staff quarters	15 Chapel

Figure 90 (above) Ground-floor plan of part of the Royal Victoria Hospital at Netley, Hampshire, showing the central administration block and one of the ward wings, as originally designed by R O Mennie in 1856.
[Plan based on The Builder, 23 Aug 1856, 458]

Figure 91 (right) Detail of the main façade of the Royal Victoria Hospital, Netley, erected in 1856–63.
[NMR BB90/9180]

Body and soul together

SPIKE ISLAND
By Philip Hoare

Fourth Estate, £17.99
ISBN 1 841 15293 5

📞 **£15.99 (free p&p) 0870 160 80 80**

Michael Arditti

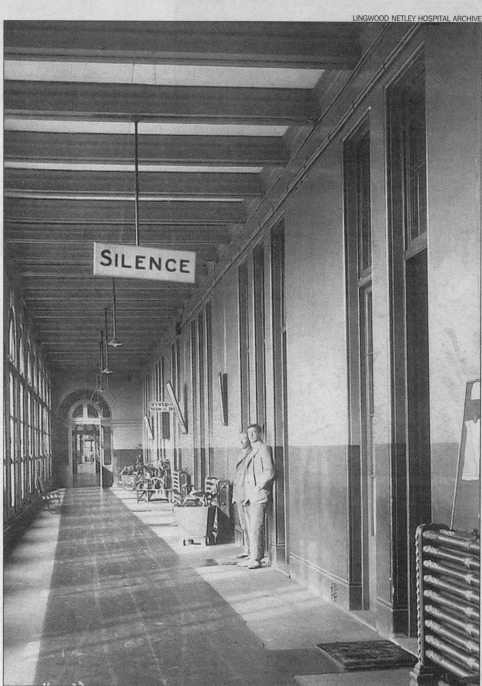

LINGWOOD NETLEY HOSPITAL ARCHIVE

The military hospital at Netley was founded after agitation from — among others — Florence Nightingale

As the biographer of Noël Coward and Stephen Tennant, Philip Hoare may have shrugged off his suburban background, but it continues to exert its hold on his imagination. Hoare was born in Sholing, outside Southampton, a town whose present respectability strives to conceal the raffish past that earned it the sobriquet Spike Island. For the young Hoare, its chief fascination was its proximity to Netley, home first to a Cistercian abbey and later to a Victorian military hospital.

Hoare's ostensible subject here is the military hospital, which was founded in 1863 under the personal patronage of the Queen and finally closed its doors a century later. But his broader aim is to use abbey and hospital as the basis for a meditation on the changing English landscape since the arrival of the Cistercians during the reign of King John. So he depicts the abbey's development from religious foundation through aristocratic residence to inspiration for art as varied as Horace Walpole's house at Strawberry Hill, William Shield's comic opera at Covent Garden and Jane Austen's *Northanger Abbey*.

He describes the hospital's establishment after agitation from, among others, Prince Albert and Florence Nightingale about the horrendous conditions suffered by convalescent soldiers. From the outset, however, its function as an expression of imperial pride took precedence over medical care. With a façade a quarter of a mile long, it was the largest hospital ever built. Its corridors were so vast that, at the end of the century, postmen would cycle along them: when the building was turned over to the US Army during the Second World War, GIs drove down them in jeeps.

Hoare charts expertly the story of the hospital, from its royal origins (Queen Victoria not only paid frequent visits but knitted a pink and white shawl to be worn by the most valiant of her wounded troops), through its social innovations (in spite of Nightingale's misgivings, it was the first military hospital to employ nurses) to its medical discoveries (prime among them being Almroth Wright's development of a typhoid vaccine). He introduces Netley's most celebrated residents — patients such as Wilfred Owen, recovering from shell-shock after the Somme, and doctors such as R. D. Laing, horrified by the inhumane treatment of psychiatric patients in the insulin ward. He charts the hospital's decline and its fitting final incarnation as a film set for the greatest of all Victorian fantasies, *Alice in Wonderland*.

Hoare has a great story to tell and he does so superbly. This is a splendid example of grassroots history. Less successful is the interweaving of his own biography with that of the buildings. While his reminiscences may guarantee authenticity in an age that values personal testimony over objective fact, both abbey and hospital — even in ruins — are strong enough to stand up without the additional support.

CHUCK KIMMERLE

he restless dead were some early explanations of the Northern Lights

Fiction

THE STREAM
By Brian Clarke
Swan Hill Press, £14.95
ISBN 1 84037 186 2

£12.95 (free p&p) 0870 160 80 80

BRIAN CLARKE, a wildlife and travel writer who specialises in fish and fishing, has produced a devastatingly effective novel which ought to be required reading for schoolchildren, government ministers, businessmen, environmentalists and anyone else who has an interest in the environment. Hailed as this generation's answer to Rachel Carson's *Silent Spring*, it spans five years in the lives of the fish, birds and insects in a river which runs past an area earmarked for a new business park. Programmed by instinct to do what they do, the creatures gradually find that life becomes more and more difficult. Clarke is careful not to identify heroes or villains, or rail against the outcome. He just sets out what happens — expertly, lyrically and with a rhythm that mirrors the patterns in the nature he describes. His prose is slightly less elegant when dealing with human dialogue, but otherwise is the perfect vehicle for conveying what occurs when instinct finds itself thwarted.

THE COMEDY MAN
By D.J. Taylor
Duck Editions, £9.99
ISBN 0 7156 3059 8

£8.99 (free p&p) 0870 160 80 80

TED KING, a quiet Norfolk lad, met the rumbustious Arthur Upward on National Service in the late 1950s. A friendship was formed, so that when Upward, an aspiring comedian, was seeking a stooge for his stage show a few years later, it was King he thought of. Thus Upward and King, one of the most famous comedy duos of the 1960s and 1970s, was born. Decades later, the past is coming back to haunt King. The BBC is putting together a documentary using archive footage, and the fraud squad is interested in some of their goings-on.

Taylor paints an evocative picture of postwar Britain: sleepy Yarmouth, where King grew up, and the provincial towns that the pair visited on tour where the "swinging Sixties" seemed a foreign country. With great invention, humour and feeling, he deconstructs what goes into creating a comedy act and the melancholy that has a large part to play.

THE DIARY OF AN AMERICAN AU PAIR
By Marjorie Leet Ford
Chatto & Windus, £10.99
ISBN 0 701 16979 6

£9.99 (free p&p) 0870 160 80 80

SUCH a title ought perhaps to raise the hackles of British readers immediately. Having cancelled her wedding and been fired by her San Francisco ad agency, Melissa decamps to Britain to work for a fading aristocratic family: remote MP husband, mother-from-hell wife, and spoilt but endearing children. In the freezing cold, decaying family pile in Scotland, the American-abroad cliché-meter might start ticking. Melissa notes the lack of hot water, the stinginess, the rigid manners and the nitpicking and bullying from her uptight boss. But although these are all reactions we might expect, Melissa is a character we're prepared to stick with as she gains in confidence and finds some Brits that she likes — although it's a mystery why she ever put up with such a dreadful family in the first place.

OUT OF IRELAND

with one hand in his pocket; that way an electric shock would travel down the body rather than across the heart. When the street lights of Omdurman ruined his observations, he asked the assistant governor of Khartoum to arrange for them to be switched off at 3 o'clock each morning.

Birkeland received only patchy recognition in his lifetime

and surgeons of the Middlesex Hospital finally prompted him to take action and work stopped at last. A committee was appointed to consider the points raised by the memorial, and while it was too late to change the basic design of the building, certain modifications were introduced. In particular, the corridor windows were replaced by large arched openings, the wards were provided with extra windows, and lobbies were introduced between the wards and the water closets. Although a government inquiry chaired by Sidney Herbert suggested that the resulting building might be better suited as a barracks, it opened to patients in 1863.[69]

Despite the controversy, the completed Netley Hospital was undoubtedly imposing (Fig 91). In the fashionable Italianate style, it was built of red brick with stone dressings, and occupied a commanding position on the edge of Southampton Water. Dominating the whole

Figure 92
The chapel is all that now survives of the Royal Victoria Hospital at Netley.
[NMR BB92/30186]

*Figures 93 and 94
A detail and ground-floor plan of the Herbert Hospital, Woolwich. The photograph shows the view through the entrance arch in the administration block looking towards the library and chapel building. It was taken in 1989, some years after the hospital had closed. By then the buildings were in a poor state of repair, but in 1991 work was under way to convert the hospital into private flats.
[Photograph NMR 89/1003; plan based on The Builder, 14 Apr 1866, 268]*

composition was the cupola of the chapel of St Luke. The chapel is all that escaped demolition in 1966, and it now stands in splendid isolation on the cleared site (Fig 92). As it was first built, the four-storeyed central block of the hospital housed officers' rooms and a swimming-pool filled with sea water. Although naval hospitals had included accommodation for sick officers from the mid 18th century, Netley was the first Army hospital to provide officers' wards. Its three-storeyed wings, each 600 ft in length, housed medical cases on one side and surgical cases on the other, and the large yard at the back was enclosed by service buildings. In the century of its existence the site expanded to include the main Army lunatic hospital, and two 20th-century hutted wartime hospitals.

The pavilion principle of planning exemplified by Continental hospitals was officially approved in the report of the Sanitary Commission, appointed 'to inquire into the Regulations affecting the Sanitary Conditions of the Army, the Organisation of Military Hospitals, and the Treatment of the Sick and

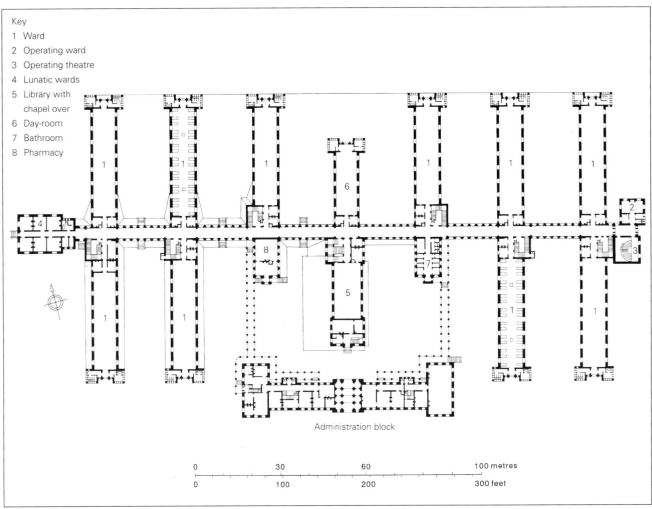

Key
1 Ward
2 Operating ward
3 Operating theatre
4 Lunatic wards
5 Library with chapel over
6 Day-room
7 Bathroom
8 Pharmacy

Administration block

0   30   60   100 metres

0   100   200   300 feet

Wounded', published at the beginning of 1858.[70] While a committee reporting on barrack accommodation in 1854–5 had recommended that 900 cu ft of air space be allocated to patients in regimental hospitals, the Sanitary Commission proposed 1,200 cu ft for all military hospitals.[71] It suggested, moreover, that the Army should maintain general hospitals during peacetime, rather than congeries of regimental hospitals, and that female nurses be introduced into general but not regimental hospital wards. More specific recommendations, affecting the fabric of existing barrack and hospital buildings, were put forward by the subsequent commission appointed 'for Improving the Sanitary Condition of Barracks and Hospitals' (Barracks and Hospitals Commission) which had begun sitting at the end of 1857. Its report was published in 1861, and an appendix appeared in 1863 dealing with specific sites.[72] By that time the Army had already erected general and regimental hospitals on the pavilion plan.

GENERAL MILITARY HOSPITALS, 1860–1914

The Barracks and Hospitals Commission Report of 1861 included designs for a pavilion-plan general military hospital at Woolwich which had begun in that year as a replacement for the late 18th-century Royal Ordnance Hospital.[73] Its architect, Captain (later Sir) Douglas Galton of the Royal Engineers, was a close associate of Florence Nightingale, had sat on the Barracks and Hospitals Commission, and was involved in the modification of Netley.[74] Ironically, he was assisted at Woolwich by R O Mennie, architect of the much-criticised Netley hospital. Upon its completion in 1865, the Woolwich hospital was named the Herbert Hospital in honour of Sidney Herbert, chairman of both the Sanitary Commission and the Barracks and Hospitals Commission, who had died in 1861.

The Herbert Hospital embodied the main principles of pavilion planning more completely than the recently built Woolwich naval hospital (see pages 85–6). It was much publicised and widely influential. Like Netley, the Herbert was an imposing, Italianate building, or rather, complex of buildings, which provided accommodation for 650 patients (Figs 93 and 94). Constructed of Suffolk white bricks, it comprised seven rows of two-storey pavilions with basements. The pavilions were built in ranks on a north–south axis and linked by a single-storey corridor running the length of the site from east to west. An administration block was centrally positioned on the north side, with a block housing the kitchen, library and chapel behind it. The link-corridor had a flat roof on which patients could stroll and take the air, and in its basement was a service passage with lifts

and chutes leading up to the main blocks above. At the western extremity of the corridor were the mortuary, operating theatre and 'offensive' wards, and at the eastern end a block containing six lunatic wards.

The main pavilions were positioned 65 ft apart, and had raised basements which accommodated a boardroom, museum, medical officers' library and an itch ward. At the inner end of every ward was a nurses' duty-room with an inspection window and a scullery. Inside the wards the majority of the beds were in pairs between the windows. Patients were allowed a cubic air space of 1,250 ft each and heating was by means of two central stoves with descending flues. Ventilators were placed high in the walls between the windows for the admission of fresh air, and shafts for the escape of foul air in the corners of the wards terminated above the roofs in louvred outlets. The walls were faced with impervious Parian cement, theoretically to prevent effluvia saturating the building. Projecting from the outer corners of the wards were sanitary towers, separated from the ward itself by L-shaped lobbies. One block contained water closets and a slop sink, the other basins and a portable bath. Between the lobbies was a recess with an arched opening, lit by a round-headed window. No day-rooms or balconies were associated with the main wards.

The Herbert was the model for the Cambridge Military Hospital at Aldershot, which was the next general military hospital to be built. As early as 1856 a pavilion-plan hospital had been designed for this site by F Warburton Stent, Clerk of Works in the Royal Engineers, but little is known about this unexecuted scheme.[75] The new hospital, replacing a collection of temporary huts, was erected in 1875–9 and had a total of 268 beds in six ward pavilions. The buildings were not without architectural embellishment, although the general effect is perhaps eccentric rather than accomplished, with a curiously disproportionate central cupola and a clock tower which would have looked less out of place on a seaside pier, perched on top of the administration block (Fig 95). The stylistic treatment was, for the most part, conservatively Classical, with rusticated window openings distinguishing the *piano nobile*, and pilasters and pediments above.

Behind the administration block were the library and dining-room and to either side were the ward pavilions. The main wards had 24 beds each, but smaller wards were provided for officers, ophthalmic cases, and prisoners. One development from the Herbert was the introduction of cross-ventilated lobbies separating the wards from the sanitary annexes, although these still projected slightly into the ward space.

As at the Herbert, no day-rooms or balconies were associated with the wards.

Extensions to the Cambridge Hospital in 1893 included two new ward pavilions, angled to the south west and the south east. They incorporated a number of innovations in their design. The water closets were on the side of the pavilion, the corner towers, with a balcony between them, containing washing facilities only and lacking the, by then, usual cross-ventilated lobbies separating them from the ward. The same design of ward block appeared at two new general military hospitals, at Colchester, built 1893–8, and the

Connaught at Aldershot of 1895–8. Both had accommodation for over 200 patients and comprised a central administration block behind which the main corridor led to flanking ward pavilions and an operating theatre.[76] These hospitals included a number of smaller special wards – at Colchester for prisoners, detainees, lunatics (with a padded cell) and ophthalmic cases (including a darkroom). The Connaught had a similar range, but had a ward for itch cases instead of for lunatics. As in the corresponding small wards of the Cambridge Military Hospital, heating was by open fires rather than stoves. The prisoners'

Figure 95
General view of the administration block of the Cambridge Military Hospital, Aldershot, Hampshire, erected in 1875–9.
[NMR BB93/21706]

Figure 96
A ward hut at the Princess Louise Hospital, Alton, Hampshire, with its sunroom to the left of the picture. The hospital was erected in 1901–3.
[NMR BB95/12081]

and lunatics' wards were preceded by transverse corridors for additional security, and the lunatics' ward had metal-framed glazing. In addition, there were the usual ancillary buildings and services, and at both sites, the patients' dining-room had an adjoining dayroom with an open balcony.

The Princess Louise Hospital erected near Alton between 1901 and 1903 was a wooden hutted hospital intended for casualties of the Boer War, although never used as such, and was a forerunner of the hutted hospitals erected during the First World War.[77] Little is known about earlier hutted military hospitals on English soil, but their various components seem to have been connected by covered ways in the manner of Renkioi. Towards the end of the 19th century, a cubic space of 600 ft per patient was still laid down for hutted hospitals, half that of permanent buildings but slightly more than the regulation hospital tent, which had 512 cu ft.[78] The wards of the Princess Louise Hospital marked an improvement on that standard, allowing 1,200 cubic feet to each patient (Fig 96). The hospital comprised three semicircular groups of ten ward blocks radiating from a curved veranda, two open to the north and one to the south. Each ward block contained a kitchen, equipment room and night-stool room, a ward with 10 beds, and a sun-room. Three parallel covered ways within each semicircle led to a bathroom, a sanitary block and a third building which served as the recreation room, medical block or administration block.

The Queen Alexandra Military Hospital on Millbank in London was built as a permanent hospital and returned to the basic pavilion-plan format of the Connaught and Colchester. Erected in 1903–5 it provided accommodation for 230 patients. White stone and red brick were used to lavish effect, particularly on the central administration block. Various refinements of detail were introduced in the design. The main wards, for example, had day-rooms rather than open balconies at their south ends, and the beds were arranged singly or in pairs to either side of sash and hopper windows, used for the first time in a general military hospital.

The Millbank hospital and the 201-bed Queen Alexandra Hospital on Portsdown Hill, Portsmouth (1904–7) were the last general military hospitals to be erected on the pavilion system, although the hospital at Fort Pitt received pavilion-plan extensions just before the outbreak of the First World War. Later general military hospitals were either hutted or occupied converted premises.

REGIMENTAL AND BARRACKS HOSPITALS, 1860–1914

Regimental hospitals, like general military hospitals, were profoundly affected by the revolutionary approach to hospital design which followed the Crimean War. A consideration of their design was initiated by the Committee on Barrack Accommodation of 1854–5, and a model plan of a 92-bed hospital was published by Dr Combe, an Army surgeon, in 1860.[79] Combe's hospital comprised three ward wings and a service wing radiating from a central administration block. It was denounced in *The Builder* for failing properly to separate the wards in the fashion of pavilion hospitals, but included one novel feature which was not taken up until some years later: the sanitary facilities occupied towers separated from the ward by cross-ventilated lobbies.[80] The report of the Barracks and Hospitals Commission, published in the following year, included model plans for regimental hospitals with 10 to 20, 60, and 120 beds.[81] According to the report, no more than 120 patients should be housed under one roof, and ward blocks should be no higher than two storeys. The single-storey pavilion hospital for 10 to 20 beds comprised a large and a small ward flanking the administrative offices, with a detached kitchen to the rear.[82] It seems to have inspired the females' hospitals erected at Woolwich and Chatham *c* 1865, in which one ward housed general and the other lying-in cases, both giving 1,350 cu ft of air space to each patient.[83]

The hospitals for 60 and 120 beds were similarly arranged, with 28-bed wards flanking a central administration block and a detached kitchen block to the rear (Fig 97).[84] The wards were almost identical to those of the Herbert Hospital. Their architect, Captain Douglas Galton, circulated a slightly improved version of the model plans through the Royal Engineers in 1862, for use at foreign stations as well as at home.[85] The first hospitals to be erected on these plans were at Hounslow Cavalry Barracks and the York Station.[86] Later examples were built at Hilsea Artillery Barracks, Portsmouth, and Lichfield Barracks.[87] The 60-bed Hounslow hospital, faced in white terracotta blocks with red-brick dressings, is one of the best-preserved examples (Fig 98).

The regimental hospital system was abolished in stages between 1870 and 1873 as part of the general reorganisation of the Army implemented by Edward Cardwell, then Secretary of State for War.[88] In the wake of these reforms numerous small establishments, more sick bays than hospitals, were erected to serve regimental districts throughout the country.[89] The majority of these buildings had an asymmetrical plan comprising an administration block and an attached single ward wing with a sanitary annexe projecting from one corner. They

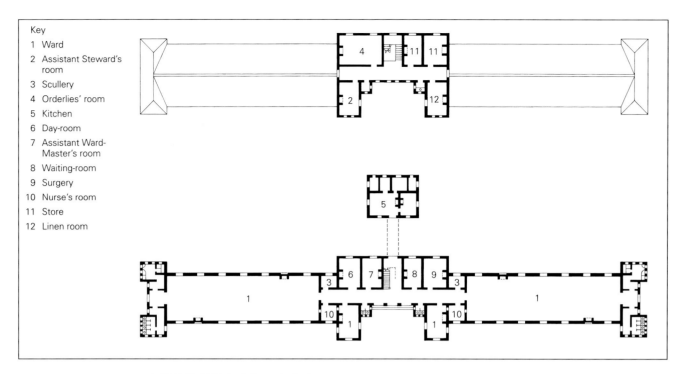

Key
1 Ward
2 Assistant Steward's room
3 Scullery
4 Orderlies' room
5 Kitchen
6 Day-room
7 Assistant Ward-Master's room
8 Waiting-room
9 Surgery
10 Nurse's room
11 Store
12 Linen room

Figures 97 and 98 Ground and first-floor plans of a regimental hospital for 60 beds, designed by Captain Douglas Galton in 1861, and a general view of the hospital at Hounslow Cavalry Barracks built to this design. The Hounslow hospital was one of the first in the country to follow Galton's model plan.
[Plans based on PP, *1861 (2839), XVI.1, 184; photograph NMR BB94/4060]*

included the Caterham Guards Depot Hospital of 1875 and the Norwich Regimental Depot Hospital of 1886.[90] Regent's Park Cavalry Barracks Hospital (1877–9) had a symmetrical plan and continued the practice of housing more than one regimental hospital under a single roof.[91] At the instigation of Major Andrew Clarke of the Royal Engineers, single-storeyed circular ward blocks were adopted by several barracks hospitals in the 1880s, for example at the Seaforth Cavalry Barracks Hospital in Liverpool of 1884.[92]

THE FIRST WORLD WAR

In 1907, in preparation for war, the Royal Army Medical Corps made arrangements to set up twenty-three Territorial hospitals, with a minimum of 500 beds each, in existing public buildings throughout the country.[93] Providing some 12,000 beds, these would augment the existing beds in military (9,000) and voluntary hospitals (10,000) available in wartime. It was recognised that many of the temporary establishments might need to be extended by hutted accommodation, so the War Office drew up

model plans (Fig 99).[94] Each ward block comprised a main ward with 24 beds, and a private or observation ward, duty-room, scullery, and sanitary facilities. The renunciation of the sanitary annexe was paralleled in certain civilian hospitals of the same date, reflecting a new confidence in plumbing (see page 11).

When war broke out in 1914, hutted hospital accommodation was erected with remarkable speed and economy in the grounds of asylums, hospitals, colleges, and also private houses such as Woburn in Bedfordshire and Cliveden in Buckinghamshire. Civilian architects were called upon to assist the War Office, and the model plan was frequently modified or improved. Most hospitals had parallel rows of pavilion wards but some, such as that erected on the outskirts of Windsor Great Park, adopted the semicircular arrangement used at Alton during the Boer War. The majority of buildings had timber frames but a variety of facing materials was used, including corrugated-iron, asbestos sheeting and brick.[95] One of the earliest hospitals to be established was the corrugated-iron Welsh War Hospital assembled at Netley in October 1914, but specially designed so that it could be moved to France or elsewhere. Its architects were E T & E S Hall, and the contractor was Humphreys of Knightsbridge, specialists in iron buildings.[96]

In 1915 several experimental open-air wards were built, with the aim of extending open-air treatment to diseases and injuries other than tuberculosis. The open-air tuberculosis wards of Addenbrookes Hospital in Cambridge, adapted in 1900 from the first-floor loggia, may have provided the ultimate inspiration for the 1,500-bed First Eastern Military Hospital, erected in 1915 on the cricket ground owned by King's and Clare Colleges in Cambridge (Fig 100).[97] This hospital scheme had been thought out years in advance by Dr Joseph Griffith, head of the Red Cross in Cambridge, and his idea was finally realised by the architect Charles Skipper.[98] The unheated 60-bed wards were open to the south, with only canvas sun-blinds suspended from the ceilings which failed to prevent the rain blowing in and flapped noisily. It was reported that the patients 'looked upon the hospital as a paradise after life in the trenches, but the nurses, who slept elsewhere in closed buildings, were adversely affected by the change of temperature'.[99] Despite their drawbacks, the open-air wards of the First Eastern were highly influential, other notable

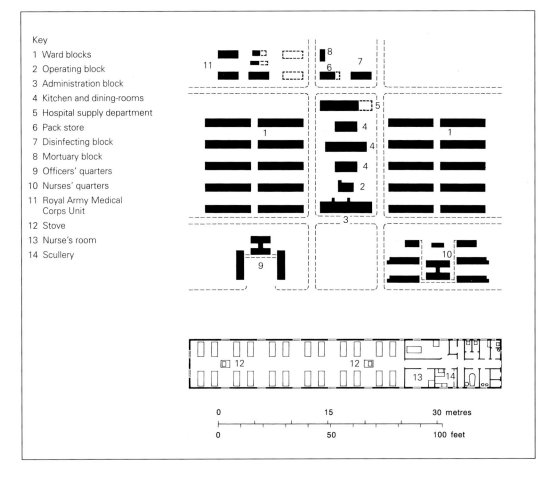

Key
1 Ward blocks
2 Operating block
3 Administration block
4 Kitchen and dining-rooms
5 Hospital supply department
6 Pack store
7 Disinfecting block
8 Mortuary block
9 Officers' quarters
10 Nurses' quarters
11 Royal Army Medical
    Corps Unit
12 Stove
13 Nurse's room
14 Scullery

0   15   30 metres
0   50   100 feet

Figure 99
Model Plan for Military Emergency Hospitals, with general layout and detail of a ward block, drawn up by the War Office in 1907.
[Plans (1:500) based on Building News, *17 Nov 1915, 566–7]*

Figure 100
This contemporary view of the First Eastern Military Hospital, Cambridge, shows the combination of open-sided ward huts and tents that occupied the site. The hospital was erected in 1915, and the ward huts were designed by a local architect, Charles Skipper.
[Wellcome Institute Library, London, L23196]

examples being erected at the Fifth Northern General Hospital (which took over the Leicester and Rutland County Asylum), and at the Third Eastern Hospital in Huddersfield. The open-air wards of the Auxiliary Home Hospital at Alderley Edge, Cheshire, were fitted with:

> *an ingenious arrangement of weather-proof shutters travelling upon and dependent from a runway or overhead monorail, running uninterruptedly around the ward outside it. The shutters are of light construction, consisting of a wooden framework panelled with asbestos sheeting, with a suitable number of windows.*[100]

A modified version of open-air wards was devised by Skipper for the Duchess of Connaught's Canadian Red Cross Hospital at Cliveden (Fig 101) where cost had not been a primary consideration.[101] The window frames were filled with gauze, theoretically to provide abundant air without draughts or dirt, and the wards were heated by radiators which were only operational for a short time while the patients were going to bed. During the summer, some patients slept on the veranda, allowing the hospital to take in more patients.

After the First World War the number of military hospitals in England was reduced, and in some stations the hospital facilities of all three services were concentrated in one establishment. This happened in Plymouth, where the Military Hospital of 1797 was closed and the military admitted to the nearby Royal Naval Hospital. By 1935, when the War Office began to prepare once more for war, there were only 3,000 equipped military hospital beds in the country.[102]

Plans to establish twenty-nine Territorial hospitals were abandoned when it was realised that emergency hospital accommodation would also be needed for air-raid casualties. The Emergency Medical Service (EMS), administered by the Ministry of Health, was set up to provide wartime hospital accommodation for the military and civilians alike (see pages 40–3). For the Army, precluded from acquiring or building new military hospitals, these arrangements were fraught with difficulties. Cases of venereal or infectious diseases and trivial sickness were not admitted to EMS hospitals, and administration and discipline proved problematic.[103] The hutted hospitals erected by the Ministry of Works under the EMS, however, can be seen as direct descendants of those erected by the War Office during the First World War.

Royal Air Force Hospitals

Throughout the First World War, the sick and injured of the Royal Flying Corps were cared for in military hospitals and those of the Royal Naval Air Service in naval hospitals. Soon after the Royal Air Force (RAF) was created on 1 April 1918, by the amalgamation of these bodies, it set up its own separate medical organisation. Initially, the RAF had no general hospitals and serious cases continued to be treated in military hospitals. RAF stations, however, were provided with small sick quarters, usually accommodated in wartime Nissen huts or other structures of a temporary nature.

One of the first purpose-built RAF station hospitals was the Combined Male and Female Hospital erected at Henlow in Bedfordshire in 1918. This small, single-storeyed pavilion-plan hospital had a central administration block and kitchen, and three main wards: a 12-bed ward for women, and 14-bed and 16-bed wards for men. Other accommodation included dining-rooms, a nurses' retiring-room, male and female officers' wings with single rooms, and an operating theatre.

The first RAF general hospital was set up at Halton Camp in Buckinghamshire in January 1919. It consisted of a series of wooden huts joined by covered ways and was augmented in 1920 by a large hospital for infectious diseases, comprising single-storeyed brick ward blocks. The general hospital huts were replaced by permanent brick buildings in 1924–7, at which time the establishment was renamed Princess Mary's RAF Hospital. The new buildings

followed the general principles of pavilion planning but had a rather unusual layout. The central section included the administrative offices, a '48-hours reception pavilion' and 'classified diseases pavilion', this last comprising ophthalmic, mental and detention wards. The hospital also included an out-patients' department, chapel, and maternity and children's wards for the families of service personnel.

The threat posed by Germany in the mid 1930s prompted a huge expansion of the RAF, including its medical services. Various alterations and additions at Halton included a new block for infectious diseases which opened in 1940. In addition new general hospitals were erected at Ely in Cambridgeshire (1939–40) and Wroughton in Wiltshire (1939–42), with identical pavilion plans. They were fine examples of International Modernism, constructed of brick with large areas of glazing – employed to striking effect in their

Figure 101
The interior of one of the wards at the Canadian Red Cross Hospital at Cliveden by Taplow in Buckinghamshire, established in 1915. The Cambridge architect, Charles Skipper, provided the plans. [Imperial War Museum, Q53611]

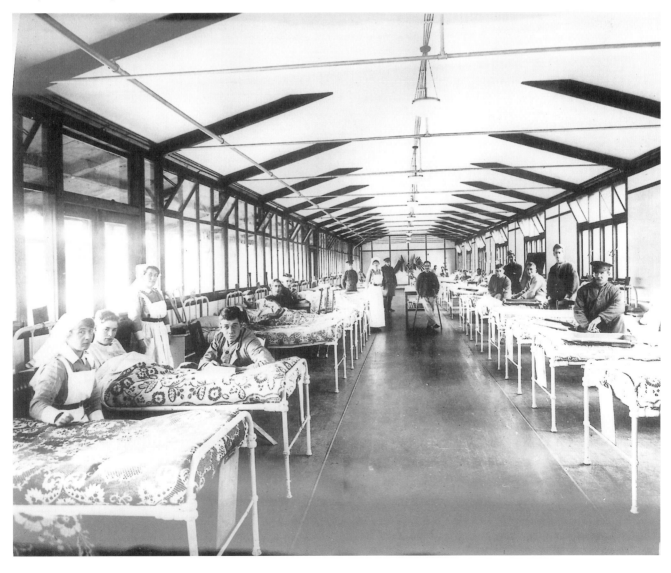

glass-brick stair towers and the curved solaria at the ends of the main wards (Fig 102). The duty-rooms, occupying a full-height bay in the centre of each ward block, separated the wings into two distinct sections. The ward services were on one side, taking up considerably more space than in early pavilion-plan hospitals since they included all sanitary facilities. Beyond the duty-rooms were wards with a balcony along one side. Glass-brick panels in the balcony floors allowed light to filter through to the ground-floor wards. Both hospitals also boasted first-floor, air-conditioned, blast-proof operating theatres.

As well as the erection of new hospitals, the expansion of the RAF led to the upgrading of station sick quarters. Several were enlarged in the 1930s to provide 50 to 100 beds and became known as station hospitals. One of these was built in 1935 at RAF Station, Henlow, to replace the Combined Male and Female Hospital. A two-storeyed brick building, it had a compact T-shaped plan and provided an out-patients' department, offices and treatment rooms on the ground floor, and two large and two small wards on the first floor. The sanitary facilities serving the wards were contained within the body of the building, and the main stair occu-

pied the rear wing. During the war additional beds were provided in adjacent temporary buildings and it was claimed that the facilities at that time 'were typical of those provided by the average cottage hospital'.[104]

Several hutted RAF hospitals were erected during the Second World War. One of the largest was the RAF General Hospital at Cosford, in Shropshire, which developed from an existing hutted station sick quarters and opened in sections from 1940 onwards. It was built to the same plan as RAF General Hospital, St Athan, in South Wales, with a zigzagging main corridor. To increase the capacity of the hospital in the course of the war, plaster patients and offensive-smelling cases were accommodated in large marquees, weather permitting.[105]

The hutted station hospitals erected in 1939–40 included those at Bridgnorth, Innsworth, Kirkham, Locking, Melksham, West Kirby, and Yatesbury. They held 100 to 200 beds, and usually included wards for medical, surgical and infectious cases, an operating theatre, labratory, and X-ray and physiotherapy departments. Ophthalmic and orthopaedic departments were also frequently provided.

Figure 102
A view of two ward wings, with their curved solaria, at the RAF General Hospital at Ely in Cambridgeshire, erected in 1939–40.
[NMR BB92/4765]

Complete Emergency Medical Service (EMS) hospitals transferred to the RAF through the Ministry of Health included those which had been erected in the grounds of Evesham and Northallerton Public Assistance Institutions.[106] Both opened to RAF patients in 1942, following alterations which brought them into line with service standards. In particular, service hospitals required much more staff accommodation than civilian hospitals, even in wartime.

One of the best-preserved Second World War hospitals, now Wymondham College in Norfolk, was handed over by the EMS to the American Air Force upon its completion in 1943. Known as the 77th USA Air Force Hospital, the wards occupied standard corrugated-iron Nissen huts, while the staff accommodation on the periphery of the site was mainly of asbestos and brick (Fig 103).

The RAF erected many different types of hut during the war, depending on the availability of materials. The most common, particularly among those erected in 1942–3, were 'SECO' (Selection Engineering Co Ltd) huts – timber-framed buildings with asbestos facings and metal windows. Twelve of these were put up at RAF General Hospital Wroughton.[107]

In the course of the war, RAF general hospitals were equipped with special departments to treat the types of injury and illness to which air crews were particularly susceptible, such as maxillo-facial and burns injuries and neurological disorders. Usually, existing buildings were adapted for these purposes. RAF hospitals managed to treat 70 per cent of RAF patients during the war, while the remainder were sent to EMS, Army or Navy hospitals.

Figure 103
A row of Nissen huts from the EMS hospital erected at Wymondham, near Norwich, in 1943.
[NMR BB93/9355]

6
Specialist Hospitals

The flourishing of medical specialism and the rise of the specialist hospital was largely a 19th-century phenomenon. Although a handful of specialist hospitals existed in England before 1800, thirty-three were founded between 1800 and 1850, and eighty-three more between 1851 and 1900; of the latter, forty-three were established in the peak period of 1850–69.[1] They were a natural development of the general hospital movement of the 18th century and an attempt to rectify its limitations.

There were three main factors contributing to their evolution. First, a growing awareness of the need to cater for the large numbers of sick, needy and diseased (other than lunatics) who were usually excluded from general hospitals: these included pregnant women, children, people suffering from venereal diseases, and those with complaints which required lengthy treatment, such as gynaecological cases and patients suffering from cancer or incurable disease. A few general hospitals had special wards and treated some cases on restrictive conditions, but most sufferers were left to seek solace at home or, where appropriate, at the workhouse. A second, associated factor was the need to develop special methods of treatment for these types of disease. It was thought that proper clinical instruction and scientific research could be ensured only if large numbers of patients with the same ailment were grouped together for observation and study. Finally, many medical men realised the opportunities for personal advancement offered by specialisation. Some of the founders and staff of specialist hospitals were also on the staff of the general teaching hospitals, and several proceeded to cultivate lucrative private practices in their chosen fields.[2]

In contrast to the general hospital movement of the 18th century, specialist hospitals were usually established not by lay philanthropists but by medical men and women: for example, Dr Charles West who founded the Great Ormond Street Hospital for Sick Children, London, in 1852, and Dr William J Cleaver, founder in 1876 of the Sheffield Children's Hospital. This gave the new institutions a more scientific status than the general hospitals, although they were often seen by the rest of the medical profession as private speculations.[3]

Nevertheless, many specialist hospitals were founded with the help of influential laymen, and the important role of philanthropy and charitable aid should not be underestimated. Both the New General Hospital (later the Mineral Water Hospital), Bath, founded in 1737, and the Sea Bathing Infirmary at Scarborough, of 1812, were set up by local gentry for the use of the poor; and the Fleming Memorial Hospital for Children at Newcastle upon Tyne, founded in 1861, was the gift of John Fleming, a retired local businessman.

Funding was provided by benefactions and subscriptions and, in some cases, appeals and charity events were arranged. Both Handel and David Garrick gave performances in aid of the London Lock Hospital, near Hyde Park Corner,[4] and the Jenny Lind Infirmary for Sick Children, Norwich, was established in 1853–4 with the help of the proceeds from two charity concerts by the famous Swedish diva. Children's hospitals in particular benefited from this kind of assistance. In 1929 Sir James Barrie made a gift of the copyright of Peter Pan to Great Ormond Street Hospital. Covering stage, film, book and (later) television rights, copyright fees contributed to a modernisation and reconstruction scheme in the 1930s.[5]

Patients came from all but the upper classes, although the emphasis was towards the necessitous poor. Many of the early sufferers admitted to the London Lock Hospital were 'naked, penniless, and starving',[6] and some children's hospitals excluded children whose parents could afford to pay for treatment elsewhere. However, 'necessitous poor' often referred to the working classes; at the Royal Sea Bathing Infirmary, Margate, only six of the forty-nine adult male in-patients recorded by the 1841 census were unemployed.[7] Many special hospitals refused entry to paupers, considering them to be less eligible for treatment.

Private wards were not unknown, and provided a valuable extra source of income. In

1869 the Samaritan Free Hospital for Women in London, established in 1847 to provide free care to poor sufferers – 'Poverty and sickness the only passport' [8] – opened a paying block for those of 'limited means'. This catered for the growing demand from a particular class of patients, such as governesses and the widows or daughters of professional men, who were unwilling to enter a public ward but could not afford private treatment at home. Thereafter there were three distinct categories of patients residing at the hospital: full paying, contributing and free.[9]

By their very nature, specialist hospitals were an urban creation, emerging in large towns and cities – London in particular – where the demand for special treatment was more acute and where there was a concentration of medical experts and students. Many began life as dispensaries in converted residential premises, providing in-patient care when demand for treatment and funding allowed. Those which succeeded either expanded haphazardly on their existing sites or commissioned new buildings. By the mid-Victorian era some of the larger specialist institutions rivalled the general hospitals in extent. This typical pattern of development was lampooned in the *British Medical Journal* in 1860:

> An energetic surgeon makes up his mind to step to fame and fortune by means of bricks and mortar. But, first of all, he must hit upon some striking speciality – the 'Dispensary for the Treatment of Inverted Eyelashes', for instance. A quiet house is taken in a side street, patrons and patronesses are canvassed for, and in an incredibly short space of time a goodly sprinkling of the aristocracy have been found to pledge themselves to serve suffering humanity. ... This goes on for a certain number of years, when it is found that eyelashes are becoming inverted in alarming numbers; indeed, there are carefully got up statistics to prove that every tenth person is suffering from this terrible disease ... in short, the dispensary must expand into a hospital. ... Such is the history of half the special hospitals ... existing in the metropolis.[10]

This was part of a concerted campaign against such hospitals waged in the pages of the medical press in the 1850s and 1860s, when specialisation was at its height. Although their pioneering role was acknowledged, increasingly it was felt within the medical profession that specialist hospitals should be superseded by special departments within the large general hospitals, where teaching was acquiring a greater prominence. Thus, one of the arguments used to justify specialist hospitals was turned against them; their existence deprived the larger hospitals of valuable cases for study and instruction, and of much-needed financial support. Their

multiplication and continued diversification was regarded as 'a scandal to the profession'.[11] It was said that many cases, such as stone, bladder and prostate complaints, could easily be treated in general hospitals, and a credulous public was being misled into believing that certain diseases could be treated only in special hospitals.[12] The foundation of a Galvanic Hospital in London in the early 1860s was the final straw for the *Lancet*: 'Next may come a Quinine Hospital, an Hospital for Treatment by Cod-liver Oil ... or by the Excrement of Boa-Constrictors.'[13]

Consequently, the late 19th century witnessed a steady growth of specialist departments and staff within general hospitals.[14] By the mid 20th century, many of the separate institutions that remained had become more closely linked with the large teaching hospitals, and were often subsumed within them. The creation, in 1948, of the National Health Service, centred and organised around a network of district general and general teaching hospitals with their own specialist departments, brought to a close the great age of the specialist hospital.

This chapter does not cover every type of specialist hospital in detail, but concentrates on the major categories. Those excluded are: skin hospitals; hospitals for stone and other genito-urinary complaints; hospitals for fistula, piles and other diseases of the rectum; foot hospitals; dental hospitals; heart hospitals; massage and galvanic hospitals and other hospitals for nervous disorders; infirmaries for diseases of the legs; nature and anti-vivisection hospitals; mesmeric infirmaries; and hospitals for the cure of disease by Swedish Gymnastics. These occur infrequently, and their origins and development are similar to those of the major types.

Maternity Hospitals

The earliest specialist hospitals to appear in England were the maternity or lying-in institutions of the mid 18th century. After the Reformation and the Dissolution of the Monasteries limited hospital accommodation for women in labour was available at St Bartholomew's and St Thomas's in London.[15] Women generally gave birth at home, where there was less risk of infection and death, but there were a great many, in particular the poor, the servant classes, and unmarried or abandoned women, for whom this was difficult, if not impossible. Nevertheless, the main justification for the establishment of separate maternity hospitals was to provide practice for the teaching and advancement of midwifery.[16]

Figure 104
General view of the main front of Robert Mylne's City of London Lying-in Hospital, erected in Old Street, Islington, in 1770–3.[Wellcome Institute Library, London, V12976]

Midwives occupied an unusual position on the fringes of the medical profession; few were properly educated and most of their specialist knowledge was acquired through experience. After the general introduction of forceps in the 1730s, there appeared a new breed of gentlemen 'man-midwives'. These were trained medical men who established schools for midwives and soon demonstrated the need for proper lying-in wards.[17] In 1739 one such 'man-midwife', Sir Richard Manningham, established a small lying-in infirmary in Westminster, which was to evolve into Queen Charlotte's Hospital.[18] By 1767 there were four separate lying-in hospitals in London, all but one in converted houses, and others were established in Newcastle, in 1760, and Manchester, in 1790.

The first purpose-built maternity hospital in the British Isles was The Rotunda, which opened in 1757 in Dublin.[19] In England, the earliest example was the Westminster New Lying-in Hospital, established by Dr John Leake, another man-midwife, and erected in 1765–7 by Richard Dixon, the hospital's surveyor. Little is known of the building, though contemporary illustrations show it to have comprised a central three-storey block connected to flanking two-storey wings, the latter probably housing the wards.[20] Its form seems to have influenced Robert Mylne's new City of London Lying-in Hospital, erected in 1770–3 on the corner of Old Street and City Road (Fig 104). Mylne's first

important commission, this idiosyncratic, yet striking, neo-Classical building was of brick, with wooden floors and inner partitions. Its simple H-plan featured wards in projecting wings either side of a central administrative section. The design was the outcome of close consultation between Mylne and leading gynaecologists,[21] one of whom, Dr Hulme, visited the recently built hospital in Westminster and advised the hospital committee on the form their new building should take. He recommended that 'it should be composed of long spacious rooms with a range of beds on castors on each side, a fire-place directly in the middle, and windows at each end with sashes letting down at the top, and a ventilator fixed in each'.[22]

There was little innovation in maternity hospital design over the next 100 years. New buildings commissioned during this period resembled general hospital or domestic models, and were inadequate in a number of ways. Queen Charlotte's Hospital in London, rebuilt in 1855–7 to designs by Charles Hawkins, had a simple arrangement of small wards and larger convalescent rooms on either side of a central corridor, with each floor connected by a central staircase. The design was criticised severely by Florence Nightingale, who stated that the structural arrangements were objectionable, 'and would be considered so in any good hospital, and nobody now-a-days would venture to include all of them in a

general hospital plan'.[23] She cited the alarmingly high death rates among the patients; 25 deaths per 1,000 deliveries, as opposed to under 10 per 1,000 for the London workhouse infirmaries, which provided maternity facilities for the pauper classes (see Chapter 4), and 5 per 1,000 among women delivered at home.[24] The principal cause of death was puerperal or childbed fever, a highly contagious and usually fatal disease of the uterus, outbreaks of which twice forced the hospital to close temporarily while modifications were made to the ventilation and drainage systems. Indeed, the ignorance and fear surrounding puerperal fever had a profound effect on the maternity hospital movement. No new institutions were founded between 1790 and 1830, and only four appeared between 1830 and 1860.[25] In Birmingham, for example, the Lying-in Hospital, founded in 1842, discontinued inpatient care purely because of the danger of infection.[26]

At some lying-in institutions, women's and children's diseases were also treated, but uniting such services in this way was not always successful. The Liverpool Lying-in Hospital was forced to close in 1881 because of infection, which was thought to be the result of combining obstetric and gynaecological cases in one building. It was superseded by two separate institutions, a Hospital for Women, founded in 1883, and a Lying-in Hospital of 1884 (see below). The major contributory factor to the rise of puerperal fever was the number of poorly designed, overcrowded and insanitary hospitals. Florence Nightingale used the example of military maternity hospitals, which had few deaths, to extol the virtues of detached blocks, a plentiful supply of fresh air, and as few beds as was viable, thereby ensuring plenty of space per patient. She also recommended separate rooms for those in labour, a facility which, at the time, was thought to be unnecessary.[27]

One of the first institutions to show the influence of these ideas was the new Liverpool Lying-in Hospital, erected in 1884 (Fig 105). The architect, E H Banner, was experienced in hospital design and had travelled widely to inspect Continental hospital architecture. His plan was dominated by the principles of separation and isolation. All the wards were for one patient only, and were arranged in two-storey ward blocks, called 'cottages', on either side of a central administrative building, and connected on both floors by covered ways. Each 'cottage' floor also contained a nurse's bedroom 'so placed that by means of inspection windows and glass panels in doors she can

see into each ward without getting out of bed'.[28] This feature, similar to the observation facilities in isolation hospitals, does not seem to have been copied in other lying-in institutions. Other staff rooms, lecture facilities and an outdoor relief station were situated in the administrative building. The cottage ambience was emphasised by the timber framing, oriel windows and clustered chimney-stacks incorporated into the brick and terracotta elevations.

The principles of separation and classification were developed at the Salvation Army Mothers Hospital, London, designed in 1913 by Alex Gordon, with expert advice from Dr Donald Mackintosh of the Western Infirmary in Glasgow. The hospital comprised a series of separate single-storey blocks or bungalows, each for a different class of patient, including those that were married, unmarried, Jewish, or experiencing complications. The bungalows each contained accommodation for twelve patients in three wards, as well as a labour room, baby-washing room and other services. Administrative and staff rooms were provided in converted semi-detached houses facing Clapton Road. Although the external treatment of the buildings was plain and utilitarian, the design was commended in the medical press.[29]

By the early 20th century, improvements in medical science had considerably reduced the number of maternal deaths, and by the 1920s and 1930s maternity wards at general and cottage hospitals were increasingly common. In addition, instead of the 19th-century emphasis on delivery, there was a growing awareness of the importance of pre-natal diagnosis and supervision, and infant care after birth. This was reflected in the rapid growth in the number

Figure 105
Ground-floor plan of the Lying-in Hospital, Brownlow Street, Liverpool, of 1884, designed by E H Banner, showing the single-bedded wards arranged in 'cottages' to either side of a central administrative and service block.
[Plan (1:500) redrawn from Burdett 1893, portfolio of plans, 91]

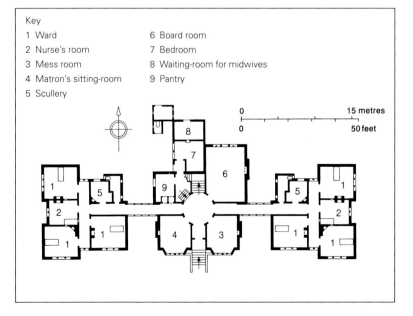

Key
1 Ward
2 Nurse's room
3 Mess room
4 Matron's sitting-room
5 Scullery
6 Board room
7 Bedroom
8 Waiting-room for midwives
9 Pantry

0   15 metres
0   50 feet

of maternity homes (often in converted houses), maternity clinics and welfare centres, and in the emergence of ante-natal clinics, pre-maternity wards and post-natal departments at maternity hospitals.[30]

Both the Liverpool Maternity Hospital, of 1924–6, by Gilbert Fraser, and the Luton Maternity Hospital, of 1936, by J W Tomlinson & K Makepeace-Warne, embodied the requirements demanded by modern maternity work. The various departments – such as administration, wards, out-patients' department and mortuary – were housed in separate blocks, at Liverpool connected by corridors, at Luton fully detached. Externally, the buildings were rather plain. The majority were of one storey and flat-roofed, with simple elevations of brick and minimal stone dressings; only the administration and staff blocks had any architectural pretensions. By 1932 the Liverpool hospital had extended its accommodation from 22 to 85 beds and 70 cots. Elsewhere in the city were an affiliated rest home, six pre-maternity centres for expectant mothers, and four district homes. At Luton, 24 lying-in and 3 isolation cases were accommodated. The main ward block was planned with a central labour unit connected by corridors to two ward wings, each with a variety of 1-, 2- and 4-bed wards, allowing for a greater classification of patients. The wards originally had doors opening on to a paved terrace which bordered the building on the southern side. A nursery was also provided and a separate ante-natal clinic was maintained in the town centre.

Women's Hospitals

Almost as controversial as maternity hospitals were separate hospitals catering for diseases of women. These first appeared in London in the 1840s, as gynaecology emerged as a distinct medical science. Although critics argued that most gynaecological complaints could be treated in existing general or maternity hospitals, few of these offered adequate facilities for scientific research.[31] Furthermore, delicate operations such as the correction of a misplaced uterus required long periods of observation and recovery which were beyond the scope of most general hospitals.[32] By 1871 there were twelve separate institutions in England catering for diseases of women, half of them in London, and all in converted premises. Their example prompted the establishment of gynaecological facilities in general hospitals; by 1873, Guy's, University College, St Bartholomew's, Charing Cross and St George's Hospitals in London all had such wards.[33]

Early women's hospitals struggled to attract funding, particularly as the phrase 'diseases of women' was often regarded as a euphemism for venereal disease.[34] When, towards the end of the century, architects began to design specialist hospitals for women, they made use of the latest trends in general hospital planning. The Elizabeth Garrett Anderson Hospital in London, founded in 1866, was the first to offer treatment to women by members of their own sex. In 1889–90 it removed to a new 42-bed building on Euston Road, designed by John McKean Brydon (Figs 106 and 107). For the somewhat narrow site, Brydon designed one long and irregularly shaped building divided into three linked blocks, a division which was more clearly defined on the first floor. This plan, a variant of the pavilion plan, featured a circular ward tower containing a ground-floor out-patients' department with a semicircular waiting-hall (Fig 108), and was closely based on Young & Hall's East Sussex, Hastings and St Leonard's General Hospital of 1885–7. The hospital committee was advised on 'sanitary and other arrangements' by Florence Nightingale and Sir Douglas Galton;[35] both would have approved of the arrangement of three separate blocks connected by corridors and covered ways, which could be sealed off to secure the isolation of any ward. In appearance, the hospital was an attractive piece of Queen Anne revival architecture, of stock brick with red-brick cornices, quoins and window dressings.

A few women's hospitals also admitted children, such as St Mary's Hospital for Women and Children in Manchester. Erected in 1905–11 to designs by John Ely, it had one wing for children containing large pavilion wards. However, the women's wards in the other two wings were considerably smaller, as this was thought to benefit such patients. Wards for either four or six patients were used in the Chelsea Hospital for Women, London, of 1914–16, designed by Young & Hall. Its form, with a central administrative block connected by corridors to flanking ward wings, was typical of pavilion-plan general hospitals. However, an unusual aspect of the design was the arrangement of the sanitary facilities, which, although separated from the wards by the principal corridor, were incorporated within the main building (see page 11).

The inter-war period saw little change in the design of women's hospitals. Both the Nottingham Hospital for Women, of 1929–30, by Harry Garnham Watkins & Albert Nelson Bromley, and the Samaritan Free Hospital for Women, Liverpool, of 1929–32, by E Kirby & Sons, were designed with pavilion-plan wards in the wings of U-shaped blocks (although at

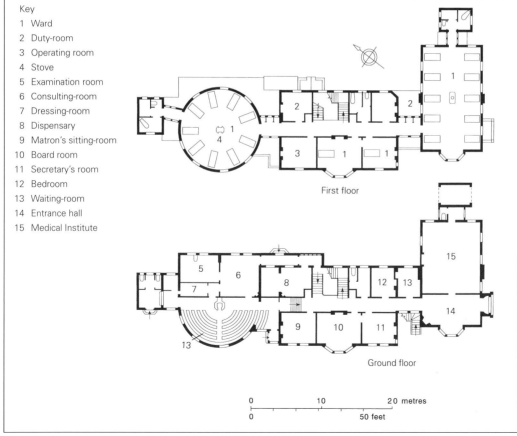

Key
1 Ward
2 Duty-room
3 Operating room
4 Stove
5 Examination room
6 Consulting-room
7 Dressing-room
8 Dispensary
9 Matron's sitting-room
10 Board room
11 Secretary's room
12 Bedroom
13 Waiting-room
14 Entrance hall
15 Medical Institute

First floor

Ground floor

0   10   20 metres
0   50 feet

*Figures 106 and 107
General view and plans
for the ground and first
floors of the Elizabeth
Garrett Anderson
Hospital, London, built
in 1889–90, and
designed by J M Brydon.
Although the hospital
remains today, the
circular ward-tower has
been demolished, as have
much of the roof-line
decorations and chimney
stacks.[Photograph GLRO,
H13/EGA/155/9/1
(Reproduced by courtesy of
Elizabeth Garrett Anderson
Hospital, UCLH NHS
Trust); plans (1:500) based
on* Building News, *10 May
1889, 650]*

109

Figure 108
Photograph of the semi-circular out-patients' waiting-room at the Elizabeth Garrett Anderson Hospital in London. The tower was later demolished to make way for a new wing built in 1929.
[GLRO, H13/EGA/156/19 (Reproduced by courtesy of Elizabeth Garrett Anderson Hospital, UCLH NHS Trust)]

Nottingham only one wing was actually built). Both had centrally placed operating-theatre suites; that at Liverpool was planned on the 'dual system', with two separate theatres, one either side of shared central auxiliary service rooms. Nurses were accommodated at Nottingham in a vacant nursing home in the grounds, and at Liverpool in the upper storeys of the administration block. For the South London Women's Hospital of *c* 1930–5, Sir Edwin Cooper adopted the established neo-Georgian manner typical of the period. He devised a large courtyard plan, incorporating earlier wards of 1916 by Marcus E Collins, but this was never completed. The need for extensive accommodation in women's hospitals was declining, as, by the 1930s, it was becoming increasingly common for women's diseases to be catered for with maternity cases in special departments attached to general hospitals.

Children's Hospitals

Having provided specialised hospital care for women in childbirth as early as the 1730s, English society waited another hundred years before attempting to ensure the survival of their offspring by providing hospitals for children. Childhood death seems to have been regarded as unavoidable. And death rates were appalling:

by 1842, of the 50,000 people who died each year in London, 21,000 were children under 10 years of age. Yet, of the 2,363 persons in London hospitals at the time, only 26 were young children.[36] Similar figures were recorded elsewhere.[37] A number of children's dispensaries had been established in the early 19th century in large cities such as London and Manchester, but these had failed to reduce the problem, which had been exacerbated by the population growth and migration which accompanied the industrial expansion of the 1830s and 1840s. There was also a need for an improved understanding of children's diseases; it was said that, 'with the exception of a ward at Guy's, the medical student may "walk" every hospital in London, and have no opportunity of seeing a single instance of infantile disease'.[38]

The first children's hospital in England was that founded in 1852 by Dr Charles West in a house in Great Ormond Street, London. West had studied children's hospitals on the Continent, where the development from children's dispensaries to hospitals had occurred much earlier. His example was quickly copied, and by 1888 there were thirty-eight children's hospitals in Britain.[39] In 1872–7 a new 120-bed hospital was erected on the Great Ormond Street site to designs by E M Barry (Fig 109). This comprised a square central section, with a chapel and kitchen on the ground floor, flanked

by rectangular ward wings terminating in corner turrets containing the baths and sanitary facilities. Each ward had 16 beds, with a cubic space allowance of 1,000 ft per patient. The principal elevation, with its round-arched windows, octagonal turrets, and steep-pitched roofs, combined elements of Italianate and Northern Renaissance architecture, and featured balconies to the wards on the first and second floors. A large out-patients' department was housed in the basement, and a separate building with isolation wards and a mortuary was planned to the north, to be connected by a short bridge. Staff and administrative accommodation was provided by renting other buildings

in the vicinity. The hospital was enlarged in 1890–3 by the addition of a new Jubilee Wing, designed by Charles Barry (which can be seen in the foreground of Figure 109). This extended the out-patients' department in the basement and provided four new large wards, with increased floor space per patient and larger windows.

Similar children's hospitals appeared throughout the country. One of the largest was the Royal Manchester Children's Hospital of 1872–8, designed by Pennington & Bridgen for 170 patients. It had six single-storey pavilion wards, each with 26 beds, connected by a series of corridors to a central administration and staff block.

Figure 109
This photograph of Great Ormond Street Hospital for Sick Children, London, was taken c 1893, and shows the Jubilee Wing, of 1890–3, by Charles Barry, to the right with E M Barry's original building of 1872–7 (now demolished), behind it to the left. [Bedford-Lemere photo, NMR BL 12041]

*Figures 110 and 111
Photograph and first-
floor plan of the
Belgrave Hospital for
Children, Lambeth, built
in 1899–1926, to
designs by Henry Percy
Adams & Charles
Holden. The hospital
closed in the mid 1980s
and the building has
recently been restored
after some years of
neglect.
[Bedford-Lemere photo,
NMR BL 29494/A; plan
from* The Builder,
*9 May 1903, 488
(NMR BB94/19969)]*

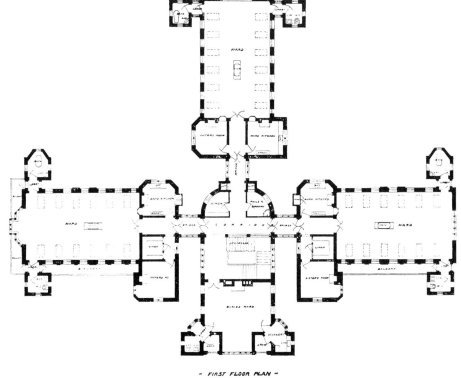

~ FIRST FLOOR PLAN ~

However, the most exciting in terms of architectural *éclat* was the Belgrave Hospital in London of 1899–1926 designed by Henry Percy Adams & Charles Holden (Figs 110 and 111). By adopting a quasi-cruciform plan, with wards radiating out from the centre, Adams & Holden aimed to obtain maximum light and air from a restricted site. One wing contained the administration block, connected by corridors on the ground floor and bridges on the upper floor to the three-ward pavilions; this allowed any ward to be isolated from the rest of the building during an outbreak of infectious disease. An out-patients' department occupied one corner of the site, with its own entrance and emergency rooms for isolation cases. The building introduced Holden as a major new innovative designer. His striking elevations, with their powerful massing of patterns of battlemented turrets, chimneys and buttresses, create a picturesque silhouette and feature many of the motifs which were to characterise his mature style.

The similarity to contemporary general hospital design is predictable, as children's hospitals were basically general hospitals with an age limit. However, some special features were required: it was common to have numerous ward-kitchens to maintain a round-the-clock supply of milk and other foods, and out-patients' departments were usually extensive, with large waiting-rooms to accommodate both patients and adult escorts. At Great Ormond Street two waiting-rooms were provided – one for regular out-patients, the other serving new admissions – in order to minimise the spread of contagious disease, an important facility considering the susceptibility of children to eruptive fevers.

Although Great Ormond Street possessed an ornate Byzantine chapel (a special gift from W H Barry, a relative of the architect, in memory of his wife), for reasons of economy, most children's hospitals were simple brick buildings, with plain interiors. The Fleming Memorial Hospital in Newcastle was a conspicuous exception (Fig 112). Fleming's generosity financed a palatial Jacobean edifice designed by Quilter & Wheelhouse and erected in 1887–8. The richly decorated interior – with panelled rooms, carved wooden chimney-pieces and strapwork iron columns – matched the Baroque exuberance of the exterior.

Figure 112
Detail of the principal elevation of the Fleming Memorial Hospital, Newcastle, built in 1887–8 to designs by Quilter & Wheelhouse.
[NMR BB93/35493]

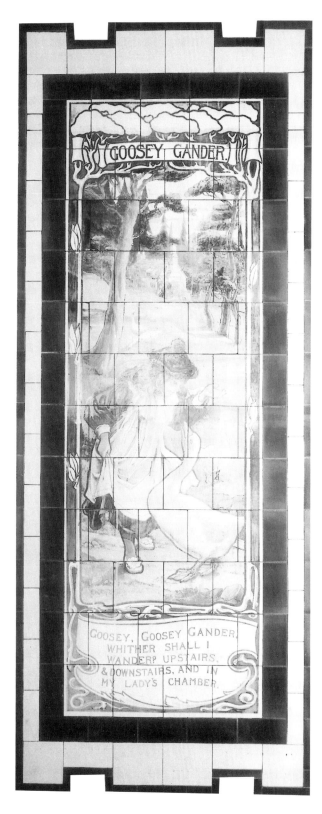

Figure 113
Decorative tile picture, designed by Gertrude Bradley, from the
babies' ward at the Belgrave Hospital for Children, Lambeth.
[NMR BB87/7492]

Despite the general tendency towards thrift, several Victorian children's hospitals decorated their wards with ceramic-tile pictures of nursery rhymes and fairy tales; the babies' ward at the Belgrave Hospital, for instance, had tiles designed by Gertrude Bradley for Simpson & Sons (Fig 113).[40] Such panels were also popular in children's wards in those general hospitals, such as Charing Cross and St Thomas's in London, which had begun to admit children.

The 20th century witnessed a growing awareness of the benefits of fresh air and sunshine, and many elements of the open-air design featured in sanatoria began to be incorporated into children's hospitals. The Children's Hospital, Birmingham, designed by F W Martin, a local architect, and built in 1913–14, featured two large pavilions set at an angle facing south. These contained long general wards, each with only one row of beds arranged along the north side so that the whole south front, which consisted of folding windows, could be thrown open to the sun and air. Some hospitals had verandas added to existing wards, while at Great Ormond Street and the Westminster Children's Hospital, large new ward blocks with open-air balconies were added during the 1930s. Even the youngest and most delicate of children were thrust into the open air. The Duchess of York Hospital for Babies, in Manchester, moved in 1920 to Cringle Hall, Levenshulme. In 1925 a new ward block, designed by Cruikshank & Seward, was erected in the grounds. This single-storey block comprised a series of south-facing wards, each with folding doors, facing on to a raised terrace where cots could be wheeled into the sunshine. The hospital specialised in the treatment of diarrhoea and rickets, and a small laboratory was provided for research into nutritional disorders.

One solution to the problem of obtaining maximum sunlight was the 'terrace' system of construction, popular in Continental sanatorium architecture, where floors were staggered to prevent the balconies of upper wards from overshadowing those below (see page 151). A rare example of this system applied to an English children's hospital was the Queen Elizabeth Hospital for Children, at Banstead Wood in Surrey. This was established in the 1930s as a country hospital for children from the East End of London, in the grounds of a house of 1884–6 by Richard Norman Shaw. New buildings, designed by H S Goodhart-Rendel *c* 1936, included a large 'terrace' ward block, originally intended to provide open-air treatment for acute cases (Figs 114 and 115).

There were to be no doors or windows, with the patients protected from the weather only by roller blinds. The wards were planned with the service rooms grouped behind them; these provided constructional support for the beams carrying the overhanging floors above, thus avoiding expensive cantilevering.

Goodhart-Rendel's buildings, which included a large vernacular-style nurses' home,

were designed to be in harmony with the existing house, partly for aesthetic reasons and partly because it was felt that the 'particular domestic note that Norman Shaw had struck would, if followed in the other buildings, reduce the unduly institutional character that might intensify the alarm that any child must feel on entering a hospital'.[41] The house, rebuilt after a fire in 1938, became the administration block.

Figures 114 and 115 General view, upper-floor plan and section of the Queen Elizabeth Hospital for Children, Banstead Wood, Surrey. The hospital buildings were erected in 1936–48 to designs by H S Goodhart-Rendel. The administration block, seen on the left of the photograph, originally occupied a house by Richard Norman Shaw, but a fire in 1938 resulted in considerable rebuilding. On the right of the photograph is the terraced ward block.
[Photograph NMR BB92/30494; plans and section (1:500) based on The Builder, *26 Mar 1948, 362]*

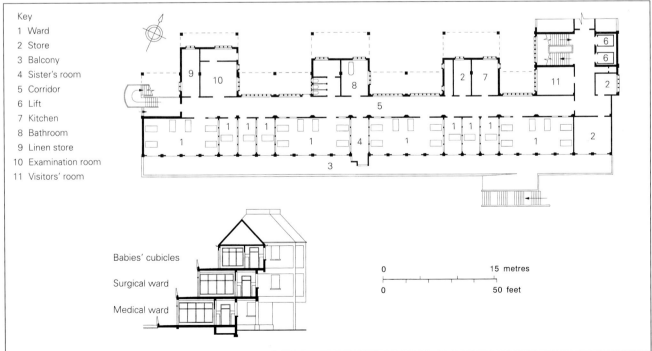

Key
1 Ward
2 Store
3 Balcony
4 Sister's room
5 Corridor
6 Lift
7 Kitchen
8 Bathroom
9 Linen store
10 Examination room
11 Visitors' room

Babies' cubicles
Surgical ward
Medical ward

Orthopaedic Hospitals

Until the 18th century the general attitude towards the welfare of cripples was one of indifference. By then, surgeons had begun to treat chronic bone and joint diseases with a combination of manipulation and corrective appliances, but the process was slow and painful – the famously club-footed Lord Byron regarded his surgeon as his 'tormentor'.[42] Hospitals for the treatment of crippled children emerged on the Continent in the early 19th century, in the wake of improved surgical techniques, but the British medical profession was reluctant to try the new methods.[43]

The first British orthopaedic hospital was an Infirmary for the Cure of Club Feet and other Contractions, which opened in a converted house in London in 1840. It was founded by Dr W J Little, who had studied in Berlin. Three similar institutions appeared during the following thirty years, all in London and all in converted houses. The established children's general hospitals offered little additional aid, as they concentrated on cases of acute disease or those needing urgent treatment. A handful of new institutions was founded during the period 1870–90, but the orthopaedic-hospital movement did not begin to flourish until the turn of the century, by which time the improvement in antiseptic surgery and the discovery of X-rays had allowed new operations for the treatment of bone disorders and paralysis to be developed, and the importance of sunshine and fresh air in the treatment of diseases had been realised.[44]

Highly influential, despite its humble beginnings, was the Home for Cripples in Baschurch, Shropshire, founded in 1900 by Agnes Hunt, who was herself disabled by hip disease. (Hunt became the Florence Nightingale of orthopaedic nursing, known to her patients as 'The Lady of the Limp'.) An empty residence was converted to provide beds for eight children, and an open-air shed was later built in the garden to accommodate those who could not be taken up the stairs of the house. The children thrived in the outdoor conditions and two further sheds were erected. Similar treatment was provided even in central London. In 1907, the Royal National Orthopaedic Hospital, an amalgamation of the three earliest London institutions, opened in a new complex of buildings in Great Portland Street, designed by Rowland Plumbe. The main ward block (Fig 116) comprised offices, staff rooms and shop fronts on the ground floor, with pavilion-type wards for men, women and children, an operating theatre and staff rooms on the floors above. The wards were arranged around a central hall and, despite the confined nature of the site, were provided with balconies and portions of flat roof for open-air treatment. A separate out-patients' department, with a large room for exercise and massage, and a home for nurses were located on the surrounding streets.

As it became clear that deformity and orthopaedic complaints were inextricably linked with poverty, poor diet and overcrowding, so the emphasis on sunshine, good food and fresh air continued to dominate their treatment. Hence the similarity of many orthopaedic hospitals to contemporary sanatoria. The King Edward VII Memorial Hospital, near Sheffield, was built in 1913–16 as an institution for the medical care and education of crippled children, to designs by A W Kenyon, a local architect. It was planned symmetrically, with single-storey wards and open-air classrooms and dining-rooms on either side of a central three-storey administration block and nurses' home. Four of the wards were grouped in V-shaped pairs at each end of the building, and all had verandas on to which the beds could be brought out. All the buildings were faced in local stone with Derbyshire ashlar dressings, in a Lutyensesque Classical style, with the verandas supported on colonnades of paired Doric columns.

The First World War did much to alter the attitude in this country towards orthopaedics. Appalling casualties from battles such as Ypres and the Somme led to the establishment of a Department of Military Orthopaedics in the British Army, with Dr Robert Jones at its head.[45] By the middle of 1917 there were ten military orthopaedic centres in Great Britain, of which four were in England – in London, Liverpool, Leeds and Bristol. Typically, wards were in wooden huts, and each centre provided massage, electrical treatment, hydrotherapy and training workshops for the rehabilitation of disabled servicemen as well as surgical operations.[46] Robert Jones's wartime experiences highlighted the lack of adequate facilities in England, and in 1919 he published proposals for a network of central orthopaedic hospitals served by local after-care clinics.[47] The country was to be divided into districts, each with an orthopaedic hospital, which was to be situated in the country for the sake of fresh air and was to comprise wooden huts, which were both effective and cheap. Each district hospital was to be served by a dozen or so out-patient clinics, which would provide preliminary examinations, minor treatments and periodic supervision. By 1923 there were fifteen such clinics in Shropshire, where the scheme started, ten in Staffordshire, and eight or nine in Oxfordshire.[48]

Figure 116
Principal elevation of the Royal National Orthopaedic Hospital, London, designed by Rowland Plumbe, and erected in 1907.
[NMR BB92/23893]

Many of the hospitals occupied disused military buildings, which were well suited to their new purpose. In 1925 the Crippled Children's Hospital, Kirkbymoorside, opened in buildings erected for servicemen at the end of the First World War in the grounds of Welburn Hall, Yorkshire. Similarly, in 1921 Agnes Hunt's cripples' home moved to a disused military hospital near Oswestry, where it reopened as the open-air Shropshire Orthopaedic Hospital, with 330 beds. The temporary buildings at Oswestry were subsequently replaced in 1931–3 by a new complex, designed by F Charles Saxon, comprising a series of single-storey ward blocks (Fig 117), arranged either side of a spinal corridor. The administration block was placed about half-way along the corridor and the staff accommodation was at one end. The layout was very close to the wartime complex, but the new wards had large, fully opening windows, sunny south-facing day-rooms and verandas. The hospital was later renamed the Robert Jones and Agnes Hunt Orthopaedic Hospital, after its founders, and new theatre, X-ray and out-patient facilities were added in 1935.

This type of arrangement, featuring long rows of low buildings situated on a semi-rural site, characterised orthopaedic hospital design of the inter-war years. Examples include the new buildings of the 1920s and 1930s for the country branch of the Royal National Orthopaedic Hospital, at Stanmore, Middlesex, designed by H F Murrell & R M Pigott, and the rebuilt Wingfield-Morris Orthopaedic Hospital (now the Nuffield Orthopaedic Centre), Oxford, of 1931–9, designed by R Fielding Dodds.

Lock Hospitals

The advent of venereal disease in Britain in the 15th century coincided with the final decline of leprosy, and some of the first unfortunates to contract the new 'French' disease were housed in obsolescent lazar houses. At least two of these properties were known as 'lock hospitals', notably 'the Loke beyonde Saint Georges barre' in Southwark.[49] Although several colourful derivations have been suggested, the word 'lock' or 'loke' appears to have referred simply to an enclosure in which the lepers were kept.[50]

In addition to their premises, the early sufferers from venereal disease inherited much of the stigma associated with lepers. Most hospitals refused to admit such patients, who were regarded as undeserving and unworthy of treatment, as well as being a danger to others. There was also the question of their smell, which was described as 'so offensive that ... where even one ward was appropriated ... it pervaded the whole house'.[51]

The first modern hospital to treat venereal disease was the Lock Hospital in London, opening in January 1747 in a house in Grosvenor Place, near Hyde Park Corner.[52] As a converted residential property, the new hospital offered nothing innovative in terms of planning, but its importance as a place of refuge was verified by its immediate success; of 695 patients received between 1747 and 1749, 646 were discharged cured.[53] To counter any possible charge that the hospital was an encouragement to vice, no patients, once cured or discharged, were allowed readmission. A small chapel was

*Figure 117
Interior of a typical open-air ward block at the Shropshire Orthopaedic Hospital, Oswestry, designed by F Charles Saxon and erected in 1931–3. This photograph, probably taken in the 1930s, clearly shows the wheels on the beds, which made them easily manoeuvrable on to the verandas.
[NMR BB90/9253]*

Figure 118
This watercolour of the
London Lock Hospital
at Paddington,
commenced in 1842,
was painted by the archi-
tect, Lewis Vulliamy.
(Reproduced by courtesy
of James Bettley)

added in 1762 and became an important element in the rehabilitation of patients; those who were physically able were required to attend all religious services. This moral aspect of the treatment was extended in 1787 when an asylum 'for those desirous of giving up their evil life' was established in a second house near by.[54] Similar hospitals appeared in other cities, such as Newcastle (1813), Manchester (1819) and Liverpool (1834).[55]

In 1842 the London Lock Hospital moved to a new building on the Harrow Road in Paddington (Fig 118). This was designed by Lewis Vulliamy as a complex for 100 men and women, with a chapel and an asylum for a further 50 women, but was built in phases as money allowed. In general, the planning was conventional, with most of the patients housed in large, dormitory-type wards. Venereal sufferers were seldom confined to bed and required less ward space than other types of hospital patient. Dominating the group of Jacobean-style buildings was a large Perpendicular chapel, emphasising the institution's proselytising zeal.

It is difficult to assess the incidence of venereal disease in Victorian England. There are no accurate figures, and deaths were not always registered correctly for fear of distressing relatives. Further hospitals opened in Leeds (1842), Bristol (1870) and Brighton (1881), and workhouses commonly included venereal wards (see Chapter 4).[56] Facilities were sometimes provided in seafaring towns and ports, where 'many foreign sailors are always found suffering from

the disease'.[57] The Royal Albert Hospital in Plymouth, of 1862–3, which was designed by Alfred Norman to accommodate general, ophthalmic and accident cases in separate wards, had one wing devoted to venereal patients. However, there seems to have been little effort on the part of the existing medical services to deal in a concerted fashion with the problem, which society was happy to ignore or to regard as a form of divine retribution. One sufferer was told by his doctor: 'You have had the disease one year, and I hope it may plague you many more to punish you for your sins and I would not think of treating you.'[58] The London Lock Hospital was only able to survive with the help of Government subsidies, in return for admitting infected servicemen. Between 1864 and 1867, 36 patients were sent by the Admiralty and 430 by the War Office, the subsidies allowing further buildings to be erected at Paddington, thus realising Vulliamy's original scheme.[59]

In 1862, No. 91 Dean Street, Soho, was acquired by the hospital and converted as a branch for male patients. In 1911–13 this was replaced by a new building, designed by Alfred Saxon Snell. The neo-Georgian main block, of red brick and stone, housed three floors of general wards, with an isolation ward and operating theatre on the fourth floor. Connected to the ward block was an out-patients' department with its own operating theatre and laboratory, reflecting the growing emphasis on out-patient care. Improved methods of treatment continued to reduce the number of complicated cases and hence the need for residential care.

By 1913 venereal disease had been identified as a major factor in the physical deterioration of the British population and a Royal Commission was appointed to investigate the matter. The outbreak of war in 1914 highlighted the problem, which was regarded as a serious threat not just to public health, but ultimately to the war effort. Military lock hospitals were eventually provided, but civilian sufferers were still turned away by many hospitals. Most tragic were the cases of congenital syphilis; in 1915 it was estimated that for every nine soldiers abroad dying every hour for their country, twelve babies died at home in the same time to their country's shame.[60] The Royal Commission's final report of 1916 recommended that clinics be established in each local-authority area, preferably at existing general hospitals, and outlined a public education campaign.[61] Legislation followed quickly, a national network of free clinics eventually was provided, and by 1952 the last of the lock hospitals had closed.

Eye Hospitals, and Ear, Nose and Throat Hospitals

Little attention was paid to the anatomy of the sensory organs in the 17th and early 18th centuries. Even by the early years of the 19th century most eye and ear complaints were treated by 'itinerant quacks', and only occasionally by qualified surgeons as a sideline.[62] However, some eye dispensaries offering out-patient treatment did appear in the later 18th century.[63]

The impetus for the establishment of eye hospitals was the return from Egypt and India of soldiers who had served in the Revolutionary and Napoleonic Wars. A large number had contracted 'Egyptian ophthalmia' (thought to be a mixed infection of prurient ophthalmia and trachoma) and on their return the disease spread throughout the country, causing many people to lose their sight (see also page 89).[64]

Three new London institutions were established specifically to meet this demand: an Infirmary for Curing Diseases of the Eye and Ear (later Moorfields Hospital), founded by Dr John Cunningham Saunders in 1804–5; the Royal Westminster Ophthalmic Hospital, founded in 1816 by Dr Guthrie; and the Ophthalmic Hospital near Regent's Park, erected in 1818 'by order of Government'.[65] Only the last was a purpose-built hospital, designed by John Nash for Sir William Adams, oculist to George IV, to replace inadequate premises at Chelsea. The new two-storey building comprised two long, barrack-like ward wings on either side of a central admin-

istrative section, prefiguring the mid-century pavilion plan. The hospital also featured a very early form of artificial heating and ventilation (see page 10).

The London hospitals, in particular that of Dr Saunders, were an encouragement to others and between 1810 and 1840 a further thirteen eye hospitals were established in England.[66] All occupied converted houses and concentrated on out-patient relief. In-patient surgery, when performed, was often confined to operations such as the removal of cataracts.[67] The Shrewsbury Eye and Ear Infirmary, established in 1818, later also treated throat disorders, and the Liverpool Ophthalmic Infirmary, of 1820, amalgamated in 1841 with a nearby ear institution to become the Liverpool Eye and Ear Hospital. Facilities for ear and throat treatment at eye hospitals became increasingly common,[68] although the interconnection of ear, nose and throat complaints also generated a need for separate ear, nose and throat hospitals (see below).

By the mid-Victorian period, some specific design features had been developed. For eye patients, a proper regulation of sunlight was paramount. Small, dimly lit wards were preferred,[69] or larger wards partitioned into smaller sections, to prevent the patients from looking directly at the glare from rows of opposing windows. Moorfields Hospital, as extended and rearranged between 1860 and 1870 by Lander & Bedells, featured partitions, and both the 88-bed Liverpool Eye and Ear Hospital (Figs 119 and 120), of 1879–81, by Christopher Obee Ellison, and the 100-bed Manchester Royal Eye Hospital, of 1884–6, by Pennington & Bridgen, had partitioned wards. However, this feature was later criticised for impeding cross-ventilation.[70] The Liverpool and Manchester hospitals also used toned or coloured glass in the windows of the patient areas, another common method of softening sunlight; green and blue were the favourite colours. The rather idiosyncratic style of the Liverpool hospital appears to be characteristic of Ellison, who designed the Shropshire Eye, Ear and Throat Hospital, Shrewsbury, of 1879–81, in a similar manner.

Operating facilities were, naturally, specialised. In Bradford, the Eye and Ear Hospital of c 1864 boasted an operating table with Graefe's contrivance for 'fixing the head between two padded boards, by the means of screws, on the principle of a book or card-press'.[71] Out-patients' departments began to grow in size, a direct result of the invention by Helmholtz in 1851 of the ophthalmoscope, an instrument which improved techniques for inspecting the eye.[72] These burgeoning departments required

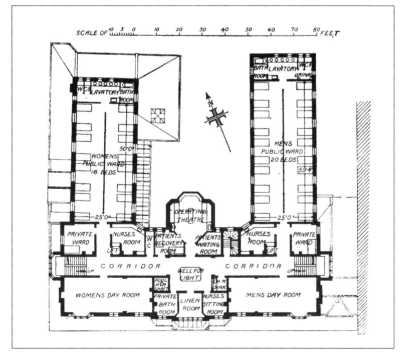

Figures 119 and 120
General view and first-floor plan of the Liverpool Eye and Ear Hospital, designed by C O Ellison and erected in 1879–81. Note the partitions down the centre of the public wards shown on the plan.
[NMR BB93/35370; plan from Burdett 1893, portfolio of plans, 104 (NMR BB94/16115)]

121

careful planning, as the majority of patients attending were blind or partially sighted. Facilities were usually situated on the ground floor, and included a waiting-hall, consulting, ophthalmoscope and minor-operations rooms, and a dispensary. The out-patients' department at Liverpool was arranged to deal with patients in a 'quiet, systematic and expeditious manner',[73] while the Royal Eye Hospital, London, of 1889–92, adopted a one-way system to prevent patients having to cross each other or retrace their steps.

The Royal Eye Hospital was designed by Keith Young, of Young & Hall, under the direction of Professor McHardy, the hospital surgeon. The careful planning of the basement and ground-floor out-patients' department was matched on the upper floors, where the general and private wards were situated. At the rear was a semicircular staircase, rising the full height of the building. This comprised two flights, one for ascent and one for descent, with a central dividing rail and swing-bars at top and bottom, to prevent collisions. The sanitary facilities were kept separate from the wards, and projected from the staircase.

Outside London, new hospital buildings were provided in centres of heavy industry, such as Liverpool (1879–81), Manchester (1884–6), Wolverhampton (1888) and Sunderland (1892–3). At the Sunderland infirmary two of the earliest benefactors were colliery owners,

although the principal subscriptions to the funds came from the workmen of the town.[74] A familiar complaint treated at the infirmary was Miner's Nystagmus, a disease afflicting only coalminers, and almost exclusively the 'hewers', who worked with picks in poor lighting conditions. The hospital also treated men from the local glassworks and shipyards, and in 1905 purchased a Haab's Electric Magnet, used to extract pieces of steel from the eyeball.[75]

As early as the 1860s, many of the London general hospitals had opened ophthalmic departments,[76] and the trend continued towards the end of the century. Few new eye hospitals appear to have been founded in the 20th century, but many existing institutions commissioned new buildings. These differed little from general hospitals in design. The new Royal Westminster Ophthalmic Hospital, London, erected in 1926–36 to designs by Adams, Holden & Pearson, was a compact, six-storey building, reflecting the contemporary interest in vertical planning (see page 37). By contrast, William & Thomas Ridley Milburn's Sir John Priestman Durham County and Sunderland Eye Infirmary of 1938–42 was a large, sprawling building (Fig 121). Milburn employed steel-frame construction, flat roofs, and brick, concrete and stone facings to create a striking Modern design which recalls Burnet, Tait & Lorne's Royal Masonic Hospital, London, of 1933 (see page 38). The infirmary comprised partitioned wards for sixty

Figure 121
General view of the Sir John Priestman Eye Infirmary, Sunderland, erected in 1938–42, to designs by W & T R Milburn.
[NMR BB93/35869]

Figure 122
The north elevation of
the Royal Ear Hospital,
in Huntley Street,
London, photographed
in 1928, the year that
the hospital opened. The
building was designed by
Wimperis, Simpson &
Guthrie, and subse-
quently became part of
University College
Hospital.
[Bedford-Lemere photo,
NMR BL 28893/3]

patients, an out-patients' department, operating-theatre suite, administration block and nurses' home. It claimed to be one of the first all-electric institutions in the country, with its own electricity sub-station, and was specially sited 2 miles from the centre of Sunderland to ensure a clean, smoke-free atmosphere.

Separate ear, nose and throat institutions were less common than their ophthalmic counterparts and tended to be small in size, often established in converted houses, such as that established in 1837 in Bath. A small number of purpose-built hospitals was erected, including a new building for the Royal National Throat, Nose and Ear Hospital, London, which had been founded in 1862 as a dispensary by Morell Mackenzie to enable him to carry out research and treatment made possible by the invention of the laryngoscope eight years earlier.[77] The new premises, built in Golden Square in 1882–3, were designed by Charles L Luck and provided both large general wards and smaller private wards. A new building in Queen-Anne style, designed by Cossins & Peacock, was erected in 1891 for the Birmingham Ear and Throat Hospital, and a large and impressive new building was provided in 1926–8 by Wimperis, Simpson & Guthrie for the Royal Ear Hospital, London (Fig 122). The latter, part of the University College Hospital complex in Bloomsbury, was a dramatic design of

four storeys and basement in red brick and artificial stone, with a bold neo-Tudor entrance front. Despite its name, the hospital also treated nose and throat patients. An out-patients' department was situated on the ground floor, with wards for men, women and children on the three upper floors. A special feature was the silence room in the basement, where extra-thick walls and floor allowed aural experiments and tests to be made in ideal conditions.[78]

Mineral-Water and Sea-Bathing Hospitals

Interest in the health-giving properties of mineral waters, whether used for bathing or drinking, was revived in England in the 16th century and led to the expansion of spa towns such as Cheltenham, Buxton, Tunbridge Wells and – most notably – Bath. By the early 18th century, hundreds of sick people were flocking to Bath every year to immerse themselves in the hot mineral waters, which were renowned for their beneficial effect on rheumatism and arthritis. Several public baths were established and royal visits helped popularise the town as a resort, with the unfortunate result that the streets became littered with cripples and beggars. With the support of Beau Nash, a 'New General Hospital', later known as the Mineral Water Hospital, was founded in an attempt to control the unwelcome annual invasion of those coming to take the waters.[79]

A handsome neo-Classical building, of two storeys over a basement, was designed by John Wood and erected in 1738–42 (Fig 123). It was faced originally with local stone donated by Ralph Allen from his quarries at Coombe Down. (Allen had earlier contracted to supply stone for the rebuilding of St Bartholomew's Hospital in London, see pages 18–20.) The building accommodated up to 150 patients, all to be non-residents of Bath and to be provided by their own parishes with three shillings 'caution money', to cover the cost of their journey home should they recover, or of their burial should they die in hospital.[80] As well as the patients' wards, situated on the ground and upper floors, the hospital contained staff rooms on the ground floor and kitchen, laundry, bakery, brewhouse, wash-room, lavatory and mortuary accommodation in the basement. Although established to give easy access to Bath's natural waters, the hospital did not provide treatment baths on the premises until 1830, when underground pipes were constructed to convey water direct from the nearby King's Bath; prior to this, patients had to walk or be carried to the public baths and pump. The hospital's popularity created problems with overcrowding and an extra storey was added in 1793. Eventually, in 1858, an adjacent site was acquired and a large new block was erected, designed by Manners & Gill, its principal façade echoing that of Wood's building (see Figure 123). The Bath Mineral Water Hospital continued to specialise in the treatment of arthritis, rheumatism, gout, paralysis and skin complaints; patients imbibed regular doses of the waters and bathed in a variety of douches, immersion baths and massage baths.

By the late 16th century, Buxton, too, had acquired a reputation as a centre for healing, prompting the 6th Earl of Shrewsbury to erect

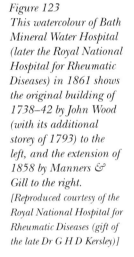

Figure 123
This watercolour of Bath Mineral Water Hospital (later the Royal National Hospital for Rheumatic Diseases) in 1861 shows the original building of 1738–42 by John Wood (with its additional storey of 1793) to the left, and the extension of 1858 by Manners & Gill to the right.
[Reproduced courtesy of the Royal National Hospital for Rheumatic Diseases (gift of the late Dr G H D Kersley)]

Figure 124
This interior view of the
Devonshire Hospital at
Buxton shows part of the
dramatic wrought-iron
dome designed by Robert
Rippon Duke. The dome
was added to the Duke of
Devonshire's former
riding-school in 1879 as
part of its conversion
into a hospital.
[NMR BB93/35369]

a hall to accommodate visitors of rank, in particular Mary Queen of Scots.[81] By the 1820s, various public baths were in existence, but no proper hospital accommodation was provided until 1858, when the Duke of Devonshire gave part of his magnificent stables and riding-school, built in 1785–90 by John Carr, to the Buxton Bath Charity. About two-thirds of the site was given initially, and was converted by Henry Currey, the Duke's architect at Buxton, and opened as the Devonshire Hospital; the remainder of the site followed in 1878. The stables had been dominated by a colonnaded circular exercise yard for the horses, and in 1879 this was roofed by Robert Rippon Duke with a spectacular wrought-iron dome, then the largest known dome in the world (Fig 124). This

central area, comprising almost half an acre, was artificially heated and ventilated and was used all year round by the patients for rest and recreation.

Sea-bathing cures had been promoted as early as 1660 at Scarborough by a Dr Wittie,[82] but it was not until the 18th century that the cult of sea bathing flourished. Dr Richard Russell of Lewes recommended the use of sea water for glandular complaints, and claimed that the sea at the small fishing village of Brighthelmstone was of an unusual saltiness, persuading his patients to bathe in it and swallow pints of it daily.[83] Under the patronage of the Prince of Wales (later George IV) the village was transformed into the fashionable resort of Brighton. Other coastal resorts, such as

Figure 125
Design for the General
Sea Bathing Infirmary
at Margate, Kent, by the
Revd John Pridden. The
infirmary opened in
1796 and pioneered the
treatment of non-
pulmonary tuberculosis
by exposure to the open
air and sea bathing.
[Wellcome Institute Library,
London, V0013929B, from
Lettsom 1801 III, between
pp 234 and 235]

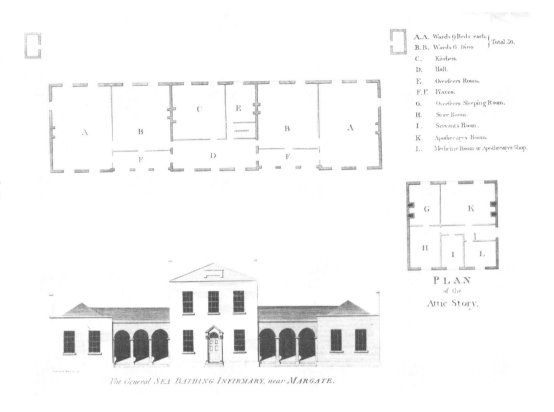

Figure 126
General view of the Royal
Sea Bathing Hospital,
Margate. In the fore-
ground of the photograph
is the south wing of the
hospital, added in the
early 19th century,
behind which the centre
range and north wing
can just be seen. The
portico was moved to this
position from the west
front of the central range
in the 1880s.
[NMR BB91/21378]

Margate, also became popular destinations, but it was usually only the wealthy who profited from the advantages of visiting the seaside. One particularly needy section of society was the large number of the poor of London who suffered from scrofula, a tuberculosis of the glands, joints and bones for which there was no appropriate treatment. John Coakley Lettsom, a prominent Quaker physician, thought that sea air and sea bathing were 'peculiarly requisite' for the treatment of scrofulous disease, and founded a General (later Royal) Sea Bathing Infirmary at Margate for this purpose.[84] Situated on the north-east coast of Kent, Margate offered sheltered conditions and a moderate climate, and was within easy reach of London by boat.

A suitable building was designed by the Reverend John Pridden, an antiquary and amateur architect, associate of Lettsom and co-founder of the hospital, and opened in 1796 (Fig 125). Its radical design embodied Lettsom's emphasis on fresh sea-air and sunshine as part of the treatment. Short open colonnades, called 'piazzas' by Pridden, adjoined 9 and 6-bed wards either side of a two-storey staff and administration block, allowing beds to be placed in the open, thus anticipating by more than a century the open-air treatment of pulmonary tuberculosis (see pages 144 ff).

Treatment at Margate was, at first, rather primitive. Patients, under the supervision of a bath nurse, were taken down to the shore and fully immersed in the water using the hospital's own bathing machine. Not surprisingly, given the nature of the English climate, the hospital opened only in the summer months until indoor salt-water baths were provided in 1858; sea water was then pumped up the 30 ft from the shore by a horse-driven pump.

By the 1850s, the hospital had been extended by the addition of two flanking wings, and transformed into a uniform piece of Greek Revival classicism (Fig 126). A monumental Doric portico, rumoured to have been salvaged from the ruins of Lord Holland's villa at Kingsgate, was attached to the entrance front and was echoed by matching Doric pilasters decorating the wings. A generous donation from Sir Erasmus Wilson, President of the Royal College of Surgeons and a director of the hospital, allowed an extensive new ward wing, with a large sea-water swimming-bath, to be erected in 1883. The architect, James Knowles junior, also designed the adjoining chapel (Fig 127), with seating in one half of the nave only, to allow patients confined to bed to attend services. The new wing had a roof-top promenade and, by enclosing the west front of the original building, created an attractive quad-

rangle; the entrance portico was then moved to its present position on the south front. The new wards, designed by Knowles under Wilson's direction, were used largely for dressing the tubercular joints and glands, and for sleeping accommodation during unusually inclement weather, as, for the most part, the patients remained both by day and night on the veranda surrounding the quadrangle (Fig 128).[85]

A similar facility existed in the north of England at Scarborough, where a sea-bathing infirmary had been set up in 1812 by a number of local gentry to cure 'sick poor who were proper objects for warm sea bathing'.[86] A new building was designed by William Baldwin Stewart in an Italianate villa style, and erected in 1859–60. Sea water was delivered to the infirmary in wooden barrels by horse and cart until 1888, after which it was pumped by gas engine from the adjacent public baths. The hospitals at Margate and Scarborough were established primarily for the treatment of scrofula and other diseases, but in later years both were used increasingly for convalescence. Sea bathing was a popular treatment at a number of convalescent institutions, and the distinction between specialist and convalescent hospitals in this field is often blurred (see also Chapter 9).

Figure 127
Interior view, looking towards the east end, of the chapel erected in 1883 at the Royal Sea Bathing Hospital, Margate, designed by James Knowles junior. [NMR BB91/20107]

Cancer Hospitals and Hospitals for Incurables

Regarded with apprehension as noxious and incurable, cancer was rarely treated in the wards of early 19th-century general hospitals. With the exception of the Middlesex Hospital in London, which opened a cancer ward in 1792, most general hospitals excluded all but the simplest surgical cases. Britain's first cancer hospital opened in 1852 in London, occupying a converted house in Fulham Road, having grown out of an out-patients' dispensary which had been established in Westminster the previous year. Its founder was Dr William Marsden, who was struck by the lack of facilities available for his afflicted wife, who died of cancer of the ovary. The new institution (known since 1954 as the Royal Marsden Hospital) offered treatment to poor sufferers free of charge, a policy declared by its original name of the Free Cancer Hospital, and encouraged study of the disease, but was not without its critics. Queen Victoria refused her patronage, regarding the hospital as superfluous, and only changed her mind when it was proven that most applicants had been turned away by general hospitals.[87]

The hospital eventually moved to a new building, capable of accommodating sixty patients, erected in 1859–60 on the other side of Fulham Road. This was designed by John Young & Son, with the help of David Mocatta. Young & Son's plan, although traditional in its arrangement of central administrative block and ward wings, was unique in that it was not rectangular but trapezoidal, without any right-angled junctions. This was apparently an attempt to make the most of the limited space available by following the existing irregular site boundaries. *The Builder* was not impressed, warning ominously that 'The mistake will be long regretted'.[88] Facilities did not differ significantly from general hospitals, with an out-patients' department in the basement and large wards on the upper floors. Aside from some primitive caustic applications for external growths, early cancer treatment focused on the relief of pain (usually with opium or cocaine) and the care of the dying, hence the lack of special rooms or design features. Externally, the building presented an unusual, polychromatic façade, with a mix of white, yellow, red and black brick, and Portland stone. A 'very favorable [sic] example of design' commented the *Building News*, omitting any mention of the crazy plan.[89]

Despite *The Builder*'s misgivings, parts of this idiosyncratically planned building were retained when the hospital was reconstructed and enlarged in 1885, to designs by Alexander Graham, a friend of Florence Nightingale (Figs 129–31). The earlier building formed the nucleus of the improved hospital, with some of the askew walls preserved behind the new façade. The old ground-floor wards were converted to new uses and two new ward wings were added to the east and west, each incorporating a degree of cross-ventilation. Improved sanitary facilities were provided in two octagonal towers, one at the end of each ward, and a small chapel was added later at the rear of the building. The new hospital, of red brick with dressings of Ancaster stone, exhibited a free mix of Jacobethan and Baroque elements, with a lively silhouette of panelled cupolas, ridge-ventilators and weather-vanes. Unfortunately, a century of alterations and additions has obliterated much of this fine frontage.

As so often happened, the emergence of a new specialist institution in the capital was the stimulus for other large cities to follow suit. Marsden's success and the growing demand for treatment prompted the establishment of cancer hospitals in Leeds (c1858), Liverpool (1862) and Manchester (1871).[90] However, none of these dealt solely with cancer (skin problems, scrofula and other chronic diseases were also treated), and none required new buildings on the scale of those in London.

The discovery at the end of the 19th century of X-rays, radioactivity and radium revolutionised the treatment of cancer. The emphasis moved away from medical care for the dying to the development of radiotherapy and more radical surgery, and a concentration on clinical laboratory research. Many of the new facilities began to be based in separate institutes or at the

Figure 128
This photograph of the children's veranda at the Royal Sea Bathing Hospital, Margate, was taken c 1900. It shows the girls tucked up in their beds in the open air, under the watchful gaze of a nurse.
[NMR BB91/21384]

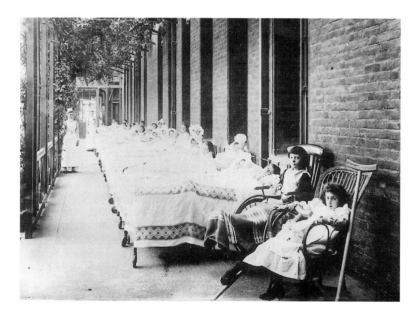

large general teaching hospitals. A new radium wing and radiotherapy institute, designed by Keith Young, was added to the Middlesex Hospital in 1897–9, and was in most respects a self-contained cancer hospital.

Radium institutes, which first appeared on the Continent, were popularised in this country by King Edward VII, who had himself been treated with radium. A handsome Baroque example was that in Riding House Street, London, designed by Thomas P Figgis & Alan Edward Mumby and erected in 1909–11. It contained separate consulting and treatment rooms (and separate entrances) for both the affluent and the needy, and was the gift of Lord Iveagh and Sir Ernest Cassel, the latter a friend of King Edward VII. Similar facilities appeared elsewhere, such as the Radium Clinic, Burnley, of 1929, which occupied a two-storey block, designed by Hitchen & Pickup, attached to the Victoria General Hospital. This was symptomatic of the general move towards concentrating services centrally, and under the National Health Service cancer treatment was gradually integrated into the large general and teaching hospitals.[91]

Figures 129 and 130
A photograph of c 1893 and ground-floor plan of the Free Cancer Hospital (now Royal Marsden), Chelsea, as rebuilt in 1885. The askew walls retained from the earlier hospital on the site of 1859–60 are shown in black on the plan.
[Bedford-Lemere photo, NMR BL 11989/A1; plan (1:500) after The Builder, 28 Apr 1860, 264 and 26 Sep 1885, 441]

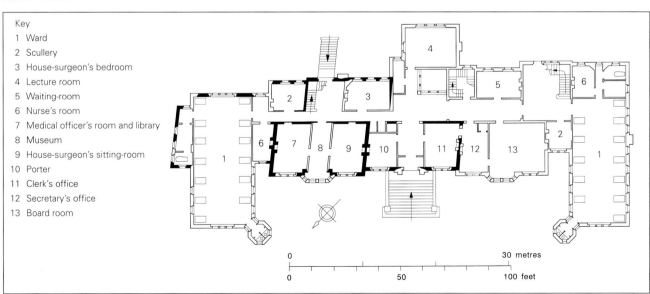

Key
1 Ward
2 Scullery
3 House-surgeon's bedroom
4 Lecture room
5 Waiting-room
6 Nurse's room
7 Medical officer's room and library
8 Museum
9 House-surgeon's sitting-room
10 Porter
11 Clerk's office
12 Secretary's office
13 Board room

Figure 131
The interior of a
women's ward at the
Free Cancer Hospital,
photographed c *1893.*
[Bedford-Lemere photo,
NMR BL 11990/6]

As with cancer patients, those unfortunate enough to suffer from incurable conditions such as rheumatism, paralysis, deformity and spinal disease or injury were unwelcome in general hospitals because of the lengthy period of time for which they required accommodation. Separate institutions for incurables began to appear in the 1850s, and were increasingly common by the 1880s and 1890s. Many were established in large houses, as at the Northern Counties' Hospital and Home for Incurables, which took over Mauldeth Hall, near Manchester, and the Royal Midland Counties' Home for Incurables, which acquired a large property known as the Arboretum, at Leamington Spa. These readily offered a comfortable domestic environment, the creation of which was to be the fundamental principle in the care of incurables. Hence the similarity of many purpose-built incurables' hospitals to domestic architecture. The Home for Incurables for the Border Counties at Carlisle, of 1884–5, was designed by George Dale Oliver in a homely version of English Gothic, while at the new Home for Incurables at Newcastle which opened in 1893, Edward Shrewbrooks opted for a simple Renaissance style. However, the latter building, despite its 'cheerful' south-facing day-rooms, relied heavily on the traditional elements of general hospital design, such as pavilion-plan wards and a wide linking corridor running the entire length of the building, for the easy movement of beds and wheelchairs.

A more successful integration of a domestic ambience with the requirements of a hospital for the care of the incurably ill was provided at the British Home and Hospital for Incurables. Originally established in a house in Clapham Rise, London, this institution moved to a new building erected in 1892–4 on a larger site at Streatham, then a suitably semi-rural district. The architect was Arthur Cawston, who shot himself, apparently accidentally, before the building was completed.[92] He was succeeded as architect to the hospital by Edwin T Hall.

At Streatham, Cawston (and Hall after him) avoided the monotony of a long, institutional corridor by designing a building composed of an asymmetrical arrangement of connected blocks, not unlike a large Victorian country house (Figs 132 and 133). Furthermore, within the ward blocks the inmates were subdivided into separate groups or 'families', each with their own sleeping accommodation, day-rooms and facilities. Equally, the exterior had little of the hospital about it. A handsome and elegant façade, in a neo-Tudor style, it featured numerous gables and dormers, with regular bays of Bath stone to relieve the predominantly red-

*Figures 132 and 133
General view and
ground-floor plan of the
British Home and
Hospital for Incurables
at Streatham, London,
designed by Arthur
Cawston, and built in
1892–4, with later addi-
tions by E T Hall of
1894–1912.*
[Perspective from Academy
Architecture *1912, 42,
118 (NMR BB94/19970);
plan (1:750) based on plan
from Burdett 1893, port-
folio of plans, 85]*

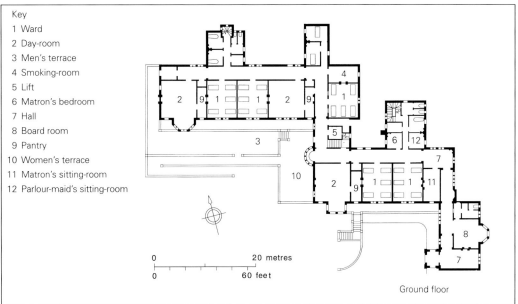

Key
1 Ward
2 Day-room
3 Men's terrace
4 Smoking-room
5 Lift
6 Matron's bedroom
7 Hall
8 Board room
9 Pantry
10 Women's terrace
11 Matron's sitting-room
12 Parlour-maid's sitting-room

0   20 metres
0   60 feet

Ground floor

brick walls. A natural fall to the west was exploited by the architect to provide spacious raised terraces, with balustrades of pink terracotta, where the patients could appreciate the surrounding garden. For those unfortunate enough to be confined to bed, windows were brought to within inches of the floor to ensure an unimpeded view. The garden itself, though attractively laid out, did not need to be extensive, as few of the patients were capable of outdoor exercise.

When officially opened on 3 July 1894 by the Princess of Wales, the hospital comprised two three-storey ward blocks with rooms for fifty patients and resident staff. Hall later added a small private chapel (1894–6) and an entertainment hall (1899), both part of Cawston's original plan but delayed until sufficient funds were available. These featured galleries at first-floor level where patients could be wheeled in directly, and the hall was leased for use by local residents, thus attracting extra revenue.

7
Hospitals for Infectious Diseases

Infectious diseases are spread in a number of ways. Diphtheria, smallpox and tuberculosis are carried on the breath; cholera, dysentery and typhoid (or enteric) fever can be caught through contact with infected faeces; scarlet fever is passed on through contact with infected material; and relapsing fever, scabies and typhus are spread by parasites.[1] Even before these diseases were identified and differentiated from each other and their methods of transmission known, attempts were made to isolate the infected from the healthy in order to give a degree of control over what were often incurable and frequently fatal ailments.

Smallpox, with its distinctive pustules and great virulence, was easily recognised, but diagnosis long remained vague of the numerous other infectious diseases, many of which had a fever as the main symptom. Indeed, until well into the 19th century, 'fever' was seen as a generalised, non-specific form of disease, spontaneously generated in foul air and putrefying matter. Typhus and typhoid fevers were the first to be separately identified in 1837, followed by relapsing fever in 1843.

Hospitals for infectious diseases needed little special planning. Their *raison d'être*, above all, was isolation. Usually some attempt was made to prevent cross-infection, particularly at hospitals where more than one type of disease was admitted. Out-patients' departments were not provided and surgery did not feature in treatment until the early 20th century. In other respects isolation hospitals were closely related to general hospitals, reflecting contemporary developments in design. Unlike general hospitals, however, most were established either by Poor Law guardians as part of the workhouse, or by local authorities. Essentially, the isolation hospital was the poor man's spare bedroom.[2] Those who could practised isolation at home, and hospitals served the working and lower classes. They were invariably erected in response to specific events, such as epidemics, which were also the spur to a growing body of legislation aimed at containing these devastating and repeated outbreaks.

Tuberculosis, which was not identified as an infectious disease until the mid 19th century, produced a quite distinctive response from the medical and architectural professions alike, and is therefore considered separately at the end of this chapter.

Hospitals for Infectious Diseases up to the Mid 19th Century

Once outbreaks of the plague ceased to occur in Britain after the 1660s, smallpox caused the greatest fear and repulsion, not least because the disease was so readily identifiable. Pesthouses provided the earliest resort for those suffering from smallpox or other infectious diseases. These were rented or even built by local communities, usually the parish. Surviving examples in Suffolk and Hampshire suggest that they were ordinary houses, commonly of two-room plan with a central staircase. The pesthouse at Framlingham, Suffolk, functioned on the usual arrangement whereby a nurse occupied the house and cared for patients sent there by the parish. It was not until the mid 18th century that more extensive isolation hospitals were erected, and these were solely for smallpox cases.

Most general hospitals attempted to exclude people with infectious diseases that might spread to and endanger the other patients. Problems inevitably arose because imperfect diagnosis often led to the admission of patients in the early stages of fever, causing infectious disease to develop among existing patients. It was common for any fever cases inadvertently admitted to be dismissed or boarded out when the nature of their illness was discovered.

The first smallpox hospital in the country was founded in 1746 in London. By the 1750s it was split between three sites: one building in Shoreditch admitted patients who had been inoculated (and were therefore suffering from the milder form of the disease), one in Islington was for convalescents, and a third, in Cold Bath Fields, Clerkenwell, was for the severest cases, who had never been inoculated. Only the last of these was a purpose-built hospital, erected *c* 1753

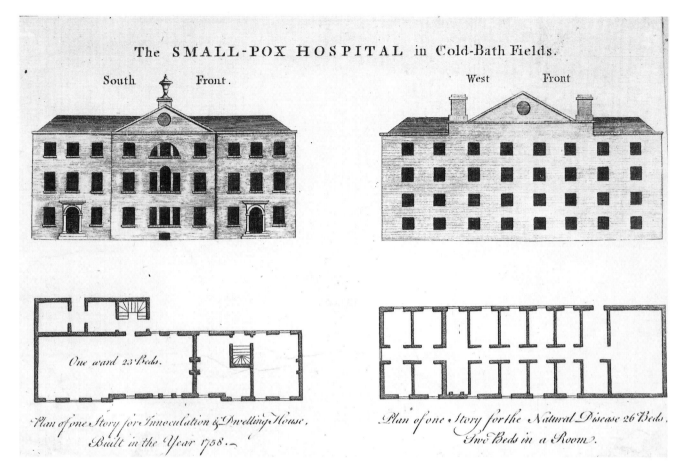

adjoining an obsolescent public house (Fig 134). The main, south elevation was in a restrained, Palladian style and the building housed large 23-bed wards on each floor. A rear wing was added in 1762 which contained a number of smaller wards placed either side of an axial corridor.[3]

The Cold Bath Fields building was eventually superseded by a new smallpox and fever hospital erected in 1793–4, near St Pancras.[4] In plan and appearance the new building resembled contemporary general hospitals, with a central three-storey, five-bay block flanked by two-storey, three-bay wings. The main wards presumably were in the wings, occupying the whole of each floor, tall round-headed windows giving generous ventilation.

Although there was a pressing need for separate hospitals to isolate and treat infectious diseases, progress was desperately slow. Many general hospitals were forced to provide fever wards as patients had nowhere else to go. At the Chester Infirmary in 1783 specific wards were set apart for infectious diseases, mainly typhus. They were situated within the main building but separated from other wards. Liverpool Infirmary followed suit in 1787, when the victims of a typhus outbreak were placed in wards improvised in the basement.

The Liverpool Fever Hospital, built at Brownlow Hill in 1801, was the first to be established for infectious diseases other than smallpox. Its arrangement of small wards on either side of an axial corridor echoed that of the rear wing added to the Clerkenwell smallpox hospital. This reflected the prevailing belief that by splitting the patients up into smaller groups the risk of cross-infection would be diminished. However, experience showed that fevers still spread through the building, and hospitals increasingly refused to admit patients suffering from certain diseases (in particular smallpox). Many of the earliest fever hospitals were known as 'houses of recovery'. Between 1802 and 1804 such hospitals were established in London, Manchester and Newcastle upon Tyne. That erected as the Newcastle House of Recovery survives (Fig 135), an austere stone building of three storeys, built outside the town walls in an 'airy and retired situation'.[5]

The house of recovery in London first occupied a house in Constitution Row, Gray's Inn Lane, 'to the great horror of its neighbours who threatened indictment and prepared for litigation'.[6] Whether or not as a result of this opposition, the fledgling fever hospital moved in 1815 to a building belonging

Figure 134
The Smallpox Hospital at Cold Bath Fields, Clerkenwell, London, now demolished. The elevation labelled 'South Front' is the original building of 1753, while that labelled 'West Front' is the west wing added in 1761. Despite the anomalies in these plans and elevations, they are probably the best surviving illustrations of this building.
[Guildhall Library, Corporation of London PR. F1/COL/FIE]

Figure 135
The Newcastle House of
Recovery, built in 1804
outside the old walls of
Newcastle upon Tyne, is
a rare survival of an
early fever hospital.
[NMR BB93/35217]

to, and on the same site as, the Smallpox Hospital at St Pancras. In the mid 19th century both hospitals were displaced by the development of the new terminus of the Great Northern Railway – now King's Cross Station. The smallpox hospital then moved to a new building in Highgate, and the house of recovery to Islington. For the latter, thenceforth known as the London Fever Hospital, Charles Fowler designed an imposing building, reminiscent of Barry's Italianate club houses (Figs 136 and 137). Whilst Fowler is perhaps best-remembered for his Covent Garden and Exeter markets, this was not his only hospital commission, having designed the Devon County Lunatic Asylum some years earlier (see page 163). The Fever Hospital was erected in 1848–9 in Liverpool Road and comprised a central three-storey administration and staff block flanked by two-storey ward blocks. Partly open single-storey corridors linked the central block to the wings, introducing an element of separation between them. The main fever wards were arranged back-to-back, a common feature of larger general hospitals of the time. To aid ventilation, the central spine-wall had a number of openings, but even this measure was not enough to save the hospital from censure

a decade later when pavilion planning was being enthusiastically welcomed as the remedy for cross-infection. Although careful provision was made for the wide separation of the sexes, different types of fever were not separated until 1862. The staff fared rather better, and cases of fever among those working in the new administration building were rare, whereas in the old building at King's Cross, the officers and servants were frequently infected.[7]

Urban areas, where epidemics were rife, saw the establishment of a number of isolation hospitals in the first half of the 19th century, but rural districts continued to rely on small pesthouses. By the early decades of the 19th century the maintenance of many of these pesthouses was in decline, and this limited local provision was largely superseded by the workhouse system (see Chapter 4). Most workhouses had at least nominal hospital accommodation, and many included separate fever blocks. As early as 1836 there was a small single-storey fever hospital at Stow-on-the-Wold workhouse in Gloucestershire. It was a simple enough building, comprising a central nurse's room with flanking wards. Elsewhere, larger fever blocks came to be built, such as that erected in the 1860s behind the infirmary at Southampton Incorporation Workhouse (see page 62).

Following devastating epidemics of smallpox, typhus and typhoid, came cholera. This was not endemic in Britain. It arrived, perhaps from Asia, in 1831, and, despite the Cholera Prevention Act of 1832,[8] there were repeated epidemics of the disease. The worst occurred in 1848–9, claiming the lives of about 50,000 people in England and Wales.[9] And this was only ten years after a particularly appalling smallpox epidemic which had killed about 42,000.[10] Early legislation tended to be well-intentioned but was often ineffectual while the erection of hospitals depended upon funds first being raised from the rates. In the midst of each succeeding epidemic local authorities throughout the country accepted that available hospital accommodation was disastrously inadequate, but they had seldom gone farther than proposing to take action before the epidemic subsided and the initiative was lost. The cholera epidemic of 1866, for example, prompted the erection of only a few hospitals, although the provisions of the Sanitary Act of 1866[11] gave town councils and local boards of health the power to provide either temporary or permanent hospitals, and justices of the peace the power to remove patients to them. None of the few cholera hospitals built in the 1860s survives. They were all quite small, the largest being the Garrison Hospital at Hull which had just 21 beds.

*Figures 136 and 137
Elevation and ground-
floor plan of the London
Fever Hospital,
Islington, designed by
Charles Fowler and
erected in 1848–9. The
plan is dominated by the
large back-to-back wards
in the two side wings.
The variety of wards
shows great care in clas-
sifying and distributing
the patients in appro-
priate accommodation.
[Elevation NMR
BB96/9814; plan NMR
BB96/9815 from* The
Builder, *12 Aug 1848,
390–1]*

PLAN OF THE NEW LONDON FEVER HOSPITAL.

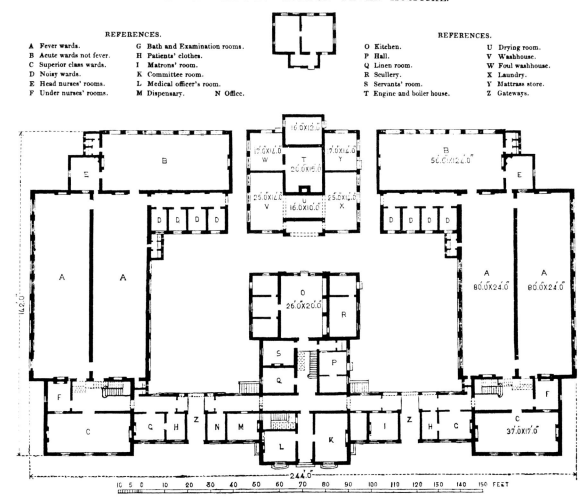

REFERENCES.

A Fever wards.
B Acute wards not fever.
C Superior class wards.
D Noisy wards.
E Head nurses' rooms.
F Under nurses' rooms.

G Bath and Examination rooms.
H Patients' clothes.
I Matrons' room.
K Committee room.
L Medical officer's room.
M Dispensary.   N Office.

REFERENCES.

O Kitchen.
P Hall.
Q Linen room.
R Scullery.
S Servants' room.
T Engine and boiler house.

U Drying room.
V Washhouse.
W Foul washhouse.
X Laundry.
Y Mattrass store.
Z Gateways.

The Metropolitan Asylums Board and Isolation Hospitals in London

London, with its special problems of scale and administrative complexity, was dealt with by separate legislation and organisation.[12] Under the Metropolitan Poor Law Amendment Act of 1867,[13] the Metropolitan Asylums Board (MAB) was set up to provide a central unified body for treating both infectious diseases and insanity within London (see also pages 173–4). During the next twenty-five years a comprehensive network of fever hospitals was created around London, linked by an efficient horse-ambulance service. These hospitals were intended for paupers only. However, the metropolitan local authorities all failed to provide for non-paupers, either under the adoptive 1866 Act, or the 1875 Public Health Act (see page 139). The MAB therefore admitted non-paupers as well, a policy that was only made legal in 1883 by the Diseases Prevention (Metropolis) Act.[14]

The initial aim of the MAB was to build three hospitals at widely separated sites, at Hampstead, Homerton and Stockwell, each with 200 beds for fever and 100 beds for smallpox cases. Considerable delays were caused by strong local opposition, in particular from the influential residents of Hampstead who objected to the close proximity of infectious patients.[15] It was not until the beginning of 1870 that the MAB managed to erect the Hampstead Smallpox Hospital. A competition for the design had been won by Pennington & Bridgen, a Manchester firm with offices in London. The intention was that the hospital should be a temporary construction, and the single-storey ward blocks of timber and iron were erected speedily in just four weeks.[16] The buildings were urgently needed, not for smallpox, but to help cope with an epidemic of relapsing fever.[17]

The hospitals at Homerton and Stockwell, known respectively as the Eastern and South-Western Hospitals, were built on a smaller scale than originally intended and were completed in 1871, by which time the epidemics of smallpox and relapsing fever had subsided. The basic layout of the fever and smallpox sections was similar to the Hampstead hospital, with a single row of parallel ward blocks joined at one end by a covered way. At Homerton the four smallpox wards radiated from a central building. The ward blocks were two storeys high, with one large ward on each floor, and a sanitary annexe part-way along one side, an arrangement found in many later hospitals built by the Board.

The smallpox epidemic of 1870 made it clear that further hospitals would be needed and in 1876–7 two were established: at Fulham (the Western Fever Hospital), and Deptford (the South-Eastern). These were designed by the resident engineers of the MAB asylums at Leavesden and Caterham, respectively J Walker and William Crickmay, and consisted of permanent administration and service buildings, to which temporary ward huts could be added in the event of another epidemic.[18] That of 1877 resulted in corrugated-iron buildings being added almost immediately.

Continuing local opposition aggravated the MAB's attempts to provide isolation hospitals, especially for smallpox. The widespread fear of the disease was exacerbated by a common misconception that it was transmitted through the air rather than by contact with an infected person. Hostility towards smallpox hospitals was compounded by a growing anti-vaccination campaign, which could only make the need for such hospitals the greater. Nevertheless, first the Hampstead, and then the Fulham hospitals were closed, and the MAB recognised that it was unlikely to be able to open a smallpox hospital near any populated area in the future.

In desperation, the MAB had borrowed the quarantine hulk *Dreadnought*, moored at Greenwich, during the epidemic of 1871–2, and during that of 1880–1 the Board borrowed two other hulks, *Atlas* and *Endymion*.[19] In 1882 they moved these last two ships from Greenwich to moorings on the south bank of the Thames in Long Reach, by Dartford, where they were joined by the *Castalia*. The *Endymion*, a 50-gun, 3,000-ton frigate, was converted to provide administrative offices, while patients were accommodated on the *Atlas*, a 100-gun ship of the line of the Nelson class. The twin-hulled *Castalia* had been built in 1874 as a cross-channel ferry. In effect she comprised two Thames barges secured side by side and had never been put into service because she gave too rough a ride. A row of five ward blocks was built across the top deck giving accommodation for a total of 150 patients (Fig 138).[20]

A river-ambulance service carried patients to the floating hospital in paddle steamers, operating from three wharves at Fulham, Blackwall and Rotherhithe, where small ambulance stations were built, each comprising an examination room, an isolation ward for patients found unfit to travel and a ward for doubtful cases.[21] The river service complemented the MAB's horse-ambulance service, inaugurated in 1881 with a station at Hackney, with others opening at Deptford in 1883, Fulham in 1884, and Homerton in 1885. Three more were added in 1896–7. These consisted of stables for up to twenty horses and staff accommodation, including a house for the resident caretaker.

At Long Reach the MAB had also purchased a little over 8 acres of land on the foreshore where a pier was constructed together with a number of auxiliary buildings to serve the hospital ships. The pier also allowed convalescent patients to be offloaded and transported to the Board's South Smallpox Camp at Darenth, a few miles to the south. This was first set up in 1881 with 300 beds in marquees supplied by Piggott Brothers and by John Edgington, the principal firms providing hospital tents.[22] The marquees were arranged in two rows and had wooden floors; each contained 20 beds, while two larger marquees served as day-rooms. The camp was replaced in 1887–1902 by permanent buildings and renamed the Southern Convalescent Hospital. These new buildings were of two storeys, with a playroom, day-room and dining-room on the ground floor and two dormitories above, a sanitary annexe projecting on one side.

Other convalescent fever cases were sent to the Northern Convalescent Hospital built at Winchmore Hill in 1885–7. This was a large complex of handsome, detached buildings of yellow stock brick with abundant red-brick dressings occupying a 36½-acre site on high ground to the north of London. Designed by Pennington & Bridgen, the hospital comprised a large administration building, detached houses for the steward and gardener, a mortuary and sixteen two-storey villas for the patients. The villas were of L-shaped plan, with two day-rooms on the ground floor and dormitories above.[23]

The combined epidemics of scarlet fever and smallpox in 1892 led to a shortage of accommodation in the Board's hospitals, and two more temporary fever hospitals were provided, the North-Eastern at Tottenham, erected in 1892, and the Fountain at Tooting, which opened in the following year. The former was designed by A & C Harston. The boiler house and associated buildings were of brick, while the rest of the hospital was constructed of timber on brick piers resting on concrete platforms (Fig 139). The Fountain, designed by Thomas Aldwinckle, was largely single storeyed and of similar construction, with walls and roofs of timber framing covered externally with boarding, felt and corrugated iron, standing on dwarf brick walls to floor level. Inside, the walls were lined with boarding and asbestos on plaster, and the floors were of wood laid on joists on sleeper walls, with a 6-in. concrete raft beneath.[24]

The crisis of 1892 also prompted the MAB to build three further permanent fever hospitals, bringing accommodation to one bed for every 1,000 of the population. The first to be erected was the Brook Hospital at Shooters Hill in 1894–6, followed by the Park Hospital, Hither Green, in 1895–7, and the Grove Hospital, Wandsworth, in 1899. Each commission went to a different architect: the Brook was designed by Aldwinckle, the Park by Edwin T Hall and the Grove by Alfred Hessle Tiltman. All the hospitals were of brick, and for the most part utilitarian in appearance, with any decoration usually restricted to a few buildings such as the

Figure 138
This photograph of the hospital ship Castalia, *moored in the Thames at Long Reach, was probably taken in the late 19th century, and shows the bizarre arrangement of the ward blocks on the ship's deck.*
[GLRO, Photographic Collection 26.16 CAS 77/1409]

Figure 139
A detail of one of the ward blocks at the North-Eastern Hospital, Tottenham, London, erected in 1892 to designs by A & C Harston. Most of the timber ward blocks were replaced by brick buildings in the 1930s. [GLRO, Photographic Collection 26.15 NCR B1757]

administration blocks and water towers. The ward blocks were of two storeys, and the Park and Grove were the first of the Board's hospitals to have sanitary annexes at the ends of the wards. At the Park, which was probably the most attractive of the three, these were used to strong visual effect (Fig 140).

The last large isolation hospitals established by the MAB were built on the site at Long Reach. In 1901 the Board reviewed the future of the hospital ships. The cost of maintenance was high, and ships were prone to fires. Furthermore, there were problems with ensuring the safety of delirious patients on board ship, delirium being one of the stages of smallpox. Tragically, two patients escaped the vigilance of the staff and threw themselves overboard. Hazards arising from bad weather and the possibility of collision also provided strong inducements for the Board to consider alternative accommodation.[25]

A massive outbreak of smallpox in 1901 stimulated the MAB to move quickly to build additional hospital accommodation ashore. A permanent hospital was planned on the portion of land at Long Reach known as Joyce Green, but in order to cope with the epidemic two temporary hutted hospitals were built near the ships. The first to be erected, known simply as Long Reach Hospital, was completed early in 1902 and provided 300 beds. The Orchard Hospital was three times the size and came into service shortly afterwards. These wooden hospitals consisted of rows of huts, with a sanitary annexe on the long side, connected by covered ways.

Plans were drawn up by A & C Harston for both the temporary hospitals and the permanent

Joyce Green. This last, the largest of the three with 986 beds, was opened at the end of 1903.[26] It comprised a series of two-storey ward pavilions, terminating in twin sanitary annexes, arranged in a V-shape. (The layout was determined by the line of the main West Kent Sewer which crossed the site.) In addition to the wards there were extensive administration, staff and service buildings.

After 1902 the incidence of smallpox declined in London. The Orchard Hospital lay empty, and Joyce Green was seldom required. Eventually, the MAB decided to reserve the two temporary hospitals for smallpox cases and use Joyce Green for other infectious diseases. From 1907 diphtheria and scarlet fever cases were received at the hospital, and later, measles and whooping-cough patients were also admitted.

Isolation Hospitals Outside the Metropolis in the Later 19th and Early 20th Centuries

From the scant provision for infectious diseases that existed outside London in the mid 19th century, an extensive network of local authority isolation hospitals had been established by the turn of the century. In the late 1860s, cholera had barely subsided before new epidemics erupted: an outbreak of relapsing fever in 1869–70 was followed in 1870 by the worst-ever epidemic of smallpox. These epidemics led to the building of a number of isolation hospitals. Many were hastily put-up, temporary structures, usually of timber or corrugated-iron construction, although a steadily increasing proportion were built of permanent materials.

A few local authorities followed the advice of a Privy Council memorandum on isolation hospitals of 1871, which suggested that village communities should maintain what amounted to pest-houses, with room for four patients.[27] One such hospital was erected at Berwick-on-Tweed in 1872. From that year hospital construction was overseen by the Local Government Board (LGB), which, until the early 1890s, gave the same advice in its memoranda as the Privy Council regarding small, local isolation hospitals. By that time almost one-fifth of the isolation hospitals in England were converted houses or other converted premises, including factories.[28]

The LGB authorised loans for isolation-hospital building and tried to apply suitable standards by withholding loan sanction where the proposed buildings were judged unsuitable. (The Board refused to sanction loans for corrugated-iron hospitals after 1900.) Nevertheless, some local authorities erected hospitals of unapproved designs at their own expense in times of emergency. Some chose to adapt existing buildings, and unwilling or impoverished rural councils were sometimes persuaded to invest in a tent or a portable cabin. These expedients rarely involved the preparation of a site, the hospital being set up near to the homes of the patients, and all have now vanished without leaving tangible evidence.

Because the miasma theory held that fevers were caused by foul air and putrefaction, earlier sanitary legislation had been directed towards removing the perceived causes of disease, and it had been assumed that once this was achieved fever hospitals would not be necessary. Gradually the miasma theory was abandoned, and the progress of medical knowledge is reflected in contemporary public health legislation. The Public Health Act of 1875[29] established a system of rural and urban sanitary authorities across the whole country. It not only gave all local authorities power to provide hospitals, but, perhaps more importantly, allowed them to borrow money for the purpose. Economy was always an important factor in local-authority hospital building. The cost of treatment could be recovered from the patients, or, if paupers, from the guardians, but in practice charging policies varied and were often flexible and generous.

Usually a smallpox hospital was the first to be built, a reflection of the public fear of the disease. The LGB always preferred smallpox hospitals to be on a separate site, but this was probably only enforced rigidly after about 1890, when the provision of hospitals for scarlet fever and other infections was increasing rapidly. Hospitals set up by small town and rural councils commonly consisted of a single block

containing two wards flanking a central duty-room, and minimal ancillary buildings. They were situated well away from most habitations and their isolated positions meant that staff accommodation was necessary. Small hospitals often had a visiting caretaker, and, when the building was in use, nurses must have attended daily. All decently designed hospitals, and all those belonging to larger authorities, combined staff accommodation with what was termed 'administration' (including matron's office, dispensary and kitchen), in one building. Single bedrooms on the first floor were the standard provision, along with a sitting-room and a dining-room served by the adjacent hospital kitchen.

In populous towns the occurrence of disease was more constant than in the countryside and there was a greater likelihood of more than one disease being prevalent at any one time. Large hospitals, with a number of separate wards, were therefore necessary. These generally comprised a separate administration block flanked by a number of detached ward blocks which were

Figure 140
General view of the sanitary towers at the ends of the ward pavilions at the Park Hospital, Hither Green, Lewisham, designed by E T Hall and built in 1895–7.
[NMR BB93/25114]

aligned north–south, as in general hospitals, so that beds on each side of the wards received equal amounts of sunlight. While the principles of ward design found at general hospitals were adopted, the detailed planning differed. One of the closest to a general hospital in design was Cheddon Road Hospital, erected by Taunton Borough in 1878. It had four wards, each occupying a single-storey pavilion of pale bricks with a pantiled roof. The pavilions were placed parallel to each other and connected by a covered way at one end. It was rare for ward pavilions at isolation hospitals to contain only one ward; two were more usual, with a duty-room between them. This was a more economical arrangement for all but the largest hospitals as it allowed each pavilion to be allocated to one disease, with one ward for men and the other for women.

Typically, many authorities were unwilling to build expensive permanent hospitals and began by erecting relatively small hospitals to which ward blocks were later added in a piecemeal fashion. Priorsdean Hospital, for example, was originally built in 1882–3 as the Portsmouth City Hospital for Infectious Diseases to the designs of a local builder, Mr Tull. To begin with it comprised just two ward blocks flanking the administration building, although the site was large enough for tents to be put up if necessary. Further ward blocks were added on the vacant land regularly until about the 1930s.

The Isolation Hospitals Act of 1893[30] had a greater impact than any previous legislation. Although it was still not compulsory for local authorities to establish hospitals for infectious diseases, it was rapidly becoming more difficult for them to avoid doing so. The 1893 Act not only enabled county councils to provide isolation hospitals, but also allowed them to compel local authorities within the county to do so. These local authorities could either act individually or combine with others to form joint districts.

The LGB maintained its supervisory role. It insisted that new hospitals should be able to treat at least three diseases at the same time, which meant a minimum of six wards arranged in three blocks – the maximum economical number of patients per ward being about twenty-four. Plans of hospitals sometimes designated pavilions as being for scarlet fever, diphtheria, measles or some other specific disease, but this must be taken as no more than an indication, for in times of epidemic, flexibility of use was essential.

Scarlet fever was the most common disease and where ward pavilions differed in size, the largest were usually occupied by such cases. As

the disease had distinct acute and convalescent phases, a day-room for convalescents featured in many scarlet-fever ward pavilions, often situated over the entrance and duty-room. In the largest institutions convalescent patients were sometimes allocated separate wards, but apart from a difference in the number of beds and of cubic space allotted to patients there is no discernible difference between them and ordinary wards. Sometimes typhoid-fever patients were given a larger amount of cubic space than other patients, which could be achieved most simply by reducing the number of beds in the ward. Diphtheria and enteric fever required the most nursing, so these wards never had more than 12 beds.

From the early 1890s up to the First World War over 300 local-authority isolation hospitals were built across the country.[31] A limited number of general layouts was adopted. Large hospitals had the blocks parallel and in rows, while smaller hospitals could employ less unfriendly arrangements around a central green or garden. A few consisted of two ward pavilions flanking a central administration block, to which they were connected by covered walkways, though this was never common in permanent hospitals. Ward pavilions were almost invariably designed according to the LGB standard plans (Fig 141). The commonest and most widely adopted of these was type C. This had first appeared in the memoranda in 1888, and after 1902 a variation was introduced with an extra single-bed ward on either side of the duty-room. Windows between them allowed the nurse on duty to keep patients under observation; the wards were therefore particularly suitable for patients who were either noisy, objectionable, paying for their own bed, or of uncertain diagnosis.

The second most commonly adopted plan was type B, published in the LGB memoranda from 1888 to 1924. Most examples of this plan type were built before 1900, after which a modification became popular whereby projecting walls in the veranda provided additional separation between the two wards. Perhaps the main advantage of the plan was its economical way of providing for several different diseases amongst a small number of patients. Consequently, it was often chosen as the 'isolation pavilion' of a hospital, as at Bagnall, Staffordshire, in 1907, and was generally reserved for rarer diseases. A larger variation, designated plan type D, which only appeared in the memorandum of 1888, placed the outer wards across the width of the block to form cross wings. This was copied by many authorities up to the First World War.

With the Board's encouragement, more or

Figure 141
Model plans of isolation-hospital ward blocks published by the Local Government Board between 1876 and 1924. These plans were extensively copied at isolation hospitals throughout the country. [Plans (1:500) based on Local Government Board memoranda On the Provision of Hospital Accommodation by Local Authorities, *1888, 1892, 1900, 1902, 1921 and 1924]*

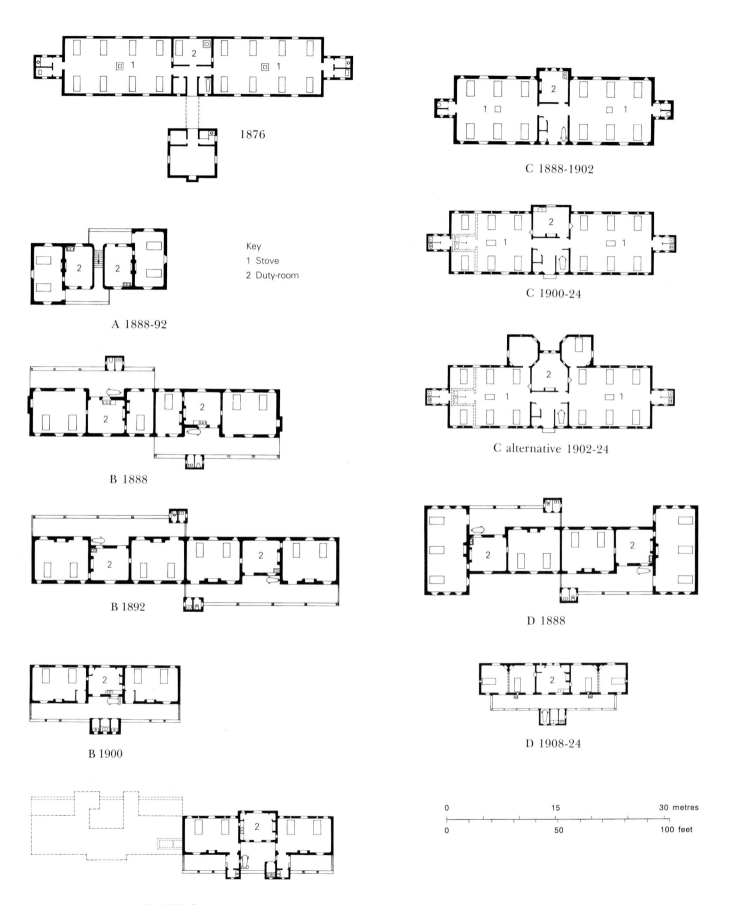

1876

C 1888-1902

A 1888-92

Key
1 Stove
2 Duty-room

B 1888

C 1900-24

C alternative 1902-24

B 1892

D 1888

B 1900

D 1908-24

B 1902-21

| 0 | | 15 | | 30 metres |
| 0 | | 50 | | 100 feet |

less comprehensive service buildings were included in every hospital, especially laundry, mortuary, disinfector and garage. A mortuary had been essential since the Infectious Diseases (Prevention) Act of 1890,[32] which decreed that the bodies of those who died from infectious diseases should be removed from the hospital directly to the place of burial. Because of the risk of infection, the mortuary was not a place for visitors, and, except in large urban hospitals, rarely consisted of more than a single room. If physical arrangements were made for relatives to view a body, they usually included a plate-glass screen to divide the two. Separate laundries for staff and patients were part of the sanitary regime, and usually had an adjoining disinfecting chamber.

Planning became more sophisticated as experience of running large isolation hospitals taught more lessons about the spread of infection and the course of the diseases. Sanitary annexes were generally at the outer ends of the wards, separated by ventilated lobbies which doubled as hand-washing rooms. Bathrooms were often contrived at the entrance to the pavilion, but the bath that they contained was usually a portable one, because it was considered preferable to bath the patient next to his bed. A bathroom next to the entrance had the advantage of allowing a departing patient to be bathed immediately before he left the hospital building. This practice became a standard part of discharge routines, which also included the separation of infected and disinfected clothing. At larger hospitals special discharge blocks were designed for this process. The Park Hospital, Reading, erected in 1904 from designs by the local firm of Charles Smith & Son, had a suite of discharge rooms attached to the porter's lodge (but with a separate entrance). It was fitted up with a bathroom flanked by dressing and undressing rooms, and a waiting-room.[33]

In the early years of the 20th century a new plan type was devised which gained increasing importance: the cubicle isolation block. In 1906 a block was erected at Walthamstow consisting of rows of single rooms reached from an external veranda. It provided a greater degree of isolation and separation than the usual ward blocks and was thus of great benefit for accommodating cases where diagnosis was uncertain. A similar block was begun at the Norwich Isolation Hospital in 1908, and the LGB published a model plan (confusingly called type D) for a simplified version suitable for smaller hospitals (see Fig 141). In 1912 a cross-shaped variant was built at Croydon, which was copied at the isolation hospitals at Portsmouth and Cambridge (Fig 142). The simpler LGB type was copied endlessly, so that by 1940 almost every hospital had at least one cubicle isolation block. They were so convenient and flexible that the proportion of beds provided in such blocks increased greatly between 1920 and 1940.

Developments Between the Wars

In 1919 the Local Government Board was superseded by the Ministry of Health. One of the Ministry's first actions was to reiterate the LGB's call for county councils to draw up schemes for the rational organisation of the treatment of infectious diseases within their areas. The amalgamation of district councils into joint districts led to larger, better-built hospitals replacing some of the less suitable early buildings. This reorganisation was made possible by improvements in transport. Motor ambulances replaced slow and uncomfortable horse-drawn ambulances during the first fifteen years of the 20th century, and the improvements in road surfaces that accompanied the contemporary increase in motor traffic made the carriage of fever patients over long distances a possibility for the first time.

New hospitals built to serve amalgamated districts were well planned and built of permanent materials, corrugated-iron falling entirely out of use. The majority were erected during the 1930s, and adopted the smooth, clean lines of the Modern Movement, so ideally suited to conveying the hygienic aspirations of these hospitals. The County Architect's department usually provided the designs, which were sometimes unsympathetically crude and sometimes cautiously up-to-date. Dereham Hospital, for

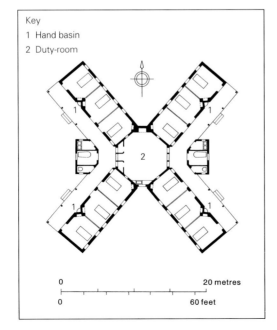

Key
1 Hand basin
2 Duty-room

Figure 142
Ground-floor plan of the cruciform cubicle isolation block erected at Cambridge Isolation Hospital in 1914–15, to designs by C Chart.
[Plan (1:500) based on
The Hospital, *26 Jun 1915, 277]*

0   20 metres

0   60 feet

example, was designed by the Norfolk County Architect, C J Norton, and opened in 1938. The ward pavilions, of utilitarian appearance and constructed of Fletton Rustic bricks under tiled roofs, were arranged in parallel rows. As usual, plenty of space was left for a future expansion that was rarely achieved.

There was also a rise in the number of notifiable infectious diseases that required isolation in hospital. This made the provision of cubicle blocks essential, as some diseases were rare and did not merit the reservation of a whole pavilion. The introduction of surgery for diphtheria as well as other ailments, including perforated bowel and erysipelas, meant that operating theatres had to be included. They were often placed at one end of a block, with a large north window.

The increased size of many hospitals led to the creation of separate nurses' homes to augment the few rooms already available. In many small hospitals a wing was added to the side or rear of the administration block, and elsewhere detached homes were built, although proximity to the administration block was usual. At Heathcote Hospital, built originally for the Warwick Joint Hospitals Board in 1887–91 to designs by Keith Young, a new nurses' home was built near the administration block in the 1930s. Large hospitals built correspondingly large homes, and changing staff–patient ratios and shorter working hours greatly increased the number of nurses working at isolation hospitals. In addition, many of the larger hospitals were recognised as training centres and required sufficient accommodation for the increased numbers of trainee nurses. Rooms for instruction and for study were essential, and recreational rooms were also provided. At Groby Road Hospital in Leicester, which had been built in 1898–1900 to designs by Blackwell & Thomson, a large new nurses' home was added in 1934 to accommodate 140 nursing and domestic staff. This tall, red-brick building has more than a hint of a neo-Georgian telephone exchange, with a nod in the direction of the Modern Movement provided by the curved staircase window (Fig 143). The home contained the usual mix of bedrooms, study-rooms and so forth, but had the less common feature of a large ballroom that could be partitioned into two unequal-sized sitting-rooms.

The introduction of antibiotics in the 1940s, which provided a new effective treatment for infectious diseases, resulted in a rapid decline in the need for isolation hospitals, and many were put to new uses or abandoned altogether. Smaller ones were often converted to house geriatric patients or the mentally handicapped.

Tuberculosis Sanatoria

Transmitted mainly by droplet infection, tuberculosis multiplies slowly, and the success of the human immune system in dealing with it depends heavily on the condition of the patient. Before Robert Koch's identification of the tubercle bacillus in 1882, pulmonary tuberculosis was known either as phthisis or, most commonly, consumption. The fashionable disease of the Romantics, it claimed the lives of Keats, Chopin and Emily Brontë. However, it was only recognised as infectious in 1865 when the French physician, Jean-Antoine Villemin, transmitted it to rabbits. Before the discovery of streptomycin in 1943,[34] successful treatment of pulmonary tuberculosis was limited to improving the patient's health so that the immune system could keep infection under control.

In the 19th century consumption was seen as a degenerative disease, caused by a weak constitution. Treatment, available to only a wealthy

Figure 143
This detail of the nurses' home at Groby Road Isolation Hospital, Leicester, shows the main entrance and curved stair tower. The home was added to the hospital in 1934.
[NMR BB93/35276]

few, consisted of a change of air, at first to the warm, dry Mediterranean but later to Alpine resorts. Because there was no hope of cure, except perhaps with the patients most recently infected, consumptives were excluded from general hospitals. The first hospitals to be established for the treatment of consumption usually attempted to recreate the desired Mediterranean temperature within closed windows. Rest and sedation aimed to combat the patients' loss of strength, and their diet was restricted, with little or no meat. These hospitals were fee-paying and thus only accessible to the middle and upper classes.

The Brompton Hospital in London was the earliest built specifically for this purpose. The Tudor-style building, of red and blue bricks with stone dressings, had a collegiate appearance (Fig 144). Erected in phases between 1844 and 1854, it was designed by Frederick John Francis to an H-shaped plan and contained small wards with up to 8 beds, each opening off a 9-ft wide corridor that doubled as a day-room. A system of forced ventilation was intended to maintain a temperature of about 61°F throughout the year, although it never worked satisfactorily. Many of the patients were mobile, hence the need for day-rooms, and a fine little Gothic chapel was built at the back of the hospital in 1849–50, designed by Edward Buckton Lamb in his idiosyncratic style (Fig 145).[35] In 1855 Lamb went on to design the Royal National Sanatorium for Consumption at Bournemouth, where he copied the Brompton formula of small wards with associated day-rooms.

Some of the later and smaller institutions were more domestic in appearance and plan,

although small wards and a controlled atmosphere remained the norm. Domesticity was taken to an extreme at the Royal National Hospital, Ventnor, established in 1869. Designed by a local architect, Thomas Hellyer, it comprised a row of eight pairs of semi-detached villas flanking a chapel, each villa having two sitting-rooms and a veranda on the ground floor facing the sea, while on the upper floors there were single bedrooms; behind were bathrooms and nurses' rooms. There was also a system of warming and ventilation by forced air.

The revolution in the design of hospitals for tuberculosis came with the widespread adoption of open-air treatment. As early as 1791 Dr Lettsom had incorporated exposure to the open air for patients with tuberculosis of the glands (scrofula) at the Royal Sea Bathing Infirmary at Margate (see page 127), and between 1840 and 1843 Dr George Bodington had used similar methods for patients with pulmonary tuberculosis in a house at Sutton Coldfield. However, these experiments were contrary to accepted medical opinion at the time, and had little immediate impact.

Open-air treatment received more serious attention after Herman Brehmer opened his first sanatorium in the mountains of Germany in 1854. Brehmer believed that consumption was absent above a certain altitude and devised a regime that entailed life in the open air, abundant food, and methodical exercise. His sanatorium at Gorbersdorf, in Germany, opened in 1859 and achieved encouragingly successful results. Brehmer's ideas proved highly influential, and a strict version of his treatment was developed by Otto Walther at the Nordrach

Figure 144
View of the principal elevation of the Brompton Hospital, London, by the architect, F J Francis, of 1844.
[Lithograph in the Scottish Record Office, RHP 14443 (Reproduced courtesy of The Duke of Buccleuch and Queensbury)]

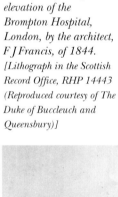

Sanatorium in the Black Forest which opened in 1889. Walther prescribed walking as the principal and carefully regulated exercise, and a nourishing diet. Nordrach Sanatorium was visited by many British patients and doctors, and spawned numerous imitators.

One of the earliest open-air sanatoria in Britain was the Manchester Sanatorium, established at Bowdon in 1884. A south-facing wing, designed on a half-butterfly plan, was added to it in 1886, consisting of two large 10-bed wards arranged on either side of a ward kitchen and bathrooms. The wards, set high above ground level on a raised basement, had casement windows reaching almost to the floor, and the patients were 'encouraged to live in the open air as much as possible'. At the centre of the wing there was a large conservatory or 'sun-bath', where the patients could 'bask in sunlight and read or play bagatelle'.[36] In both its design and medical regime, this hospital set the standard for nearly all subsequent sanatoria in England.

At first it had been thought that high altitudes destroyed tuberculosis. However, while many patients did indeed improve or even were cured in these mountain sanatoria, by no means all of them recovered, and the altitude theory had to be dismissed. Fresh mountain air, at any altitude, had sufficiently beneficial effects to remain an important curative element, though further experiments were made to find locations or treatments that would either cure or arrest the progress of this disease. Brehmer's pupil Peter Dettweiler advocated rest rather than exercise, together with sun and open air, preferably in a forest – the vapours from pine trees were thought to be particularly efficacious.

For the most part these sanatoria were still aimed towards the comparatively wealthy, but in 1892 Dettweiler opened the first sanatorium for working-class patients, at Ruppertshain in southern Germany. This economically designed structure proved highly influential, although it was a few years before a similar establishment was erected in this country.

Towards the end of the century it was recognised that neither a specific type of climate nor high altitude were essential curative factors, but simply a plentiful supply of fresh air. This realisation led to a rapid escalation in the number of sanatoria in Britain. A farm at Downham in Norfolk, which was less than 100 ft above sea level, was the site chosen by Dr Jane Walker in 1898 at which to conduct open-air treatment on a small number of patients. Her success there led her to establish the East Anglian Sanatorium for paying patients and Maltings Farm Sanatorium for the poor. Both sanatoria were situated on a large estate near Nayland in

Suffolk. The East Anglian Sanatorium was built in 1899–1901 and was designed to Dr Walker's specifications by Smith & Brewer, with something of the same flair and stylish lines of their recently completed Mary Ward Settlement in London. On its long front elevation, the windows of the upper floor are set high under sweeping eaves. The patients' rooms were all on this side, with a long access corridor behind them. Originally, a few of these south-facing rooms were allocated to doctors and staff, although it became more common to relegate all staff to accommodation at the back of the building. A wing on the north side of the sanatorium contained the kitchen and service rooms as well as a large dining-hall and billiard room.

Open-air treatment was not restricted to purpose-built sanatoria. It could be carried out to a limited extent in a patient's own home, and was taken up for tuberculosis cases in work-houses and mental hospitals. Throughout the

Figure 145
The Brompton Hospital chapel was added in 1849–50 to designs by E B Lamb and altered by William White in 1891–2. This photograph shows the interior looking west.
[GLRO: GLC photograph 71/1681]

Figure 146
General view of the
south front of Mundesley
Sanatorium (now
Mundesley Hospital),
in Norfolk, built in
1899, supposedly to the
design of the
sanatorium's founder,
Dr Burton-Fanning.
The construction was
carried out by the
specialist firm of
temporary-building
suppliers, Boulton &
Paul.
[NMR BB92/7241]

second half of the 19th century a high proportion of the inmates of workhouses were suffering from tuberculosis, sent there because they were no longer able to work and support themselves. Usually they were mixed with ordinary patients in the general wards. At the turn of the century a number of guardians in London and the larger towns set aside special wards for tubercular inmates (see page 73). These were usually adapted for their new purpose by the insertion of french windows, although open-air treatment could be, and frequently was, given by simply leaving windows open.[37]

At the same time some general hospitals began to accept tuberculosis cases for open-air treatment. Sheffield Royal Infirmary was the first, in May 1899, using a ward where half of the windows were kept permanently open; the paths in the grounds were also improved and wooden shelters provided. Twelve months later a first-floor loggia at Addenbrooke's Hospital, Cambridge, was adapted for open-air treatment, and in September 1900 the Royal Berkshire Hospital at Reading refurbished balconies for the same purpose. These adaptations remained exceptional, and were only for patients in the early stages of the disease.

Between 1891 and 1911 over fifty hospitals treating tuberculosis were established in England and Wales, either privately or by voluntary subscription. Mundesley Sanatorium (Figs 146 and 151) was unusually lavish in its

provision of a south-facing bedroom and sitting-room for each of its twelve patients. This 'private institution for well-to-do patients' was established by Dr F W Burton-Fanning of Norwich, who is said to have designed the main building in 1898.[38] With its weather-boarding, mock half-timbering, and broad gables, it echoes a *châlet Suisse*, and perhaps this was a deliberate ploy to recreate the atmosphere of the Continental sanatoria and woo a high-class clientele. The construction was carried out by Boulton & Paul, a well-known firm supplying temporary buildings that was based locally. The Mundesley design later appeared in their catalogues as Hospital No. 154. The high fees charged by Burton-Fanning deterred most potential patients and he was soon forced to convert the sitting-rooms to additional bedrooms and reduce his fees. One of the innovations at Mundesley, invented by Burton-Fanning, were wooden shelters that could be turned to face away from the wind, and in which patients could spend the whole day, and even the night (Fig 147). Such shelters, whether movable or fixed, were relatively inexpensive and soon became popular.

Sanatoria designed for the poorer classes, and with limited funding, were necessarily simpler but followed the same basic principles of design. Single-storey timber-framed structures were the most common, and sectional buildings clad in wood or corrugated-iron were supplied

by firms such as Boulton & Paul or Humphreys of Knightsbridge. Working-class patients at Maltings Farm were housed in wooden buildings, and a barn was adapted to serve as a dining-room. Similar economical measures were taken at Kelling Sanatorium, near Cromer in Norfolk, established by the ever resourceful Burton-Fanning for 'persons unable to pay the fees commonly current at private institutions'.[39] Kelling opened in 1903 in a converted house to which ward wings were added to designs by Clare & Ross, architects specialising in economic housing. They gave physical form to the ideas of Burton-Fanning, providing open-fronted sleeping-rooms protected by a continuous veranda.

Verandas, balconies, and sun-trapping butterfly plans, together with revolving shelters, became standard features of sanatoria. These were put to good architectural effect in a number of instances, and some of the early 20th-century sanatoria are among the most attractive hospital buildings. Frimley Sanatorium in Surrey by E T Hall of 1901–5, Mount Vernon in Middlesex by Frederick Wheeler of 1902 (Fig 148), and Adams & Holden's King Edward VII Sanatorium at Midhurst in Sussex of 1903–6, are three of the finest. With a relatively ambulant and captive population, a chapel was also a common feature, though few were as accomplished as those at Mount Vernon and Midhurst.

At Mount Vernon, Wheeler created a superb Arts & Crafts chapel, closer in scale to a parish church (Fig 149), while the chapel at Midhurst was designed on the open-air principle, with two naves converging at a central preaching space to create a V-shaped plan (Fig 150). The southern sides were originally formed of open arcades, though these have since been sympathetically glazed.

At first the undoubted success of sanatoria generated great optimism. A high proportion of 'suitable patients' – that is, those in whom the disease was not too far advanced – secured a remission during the standard stay of twelve to fifteen weeks. Furthermore, developments in the use of X-rays and surgery were seen as potentially useful means of treating and diagnosing the disease. The new technique of artificial pneumothorax, which involved collapsing the lung in order to rest it, was the most notable of these. Such radical thoracic surgery was only possible with the use of X-ray equipment. X-rays had been discovered in 1895, but they were of limited use at first due to the long exposures required, the difficulty of obtaining a sufficiently clear image, and the uncertainties of interpreting X-rays showing soft tissue. It was not until 1910 that the pneumothorax operation was first performed successfully in England (at Mundesley and the Brompton), but it was practised widely during the First World War and

Figure 147
Revolving sleeping-chalets for tuberculosis patients at Mundesley Hospital, Norfolk, probably designed by Dr Burton-Fanning in about 1900.
[NMR BB92/7249]

*Figure 148 (opposite)
View of the south front of
Mount Vernon
Sanatorium (now
Mount Vernon
Hospital), Northwood,
in the London Borough
of Hillingdon. The
sanatorium was
designed by Frederick
Wheeler and built in
1902.*
[NMR BB92/16094]

*Figure 149 (left)
The chapel at Mount
Vernon Sanatorium was
built of knapped flint
with yellow stone dress-
ings. In 1987–8 it was
converted into a library
and conference centre by
Bill Miller Associates.*
[NMR BB92/16103]

Figure 150
The south elevation of
the open-air chapel built
at the King Edward VII
Sanatorium, Midhurst,
West Sussex, designed by
Adams & Holden and
built in 1903–6.
[NMR BB92/26949]

was the major advance in treatment in the inter-war period. Despite this fact, the procedure was expensive, not entirely safe, and only suitable for about 10 per cent of patients. As it required highly skilled doctors with well-equipped theatres and X-ray facilities to help control the operation, this treatment tended to be offered only in a few of the larger hospitals or sanatoria.

For the majority of patients, treatment still relied on exposure to the elements, rest, and a nourishing diet. But many relapsed on returning home and resuming work, or were unable to afford to spend a sufficient length of time at a sanatorium. Attempts to combat these limitations concentrated on prolonging treatment at sanatoria and monitoring patients once they had been discharged. A few institutions created colonies. One of the earliest and most extensive was the Cambridge Tuberculosis Colony originally established in 1916 at Bourn, which moved to Papworth in 1918. Its main purpose was to rehabilitate sufferers, and patients were trained in a variety of trades, from carpentry to boot-repairing, and from cabinet-making to farming. Such occupational and recreational therapies were widely adopted. The variety of activities on offer at Mundesley Sanatorium was depicted in a charming view of the hospital painted *c* 1930 (Fig 151).

Concurrently with the advances in treatment, legislation was introduced in an effort to bring these benefits to a wider section of the population. The National Insurance Act of 1911 made local authorities responsible for providing tuberculosis treatment for people insured under the scheme, with the Local Government Board acting as the supervising body (from 1919, this function was taken over by the Ministry of Health). Under the terms of the Act, the LGB could repay three-fifths of the capital costs of building or extending sanatoria, up to a maximum of £90 a bed, and half the cost of treatment. This put the Board in a strong position to insist that county councils should prepare schemes for the treatment of tuberculosis in their areas, including dispensaries for out-patients as well as sanatoria for in-patients.

As a result, much of the accommodation for patients suffering from tuberculosis built in response to the Act was at infectious diseases hospitals. This allowed local authorities to economise on administrative and service buildings. Many existing isolation hospitals had vacant space which had been left for tents or new wards, and the reduced incidence of other infectious diseases made ward blocks available. At Groby Road Hospital in Leicester, for example, it was calculated that the decline in the number of scarlet-fever patients made at least one of four pavilions available for tuberculosis. A pavilion was simply converted by adding wide verandas and dropping some window-sills to ground level.

Tuberculosis blocks added to isolation hospitals tended to be of simple design and offered limited therapies, concentrating on open-air treatment. Only the largest, such as Leicester,

had theatres of any size, although many seem to have had some provision for minor operations. The pavilion added in 1913 to Hill Top Isolation Hospital, Bromsgrove, was typical. Designed by A K Rowe, it was a small single-storey block with wards opening on to a front veranda and a narrow rear veranda for staff access. Separate circulation for staff was provided to minimise their contact with the disease.

The counties' and county boroughs' responsibilities were broadened by the 1921 Public Health (Tuberculosis) Act[40] which made treatment available to all, irrespective of whether or not they were insured, and almost all sanatoria after 1920 were built by county and county borough councils.

As with local-authority isolation hospitals at this period, a process of reorganisation and centralisation occurred. This became all the more vital when county councils were given responsibility by the Local Government Act of 1929 for Poor Law patients,[41] amongst whom were large numbers suffering from tuberculosis. Plans had to be made for their accommodation, and they were progressively moved from workhouses into new sanatoria. In order to obtain a large enough site, councils often acquired a small country house and its land; the house was used for staff and the first patients, and gradually more suitable accommodation was added in the grounds. There were generally two phases of building. In the first phase, familiar sanatorium-type structures were erected, often of one storey, offering open-air treatment. Later, notably in

the 1930s, larger buildings were added, usually of two storeys, providing a very large number of beds, and also offering a progressively greater degree of surgical treatment.

During the 1930s multi-storeyed ward blocks were erected at a few sites which were designed with each floor stepped back to create terraces. The Bernhard Baron Hospital, part of the Papworth Colony, adopted this form. Built in 1932–4, it provided 84 beds for male patients. Large double doors in the wards opened on to the terraces. Similarly, at the Poole Sanatorium at Middlesbrough, ward blocks with extensive roof-terraces were designed by William & Thomas Ridley Milburn (Fig 152). This smart collection of Modern Movement buildings was erected between 1938 and 1947.

Innovative planning is also evident at Rochford Hospital where a highly original building was produced by the architect F W Smith for tuberculosis patients. Completed in 1939, it had a V-shaped plan with square wards stepped back *en échelon* to either side of a central rounded point, in a striking design which aimed to admit a maximum amount of sunlight into the wards (Fig 153).

All the sanatoria considered so far were concerned with the treatment of pulmonary tuberculosis, but during the inter-war period the treatment of non-pulmonary tuberculosis expanded considerably. The disease attacked parts of the body other than the lungs, causing physical deformities; these were particularly notable, and treatable, among children (see

Figure 151
This bird's-eye view of Mundesley Sanatorium in Norfolk, painted c 1930, shows Burton-Fanning's building of 1899 to the left and various later additions. The revolving shelters can be seen in the foreground to the left of the picture, and the artist has provided a series of vignettes showing the various activities of the patients.
[NMR BB92/7262]

Figure 152 (above)
General view of the ward
block for adults at the
Poole Sanatorium,
Middlesbrough, designed
by W & T R Milburn
and erected in 1938–45.
[NMR BB93/20214]

Figure 153 (right)
The tuberculosis block at
Rochford Hospital,
Essex, built in 1938–9,
to a highly unusual
design by F W Smith.
[NMR BB92/5877]

page 114). Open-air treatment was suitable for some forms of this tuberculosis, but traction and surgery were often employed. At first the principal hospitals for non-pulmonary tuberculosis were private and voluntary, the local authority sanatoria concentrating on pulmonary tuberculosis.

At Alton, in Hampshire, the Lord Mayor Treloar Hospital had been established in 1907 for the treatment of children suffering from non-pulmonary tuberculosis in buildings originally erected for casualties of the Boer War. Between 1929 and 1939 the hospital was largely rebuilt, the architect H C Smart working to a brief prepared by Henry Gauvain, the medical superintendent. Gauvain attempted to treat most conditions by sunlight, both real and artificial, in combination with minimal surgery and maximum traction. The buildings were designed to fit Gauvain's methods. The main range consisted of a row of five blocks, each containing a pair of wards with service rooms to the north and a broad terrace with deep verandas to the south. These verandas were roofed with Vitaglass, which transmitted ultra-violet light, and the outer half could be retracted under the upper half in fine weather. The basement of one block contained a light department, equipped with Finsen lamps for artificial-sunlight treatment. Because the patients were all children, movable screens allowed the blocks to be opened up or subdivided for classes.

Local authorities treated more surgical tuberculosis, affecting the limbs, after the mid 1920s. But the backlog of untreated cases, especially children, was soon reduced, helped by a falling birth-rate and a reduction in the incidence of the disease.

Tuberculosis was effectively conquered by the discovery of streptomycin, but a number of the largest sanatoria retained an important role within the health service because of the surgical skills developed by their staff. Thus both Harefield and Papworth became leading hospitals in heart surgery. Nevertheless, most sanatoria, and indeed isolation hospitals, have long ceased to be required for their original purposes, and where the buildings survive at all many have become home to a geriatric or long-stay unit, or a centre for the disabled.

8
Mental Hospitals

All the hospital types so far discussed have had one common aspect: they were each designed for the physically ill. As such, they have many similar features, as developments in planning were readily adaptable for hospitals accommodating general medical, surgical or specialist cases. Whilst hospitals for the mentally ill can also be seen to adopt many of the general principles of hospital planning – notably in relation to ventilation and sanitation – their very different function naturally produced a quite distinct architectural response.

The earliest asylums were designed with security as the overriding requirement. Understanding of mental illness was limited, and public prejudice widespread. If it was difficult to find good nursing staff for general hospitals, it was doubly hard to find sympathetic, reliable and educated staff for asylums, where the nurses were little more than 'keepers'. For the most part, conditions in the early asylums were atrocious, and so-called scientific treatments would seem barbaric today. Nevertheless, a few pioneering individuals strove to improve the methods by which lunatics were treated and the accommodation which confined them. In the late 18th and early 19th centuries, the most influential were two Frenchmen, Philippe Pinel and Jean Étienne Esquirol, and their work was continued in this country by men like William and Samuel Tuke and John Conolly.

As with the development of medicinal cures for physical illnesses, which is a relatively modern phenomenon, it is only in the recent past that drugs have been developed for a large number of mental illnesses. Thus, the ever-expanding asylums of the Victorian era gradually were emptied of newly treatable cases in the 20th century, a process which has continued with the policy of 'care in the community'.

Bedlam and the Early Asylums

Bedlam was to become synonymous with the mad and madhouses. More than any other hospital for the mentally ill, Bedlam, Bethlem or Bethlehem Hospital, as it was variously known, worked its way into popular imagination, art and literature.

The origins of this hospital can be traced back to the hospital of St Mary of Bethlehem. The City of London became involved in the administration of the hospital in the mid 14th century, and, by the early 1400s, Bethlem was specialising in the care of the insane.[1] It escaped suppression at the Dissolution, and in 1553 was incorporated by Edward VI in a collective charter with Christ's Hospital, St Thomas's and Bridewell as one of the Royal Hospitals.[2]

By the 1670s the hospital was in a deplorable condition and in 1674 the court of governors resolved that 'the Hospitall House of Bethlem is very old weake & ruinous and to small & streight for keeping the great numb of Lunatikes as are therein att psent'.[3] It was therefore decided to provide new premises elsewhere.

The new building (see Figure 2), erected in 1675–6, could not have contrasted more strongly with the old. It was designed on a palatial scale by Robert Hooke, and was among his finest architectural works. There was sufficient accommodation for 120 patients, and the hospital's main elevation, punctuated by square pavilions, shows Dutch and French influences, in particular the Palais des Tuileries begun by Philibert de l'Orme in the 16th century. It was supposedly the similarity to the Tuileries which so offended Louis XIV that he ordered 'a plan of St James's Palace to be taken for offices of a very inferior nature'.[4] In England, however, the new Bethlem was widely admired, John Evelyn describing it as 'magnificently built, & most sweetly placed in Morefields'.[5]

The area in front of the hospital was enclosed by a screen wall, in the centre of which were large ornamental iron gates. Resting on the broken pediment of the gateway were two Portland stone figures of madness, carved by Caius Gabriel Cibber. They were supposedly modelled on inmates of the hospital, one of whom was reputedly Oliver Cromwell's porter.[6]

The hospital itself was largely of two storeys over a basement, constructed of brick with free-stone dressings. The central and end pavilions were ornamented by Corinthian pilasters supporting segmental pediments, each containing

the Royal Arms or Arms of London, carved in stone. In the hall, the various benefactors were commemorated by tablets bearing their names, linked together by carved cherubs' heads. The steward's office was at the front of the building, together with the physician's and apothecary's room in which new admissions were examined and from which patients were discharged. To the rear of the hall was a grand staircase which ascended to the committee-room, dignified by an ornamental plaster ceiling. The hall also gave access to the patients' accommodation on either side, which comprised a combination of galleries and cells which was to remain the standard form in asylum design for almost two centuries. The cells, which served as bedrooms for the inmates, measured 12 ft 6 ins by 8 ft and were lit by small, unglazed windows, set high in the walls. The galleries were approximately 320 ft long, 16 ft wide and 13 ft high, and were designed to serve both as corridors of communication and as an alternative place of exercise to airing-courts in bad weather.[7] In practice, many of the inmates remained in their cells day and night, often chained to their beds, and only those that were considered to be quiet or convalescent were allowed 'the liberty of the gallery'.[8] The galleries were used mostly by visitors: from them they could safely peep into the cells through 'wickets' or spy-hatches. Some accommodation for staff seems to have been provided in the attic of the central pavilion, while the basement contained the kitchen and laundry, although parts were let to the East India Company for storing pepper.[9]

The eighth scene of Hogarth's *A Rake's Progress*, painted in 1732–3, was set in one of the new men's wards, erected at the east end of the asylum in 1725. A corresponding block for women was erected at the west end in 1733. Classification of the patients was still very much in its infancy. There was no precise definition of insanity or lunacy at this date, but a distinction was made between mental illness developed in later life which might be deemed curable, and idiocy or imbecility (later termed 'mental deficiency'), which was usually apparent from birth and judged to be incurable. In addition, certain cases were excluded, namely: 'mopes', idiots, women-with-child, persons afflicted with the palsy or venereal disease, subject to convulsive or epileptic fits and such as are 'weak through old age or long illness.'[10]

For a long time Bethlem was the only charitable or public hospital for the mentally ill. In the 18th century there was a rapid growth in the foundation of private madhouses, usually in converted premises, but few other asylums were established for the poor. One of the earliest was the Bethel Hospital, founded in Norwich in 1712 by Mary Chapman, whose concern for the plight of lunatics arose from her experience of mental instability amongst her relatives.[11] In that year a contract was drawn up by her agent with Richard Starling, carpenter, and Edward Freeman, mason, to build the hospital, which was to care for lunatics (as opposed to congenital idiots or the merely simple-minded), from the Norwich area. Bethel hospital is of two storeys and attics constructed of red brick with a tiled roof (Fig 154). The original plans do not survive but the hospital seems to have been U-shaped, the wings extending north towards the street. Inside there is little evidence of the original arrangements, but the building contract of 1712 specified that there should be a central passage with three rooms on either side and a similar arrangement on the first floor. Projecting south wings were added in the mid 18th century, one of them containing the committee-room. The north side of the hospital was obscured by a new wing built in 1899.

In London, St Luke's Hospital for Lunatics, established in 1750, became a notable rival of Bethlem. George Dance the elder provided the design for this austere symmetrical building of three storeys with minimal Palladian details.[12] The hospital was intended originally for just twenty-five patients who were to be of the 'middle classes', appealing to those 'not rich enough to send their relations to private institutions and too proud to allow them to be classed as parish poor'.[13] In 1753 the number of inmates was increased to seventy and the building was enlarged in 1754. By 1780 it housed about eighty curable and thirty incurable patients, but in that year a site was acquired for a new building in Old Street. Dance's son, also George, was requested to draw up plans, and the most economical of his designs was adopted. Built in 1782–7, this long, roughly rectangular building of three storeys had a forbidding aspect, with tier upon tier of windows set in relieving arches (Fig 155).

In the central block the ground floor was given over to the offices of the master and apothecary, a dining-room and visitors' room. On the first floor were the committee-room, a waiting-room and physicians' office, and on the upper floor were five bedrooms, presumably for staff. The wings on either side of this central

Figure 154
This general view of
Bethel Hospital,
Norwich, shows the
south elevation with the
wings that were added
in the mid 18th century.
The central range is part
of the original hospital,
dating from 1712.
[NMR BB92/7007]

section contained the patients' accommodation (Fig 156). John Howard, the prison and hospital reformer, noted that there were:

> on each of the three floors, three long galleries and
> wings, with opposite cells for the patients ... in
> each gallery there are thirty-two cells which are
> arched, boarded and wainscoted (ten feet four
> inches by eight, and thirteen feet three inches high)
> and each cell has a window outward, and a large
> aperture over the door, with inside wire lattice to
> the iron bars, to prevent accidents, and (very
> properly) no shutters.[14]

The galleries were 15 ft wide and each contained a privy and two sitting-rooms, one for quiet and the other for turbulent patients. Water was supplied to the galleries from cisterns in the attics, which were filled by 'four machines or forcing pumps', and there was also a 'new, but very inconvenient bath'.[15]

From the mid 18th century further asylums were established, including those at Manchester (*c* 1766), Newcastle (1767), and Liverpool (1792). Those at Manchester and Liverpool were founded in connection with the general infirmaries there. The most notorious of the early asylums, however, was that built in York in 1772–6 (Fig 157), designed by John Carr with accommodation for fifty-four patients. Carr's experience of building

large Palladian houses, such as Harewood, is reflected in the principal elevation, which also closely resembled his earlier design for Leeds Infirmary. The main front at York was dominated by a Tuscan portico over the central three bays, and the *piano nobile* was defined by round-headed windows. The central entrance gave access to a broad axial corridor with a window at each end, and the main stair in the centre. (The stair was later moved to a new wing built to the north.) The first ten patients were admitted in 1777 at a charge of 8s per week. From the beginning it had been intended that the asylum should be for the benefit of pauper lunatics but by 1784 difficulties in funding led the governors to agree to take in a limited number of higher-class patients paying inflated fees. Although the asylum had been established with good intentions, and its rules of management had attempted to safeguard against abuses, by the last decade of the 18th century conditions were appalling and the management corrupt.

The suspicious death of a member of the Society of Friends, Hannah Mills, while a patient at the York Lunatic Asylum, prompted local Quakers to set up their own institution in the city in 1792. The Retreat (Fig 158), financed and administered by Quakers, was intended as

'a retired Habitation, with necessary advice, attendance, &c. for the Members of our Society ... who may be in a state of Lunacy, or so deranged in mind (not Idiots) as to require such provision'.[16] The plans for this influential asylum were drawn up by a little-known architect and builder from London, John Bevans, a Quaker himself. Bevans worked closely with William Tuke, the principal founder, to produce an unpretentious building with a plan similar to the York Lunatic Asylum. The plan was not remarkable, and was criticised by James Bevans (who may, or may not, have been a relation) in his evidence to the Parliamentary Select Committee on Madhouses in England of 1815.[17] It was rather the humane treatment, or 'moral management', of the patients which attracted attention. Indeed, Samuel Tuke, grandson of The Retreat's founder,

claimed that 'an inferior plan well executed may be more beneficial than a better system, under neglected management'.[18]

Apart from the Tukes, one of the most influential figures in the early history of asylum building was Dr Edward Fox, who established a private asylum, Brislington House, near Bristol, in about 1804. To provide distinct classification of the patients, the asylum was designed as a group of detached houses, with each class inhabiting a different house with its own garden court where the patients could take their exercise. These courts were thoughtfully laid out with both the security and the enjoyment of the patients in mind: 'the ground ... is elevated, so that they can view the surrounding country, while a border sloping towards the wall secures them from an escape.'[19] This was an arrangement which

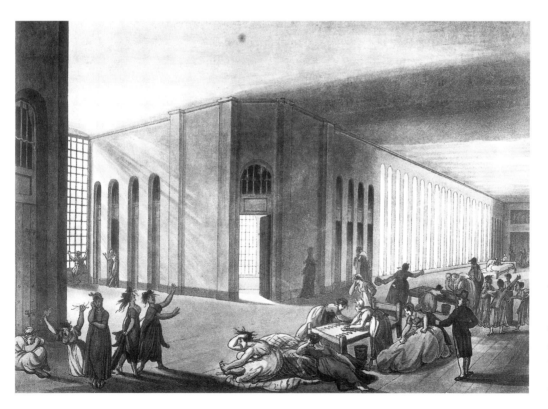

Figure 155
Engraving of the principal elevation of St Luke's Hospital, Old Street, London, built in 1782–7 to designs by George Dance the younger. The hospital remained on this site until 1917, when the building became the Bank of England's printing-works. It remained in the Bank's occupation until 1956, but has now been demolished.
[Wellcome Institute Library, London, V13204]

Figure 156
This aquatint by Thomas Rowlandson of c 1809 depicts one of the galleries in St Luke's Hospital, London.
[Wellcome Institute Library, London, V13209]

Figure 157
General view of the principal elevation of the York Lunatic Asylum (now Bootham Park Hospital), erected in 1772–6 to designs by John Carr. In the background, on the right-hand side of the photograph, can be seen part of the north wing added in 1817 for female patients, one of many later additions on the site.
[NMR BB94/990]

featured in many later county asylums. (The separate houses at the Brislington asylum subsequently were joined together and remodelled.)

In addition, small houses on each side of the asylum served as infirmaries and some detached houses on the estate were used for 'members of the nobility' who were accommodated 'with servants from the institution'. Brislington House was also notable as an early instance of fireproof construction: the staircases, doors, joists, and window-frames were all made of iron and the floors of a composition of stucco and plaster of Paris.[20]

Fox's use of separate houses may have been inspired by French asylums, notably La Salpêtrière in Paris. The latter had been extended in 1786 by François Viel, who designed a series of *loges* or detached blocks. These were assigned to different categories of patients, as at Bristol, but the *loges* were all built to the same design and were of one storey. Railings between the blocks further separated the curable, incurable, melancholy, agitated, idiots, escapees and 'sowers of discord'.[21]

The Rise of the County Asylum

At the beginning of the 19th century many private institutions for the insane had poor reputations. In 1809 Andrew Duncan the younger, who, like his father, was a physician and professor at Edinburgh University, commented that:

In reality excellent private madhouses are to be met with, in various parts of the country, but ... some of them are disgraceful nuisances and they are liable to the greatest abuses. From improper construction, being almost never built on purpose, they are deficient in accommodation for the patients, and insufficient for public security. Instances of lunatics escaping from private madhouses do not infrequently occur; while, on the other hand, unnecessary, or hurtful coercion must often be employed, to make up for the defects of the building.[22]

It was the gradual awareness of the terrible conditions prevailing in some of the existing asylums, and particularly in the numerous private madhouses (primarily run for profit), which finally provoked a call for legislation to safeguard the welfare of lunatics. Prior to the 19th century, the law had little to do with the mentally ill. The Vagrancy Act of 1744,[23] which had amended the law relating to rogues, vagabonds, and other 'idle and disorderly persons', had enabled Justices of the Peace to apprehend pauper lunatics and have them confined, if necessary in chains, 'in some secure place'. In addition, there was an Act for Regulating Private Madhouses of 1774,[24] but this only related to the London area and was principally concerned with protecting wealthy sane people from being locked up by scheming relatives. The only other legislation relating to the care of the insane in existence at the beginning of the 19th century was the Criminal

Lunatics Act of 1800,[25] which merely suggested that criminals proven insane might be detained 'at His Majesty's pleasure'.

Parliament's first genuine attempt to address the question of the care of the insane was made in 1807, when a Select Committee was appointed to enquire into the state of criminal and pauper lunatics in England and Wales. The Committee was chaired by Charles Williams-Wynn, then Under Secretary of State for the Home Department, and his efforts, together with those of the group of fellow humanitarians who formed the Committee, resulted in the County Asylums Act of 1808.[26] Wynn's Act allowed counties to establish asylums for pauper lunatics but did not make such provision mandatory, and gave no assistance to architects regarding the design of suitable buildings. It did, however, insist upon the provision of regular divine service for the inmates, largely as a result of Dr Fox's evidence that it had a beneficial and calming effect. Fox claimed that Brislington House was the first to establish such a service.[27]

Over a dozen county asylums were established in the thirty years after Wynn's Act. At first, architects had to look to existing institutions, and authorities such as Dr Fox, for inspiration. The Chairman of the Committee of Governors for Nottingham County Asylum, Dr Storer, corresponded with Fox on several points of asylum building. He queried the use of iron for fireproofing, the need for galleries, and methods of ventilation. Dr Fox was warm in his praise of iron used in construction, which he considered 'did not only serve to alleviate the dangers from fire, but also from lice and vermin'. However, he was against galleries, condemning those he had seen at asylums in London, York, Manchester and Liverpool, as 'cold and comfortless, subject to currents of cold air without the cheering influence of light and heat from the sun'.[28]

Nevertheless, Richard Ingleman's design for the Nottingham County Asylum was basically of the Bethlem type, or corridor plan. Erected in 1810–12, it comprised on each floor 'a long and airy corridore, which leads to each range of cells, airy, cool and comfortable, and affording accommodation for fifty-six patients'.[29] A greater attempt seems to have been made to classify patients than hitherto: 'its general plan is to provide separate and distinct wards for male and female lunatics, distributed into classes, as well as for the convalescents and incurables, and also separate and distinct airing grounds for the male and female convalescents.'[30] There were three classes of patients: parish paupers, second-class patients with limited means, and first-class patients in affluent circumstances who enjoyed better accommodation, 'with a separate table'.[31] Although the asylum opened in February 1812, a system of heating and ventilation was not installed until 1816.

Early improvements included a boundary wall, which put a stop to 'those insults and interruptions which were formerly offered to the patients from the road', and the introduction of basic occupational therapy in the form of knitting, cotton-winding and such like.[32] As with many of the earlier, relatively small asylums, the number of patients seeking admission steadily rose. Continued overcrowding led to the establishment of a separate asylum for first and second-class patients which opened in 1859 as the Coppice Hospital. A further asylum was erected for the Borough of Nottingham in 1875–80 and a new county asylum was built in 1899–1902. The original asylum was subsequently demolished. This pattern of development is mirrored in most English counties.

Figure 158
General view of the main elevation of The Retreat, York, designed by John Bevans, and erected c 1792, showing the asylum as first built. Although much of the original building remains, there have been many alterations and additions, the earliest of which date from about 1800.
[NMR BB91/17035]

Figure 159
Elevation and plan of the new Bethlem Hospital built at St George's Fields, Southwark, in 1812–15, designed by James Lewis. The combination of single cells and galleries had been established in the earlier Bethlem Hospital, and remained typical of asylums built during the early and mid 19th century. This arrangement was generally termed the 'corridor plan', as the galleries also served as the main corridors.
[PP 1814–15 (296), IV.801, 1031, pl vii, (British Library, BS Ref 1/4, pl VII)]

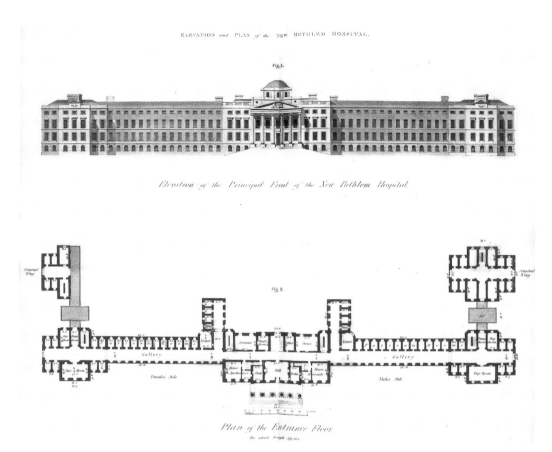

As the Nottingham County Asylum was being completed, a new Bethlem Hospital was rising in St George's Fields (Fig 159). Robert Hooke's building had fallen into a sad state of repair, and a competition for the design of a new building was held in 1810, James Lewis, the hospital's surveyor, drawing up the final plans and elevations, based on the three winning designs.[33] The opening of the new asylum coincided with the publication of the Select Committee Report on Madhouses in England of 1815, in which it was condemned by James Bevans. He was critical of the asylum's excessive expense, which he believed was occasioned by 'the very unnecessary thickness of its walls', and he thought that many of the apartments were extremely gloomy, particularly those overshadowed by the 'immense portico that is in front of the building'. Other objections included inadequate classification of the patients due to an absence of separate staircases to each of the galleries, the lack of glass in the major part of the windows in the patients' sleeping-rooms, and the way in which the front windows were closed up, preventing the patients from looking out of them. In addition he considered that the fireproofing was inadequate and the privies were badly positioned.[34]

In design, the new Bethlem Hospital was neither so very different, nor so very much worse, than other asylums built both before and after. It followed the accepted corridor plan, with a central administration block flanked by the patients' accommodation, arranged with a gallery on one side and single cells on the other. At the extreme ends of the building were short wings with cells on both sides of a central corridor, and a small block for criminal lunatics was also planned with cells on both sides. A chapel was provided under the shallow dome which originally crowned the building. This 'species of pumpkin-shaped cupola' attracted the attention of the Government in 1812, when it was proposed that a semaphore should be erected upon it to warn of attack from France.[35] The dome was rebuilt in 1844–6 to designs by Sydney Smirke when the chapel was enlarged.[36]

In the 20th century Bethlem relocated once more when extensive new buildings were erected in 1928–30 at Monks Orchard, Croydon. After the move, parts of the old building were demolished before it became home to the Imperial War Museum.

The ease with which criminal lunatics had been accommodated at Bethlem Hospital, where they were provided with the same type of accommodation as the rest of the inmates,

is indicative of the close relation between early asylum plans and prison design. This was the inevitable result of the need to supervise a large number of often violent patients by a small number of untrained staff, and it was thus that Jeremy Bentham's writings expounding the principle of the panopticon were adopted and adapted by both prison and asylum architects.[37] The panopticon comprised a circular tower with a central core from which the overseer could observe not only the prisoners, who were placed in cells in a circle around him, but also the other keepers. One circular asylum, the Narrenthurm, was built in Vienna in 1784. This massive tower, of five storeys with a yard in the centre, provided 250 beds in a combination of wards and single cells, with a corridor running around the inner wall from which the cells radiated outwards.

In both prisons and asylums the panopticon principle was most satisfactorily realised when transformed into the radial plan, where a central hub, occupied by the staff, was surrounded by wings containing galleries and cells for the patients. A remarkable and early example of a building for lunatics planned on the radial principle was built at Guy's Hospital in London (Fig 160). From its foundation it had been intended that Guy's should admit lunatics, a class of patient excluded from the nearby St Thomas's. In 1797 a detached block for lunatics was erected on the south side of the main building. It had just two short wings containing the patients' accommodation, set at an angle to the central ancillary rooms. The plan, reproduced in the Parliamentary Select Committee Report of 1815, impressed James Bevans, who considered it to be the best building for the insane in or near London. Its greatest defects seemed to be a lack of classification of the patients within the building, hardly surprising considering its size, and the lack of heating in the patients' bedrooms.[38]

The first asylum with a fully developed radial plan was erected in Glasgow in 1810 to designs by William Stark.[39] It comprised a central tower containing the offices and keepers' apartments from which radiated four wings, with single cells on one side and galleries on the other. Although comparable radial plans were later adapted for workhouses and prisons, the only fully radial asylum erected in England was the Cornwall Lunatic Asylum at Bodmin, designed by John Foulston (Fig 161). Built between 1817 and 1820, the asylum comprised six wings radiating from a polygonal hub with an administration block on the south-east side containing the main

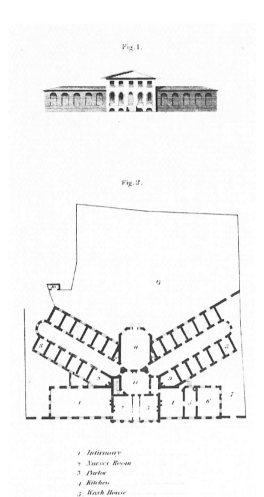

Figure 160
Elevation and plan of the lunatics' block built at Guy's Hospital, London, in 1797. The building was demolished in the early 20th century to make way for the electrical and massage department.
[PP 1814–15 (296), IV.801, 1031, pl iii, (British Library, BS Ref 1/4, pl III)]

Fig.1.

Fig.2.

1 Infirmary
2 Nurses Room
3 Parlor
4 Kitchen
5 Wash House
6 Drying Room
7 Drying Ground
8 Rooms for Washing of Patients
9 Keepers Sleeping Rooms
10 Water Closets
11 Patients Day Room
12 Matrons Day Room
13 Airing Ground

entrance. The asylum had sufficient accommodation for approximately 112 patients who were classed as pauper, subscription and superior.[40] Convalescent cases were allocated the ground floor of one wing and 'the incurable or worst description of patients' were separated from the rest of the inmates. Incontinent patients were allocated a small dormitory at the end of a wing, and cells for the violent or noisy were also kept at a distance.[41]

Supervision was the keynote of the design, in keeping with Benthamite principles. The keepers' rooms had an inspection window from which the keeper could overlook the dayroom and the gallery. In addition, the keepers were themselves kept under the supervision of

*Figures 161 and 162
Ground-floor plan and
section of the Cornwall
Lunatic Asylum (later St
Lawrence's Hospital),
Bodmin, designed by
John Foulston and built
in 1817–20. Foulston's
section demonstrates the
ease with which each
wing could be kept under
surveillance by the
governor and matron.
[Plan (1:1000) redrawn
from Foulston 1838; elevation and section, British
Library 560* e30, Foulston
1838, pls 104,106]*

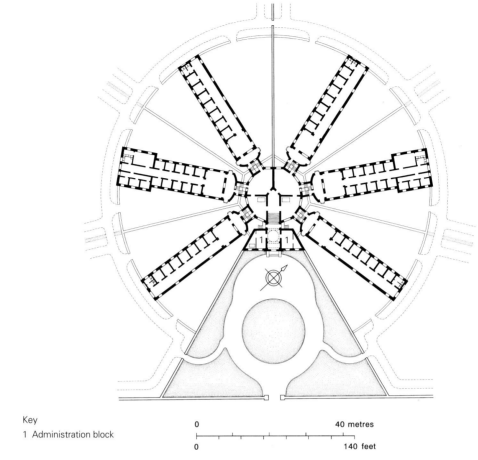

Key
1 Administration block

0   40 metres

0   140 feet

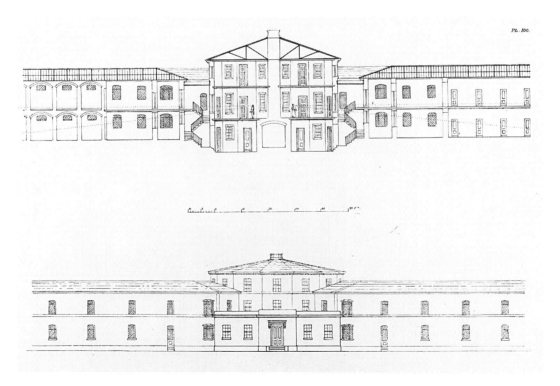

the governor and matron through a further series of inspection windows in their apartments in the central hub. This point was neatly illustrated by Foulston's section which includes the figures of the governor and matron with dotted lines showing the extent of their view (Fig 162).

Although radial plans were proposed for subsequent asylums, such as the double radial submitted in the competition for the proposed Middlesex Asylum in 1827, they were never adopted. The last asylum to be built on a variation of the radial plan was the Devon County Asylum at Exminster (Fig 163). It was designed in about 1842 by Charles Fowler, who attempted to combine the advantages of radial plans, where all the patients' apartments were within easy reach of the administrative centre, with the corridor plan, which was less cramped. The administrative offices were placed at the centre, surrounded on three sides by a U-shaped range from which six wings radiated. The wings contained the patients' single cells, a gallery, and two wards at the end with five and seven beds in each.

A more widely copied plan-type in the early 19th century was that devised by the well-established York-based architects, Charles Watson & James Pigott Pritchett, for the West Riding Pauper Lunatic Asylum at Wakefield. The County Magistrates held a competition for the design in 1816, for which Samuel Tuke drew up the instructions and which he helped to assess. Tuke emphasised that architects should pay strict attention to facilities for the inspection of both the patients and the attendants. In preparation for the task, Watson and Pritchett visited 'several of the best constructed asylums in the Kingdom, particularly the celebrated one at Glasgow'.[42]

Figure 163
This aerial photograph of the Devon County Asylum, Exminster, clearly shows its unusual plan, with the patients' accommodation ranges radiating outwards from the central administrative and service buildings. The asylum (later Exe Vale Hospital) was designed by Charles Fowler and built in 1842–5.
[NMR BB95/10489]

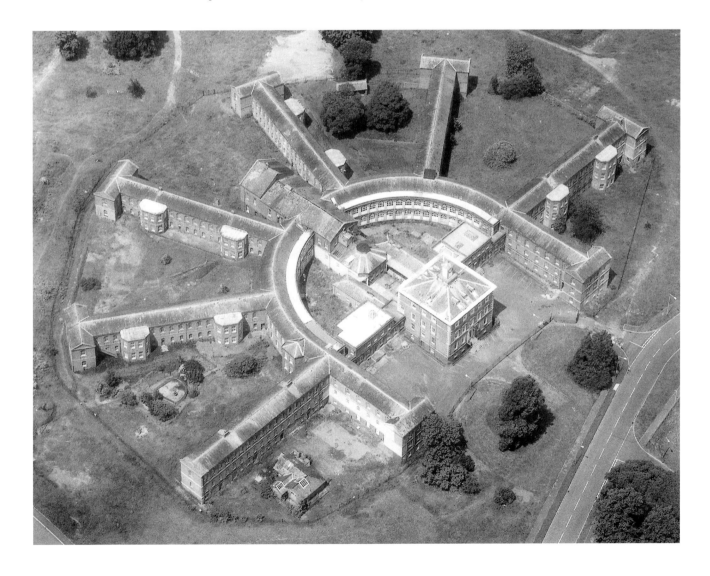

Figure 165 (opposite)
The administration
block of the Surrey
County Asylum (later
Springfield Hospital),
Wandsworth, London.
The asylum was built in
1838–41 to designs by
William Moseley, and
was greatly extended
over the succeeding
decades.
[NMR BB91/25936]

The Wakefield asylum was designed on an H-shaped plan to contain 150 pauper lunatics, with an equal number of each sex (Fig 164). The central range, on a roughly east–west axis, contained the main entrance and the apartments of the superintendent and matron. At each end were octagonal towers with a spiral stair at the centre, echoing Stark's central tower at Glasgow. The wings extending from the tower to the north and south contained the usual combination of single cells on one side with a gallery on the other.

A number of later asylums were modelled on Wakefield. Elements of it can be traced in the winning plans by William Alderson of 1827 for the Middlesex Asylum at Hanwell, particularly the octagonal towers. William Burn used it as the model for the Crichton Royal Asylum in Dumfries of 1834, and similar features were adopted by R N Clark for the Oxford County Asylum of 1844.

While Wynn's Act prompted the establishment of many county pauper asylums, charitable and private asylums continued to be founded for the mentally afflicted who were able to pay something towards their care. The Lawn, an asylum at Lincoln, was established by the physicians and surgeons of the County Hospital to care for patients of educated and cultured backgrounds with modest means.[43] Richard Ingleman, architect of the Nottingham County Asylum, drew up plans for the new building *c* 1818. Of three storeys with flanking two-storey wings, The Lawn closely echoed The Retreat, although an Ionic portico on the south elevation provided an air of greater distinction.

Contemporary with The Lawn was an asylum built at Oxford under the aegis of the Radcliffe Infirmary for indigent, but not pauper, lunatics.

Richard Ingleman was once more the architect selected; he surveyed the original location chosen for the asylum in 1813 and provided the plans for the final site, acquired between 1819 and 1821. Ingleman's design was almost identical to The Lawn, the bow-windowed keepers' rooms and central apartment on the north elevation being distinctive features of both.

As the 19th century progressed the benefits of establishing a county asylum became more widely appreciated and new asylums tended to be planned on a larger scale. When the Surrey County Asylum opened in 1841 it provided nearly 350 beds. It was designed in 1838 by William Moseley, surveyor to the County of Middlesex, who had previously designed the Middlesex House of Correction.[44] The central administrative section (Fig 165) had a chapel on the first floor, and was flanked by wings containing the patients' accommodation designed on the usual corridor plan. The numerous ancillary and service buildings were indicative of the increasing self-sufficiency of asylums and included a kitchen, scullery, stores, boiler and engine houses, blacksmith's shop, laundry, wash-house, coal store, and mortuary. In addition there were workrooms in the basement at the far ends of the main building. In the grounds there were kitchen gardens and orchards, and old farm buildings on the edge of the site were retained, providing therapeutic work for the inmates, as well as provisions for the institution.

The Lunatic Asylums Act of 1842,[45] together with the consolidating Act of 1845,[46] made the provision of asylums for pauper lunatics compulsory, and instituted a body of Commissioners in Lunacy who were to inspect all asylums and madhouses twice a year. By 1850 about fifteen large new asylums, designed on the corridor

Figure 164
General view of the West
Riding Pauper Lunatic
Asylum at Wakefield
(later Stanley Royd
Hospital), West
Yorkshire, designed by
Watson & Pritchett and
built in 1816–18.
[Photograph from
University of St Andrews
Library]

plan, had either been built or were in the course of erection. The Somerset County Asylum at Wells of 1844–7 is one of the more architecturally distinguished examples (Fig 166). Scott & Moffatt employed a Jacobean style for the pinkish-brown stone buildings with their greyish-yellow ashlar dressings. The chapel, added in about 1870, has the unusual feature of covered bridges linking it to the main building.

Colney Hatch Asylum, the second to be provided for the county of Middlesex, was one of the most widely publicised of this period (Fig 167). It closely reflected the writings of John Conolly, Medical Superintendent of Hanwell Asylum and champion of the humane treatment of lunatics by methods of non-restraint:

> Among the various forms of asylums adopted by architects, I believe there is none so convenient as one in which the main part of the building is in one line ... a building of this shape, long and narrow, consisting of a succession of galleries or corridors, with bedrooms on one side only, may be moderately perflated by every wind that blows – an advantage extremely salutary to those who pass their whole time in it.[47]

Colney Hatch included a number of innovations in its plan. Indeed, much of its renown rested on its exceptionally long corridor, measuring well over a quarter of a mile and running along the entire north front (Fig 168).[48] The staff were to traipse along this corridor to get from one end of the building to the other, and avoid using the patients' galleries for this purpose, thus allowing the galleries to become more akin to day-rooms.

Colney Hatch was designed in 1848 by S W Daukes, a pupil of J P Pritchett, and was the focus of a lengthy debate on whether two or three storeys were preferable in such an institution. Conolly recommended no more than two storeys and a maximum of 300 to 400 patients. Such advice was all too often abandoned when cost-conscious committees, faced with growing numbers of patients, chose to extend existing asylums rather than build new ones. Thus, once-manageable buildings grew to colossal proportions.

The building which most closely followed Conolly's idea of the perfectly planned asylum was that erected near Mickleover for the county of Derby, where he was able to advise the

Figure 167
Colney Hatch Asylum (later Friern Hospital), London Borough of Barnet, designed by S W Daukes and built in 1848–51.
[NMR 4898/55]

Figure 166 (opposite)
The administration block of the Somerset County Asylum (later Tone Vale Hospital), Wells, designed by Scott & Moffatt and built in 1844–7.
[NMR BB91/26006]

Figure 168
View along the main corridor of Colney Hatch Asylum. The honeycomb-vaulted ceiling was a type of fireproof construction which was also employed at other hospitals of the mid 19th century.
[NMR BB92/24348]

building committee. His recommendations covered most aspects of design, from the size of the galleries – which he considered should be large enough to allow the patients to dine in – to the proportion of single rooms to dormitories.[49] The building committee did not, however, rely completely on his advice. Its members also visited existing asylums at Wakefield, Nottingham and Gloucester, and adopted the same ventilation system as several other recently erected public buildings (see pages 9–10).[50] The plans for Derby County Asylum were drawn up by Henry Duesbury in 1844, but various delays affected the progress of the building which did not open until 1851. It was thought to be the first asylum to be designed with a recreation hall, and, like Colney Hatch, had corridors for the staff, to avoid using the galleries as common passageways. Aesthetically, Duesbury claimed that he had 'aimed to individualize each [wing], to give to each an expression of homeliness, to produce shady spaces and warm corners, and to avoid the oppressiveness, to those who inhabit the building, of a grand façade and gigantic institution'.[51]

The corridor plan continued to evolve slowly through the 1850s. The Sussex County Asylum at Haywards Heath, designed in 1856 and completed in 1859, comprised large day-rooms, distinct from the old galleries, and dormitories in addition to single rooms. The introduction of dormitories was considered to be an improvement 'calculated to promote as far as possible the comfort of the unhappy inmates', as it allowed groups of quieter patients to be separated from the rest.[52] Turbulent cases were further removed to a separate one-storey block. All the main wards and day-rooms faced south, commanding fine views of the South Downs. The asylum was designed by Henry Edward Kendall, its Italianate polychromatic elevations contrasting with his earlier Tudor-style asylum of 1849 at Warley in Essex. For pauper asylums, the style of the buildings was usually of little consequence, so long as they were cheap.

The Sussex County Asylum seems to have been the first designed with a detached chapel from the outset (Fig 169). Whilst the Commissioners in Lunacy insisted on the provision of a chapel, it was not until 1887 that they recommended that it should be detached (see pages 175–6). For the Sussex Asylum chapel, Kendall adopted a similar northern Italian Gothic style to the main building, in polychrome brick, complete with striped campanile and Lego-like cornices.

The asylum's medical superintendent, C Lockhart Robertson, was particularly proud of its convenient site:

A large number of the English county asylums have the disadvantage of an isolated site; the Essex is the only asylum I can recall, which is less than three or four miles from the county town, and in this instance it is near that poor little place Brentwood, instead of Colchester or Ipswich. Four miles, and the worst road in England, lie between the county asylum and the city of Oxford; the Cambridge Asylum is [a] good four miles from that seat of learning, and so also the asylum at Michelover [sic] from Derby, Bracebridge from Lincoln, &c., &c.[53]

In contrast, the Sussex County Asylum was close to a central railway station and 'within an hour's ride of the great metropolis, which is after all, the centre of everything in England'.[54] Proximity to a railway became a prerequisite for county asylums from the later 19th century, when they were invariably situated well away from any towns or cities. Indeed, it was common for asylums to establish their own branch line, either for the convenience of transporting patients and staff or for the delivery of supplies, in particular coal to stoke the great boiler houses that served these vast institutions.

Despite the rapid increase in the provision of asylums throughout the country during the 19th century, particularly following the passing of the Lunacy Acts of the 1840s, private asylums continued to fulfil the need for paying patients whose relatives and friends sought more congenial surroundings for them. Coton Hill Asylum, Stafford, designed by Fulljames & Waller, opened in 1854 'on a scale suitable to various classes of society'.[55] In fact there were three classes of accommodation offered: high-class patients occupied suites of apartments (including rooms for their private attendants or servants and a private garden); second-class patients were provided with single bedrooms and a communal gallery, as well as a sitting-room, library, dining-room and billiard-room, music-room and drawing-room;[56] and for third-class patients there were simpler galleries with associated sleeping-rooms.

Wonford House at Exeter was similarly planned. An imposing Jacobean-style stone building, it was erected in 1865–9 to replace the nearby St Thomas's Lunatic Asylum for private patients. The plans were prepared by William F Cross for 120 inmates whose accommodation was arranged in suites of rooms to one side of the principal corridor, with most of the bedrooms and dormitories on the upper floors.

Although a greater degree of ornament might be expected in private asylums than in pauper asylums, the Royal Holloway Sanatorium surpasses all expectations. Founded by Thomas Holloway, of Holloway's Pills fame, the asylum was established for the 'unsuccessful of the middle classes', and sumptuous apartments with lavish decoration were provided for their accommodation.[57] The architect William Henry Crossland designed this vast Gothic pile, erected in 1879–84 on high ground near Egham in Surrey, with an imposing entrance block modelled on the Cloth Hall at Ypres (Fig 170). The plan is less remarkable than the ornamentation of its principal apartments (Fig 171). The walls and ceilings of the entrance hall, grand staircase, dining-hall and recreation hall were covered with paintings, gilding, 'arabesques' and panelled tracery.[58]

Private philanthropy was also responsible for the first asylums for idiots and imbeciles, that is, for those who were classed as mentally deficient rather than mentally ill. In the same way that specialist hospitals were established to provide for patients excluded from general hospitals, asylums for idiots were established to provide for a class of patient generally excluded from

the county asylums. In a letter to Williams-Wynn published in the Select Committee Report of 1807, Dr Halliday noted that in Suffolk, 'with regard to the Idiots, I may observe that the greater part of them are kept in the workhouses as common paupers, without receiving any more than common attention, and without being separated from the general mass'.[59] The Poor Law Amendment Act of 1834[60] attempted to address the problem by preventing dangerous lunatics, insane persons or idiots from being detained in a workhouse for more than fourteen days. However, as this was generally interpreted as applying to dangerous cases only, many quiet and chronic cases continued to be lodged there.

The plight of idiot children was particularly pressing, but the earliest efforts to provide for them came from individual philanthropists. Dr Andrew Reed was one of the first to devote his energies to this cause. A remarkable man, he founded a number of asylums for orphans in the London area as well as the Royal Home and Hospital for Incurables, in Surrey. In 1847

Figure 169
The chapel at Sussex County Asylum, Haywards Heath, designed by H E Kendall and built as part of the large asylum complex of 1856–9.

[NMR BB93/20771]

Figures 170 and 171
The photograph on the left shows the main entrance block of the Royal Holloway Sanatorium; the tall traceried windows at first-floor level lit the the recreation hall, the lavish interior of which is pictured above. The building was designed by W H Crossland and built in 1879–84. Both of these photographs were taken in the early 1980s following the hospital's closure, after which the building remained empty for many years. The condition of the fine interiors drastically deteriorated but recently a major scheme has taken place to convert the surviving buildings into private residences. The former chapel now houses a sports hall, and an indoor swimming-pool has been inserted into the former dining-hall.[NMR BB83/5908 and 5922]

Figure 172
General view of the principal elevation of Royal Earlswood Asylum (now Royal Earlswood Hospital), Reigate, Surrey, designed by W B Moffatt and built in 1852–5.
[NMR BB93/5107]

he 'conceived the idea of attempting to ameliorate the condition of the most helpless of all afflicted human beings – the idiot',[61] and in the following year he established a small asylum in a house in Highgate. This modest beginning soon led to the erection of an impressive and vast specialist asylum in Surrey, originally known as the National Model Asylum for Idiots, later the Royal Earlswood (Fig 172). It was designed in 1852, in the style of the prodigy houses of the late Elizabethan and Jacobean period, by W B Moffatt, whose partnership with Scott had been dissolved in 1846. Erected with considerable financial aid from the London livery companies, it was officially opened by Prince Albert in July 1855 and provided accommodation for 400 inmates.

Idiots were usually considered to be incurable and incapable of improvement. However, Reed's model asylum was designed not only 'to afford shelter to the helpless sufferer; but by the application of the best scientific and medical skill to elevate him to physical enjoyment and rational life'.[62] Reed travelled extensively throughout Britain, on the Continent and in America, in the hope of finding other institutions where progress had been made in the treatment of idiots, but met with little success. The system which he devised comprised an attempt at education in the schoolroom and physical exercise in the gymnasium. He was also a pioneer of industrial therapy, providing workshops in 1861 'where the world's outcasts are taught by skilled instructors in carpentry, shoemaking, tailoring, mat-weaving, basket-making, brick-laying and household work'.[63] Farm labouring was also encouraged.

Reed's example was followed with the establishment of other such charitable asylums. The grandeur of the Royal Albert Asylum in Lancaster similarly served to advertise the charity. This imposing building, which operated on the model of Earlswood, was designed by Edward Graham Paley in 1867. In the following year Dr John Haydon Langdon-Down founded Normansfield Hospital as a private sanatorium for mentally afflicted children of aristocratic or wealthy parentage. Normansfield was established in an unfinished house near the Thames at Hampton Wick. It was completed and adapted by Rowland Plumbe, whose additions included a lavishly decorated entertainment hall of 1877. In effect a private theatre, its provision reflected the interest in amateur theatricals of the Langdon-Down family. Langdon-Down himself had been the medical superintendent at Earlswood from 1858. He pioneered the study and classification of mental handicap, giving his name to Down's Syndrome.

The Evolution of Asylum Design in the Later 19th and Early 20th Centuries

Throughout the 19th century the number of certified lunatics steadily increased. No matter how many more asylums were erected, further accommodation was always required. The reasons for this apparent increase in insanity are open to debate;[64] the consequence, however, was straightforward – more asylums were erected, and existing ones were extended. New asylums tended to be larger than before, and as their size and the number of their inmates rose the easier it became to provide discrete accommodation for the different classes of patients, resulting in further experiments in planning.

From the 1860s pavilion planning dominated the design of hospitals for the physically ill, and in asylums too, its influence is noticeable. Only a very few asylums were built to an outright pavilion plan, and these had a limited function, admitting only quiet, chronic cases or the mentally handicapped. Experience had shown that quieter patients did not need to be confined to single rooms, but benefited from being accommodated in larger wards or dormitories. The first asylums devoted entirely to pauper imbeciles were therefore built to a variation of the pavilion plan. This essentially comprised broad ward pavilions, where, instead of two rows of beds placed along the long walls, four rows were packed in, with an iron screen along the

centre separating the two additional central rows (Fig 173). In this way, as many as 80 beds could be provided in one ward or dormitory. As the inmates were not physically ill, official recommendations concerning the cubic feet of air per person in medical or surgical wards were ignored in favour of the less generous allowance for workhouse dormitories (see Chapter 4). Indeed, broad ward or dormitory pavilions of this type were erected at many of the larger urban workhouses.

The Commissioners in Lunacy had first turned their attention to the special needs of the large numbers of idiots and imbeciles in about 1859, when they recommended 'the erection of [an] inexpensive building adapted for the residence of idiotic, chronic and harmless patients' which would provide an intermediate type of accommodation, between the workhouse and the curative asylums.[65]

The first pavilion-plan asylums were built at Leavesden and Caterham, established by the newly created Metropolitan Asylums Board (MAB). The MAB was set up to provide asylums for London's pauper lunatics and fever hospitals for paupers suffering from infectious diseases (see page 136). Their asylums at Leavesden and Caterham were both designed in 1868 by John Giles, of Giles & Biven, to provide 1,500 beds. Each large complex was symmetrically planned along a roughly north–south axis. The ward pavilions, of three storeys with hipped roofs and streaky-bacon brickwork, were linked together

Figure 173
This photograph, taken in the 1930s, of a ward at Banstead Asylum in Surrey (now demolished), shows how pavilion wards were adapted for asylums, with four rows of beds crowded into the ward. Banstead was built in 1873–7 as the third Middlesex County Asylum to designs by the County Surveyor, F H Pownall.
[GLRO 26.21 BAN A3611 80/4809]

Figure 174
These four block
plans of asylums
demonstrate the
development of
the échelon plan,
the most widely
adopted plan-type
for asylums in the
late 19th and
early 20th
centuries.

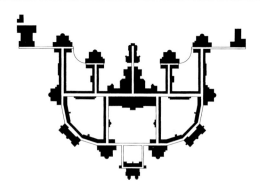

A   The fourth Lancashire County Asylum at Whittingham,
designed by H Littler and built in 1870–3

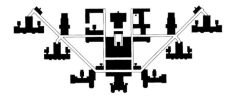

B   Gloucestershire County Asylum, at Barnwood, Gloucester,
designed by John Giles & Gough and built in 1880–3

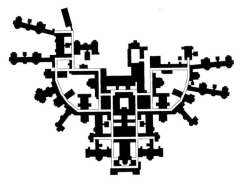

C   The Surrey County Asylum at Cane Hill, designed by
C H Howell and built in 1883–4

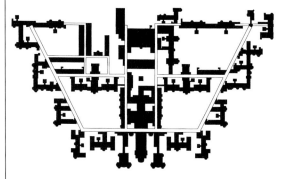

D   Claybury Asylum (later Claybury Hospital), Woodford, London
Borough of Redbridge, designed by G T Hine and built in 1889–93

by single-storey enclosed corridors, and arranged in ranks flanking a central range comprising the administration block, kitchens, stores, laundry and ancillary buildings. This economic model was copied at Banstead Hospital in Surrey, built as an overflow asylum for Middlesex County to accommodate incurable non-dangerous patients. It was reused by the MAB as late as 1899 at Tooting Bec Hospital in Wandsworth as an infirmary for sick imbeciles (later used to accommodate those suffering from senile dementia). Many aspects of pavilion planning were taken up in ordinary asylums, notably the sanitary annexe, which became a standard feature of new designs. Sanitary annexes were also commonly added to existing buildings usually as part of a much-needed overhaul of the sanitation.

The so-called detached block system, which enjoyed something of a vogue in the late 1860s and 1870s, occupies a transitional place between the tried and tested corridor plan and the 'échelon' arrangement. For the second Cheshire County Asylum at Macclesfield, built in 1868–71, Robert Griffiths designed a series of tall villa-like blocks. Arranged in a line along the south front of the complex, their three-bay façades with full-height canted bay windows had quite a convincingly domestic appearance. A series of day-rooms was provided on the ground floor with wards or dormitories above. Henry Littler designed similar villa-like blocks for the fourth Lancashire County Asylum at Whittingham in 1869 (Fig 174A).[66] Indeed, the overall layout of this asylum can be seen as the forerunner of the échelon plan, which, in the late 19th century, was to asylums what the pavilion plan was to general hospitals. Figure 174 gives an indication of how this plan-type evolved.

The first true échelon-plan asylum was designed by John Giles & Gough for the Gloucestershire County Asylum in 1879 (Fig 174B). Here the series of blocks to accommodate the patients was arranged *en échelon* and linked by a single-storey corridor. This arrangement preserved an uninterrupted southern aspect. Each block was designed to meet the requirements of different types of patients. For infirm cases a combination of single rooms, small dormitories, day-rooms and padded rooms was provided on the ground floor, with further dormitories and associated day-rooms above. Epileptics were allocated separate blocks, one containing day-rooms, the other dormitories. These dormitory blocks were placed to the north of the main link corridor, as no view was necessary, and were arranged on the pavilion principle with 60 beds arranged in four tightly

Figure 175
Interior of the recreation
hall at Claybury
Asylum, London
Borough of Redbridge,
designed by G T Hine
and built in 1889–93.
At the other end of the
hall is a stage, with a
grand proscenium arch
topped by a bust of
Shakespeare. The hall
measures 120 ft long,
60 ft wide and 40 ft
high and was designed
to accommodate 1,200
people.
[NMR BB91/17359]

packed rows. Chronic patients were given a combination of day-rooms with dormitories above. In the end Giles & Gough's scheme was never completed, and of the patients' accommodation only the infirmary blocks and one of the epileptic blocks were built.

Cane Hill, the third Surrey County Asylum, was another prototype échelon plan (Fig 174C). It was designed in 1883–4 by Charles Henry Howell, who had been the County Surveyor for Surrey since 1860, and was also architect to the Commissioners in Lunacy. Howell incorporated elements of the earlier Devon County Asylum (see Figure 163), where the patients' pavilions radiated from a semicircular corridor. At Cane Hill the layout was adapted by reshaping each pavilion to suit different classes of patients. Elsewhere, dormitory pavilions for working, chronic or epileptic patients were incorporated to more traditional overall designs.

The first large-scale échelon-plan asylum, accommodating over 2,000 patients, was erected at Claybury, near Woodford, then in Essex (Figs 174B and 9). It was designed in 1887–8 by George T Hine, a prolific asylum architect, as the fourth Middlesex County Asylum. Built on the estate of Claybury Hall, this late 18th-century mansion was converted and extended for private patients. Typically, the asylum was virtually self-sufficient, with its own farm, large kitchens, stores, and

bakery, boiler house and no less than three water towers. At the heart of the asylum was a magnificent recreation hall capable of seating 1,200 patients (Fig 175). The decoration was of high quality, with panelled walls of polished oak and an elliptical ceiling ornamented with Jackson's fibrous plasterwork.[67] Attractive surroundings for the patients had become an integral part of the philosophy of asylum design by the later 19th century, when their beneficial effects on the treatment of mental illness, even for the poorest classes, were widely canvassed:

> The modern treatment of lunacy demands also more provision for the embellishment of the asylum than is to be found in the barrack like interiors of our older institutions. Hence the interior of Claybury Asylum is almost palatial in its finishings, its pitch-pine joinery, marble and tile chimney-pieces, and glazed brick dados, so much so that some of the visitors rather flippantly expressed a desire to become inmates.[68]

Sadly, this philosophy was often lost sight of in the pursuit of strict economy.

The chapel at Claybury was linked to the main complex by a corridor. By 1887 this was against the advice of the Commissioners in Lunacy, who recommended that chapels should be detached and able to hold about three-quarters of the patients: 'It should have the usual character and arrangement of a

Figure 176
The chapel at the City of London Asylum (later Stone House Hospital), Dartford, in Kent, designed by A Murray and built in 1898–1901. The asylum opened in 1866, the original buildings being designed by the City Architect, James Bunning, although many additions and alterations were made later.
[NMR BB92/12164]

church, and contain no special or peculiar provision for the separation of the sexes, though with distinct entrances. Small rooms or lobbies should be provided near the door, to which epileptic patients seized by a fit during service may be removed.'[69] The chapel added to the City of London Asylum, at Dartford, is a particularly good example. It was designed by Andrew Murray and dedicated by the Bishop of Rochester in May 1901. The 'distinct entrances' for men and women are a dominant feature of the west elevation (Fig 176).

The arrival of the échelon plan, which could economically house such large numbers, coincided with the Local Government Act of 1888,[70] which transferred the obligation to provide public asylums from the Justices of the Peace to the new county and borough councils. The increased funding available led to a boom in asylum building, and nearly all adopted the échelon plan. Between 1888 and the First World War, twenty-five were built with this layout – twelve of them designed by Hine. Of the five asylums erected by the London County Council (LCC) on the Horton Estate at Epsom between 1897 and 1924, three featured near-identical

échelon plans. This concentrated 'infliction of insane Londoners upon an unoffending country town' was censured in the press when the fifth of these asylums was being contemplated.[71] At that time there were already about 5,400 patients and 1,000 attendants residing in the asylums at Epsom. Together with staff, the total population of the hospitals still accounted for over 10 per cent of the borough in the 1960s.[72]

Given the rural settings of the majority of asylums, the provision of staff accommodation was imperative. As the size of asylums increased and the size of the staff grew, separate buildings were provided which not only contained sleeping accommodation but day-rooms and mess rooms. Senior staff, such as the medical superintendent and steward, were provided with detached houses set away from the main building. The imposing medical superintendent's house at the Somerset County Asylum is a good example: of two storeys and attics it resembled a private villa of generous proportions (Fig 177). The house was added by Hine in 1901 as part of a general modernisation programme and was intended to free rooms at the heart of

Figure 177
The former Medical
Superintendent's House
built in 1901 to designs
by G T Hine for the
Somerset County Asylum
at Wells (see Figure
166).
[NMR BB92/11842]

the building adjoining the main entrance (the traditional location for senior staff apartments earlier in the century).

Towards the end of the 19th century, a further new plan-type that seemed particularly suitable to epileptics and the mentally handicapped was attracting attention in England. This was generally termed the 'colony system' and comprised detached blocks or villas, which were scattered over the site in an effort to diminish still further an institutional appearance. Asylums designed on the colony system had been developed in Germany in the late 1870s, inspired by the success of the Geel Colony in Belgium, which was said to have originated in medieval times after an Irish Princess was martyred there. She was later canonised and her shrine gained the reputation of curing the insane, whereupon Geel became a place of pilgrimage for lunatics. These lunatic pilgrims were boarded in the village, which gradually developed into a mental colony. The Belgian government intervened in the 19th century to the extent of placing the colony under the control of a Commissioner and a Board of Governors.[73]

Colonies became increasingly popular, both on the Continent and in America, particularly for epileptics. In general, epileptic patients were placid, willing to give assistance to others, and good workers, and were therefore most likely to appreciate and respond to the greater freedom and more home-like surroundings offered by a colony-plan asylum. By the turn of the century the best-known epileptic colonies abroad were Bielefeld in Germany and the Craig Colony, New York. In England, the National Society for the Employment of Epileptics established a home at Chalfont St Peter, Buckinghamshire, in 1884. Originally consisting of a single villa of temporary iron construction, further villas were built later as funds allowed until a substantial colony evolved.

The LCC established St Ebba's Hospital at Epsom along the lines of the Chalfont Colony.[74] The plans were drawn up by the LCC's asylums engineer, William Charles Clifford Smith, and were approved towards the end of 1900. Although it had originally been intended that the colony should be solely for male epileptics, it was decided that a small

number of females should also be accommo-dated. Their presence, the LCC argued, would be beneficial as they would be able to give assis-tance in the kitchen and laundry, and repair clothing. Work was the main emphasis of the colony system; while the women washed and sewed, the male patients were employed full-time on the surrounding farmland. The original complex at St Ebba's was relatively small, providing accommodation for 60 females and 266 males in eight detached villas. These had an attractive appearance, reminiscent of garden-suburbs Arts & Crafts, an association encour-aged by giving each villa the name of a tree.

Similar colonies were founded elsewhere, including the David Lewis Manchester Epileptic Colony of 1900–4 (Fig 178). Substantial funding was provided by the David Lewis Trustees who, in return for their invest-ment, took charge of the planning and erec-tion of the colony. They selected a London architect, Alexander Graham, who had some experience in hospital design (see page 128), and arranged two deputations to visit similar institutions on the Continent and in America. The stockbroker-Tudor style adopted by Graham for this extensive group of largely one and two-storey buildings, gives the colony a

suburban air which is reinforced by the neat paths and clipped lawns between the buildings.

The Idiots Act of 1886[75] had attempted to make the distinction between idiocy and lunacy but it had little tangible effect. At the turn of the century the condition of all those consid-ered to be mentally deficient, whether described as idiots, imbeciles or the feeble-minded, was given fresh consideration. The Elementary Education (Defective and Epileptic Children) Act of 1899[76] instituted a few special schools for mentally deficient children. These were, however, mostly in the London area. Mary Dendy was one of a growing number of people who recognised that residential care for such children was necessary in addition to special education, and it was largely through her efforts that the Sandlebridge Boarding Schools were established at Great Warford in Cheshire. The Manchester architects Walter & George Higginbottom were appointed in 1899 and they drew up plans for a small day-school and two boarding-houses. The houses were completed in 1902, on a site to the north of the David Lewis Colony, and closely echoed the colony in appearance. Each house had a day-room and dining-room on the ground floor, together with kitchen, laundry and staff rooms.

Figure 178
This aerial perspective of the David Lewis Manchester Epileptic Colony at Sandlebridge, Cheshire, shows the neat layout of the villas, administrative and service buildings. The colony was designed by A Graham and built in 1900–4.
[NMR AA92/2114]

Figure 179
A typical row of villas at
the Prudhoe Hall
Colony,
Northumberland,
designed by J H Morton
& J G Burell and built
in 1918–23.
[NMR BB93/20247]

On the first floor there was one large dormitory for the children, together with a sickroom, nurses' room and staff bedrooms.

In 1904 a Royal Commission was appointed to enquire into the care of the feeble-minded. It concluded that delinquency, alcoholism and illegitimate births, which were common amongst the feeble-minded, were conditions exacerbated by the fact that most were left to their own devices within the community. It also considered that although heredity was an important factor in mental deficiency, sterilisation, as advocated by the Eugenics Education Society, should not be contemplated. The Royal Commission's Report was published in 1908 but its recommendations were not taken up until 1913 when the Mental Deficiency Act[77] came into force. Thereafter local authorities were obliged to provide accommodation for 'the care and protection of the mentally deficient classes whose removal from undesirable surroundings is necessary in their own interests and that of society'.[78]

Even by the early years of the 20th century the distinction between mental deficiency and insanity was unclear. For the Mental Deficiency Act to be effective a more precise definition was required. The Royal College of Physicians was consulted and eventually four classes of the mentally deficient were identified and defined: idiots, imbeciles, feeble-minded persons, and moral defectives. In each case the condition must have existed since birth or an early age.[79]

The Orwellian-sounding Board of Control, which replaced the Commissioners in Lunacy as the governing body in 1914, recommended the colony system for new institutions. The Board considered that it allowed 'better classification and training' and ensured that the inmates were happier and more contented than in institutions of the barracks type.[80] Three basic types of accommodation were thought necessary, for children able to attend school or occupation classes; adults capable of work or occupation; and idiots, incapable of anything, the bedridden, very young children and 'chair cases'.[81] Within these groups, further classification was desirable to separate the old from the young, the quiet from the turbulent. A hospital for sick and tubercular cases with separate provision for infectious cases, school buildings, a central hall, workshops, and the usual administrative and ancillary buildings were also required.

The First World War precluded most local authorities from taking up their new responsibilities, and the shortage of labour, coupled with inflated building costs, caused further delays. However, during the 1920s more than a dozen mental deficiency institutions were commenced, often in a converted mansion house, which gradually evolved by building a few villas at a time. One of the earliest, the Prudhoe Hall Colony in Northumberland (Fig 179), was established in 1914 by the Northern Counties Joint Poor Law Committee and built to the designs of J H Morton & J G Burell.

Most colonies were established by local authorities, and when the Local Government Act of 1929[82] transferred all property belonging

to the former Poor Law authorities to county or county borough councils, the sudden acquisition of institutions enabled them to review their provision for the mentally ill or deficient. The Act also prompted the Board of Control to revise its guidelines for the arrangement of mental deficiency colonies. Interestingly, in the light of the emergence of International Modernism, one of the new stipulations made by the Board was that 'flat roofs should not, under ordinary conditions, be adopted'.[83]

About a dozen mental deficiency colonies were established during the 1930s, most of them vast undertakings providing near-identical accommodation. Meanwood Park Colony is typical (Fig 180). It was established by Leeds Corporation in 1919 when Meanwood Hall, about four miles from the city, and its 74-acre estate were leased, and the Hall altered to accommodate eighty-seven adults. In 1928 a limited competition was held for the development of a colony on the site, which was awarded to H Carter Pegg & J M Sheppard. Their design comprised three main groups of two-storey villas, each accommodating sixty patients, with

service buildings, workshops, recreation hall, hospital, school and two single-storey villas for the lowest-grade patients. Construction work was carried out in two phases, the first completed in 1932, the second in 1941. The buildings were utilitarian, in a simplified neo-Georgian style, and constructed of brick with tiled roofs and timber sash windows. The recreation hall at the colony could seat 600 people, the floor was suitable for dancing, and there was a fully equipped stage. It was also intended to serve as the chapel and was thus the focus of the colony's social life.

Although there had been a massive expansion in the variety of care offered for those suffering from mental illness, whether publicly or privately funded, there were still aspects which, for the most part, had been neglected. Henry Maudsley sought to create a new type of specialist mental hospital when, in 1907, he offered the LCC £30,000 to establish a hospital for the early treatment of cases of acute mental disorder. Maudsley considered that in many cases of acute insanity a recovery could be made within a short space of time, usually under three

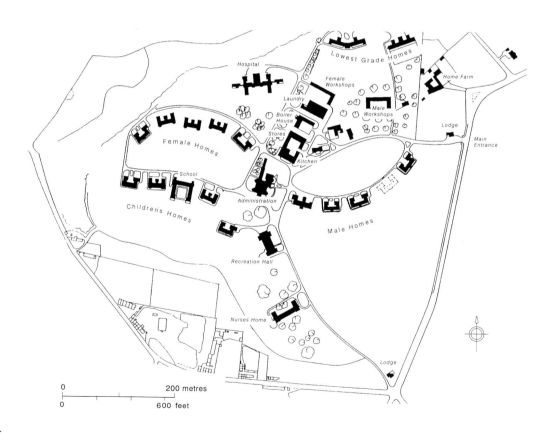

Figure 180
Site plan of Meanwood Park Colony, Leeds, designed by H Carter Pegg & J M Sheppard and built in phases between 1928 and 1941. It was typical for such colonies to be laid out with the buildings on sweeping curves, in an effort to soften their institutional appearance.
[Plan based on The Builder, 3 Oct 1941, 303]

months, but that the chances of such a recovery were diminished once the patient had been committed into a large asylum 'in which multitudes are congregated and such individual treatment is almost impracticable'.[84] He also aimed to promote research into mental illness and intended that the new hospital should serve as an educational establishment for medical students. Because of administrative delays, the site was not chosen until 1911 and the new buildings were only completed after the outbreak of the First World War, when they were immediately handed over to the military. The Maudsley Hospital finally opened in 1923.

Similarly, new ground was broken in the 1940s when the York Clinic for psychological medicine was established at Guy's Hospital in London. This was the first time that such a clinic had been built as part of a general hospital and as an integral part of a hospital's medical school. The clinic was designed to treat various mental illnesses, from mild nervous disorders to more severe cases of mental alienation, but excluded patients who required certification. The plans for the building were drawn up by William Walford & J Murray Easton, who employed steel-frame construction with brick-panel filling and russet-coloured facing bricks. The principal elevation on the east was roughly symmetrical, the main feature being the balconies in the centre portion of the first and fourth floors.

Within the clinic a simple classification system was adopted by allocating a different floor to different cases. Thus, on the first floor there were psycho-neurosis patients, on the second floor male patients requiring close care and observation, on the third floor female patients of this class, and on the fourth floor, disturbed cases. As the patients attending the clinic were physically well there was a greater emphasis on recreation spaces. A gymnasium and dining-room were provided in the basement and, on the roof there were two glass-enclosed areas, and one open section, for games such as deck-tennis and badminton. For the security of the patients, the open areas were protected by parapets and unclimbable fencing.[85]

The York Clinic represented the new attitude to mental illness. By the early 1950s fundamental changes were occurring, new drugs were introduced and mental hospitals began to allow patients more liberty to rejoin society, working with the local community services. In 1961, Enoch Powell, as Minister of Health, addressed the Annual Conference of the National Association for Mental Health and announced that mental hospitals had had their day and should be replaced by wards or wings in general hospitals. This was followed in 1963 with the government's publication of *Health and Welfare: The Development of Community Care*. The movement towards 'care in the community' had begun.[86]

9
Convalescent Homes and Hospitals

Prior to the establishment of convalescent homes in the mid 19th century, for most poor patients discharge from hospital meant a return to overcrowded, insanitary surroundings and inadequate food, conditions that severely hampered their chances of recovery. Although a few early voluntary hospitals did accept convalescents, they were accommodated with the general patients in the main wards. In the late 18th century some general hospitals began to provide convalescent wards, and, in the mid 19th century, they were included in a few of the more enlightened workhouse infirmaries. They were far from common, however, and in 1860 Dr Henry Browne, Physician to the Manchester Royal Infirmary, complained that 'the absence of day rooms and convalescent wards, where patients can eat and spend their time in pleasant and useful occupations, away from their bed rooms and the presence of distressing cases, is felt constantly in crowded hospitals'.[1]

The first home in England entirely devoted to the care of convalescents was founded largely through the efforts of Theodore Monro, a medical student at St Bartholomew's Hospital in London, who was appalled by the lack of aftercare for patients there. In 1840 he arranged to send patients from London to stay with families in Harrow Weald, where his elder brother was vicar, in order to help speed their recovery. In the following year he played a key part in the establishment of the Metropolitan Convalescent Institution. Originally occupying a vacant workhouse in Carshalton, it was intended 'to provide an asylum in the country for the temporary residence of the convalescent and debilitated poor', as it was recognised that the patients' recovery to full health was 'impracticable in the hospitals and at their own unhealthy and ill-provided homes, but may be speedily effected by pure air, rest and nutritious diet'.[2] In 1853 the institution moved to a purpose-built home on a more salubrious site in the leafy Surrey countryside near Walton-on-Thames (Fig 181). Joseph Clarke, whose 'Gothic proclivities were well-known', nevertheless supplied an Italianate design for the building, which differed from contemporary general hospitals only in its provision of day-rooms and a dining-hall in addition to the wards.[3]

Despite the long-standing concern which many physicians and surgeons felt at the lack of convalescent care, the Metropolitan Convalescent Institution had no immediate imitators. However, in 1860 Joseph Adshead, a member of the board of the Manchester Royal Infirmary, presented his 'plea for the establishment of a convalescent hospital for Manchester and its surrounding districts' to the Manchester Statistical Society – already an important forum for the promotion of pavilion planning in hospital design.[4] Adshead recognised that a convalescent home in a healthy locality would not only facilitate a swift return to health for patients sent there, but also increase the overall number who could be treated in the infirmary, by enabling patients to be discharged sooner.

Adshead produced a design for a convalescent hospital for 136 patients on the pavilion principle. Like the Metropolitan, its conventional plan made only minor concessions to its specialised function. Apart from balconies, the only obviously convalescent feature was a small day-room or dining-room associated with each ward, large enough for only a handful of patients. The scheme was not executed, despite the interest of Florence Nightingale, who 'greatly improved' the plan by her 'valuable suggestions'.[5]

Florence Nightingale's involvement with the Manchester scheme reflected a wider concern with convalescent institutions, of which she was a powerful advocate, declaring that 'every hospital should have its convalescent branch, and every county its convalescent home'.[6] By 1863 her earlier enthusiasm for Adshead's plans had been replaced by a conviction that the pavilion plan, *de rigueur* for general hospitals, should be shunned in favour of domesticity.[7] Indeed, her own concept of a model convalescent home comprised a group of cottages (Fig 182).[8] Working plans by a Mr Thomas of the War Office were drawn up to Nightingale's recommendations, and freely adapted by T H Wyatt for the Herbert Memorial Convalescent Home in

Bournemouth, built in 1865–7. However, the plan was not copied elsewhere. Nightingale's belief that it could be easily extended was misguided, and it was rejected for the large institutions, some with over 100 beds, which began to appear in the mid 1860s.

Although initial progress was slow, convalescent homes were founded at a steady rate from 1870. The majority owed their existence to private philanthropy. While gifts from wealthy benefactors and a variety of other sources paid for buildings, frequently more money had to be raised to cover daily running costs. In addition, those patients not admitted by subscribers' letters were expected to contribute to the cost of their stay.

A fundamental factor governing the design of convalescent homes was the mobility of the patients, who were neither expected, nor encouraged, to remain in their beds during the day. As a result, day-rooms, dining-rooms and attractive grounds were common features in the earlier homes and, together with a chapel, were often the only features specifically suited to the needs of convalescents, even at the larger institutions. However, by the late-Victorian and Edwardian eras the range of amenities available at convalescent homes had grown to include billiard rooms, libraries, smoking-rooms and entertainment halls.

Atkinson Morley's Convalescent Hospital at Wimbledon, which took patients from St George's Hospital, Westminster, was one of the earliest to be built on a large scale. Designed by Edward Kelly, it was erected in 1867–9 on Copse Hill, a site which sloped gently to the south. As the hospital had been envisaged for patients 'whose cures have not been completed'[9] it contained large wards of between 15 and 22 beds which could be observed from adjoining nurses' rooms. A change of air in this pleasant location was considered an important element in hastening the patients' recovery. Indeed, most convalescent homes were situated in the countryside or by the sea, where rest, graduated exercise, fresh air and wholesome food could help overcome the debility resulting from illness or surgery. This emphasis on pure country air also reflected the mid 19th-century debate on removing all large hospitals from towns or populous suburbs.[10]

The spa towns and seaside resorts popularised in the mid 19th century by 'private convalescents', who had been sent by their doctors to 'take the waters', were natural locations for

Figure 181
The principal elevation of the Metropolitan Convalescent Institution at Walton-on-Thames, Surrey, designed by J Clarke. In 1852–4 this central three-storey block and the flanking nine-bay wings were built, but in 1861–8 two further wings were added (one at each end of the building), which had been part of Clarke's original scheme.
[NMR BB93/28464]

convalescent homes. Indeed, some of these homes combined convalescent and bathing facilities, and are difficult to differentiate from specialist hospitals offering sea-water or mineral-water treatment as a cure for diseases such as scrofula (see pages 124–7). The Prudhoe Memorial Convalescent Home at Whitley Bay, built in 1867–9 for patients discharged from Newcastle Infirmary, or suffering from scrofula and similar diseases, had sea-water and fresh-water baths, as did those in other coastal resorts such as Redcar, Mablethorpe and Silloth.

At first, convalescent homes differed little in appearance from contemporary general hospitals, but this soon changed. For the Cookridge Convalescent Hospital near Leeds, erected in 1868–9, Richard Norman Shaw created an elevation which is far from institutional, although it had a straightforward pavilion plan. He imported a Kentish vernacular style to Yorkshire, mixing hung-tiles with the local stone. The sloping site enhances the sense of height in the building, which is imposing yet picturesque.[11]

In their planning, too, convalescent homes eventually became less institutional. From the 1870s onwards an increasing number of them reflected a clearer understanding of the needs of convalescents, particularly in the types and sizes of wards. A better range of accommodation evolved to meet the requirements of different illnesses and stages of convalescence. Recent admissions were kept under observation in large wards, and as patients regained health and strength they could be moved to smaller rooms. One of the first buildings to incorporate these developments was the Barnes Convalescent Home at Cheadle, established in connection with the Manchester Royal Infirmary. This vast Gothic building was designed by Lawrence Booth, of Blackwell & Booth, and built in 1871–5. In addition to pavilion wards, small, 3-bed wards were also provided, each occupying a narrow gabled bay. This arrangement was modelled on the Male Convalescent Institution at Vincennes, outside Paris, to which Florence Nightingale had drawn attention in 1863.[12]

This combination of large and small wards remained popular in convalescent homes built in the late 19th and early 20th centuries. Ida Hospital at Cookridge (Figs 183 and 184), with its clusters of half-timbered gables, clearly in imitation of Norman Shaw's earlier hospital on the same site, is a good example. Built in 1887–8 to designs by Chorley & Connon, it

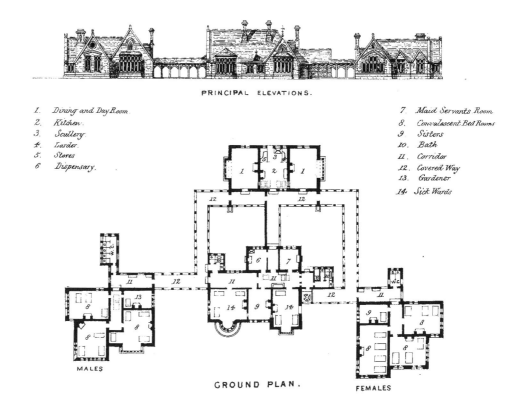

Figure 182 Elevation and plan of a convalescent hospital arranged as cottages, designed by 'Mr Thomas of the War Office' on Florence Nightingale's instructions. [Nightingale 1863, Plan No. X (Wellcome Institute Library, L0023807B)]

A DESIGN FOR CONVALESCENT HOSPITAL ARRANGED AS COTTAGES.

PRINCIPAL ELEVATIONS.

1. Dining and Day Room.
2. Kitchen.
3. Scullery.
4. Larder.
5. Stores
6. Dispensary.

7. Maid Servants Room.
8. Convalescent Bed Rooms.
9. Sisters
10. Bath
11. Corridor
12. Covered Way
13. Gardener
14. Sick Wards

MALES

GROUND PLAN.

FEMALES

*Figures 183 and 184
South elevation and
ground-floor plan of Ida
Hospital, Cookridge,
Leeds, designed by
Chorley & Connon and
built in 1887–8.
[Photograph NMR
BB92/9437; plan (1:750)
from Burdett 1893,
portfolio of plans, 97
(BB94/16113)]*

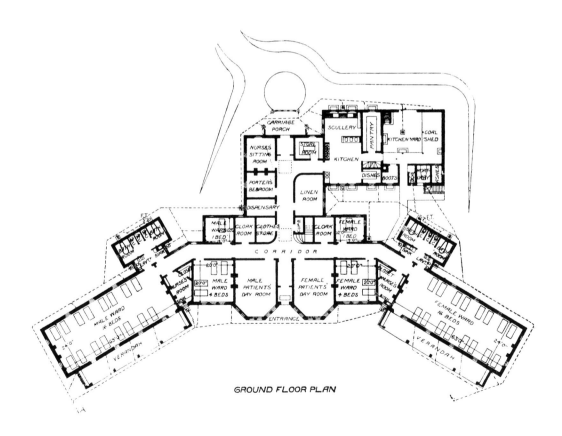

GROUND FLOOR PLAN

provided 42 beds arranged in four small wards in a central block and two large pavilion wards on either side. As the home was intended for 'semi-convalescents', most wards were supervised from nurses' rooms. Verandas were available for the use of patients, and a half-butterfly plan, with the pavilion wards angled southwards, was adopted 'for the purpose of allowing a more even distribution of sunlight than would result from keeping the front in one line'.[13] Although perhaps a little optimistic for the Yorkshire climate, such a plan was ideally suited to convalescent patients who could sit out and enjoy the sunshine. This is an early use of what became a standard form for the sanatoria of the 1890s, pre-dating its vogue in Arts & Crafts domestic architecture, where butterfly plans were used to stunning effect by E S Prior (at The Barn in 1895) and Edwin Lutyens (at Grey Walls in 1900).

The smallest convalescent homes were almost indistinguishable from cottage hospitals and indeed there were a few combined cottage-and-convalescent institutions. When the Bealey Memorial Convalescent Hospital at Radcliffe opened in 1903 it provided just 9 beds in two short pavilion ward-wings and a single room in the administration block.

Not all convalescent homes were for patients from general hospitals. Separate homes were also established for particular conditions or types of illness, and for certain groups of people. The National Hospital for the Paralysed and Epileptic, in central London, built a convalescent home in East Finchley (Fig 185), then a suitably semi-rural location, to replace two villas which had previously been used to house female convalescent patients. The new home was built to the designs of Robert Langton Cole and opened in 1897. Largely two-storeyed, it was of brick with tile-hanging and half-timbering in a stockbroker-Tudor manner that contrasted strongly with the distinctly urban and formal appearance of the parent hospital.

Some homes were intended specifically for children, and a few, such as the Hornsea Children's Convalescent Home of 1907–8 in the East Riding of Yorkshire, provided limited treatment for bone diseases. These homes differed little from the first children's orthopaedic hospitals, and all of them offered the same kind of quasi-medical treatment, heavily dependent upon fresh air and sunshine. Single-sex homes were also provided. The Florence Ada Monica Rathborne Convalescent Home (Fig 186), designed by Wilfrid R Mosley of Slough, and erected in 1912–13, was the first reserved for women and children. It is typically domestic in appearance; described as 'an adaptation of the

Figure 185 (opposite, top left)
A detail of the National Convalescent Home, East Finchley, in the London Borough of Barnet, built in 1893–7 to designs by R Langton Cole. The gabled wing with the tall roof-ridge ventilator contains the dining-hall.
[NMR BB93/20838]

Figure 186(opposite, bottom left)
A detail of the front elevation of the Florence Ada Monica Rathborne Convalescent Home, at Parwich, Derbyshire, built in 1912–13 to designs by W R Mosley.
[NMR B93/35603]

Figure 187 (top left)
General view from the sea front of the Rustington Convalescent Home, at Rustington in West Sussex, built in 1897 to designs by Frederick Wheeler.
[NMR BB92/26900]

Figure 188 (bottom left)
The Lancashire and Cheshire Miners' Convalescent Home, Blackpool, designed by Bradshaw, Gass & Hope and built in 1925–7.
[NMR AA93/1046]

Figure 189
This striking detail of
St Dunstan's Home on
the Sussex coast at
Rottingdean shows the
central part of the main
west front. The building
was designed by the pres-
tigious firm of Sir John
Burnet, Tait and Lorne
and opened in 1939.
[NMR BB96/5593]

style prevalent in Derbyshire country manor houses of the Jacobean period', it aimed 'to avoid the appearance of a public institution, in order to ensure a home-like character'.[14] The home was situated on an elevated site that afforded 'a grand view towards the south of Derbyshire dale scenery'.[15] It provided accommodation for twenty-three patients in a number of small bedrooms, containing from 2 to 5 beds, in accordance with Florence Nightingale's ideals, and all but two of the bedrooms were on upper floors.

The Zachary Merton Convalescent Home for women at Rustington in West Sussex, was one of six provided by the Zachary Merton Trust. Built in 1936–7, it provided 30 beds for mothers and babies, with separate accommodation for toddlers. Although the home was open to patients from anywhere in Britain, a number of the larger London hospitals funded half the beds at the home on a yearly basis. A further 8 beds were reserved by Metropolitan Boroughs to provide convalescent beds in association with their Maternity and Child Welfare Centres.

Separate homes for men became increasingly common with the provision of homes for groups of workers such as printers, railwaymen, merchant seamen, factory workers and coal miners. The Rustington Convalescent Home (Fig 187), established 'for working men from all parts',[16] was founded and endowed in 1897 by Sir Henry Harben, Chairman of the Prudential Assurance Society. It was designed by Frederick Wheeler, a little-known architect of some ability who handled a free style with considerable flair. Built on a generous seaside site, Rustington Home is a handsome asymmetrical building. Unusually, it provided a high proportion of single bedrooms, and the remainder had either 2 or 4 beds. From the first this was one of the more luxurious establishments, where a 'moderate' fee was charged for admission, and after Sir Henry's death it was entrusted to the wealthy Worshipful Company of Carpenters of London, which still owns and maintains the building.

The palatial Lancashire and Cheshire Miners' Convalescent Home in Blackpool was unrivalled in scale and in the comprehensive range of facilities offered when it was completed in 1927 (Fig 188). Paid for from the Miners' Welfare fund – established by a levy on coal – the home was designed by Bradshaw, Gass & Hope in a freely adapted 'Wrenaissance' style. Standing stolidly on the sea front, it could easily have been mistaken for a high-class hotel. Aside from rooms in which to smoke, read or play billiards, it provided a winter garden and a concert hall with a stage, retiring rooms and cinema. In comparison with the relatively spartan arrangements and facilities of the first convalescent institution at Walton-on-Thames, it illustrates how far the treatment of convalescents developed in less than a century.

But, for sheer bravura, the most impressive convalescent home of the inter-war period was St Dunstan's Home at Rottingdean on the Sussex coast, designed by Sir John Burnet, Tait & Lorne (Fig 189). Serving as a convalescent and holiday home for blind ex-Servicemen, this show-piece of International Modernism, completed in 1939, had flat roofs set back to form terraces and winter gardens, carefully enclosed for the protection of the occupants. As well as the usual wards and recreation rooms, additional facilities had to be provided, and aspects of the design were specially adapted for the blind. Kennels for guide-dogs were included in the basement, handrails were fixed to the walls and all projecting wall corners were rounded to minimise the risk of blind persons running into sharp obstacles.[17]

Notes and References

The following abbreviations have been used here and in the Bibliography:

B *The Builder*
BMJ *British Medical Journal*
GLRO Greater London Record Office (now London Metropolitan Archives)

NMR National Monuments Record
PP Parliamentary Papers

PRO Public Record Office
VCH *The Victoria History of the Counties of England*

Acts of Parliament have been referenced in line with standard historical convention as follows:
Local Government Act 1929: 19 Geo V, c.17

1 Historical Context

1 Knowles and Hadcock 1971, 41–2.
2 Pinker 1966, 56–7, 62; Watkin 1978, 8, 23, 56.
3 Carlin 1989, 22–3; Knowles and Hadcock 1971, 41–2.
4 Firth 1992, 260.
5 See Slack 1985; Ballon 1991, 166–98.
6 Smith, J R 1987, 13.
7 Cartwright 1977, 101.
8 Pringle 1752, 8.
9 Howard 1784, 3.
10 Ibid, 388–9, pls 21 and 22.
11 Roberton 1855–6, 133–48.
12 *PP* 1857–8 (2318), XVIII.1.
13 *B*, 2 Nov 1878, 1140.
14 See Taylor 1988.
15 Buchan 1891, 138.
16 Anon 1846, 29.
17 Chabannes *c*1818.
18 Friedman 1984, 214.
19 Fox and Fox 1836, 4–6.
20 Stark 1810.
21 Hine 1901.
22 Quoted in Milburn 1913, 300.
23 See Parry-Jones 1972.

2 General Hospitals

1 GLRO, H1/ST/A1/6, 27 Apr 1693, fol 54.
2 GLRO, H1/ST/D33/3, 14 Nov 1700, fol 27.
3 See Rose 1989.
4 St Bartholomew's Hospital Archives, HA 1/10, Minutes of the Court of Governors, July 1729, fol 197.
5 St Bartholomew's Hospital Archives, HA 19/10 and HA 19/29–31, agreement with and letters from Ralph Allen.
6 Oswald 1961, 1199.
7 Ibid.
8 McLoughlin 1978, 18.
9 Ibid, 73–4.
10 Frith 1961, 7.
11 Ibid, 10.
12 Colvin 1995, 604.
13 VCH *Staffordshire* VIII, 1963, 160; Hordley 1902, 9–10.
14 Hordley 1902, 15–16.
15 *PP* 1864 (3416), XXVIII.1, Appendix No 15, 594.
16 *B*, 11 Jan 1879, 51.
17 *B*, 5 Oct 1844, 510.
18 *B*, 17 Apr 1858, 261.
19 *B*, 5 Jun 1858, 394.
20 *B*, 30 Jun 1866, 485.
21 Walford 1897 VI, 419.
22 Abel-Smith 1964, 137.
23 GLRO, H1/ST/A10/1, 60.
24 *The Hospital*, 25 Mar 1916, 584.
25 *B*, 17 Jul 1897, 42.
26 Ibid, 42.
27 19 Geo V, c.17.

28 *Architects' Journal*, 18 Sep 1929, 410–15; *B*, 28 Jun 1935, 1202.
29 *Architects' Journal*, 24 Jun 1937, 1125–6, 1143, 1161; *Architectural Review* **74**, Aug 1933, 50–7; *B*, 16 Oct 1931, 620 and 22 May 1936, 1057.
30 Westminster Hospital Board nd.
31 *B*, 15 Jul 1938, 100–16; Barnes 1952.
32 *B*, 9 Oct 1942, 309.

3 Cottage Hospitals

1 Napper 1864; Swete 1870, 20–5, 69–71.
2 Napper 1864, 5.
3 Ibid, 5–6.
4 Ibid, 6.
5 Ibid, 9.
6 Waring 1867, 6.
7 Ibid, 8.
8 Swete 1870, 125.
9 Ibid, 133.
10 Dennison 1963, 17–18.
11 Guy 1984, 4.
12 Napper 1864, 8.
13 Ibid, 7.
14 Burdett 1896, 44.
15 Burdett 1880, 101.
16 The Revd B Lambert quoted in Goodliffe 1948, 3.
17 Swete 1870, 32.
18 Ibid, 40.
19 Burdett 1896, 83, 85.
20 Ibid, 149.
21 Swete 1870, 44–5, 145–6.
22 Waring 1867, 25.
23 Burdett 1880, 412.
24 Swete 1870, 167.
25 Burdett 1880, 417.
26 Burdett 1896, 132.
27 Swete 1870, 57.
28 Ibid, 108; Burdett 1880, 449–51.
29 8 and 9 Geo V, c.29.
30 10 and 11 Geo V, c.50.
31 *B*, 10 Jan 1947, 46.

4 Workhouse Infirmaries

1 4 and 5 William IV, c.76.
2 Nicholls, G 1898, 161, 167, 233.
3 9 Geo I, c.7.
4 22 Geo III, c.83.
5 Neate 1967, 7–9.
6 Colvin 1995, 1042.
7 GLRO, P89/MRY1/694.
8 Suffolk Record Office (Lowestoft Branch), 36/AH5/1/1.
9 See Marshall, J D 1961.
10 4 and 5 William IV, c. 76; *PP* 1834(44), XXVII.1.
11 Nicholls, G 1898, 319–20.
12 Checkland and Checkland 1974, 429–38.

13 Ibid, 437–8.
14 *PP* 1835 (500), XXXV.107, 17 and Appendix (A.), No 10; *PP* 1836 (595), XXIX.Pt.I.1, 23 and Appendix (A.), No 15.
15 Dickens 1976, 346, fig 6.
16 *PP* 1835 (500), XXXV.107, Appendix (A.), No 9, 59.
17 Colvin 1995, 577.
18 Thompson 1980, 76, pl 8.
19 Anon 1988; Royal Institute of British Architects 1993, 979.
20 Somerset Record Office, D/G/WE/32/1; plan redrawn and published in Anon 1988.
21 Anon 1988.
22 Cole 1980, 186, footnote 5.
23 Scott 1879, 76–83.
24 Morrison 1997, 184–203.
25 *PP* 1836 (595), XXIX.Pt.I.1, Appendix (C.), 450.
26 Flinn 1976, 45–66.
27 Colvin 1995, 717–18.
28 *B*, 18 Oct 1879, 1161.
29 *PP* 1867–8 (4), LX.325, 129.
30 Pass 1988, 89–92.
31 Ibid, 91 (citing letter of 23 Jul 1865, John Rylands University Library of Manchester, ms 1154).
32 *Lancet*, 1 Jul 1865, 14–22; 15 Jul 1865, 73–6; 29 Jul 1865, 131–4; 12 Aug 1865, 184–7; 26 Aug 1865, 240–3; 9 Sep 1865, 296–8; 23 Sep 1865, 355–7; 4 Nov 1865, 513–15; 23 Dec 1865, 711–14; 27 Jan 1866, 104–6; 17 Feb 1866, 178–80; 7 Apr 1866, 376–8; 1 Sep 1866, 235–6.
33 Ibid, 1 Jul 1865, 15.
34 Ibid, 1 Jul 1865, 18.
35 Hart 1865–6.
36 Ibid.
37 *PP* 1866 (372), LXI.171; *PP* 1866 (387), LXI.389.
38 *PP* 1867 (18), LX.119.
39 *PP* 1867 (3786), LX.185.
40 30 Vic, c.6.
41 Hodgkinson 1967, 499–522.
42 *PP* 1868–9 (4197), XXVIII.1, 15–18.
43 Abel-Smith 1964, 95.
44 *B*, 22 Feb 1868, 139.
45 *Illustrated London News*, 2 Dec 1871, 535, 537; GLRO, LCC/AR/CB/3/1/17, plan of *c*1930.
46 Snell, H S 1881, 1–4.
47 Ibid, 21–2; Mouat and Snell 1883, 62–5.
48 Knight's Guide 1889, 47; Freeman 1904, 44.
49 *The Hospital*, 20 Nov 1886, 124.
50 Pevsner 1952, 304.
51 *PP* 1867 (3786), LX.185, 64–79.
52 Crowther 1981, 178.
53 Snell, H S 1881, 13–15.
54 Taylor 1988, 434–5: *BMJ*, 3 May 1884, 876: *Lancet*, 5 Apr 1884, 625.

55 *Building News*, 28 Feb 1890, 305; Taylor 1988, 436.
56 *B*, 27 Feb 1914, 249.
57 *Lancet*, 28 Sep 1867, 396–7; 5 Oct 1867, 433–4; 19 Oct 1867, 496–8; 2 Nov 1867, 555–6; 9 Nov 1867, 585–6.
58 *PP* 1867-8 (4), LX.325.
59 *PP* 1868–9 (4197), XXVIII.1, 47–51.
60 Knight's Guide 1889, 44.
61 *Building News*, 6 Feb 1914, 190; *B*, 9 Jun 1916, 426.
62 Knight's Guide 1889, 47.
63 Snell, A 1905, 16.
64 *B*, 23 Dec 1876, 1235.
65 Burdett 1891–3 III, 85–90.
66 Ibid, 85.
67 *Tuberculosis* **3**, 1904–6, 4.
68 *B*, 1 Aug 1903, 142.
69 Weatherley 1904–6, 66–85.
70 *PP* 1909 (4499), XXXVII.1.
71 Crowther 1981, 182.
72 *PP* 1924 (2218), IX.751, 103; *PP* 1924–5 (2450), XIII.311, 115.
73 *B*, 17 Oct 1924, 592.
74 *B*, 29 Apr 1927, 700.
75 19 Geo V, c.17.
76 Crowther 1981, 112.

5 The Hospitals of the Armed Forces

1 Keevil 1958, 13–14.
2 Ibid, 103–6.
3 *King's Works* V, 151.
4 Coad 1989, 318–21, 333–9.
5 Ibid, 146–7.
6 Pugh 1976, 104, fig 1.
7 Lloyd and Coulter 1961, 199.
8 Ibid, 194–5.
9 Revell 1984, 11–13.
10 PRO, ADM 98/2, 331.
11 Tait, W 1905, 16.
12 Devon Record Office, 81H/4/11.
13 PRO, ADM 140/321 (2).
14 Ibid, ADM 140/321 (1).
15 Lloyd and Coulter 1961, 217.
16 Ibid, 229–30.
17 Howard 1784, 389.
18 Thompson and Goldin 1975, 150, fig 154.
19 Ibid, 146.
20 Ibid, 128–46.
21 Lloyd and Coulter 1961, 235–40, 245–7.
22 PRO, ADM 140/323–6.
23 Ibid, ADM 98/14, 463–9.
24 Ibid, ADM 98/14, 48.
25 Ibid, ADM 140/131, parts 1 and 2; Ibid, ADM 140/130, 132–6.
26 Ibid, ADM 140/137, parts 1–3; Ibid, ADM 140/138.
27 Ibid, ADM 140/140–1.
28 Ibid, ADM 140/394 and 396.
29 Lloyd and Coulter 1961, 213–14.
30 PRO, ADM 140/121 (1–10).
31 *PP* 1857–8 (2318), XVIII.1, Appendix XLIII, 461–2.
32 *B*, 3 Apr 1858, 238; 11 Feb 1860, 94; 25 Feb 1860, 113–14.
33 Ibid, 25 Feb 1860, 113.
34 Ibid, 25 Sep 1858, 643.
35 Ibid, 29 Jul 1905, 132–3.
36 Coulter 1954, 310–70.
37 Cantlie 1974 I, 23, 33–5.
38 Brocklesby 1764, 54–5.
39 *PP* 1863 (3084), XIII.117, 180.
40 Cantlie 1974 I, 44–6.
41 Pringle 1752, 125–35.
42 Cantlie 1974 I, 172.
43 Ibid, 191.

44 *PP* 1861 (2839), XVI.1, 127.
45 PRO, WORK 41/652.
46 Cantlie 1974 I, 192, 217.
47 Ibid, 184–5.
48 Department of the Environment, *Lists of Buildings of Special Architectural or Historic Interest*; Cantlie 1974 I, 192, 195–6.
49 Cantlie 1974 I, 273–81, 421.
50 Cooper 1974.
51 *PP* 1857–8 (2318), XVIII.1, Appendix XLIII, 462.
52 Ibid, XVIII.1, Appendix XLIII, 461–3.
53 Ibid, XVIII.1, xxxv, 222–4; Nightingale 1863, 37, fig 4; Burdett 1891–3 III, 740–2.
54 *B*, 25 Sep 1858, 641.
55 *PP* 1861 (2839), XVI.1, 124–5; *B*, 6 Dec 1862, 872–4.
56 PRO, WORK 43/166.
57 Ibid, WORK 43/115.
58 *PP* 1861 (2839), XVI.1, 125; *B*, 6 Dec 1861, 959.
59 Nightingale 1859*b*, 6.
60 Parkes 1857, 17, 26.
61 Brunel 1855, 5–6.
62 Binney 1858, 56–7; Herbert 1972, 19.
63 Anon 1856.
64 *B*, 23 Aug 1856, 457–9 and 20 Sep 1856, 509–11.
65 Roberton 1855–6.
66 *B*, 13 Jun 1857, 341; *BMJ* 30 May 1857, 459.
67 Woodham-Smith 1950, 266–9.
68 Ibid, 276.
69 *PP* 1857–8 (2401), XIX.325.
70 *PP* 1857–8 (2318), XVIII.1.
71 *PP* 1854–5 (405), XXXII.37, xi; *PP* 1857–8 (2318), XVIII.1, lxxvii.
72 *PP* 1861 (2839), XVI.1; *PP* 1863 (3084), XIII.117.
73 *PP* 1861 (2839), XVI.1, 194–5.
74 Galton 1865.
75 *PP* 1857–8 (361), XXXVII.101, 1–3; *B*, 11 Jul 1857, 396; *The Civil Engineer and Architect's Journal* **21**, 1858, 287–8.
76 For Colchester: NMR, PSA Collection CTR 1–70; PRO, WORK 43/421–3. For Connaught: NMR, PSA Collection ALD 1344–66.
77 *BMJ*, 18 Jul 1903, 163–4.
78 Burdett 1891–3 III, 728: *PP* 1861 (2839), XVI.1, 200.
79 *PP* 1854–5 (405), XXXII.37, xi; *B*, 22 Sep 1860, 606–8.
80 *B*, 13 Oct 1860, 649–50.
81 *PP* 1861 (2839), XVI.1, 183–5.
82 *PP* 1861 (2839), XVI.1, 183, fig 85.
83 Nightingale 1871, 41–2; Gavourin nd.
84 *PP* 1861 (2839), XVI.1, 184–5, figs 86 and 87.
85 *B*, 6 Dec 1862, 872–4.
86 PRO, WORK 43/48.
87 NMR, PSA Collection, PTM 285, BHM 9–29; PRO, WORK 43/400–1.
88 Cantlie 1974 II, 272–8.
89 Burdett 1891–3 III, 742.
90 PRO, WORK 43/5 and WORK 43/692; NMR, PSA Collection CTR 71–2.
91 PRO, WORK 43/118–19; Burdett 1891–3 III, 742–3.
92 *B*, 15 Nov 1884, 673–4.
93 *The Hospital*, 10 Oct 1914, 33–4.
94 *Building News*, 17 Nov 1915, 552–5.
95 *B*, 27 Sep 1918, 191.
96 *The Hospital*, 24 Oct 1914, 95.
97 *Building News*, 10 Nov 1915, 524; *B*, 12 Nov 1915, 342; Saundby 1914, 942–3.
98 *Building News*, 10 Nov 1915, 524 and 29 Dec 1915, 741.
99 Ibid, 10 Nov 1915, 524.

100 *Lancet*, 25 Dec 1915, 1405.
101 *Building News*, 17 Nov 1915, 554–5.
102 Crew 1953–5 I, 98.
103 Ibid, 384–9.
104 Welch 1954, 213.
105 Ibid, 195.
106 Ibid, 203–6, 229–32.
107 Air Ministry 1956, 117.

6 Specialist Hospitals

1 Kershaw 1909, 62–72.
2 Granshaw 1989.
3 *BMJ*, 30 Oct 1886, 806.
4 Bettley 1984, 169.
5 Higgins 1952, 44–5, 59–60.
6 *BMJ*, 6 Jul 1946, 16.
7 Whyman 1981, 720–3.
8 *The Hospital*, 13 Apr 1895, 31.
9 Winterton 1961, 5.
10 *BMJ*, 16 Jun 1860, 458.
11 *Lancet*, 26 Dec 1857, 650.
12 Ibid, 2 Jan 1858, 20–1.
13 Ibid, 14 Feb 1863, 183.
14 *BMJ*, 2 Feb 1867, 125–6.
15 Peachey 1924, 73.
16 Anon 1808, 7.
17 Gunn 1964, 77–8.
18 Manningham 1744, 27–8.
19 Gunn 1964, 78–9.
20 Survey of London XXIII, 1951, pl 27.
21 Richardson 1955, 25.
22 Cannings 1922, 13.
23 Nightingale 1871, 39.
24 Ibid, 11–14.
25 Kershaw 1909, 62–72; Gunn 1964.
26 Gunn 1964, 91.
27 Nightingale 1871, 41–8, 62–81.
28 Burdett 1891–3 IV, 293.
29 *The Hospital*, 25 Oct 1913, 96.
30 Ballantyne 1921; Francis 1955, 115.
31 *Lancet*, 9 Jan 1858, 47.
32 Winterton 1961, 6.
33 Ibid, 4.
34 Ibid, 3.
35 *B*, 11 May 1889, 363.
36 *BMJ*, 27 Jun 1908, 1610.
37 Robinson 1934, 66.
38 *Lancet*, 18 May 1850, 602.
39 Franklin 1964, 103, 112.
40 For a survey of tiled pictures see Greene 1987.
41 *B*, 26 Mar 1948, 365.
42 Little 1928, 25.
43 *Lancet*, 3 Feb 1838, 669.
44 Menzies 1961, 11–17.
45 Lynn-Thomas 1928, 423.
46 Mackenzie, W C 1917, 676–7.
47 Jones and Girdlestone 1919, 457.
48 Watson 1934, 246–8.
49 Honeybourne 1963, 8–9.
50 Ibid, 51, note 1.
51 Wyke 1975, 75.
52 For a detailed history of the London lock hospitals see Bettley 1984.
53 Evans and Howard 1930, 146.
54 Burdett 1891–3 IV, 308.
55 Wyke 1975, 73.
56 Ibid, 73; Fessler 1951, 154.
57 Oppert 1883, 72.
58 Alder 1980, 206.
59 Bettley 1984, 172.
60 Tomkins 1993, 383; Osler 1917, 694.
61 *PP* 1916 (8189), XVI.1.
62 Stevenson and Guthrie 1949, 61; Fraser, Sir F R 1964, 173.
63 Abel-Smith 1964, 24.

64 Collins 1929, 6–8; Kershaw 1909, 27–8.
65 Chabannes c1818.
66 Kershaw 1909, 62–4.
67 Anon 1810, 5.
68 Kershaw 1909, 68–72.
69 Oppert 1883, 70; Burdett 1891–3 IV, 309.
70 Burdett 1891–3 IV, 310–12.
71 Oppert 1883, 106.
72 Fraser 1964, 174.
73 B, 27 Apr 1878, 427.
74 Robinson 1936; *Sunderland Daily Echo*, 13 Oct 1893.
75 Robinson 1936.
76 *Medical Times and Gazette*, 5 Jan 1867, 5.
77 *BMJ*, 5 May 1962, 1266.
78 *Architectural Review* **63**, Feb 1928, 63.
79 Kirby 1925, 123; Kersley and Cosh 1965, 4.
80 Kirby 1925, 123; Kersley and Cosh 1965, 6.
81 Thornes and Leach 1991, 257–8.
82 Hembry 1990, 211.
83 Turner, E S 1967, 98–100.
84 Lettsom 1801 III, 236.
85 PP 1907 (3657), XXVII.1, 406–7.
86 *The Mercury*, 5 Nov 1983, 13.
87 Murphy 1989, 223–4.
88 B, 28 Apr 1860, 264.
89 *Building News*, 2 Dec 1859, 1089.
90 Murphy 1989, 225.
91 Ibid, 233–4.
92 B, 16 Jun 1894, 467.

7 Hospitals for Infectious Diseases

1 Kiple 1993.
2 Jones 1905.
3 Highmore 1814, 274–94; Chamberlain 1770, 604.
4 Highmore 1814, 293–4.
5 Mackenzie 1827, 516–7.
6 PP 1882 (3290), XXX.Pt.II.1, 157.
7 B, 12 Aug 1848, 391–2 and 6 Jun 1857, 320–1.
8 2 William IV, c.10.
9 Cartwright 1977, 105–6.
10 Smith J R 1987, 13.
11 29 and 30 Vic, c.90.
12 Ayers 1971.
13 30 Vic, c.6.
14 46 and 47 Vic, c.35.
15 Ayers 1971, 31–3.
16 *Illustrated London News*, 7 Oct 1871, 345–6.
17 Ayers 1971, 34.
18 GLRO, Metropolitan Asylums Board *Minutes*, 4 Dec 1875, 491.
19 Ibid, Metropolitan Asylums Board *Minutes*, 11 Jun 1881, 300; 17 June 1881, 313.
20 Burne 1989, 45.
21 Ayers 1971, 80.
22 GLRO, Metropolitan Asylums Board *Minutes*, 9 May 1881, 135–6.
23 B, 15 Oct 1892, 306; 15 Dec 1883, 809.
24 GLRO, LCC/AR/CB/4/3/137; B, 4 Nov 1893, 343.
25 Burne 1989, 50.
26 Ayers 1971, 181.
27 PP 1871 (349), XXXI.763; *Lancet*, 26 Aug 1871, 309.

28 PP 1895 (7906), LI.391.
29 38 and 39 Vic, c.55.
30 56 and 57 Vic, c.68.
31 Pinker 1966, 57.
32 53 and 54 Vic, c.34.
33 *The Hospital*, 5 Jan 1907, 253.
34 Waksman 1964.
35 Survey of London XLI, 1983, 130–9.
36 Anon c1892.
37 Weatherley 1905–6, 66.
38 Pearson 1913–14; Anon nd.
39 PP 1907 (3657), XXVII.1.
40 11 and 12 Geo V, c.12.
41 19 Geo V, c.17.

8 Mental Hospitals

1 Orme and Webster 1995, p.119; VCH *London* I, 1909, 495–8.
2 Copeman 1964, 32.
3 Bethlem Royal Hospital Archives, Court of Governors' *Minutes*, 23 Jan 1674.
4 Highmore 1814, 14.
5 De Beer 1955 IV, 134.
6 Bowen 1783, 5.
7 Ibid, 9.
8 O'Donoghue 1914, 209.
9 Ibid, 206–10.
10 Highmore 1814, 17–18.
11 Hooper 1898, 126.
12 Stroud 1971, 49–50.
13 French 1951, 44.
14 Howard 1791, 139–40.
15 Ibid, 140.
16 Tuke 1813, 26.
17 PP 1814–15 (296), IV.801, 26.
18 Tuke 1813, 47–8.
19 Quoted in Harwood 1986 pt 1, 79.
20 Fox and Fox 1836, 4–6.
21 Thompson and Goldin 1975, 56.
22 Duncan 1809, 18.
23 17 Geo II, c.5.
24 14 Geo III, c.49.
25 39 and 40 Geo III, c.94.
26 48 Geo III, c.96.
27 Fox and Fox 1836, 9.
28 Inkster 1971, 3.
29 Laird 1820, 131.
30 Ibid, 131.
31 Hunter 1918, 9–10.
32 Orange 1840, 924.
33 Survey of London XXV, 1955, 77.
34 PP 1814–15 (296) IV.801, 26.
35 O'Donoghue 1914, 303.
36 Survey of London XXV, 1955, 79.
37 Bentham 1791.
38 PP 1814–15 (296) IV.801, 26, 193.
39 Stark 1810.
40 Andrews 1978, 34–5.
41 Foulston 1838, 69.
42 Watson and Pritchett 1819.
43 Melton 1969, 5.
44 Springfield Hospital Archive, *Surrey Lunatic Asylum Annual Report* 1848, 18–19.
45 5 and 6 Vic, c.87.
46 8 and 9 Vic, c.100.
47 Conolly 1847, 12.

48 B, 5 Jul 1851, 415.
49 Anon 1844, 3–5.
50 Anon 1844, 6–11.
51 Ibid, 1–17; Anon 1846.
52 Lower 1870 II, 270.
53 Robertson 1860, 263.
54 Ibid, 263.
55 B, 30 Sep 1854, 509.
56 Ibid, 509.
57 B, 24 Aug 1872, 665.
58 Ibid, 7 Jan 1882, 23.
59 PP 1807 (39) II.69, 13.
60 4 and 5 William IV, c.76.
61 *Illustrated London News*, 15 Mar 1862, 269.
62 Ibid, 269.
63 Ibid, 269.
64 For a discussion of the rising numbers of the mentally ill during this period see Scull 1993, 334–74.
65 PP 1859 (228), IX.1, 37.
66 Anon 1973, 9.
67 B, 30 Jul 1892, 88.
68 Ibid, 88.
69 Quoted in Harwood 1986 pt 1, 153.
70 51 and 52 Vic, c.41.
71 B, 9 Mar 1907, 289.
72 Pevsner and Nairn 1971, 216.
73 Parry-Jones 1981, 201–3.
74 London County Council *Minutes*, 20 Dec 1898, 1540.
75 49 and 50 Vic, c.25.
76 62 and 63 Vic, c.32.
77 3 and 4 Geo V, c.28.
78 City of Leeds 1932, 6.
79 Jones, K 1972, 204.
80 Board of Control 1925, 1.
81 Ibid, 3.
82 19 Geo V, c.17.
83 Board of Control 1930, 12.
84 London County Council *Minutes*, 18 Feb 1908, 282.
85 B, 30 Jun 1944, 518–21.
86 Jones 1972, 226–325.

9 Convalescent Homes and Hospitals

1 Adshead 1860–1, 28.
2 Quoted in Smith, J 1990, 1.
3 B, 24 Jul 1852, 468 and 17 Mar 1888, 198.
4 Adshead 1860–1.
5 Ibid, 41–2.
6 Nightingale 1863, 107.
7 Ibid, 107–16.
8 Ibid, 112–13, plan no X.
9 PP 1864 (3416), XXVIII.1, Appendix No 15, 480.
10 See Taylor 1991, 119–20.
11 Saint 1976, 65–7.
12 Nightingale 1863, 110–12, 116–23, fig 26.
13 B, 17 Mar 1888, 197.
14 *Building News*, 14 Aug 1914, 209.
15 B, 14 Aug 1914, 175.
16 Ibid, 3 Apr 1897, 324.
17 Ibid, 7 May 1937, 981 and 5 May 1939, 850–4.

Bibliography

The list below contains works cited in the text and notes and further reading.

Abel-Smith, B 1964. *The Hospitals 1800–1948*

Ackerknecht, E H 1982. *A Short History of Medicine*

Acland, H W 1875. *Thoughts on Provincial Hospitals, With Special Reference to Oxford*

Adams, H P 1908. 'Notes on the construction of cottage hospitals'. *BMJ*, 20 Jun 1908, 1476–9
  1929. 'English hospital planning'. *Journal of the Royal Institute of British Architects*, 3 ser **36**, 15 Jun 1929, 575–605 and 29 Jun 1929, 628–55

Adshead, J 1860–1. 'A plea for the establishment of a convalescent hospital for Manchester and its surrounding districts'. *Transactions of the Manchester Statistical Society*, 23–45

Aikin, J 1771. *Thoughts on Hospitals*

Air Ministry 1956. *The Second World War, 1939–45, Royal Air Force Works*

Alder, M W 1980. 'The terrible peril: a historical perspective on the venereal diseases'. *BMJ*, 19 Jul 1980, 206–11

Andrews, C T 1975. *The First Cornish Hospital*
  1978. *The Dark Awakening*

Anning, S T 1963–6. *The General Infirmary at Leeds*, 2 vols

Anon 1808. *An Account of the British Lying-in Hospital for Married Women …*

Anon 1810. *London Infirmary for Curing Diseases of the Eye, No. 40, Charter-House-Square; Under the Direction of Mr Saunders … instituted, 1804 …*

Anon 1844. *Report on the Proposed Pauper Lunatic Asylum for the County of Derby.* (Derbyshire Local Studies Library)

Anon 1846. *Derby Proposed Lunatic Asylum. Copies of the Objections of the Commissioners in Lunacy to the Plans, and of the Answers of the Architects.* (Derbyshire Local Studies Library)

Anon 1853. *First Report of the Derbyshire County Lunatic Asylum.* (Derbyshire Local Studies Library)

Anon 1856. *Report on and Details of the Plans of the Victoria Military Hospital at Netley on the Southampton Water*

Anon 1871. *Report of the Building Committee of the Prudhoe Memorial Convalescent Home, Whitley, North Shields*

Anon *c*1892. *Sketches of the Manchester Hospital for Consumption and Diseases of the Chest and Throat*

Anon 1925. *The Book of Bath.* (Written for the Ninety-third Annual Meeting of the British Medical Association held at Bath in July 1925)

Anon 1973. *Whittingham Hospital. One Hundred Years 1873–1973*

Anon 1988. *Priory Hospital, Wells*

Anon nd (after 1945). *The Mundesley Sanatorium. Prospectus*

Austoker, J 1988. *A History of the Imperial Cancer Research Fund 1902–1986*

Ayers, G M 1971. *England's First State Hospitals and the Metropolitan Asylums Board 1867–1930*

Ballantyne, J W 1921. 'The maternity hospital, with its ante-natal and neo-natal departments'. *BMJ*, 12 Feb 1921, 221–4

Ballingall, G 1851. *Observations on the Site and Construction of Hospitals*

Ballon, H 1991. *The Paris of Henri IV*

Barnes, S 1952. *The Birmingham Hospitals Centre*

Bentham, J 1791. *Panopticon; or, the Inspection-house.* (Originally written as a series of letters in 1787)

Bettley, J 1984. 'Post Voluptatem Misericordia: the rise and fall of the London Lock Hospitals'. *London Journal* **10**, No. 2, Winter 1984, 167–75

Bevan, H 1847. *Records of the Salop Infirmary*

Binney, Capt 1858. 'Report on hutting made by the board of officers assembled in the Crimea, and observations and suggestions on the subject'. *Professional Papers of the Corps of Royal Engineers*, n ser **7**, 1858, 53–63

Blomfield, J 1933. *St George's, 1733–1933*

Board of Control 1925. *Revised Suggestions as to the Arrangement of Colonies for Mental Defectives*
  1930. *Further Revise of Suggestions as to the Arrangement of Colonies for Mental Defectives*

Bowen, T 1783. *An Historical Account of the Origin, Progress, and Present State of Bethlem Hospital …*

Brocklesby, R 1764. *Oeconomical and Medical Observations, in Two Parts. From the Year 1758 to the Year 1763, inclusive, Tending to the Improvement of Military Hospitals, and to the Cure of Camp Diseases, incident to Soldiers*

Browne, W A F 1837. *What Asylums Were, Are and Ought to Be*

Brunel, I K 1855. *Brunel's Large Sketchbook No. 9.* (University of Bristol Library)

Buchan, W P 1891. *Ventilation*

Burdett, H C 1877. *The Cottage Hospital*
  1880. *Cottage Hospitals*, 2nd edn
  1891–3. *Hospitals and Asylums of the World*, 4 vols and portfolio of plans
  1896. *Cottage Hospitals*, 3rd edn
  1924. *Hospitals and Charities*

Burne, J 1989. *Dartford's Capital River*

Bynum, W F *et al* (eds) 1985–8. *The Anatomy of Madness*, 3 vols

Cameron, H C 1954. *Mr Guy's Hospital 1726–1948*

Cannings, R B 1922. *The City of London Maternity Hospital: A Short History*

Cantlie, N 1974. *A History of the Army Medical Department*, 2 vols

Carlin, M 1989. 'Medieval English hospitals'. In Granshaw and Porter 1989, 21–39

Cartwright, F F 1977. *A Social History of Medicine*

Chabannes, Marquis de *c*1818. A*ppendix to the Marquis de Chabannes' Publication, on Conducting Air by Forced Ventilation … Published in 1818.* (Unpaginated)

Chamberlain, H 1770. *A New and Compleat History and Survey of the Cities of London and Westminster*

Checkland, S G and Checkland, E O A (eds) 1974. *The Poor Law Report of 1834*

City of Leeds 1932. *Mental Health Services Committee. Official opening of the Meanwood Colony Extensions, Meanwood, Leeds on 3 October 1932*

Clark-Kennedy, A E 1962–3. *The London*, 2 vols

Clay, R M 1909. *The Mediaeval Hospitals of England*

Coad, J G 1983. *Historic Architecture of the Royal Navy*
  1989. *The Royal Dockyards 1690–1850: Architecture and Engineering Works of the Sailing Navy*

Cole, D 1980. *The Work of Sir Gilbert Scott*

Collins, E T 1929. *The History and Traditions of the Moorfields Eye Hospital*

Colvin, H M 1995. *A Biographical Dictionary of British Architects, 1660–1840*, 3rd edn

Combe, M 1860. 'Plan proposed for the hospital of a regiment'. *B*, 22 Sep 1860, 606–8

Conolly, J 1847. *The Construction and Government of Lunatic Asylums and Hospitals for the Insane*

Cook, E T 1913. *The Life of Florence Nightingale*, 2 vols

Cooper, J 1974. *Fort Pitt, Some Notes on the History of a Napoleonic Fort, Military Hospital and Technical School.* (Unpaginated typescript)

Cope, Z 1954. *The History of St Mary's Hospital Medical School*

Copeman, W S C 1964. 'The Royal Hospitals before 1700'. In Poynter 1964, 27–41

Coulter, J L S 1954. *The Royal Naval Medical Service. Vol 1*

Crew, F A E 1953–5. *The Army Medical Services*, 2 vols

Crowther, M A 1981. *The Workhouse System, 1834–1929: The History of an English Social Institution*

Dainton, W C 1961. *The Story of England's Hospitals*
Davidson, M 1954. *The Brompton Hospital*
De Beer, E S (ed) 1955. *The Diary of John Evelyn*, 6 vols
Dennison, E J 1963. *A Cottage Hospital Grows Up: The Story of the Queen Victoria Hospital East Grinstead*
Dickens, A 1976. 'The architect and the workhouse'. *Architectural Review* **160**, Dec 1976, 345–52
Digby, A 1978. *Pauper Palaces*
Dormer, E W (ed) 1937. *The Story of the Royal Berkshire Hospital 1837–1937*
Duncan, A 1809. *Observations on the General Treatment of Lunatics as a Branch of Medical Police*
Dunn, C L (ed) 1952–3. *The Emergency Medical Services*, 2 vols
Du-Plat-Taylor, F M *et al* 1930. *Cottage Hospitals*

Eade, P 1900. *Norfolk and the Norwich Hospital*
Emrys-Roberts, M 1991. *The Cottage Hospitals 1859–1990*
Evans, A D and Howard, L G R 1930. *The Romance of the British Voluntary Hospital Movement*

Fermer, H 1990. 'Foredown Isolation Hospital'. Sussex Industrial History **20**, 1990, 15–34
Fessler, A 1951. 'Venereal disease and prostitution in the reports of the Poor Law Commissioners, 1834–1850'. *British Journal of Venereal Diseases* **27**, No. 3, Sep 1951, 154–7
Firth, C H 1992. *Cromwell's Army*, 3rd edn
Flinn, M W 1976. 'Medical services under the New Poor Law'. In Fraser, D 1976, 45–66
Forty, A 1980. 'The modern hospital in England and France: the social and medical uses of architecture'. In King, A D 1980, 61–93
Foulston, J 1838. *The Public Buildings Erected in the West of England*
Fox, F and Fox, C 1836. *History and Present State of Brislington House near Bristol, an Asylum for the Cure and Reception of Insane Persons*
Francis, H H 1955. 'The history of obstetrics and gynaecology in Liverpool'. *Sphincter* **17**, No. 3, June 1955, 114–20
Franklin, A W 1964. 'Children's hospitals'. In Poynter 1964, 103–21
Fraser, D (ed) 1976. *The New Poor Law in the 19th Century*
Fraser, Sir F R 1964. 'The rise of specialism and special hospitals'. In Poynter 1964, 169–85
Freeman, A C 1904. *Hints on the Planning of Poor Law Buildings and Mortuaries*
French, C N 1951. *The Story of St Luke's Hospital*
Friedman, T 1984. *James Gibbs*
Frith, B 1961. *The Story of Gloucester's Infirmary.* (Gloucester, Stroud and the Forest Hospital Management Committee)
Frizelle, E R and Martin, J D 1971. *The Leicester Royal Infirmary 1771–1971*

Galton, D 1865. *Report to the Right Hon The Earl de Grey and Ripon, Secretary of State for War, Descriptive of the Herbert Hospital at Woolwich*
1869. *An Address on the General Principles Which Should be Observed in the Construction of Hospitals*
1893. *Healthy Hospitals. Observations on Some Points Connected with Hospital Construction*
Gaskell, E 1964. 'Bibliography of hospital history'. In Poynter 1964, 255–79
Gavourin, B nd. *The Birth of One, Margaret Sandom, and Relevant Matters*
Goodliffe, C H 1948. *A History of Tamworth Hospital.* (The Tamworth Herald Co Ltd)
Granshaw, L 1989. '"Fame and fortune by means of bricks and mortar": the medical profession and specialist hospitals in Britain, 1800–1948'. In Granshaw and Porter (eds) 1989, 199–220
1992. '"Upon this principle have I based a practice": the development and reception of antisepsis in Britain, 1867–90'. In Pickstone 1992, 17–46
Granshaw, L and Porter, R (eds) 1989. *The Hospital in History*
Graves, C 1947. *The Story of St Thomas's 1106–1947*
Gray, A S 1985. *Edwardian Architecture: A Biographical Dictionary*
Greene, J 1987. *Brightening the Long Days: Hospital Tile Pictures*
Gunn, A 1964. 'Maternity hospitals'. In Poynter 1964, 77–101

Guy, J R 1984. *Mr Bird and His Infirmary: Crewkerne Hospital 1866: 1904: 1984*
Hake, A E 1892. *Suffering London*
Hart, E 1865–6. 'The condition of our state hospitals'. *Fortnightly Review* **3**, 15 Nov 1865–1 Feb 1866, 217–26
1866. 'Metropolitan infirmaries for the pauper sick'. *Fortnightly Review* **4**, 15 Feb 1866–1 May 1866, 459–63
Harwood, E 1986. The history and plan forms of purpose-built lunatic asylums, with a study of their conservation and reuse. (Unpublished thesis, Architectural Association, London)
Haskins, C 1922. *The History of Salisbury Infirmary*
Hembry, P 1990. *The English Spa, 1560–1815: A Social History*
Herbert, G 1972. *Prefabricated Structures for the Crimean War.* (Thesis, Centre for Urban and Regional Studies, Israel Institute of Technology, Haifa)
Higgins, T T 1952. *'Great Ormond Street' 1852–1952*
Highmore, A 1814. Pietas Londinensis: *The History, Design, and Present State of the Various Public Charities in and near London ...*
Hine, G T 1901. 'Asylums and asylum planning'. *Journal of the Royal Institute of British Architects*, 3 ser **8**, 23 Feb 1901, 161–84
Hodgkinson, R 1967. *The Origins of the National Health Service. The Medical Services of the New Poor Law, 1834–1871*
Holmes, G 1954. *The National Hospital, Queen Square, 1860–1948*
Honeybourne, M B 1963. 'The leper hospitals of the London area'. *Trans London Middlesex Archaeol Soc* **21**, Part 1, 1963, 3–61
Hooper, J 1898. *Norwich Charities: Short Sketches of their Origin and History*
Hordley, R 1902. *A Concise History of the Rise and Progress of the North Staffordshire Infirmary and Eye Hospital ...*
Howard, J 1784. *The State of the Prisons in England and Wales, with Preliminary Observations and an Account of Some Foreign Prisons and Hospitals*
1791. *An Account of the Principal Lazarettos in Europe ... Together With Further Observations on some Foreign Prisons and Hospitals; and Additional Remarks on the Present State of Those in Great Britain and Ireland.* (First published in 1789, 2nd edn with additions 1791)
Hume, W E 1951. *The Infirmary, Newcastle Upon Tyne, 1751–1951*
Hunter, D 1918. *A History of The Coppice, Nottingham*
Hunter, W 1914. *Historical Account of Charing Cross Hospital and Medical School*
Hurwitz, B and Richardson, R 1989. 'Joseph Rodgers and the reform of workhouse medicine'. *BMJ*, 16 Dec 1989, 1507–10

Inkster, I 1971. Notes on finance, building and technology in the early history of the lunatic asylum near Nottingham. (Typescript, Dept of Econ Hist, Univ of Sheffield) (Nottinghamshire Archives, SO/40 1/50/4/1)

Jewesbury, E C O 1956. *The Royal Northern Hospital 1856–1956*
Jones, H 1905. In discussion of paper by D Davies, *Transactions of the Sanitary Institute* **26**, 261
Jones, K 1955. *Lunacy, Law and Conscience, 1744–1845*
1972. *A History of the Mental Health Services*
Jones, R J and Girdlestone, G R 1919. 'The cure of crippled children. Proposed national scheme'. *BMJ*, 11 Oct 1919, 457–60

Keevil, J J 1958. *Medicine and the Navy, 1200–1900 2 (1649–1714)*
Kershaw, R 1909. *Special Hospitals. Their Origin, Development, and Relationship to Medical Education ...*
Kersley, G D and Cosh, J A 1965. *The History of the Royal National Hospital for Rheumatic Diseases, Bath*
King, A 1966. 'Hospital planning: revised thoughts on the origin of the pavilion principle in England'. *Medical History* **10**, 360–73
King, A D (ed) 1980. *Buildings and Society. Essays on the Social Development of the Built Environment*
King's Works. *The History of the King's Works.* Vol V (Gen ed H M Colvin 1976)
Kiple, K F (ed) 1993. *Cambridge World History of Human Disease*
Kirby, T 1925. 'The Royal Mineral Water Hospital: a national hospital for rheumatic diseases'. In Anon 1925, 123–9
Knight's Guide 1889. *Knight's Guide to the Arrangement and Construction of Workhouse Buildings*

Knowles, D and Hadcock, R N 1971. *Medieval Religious Houses: England and Wales*, 2nd edn

Laird, Mr 1820. *A Topographical and Historical Description of the County of Nottingham* ...

Langdon-Davies, J 1952. *Westminster Hospital. Two Centuries of Voluntary Service 1719–1948*

Lettsom, J C 1801. *Hints Designed to Promote Beneficence Temperance & Medical Science*, 3 vols

Little, E M 1928. 'Orthopaedics before Stromeyer'. In *The Robert Jones Birthday Volume: A Collection of Surgical Essays*, 1928, 1–26

Lloyd, C and Coulter, J L S 1961. *Medicine and the Navy 1200–1900. Vol III. 1714–1815*

London County Council 1949. *The L.C.C. Hospitals. A Retrospect*

Loudon, I S L 1978. 'Historical importance of outpatients'. *BMJ*, 15 Apr 1978, 974–7

Lower, M A 1870. *A Compendious History of Sussex*, 2 vols

Lynn-Thomas, J 1928. *'An appreciation'*. In *The Robert Jones Birthday Volume: A Collection of Surgical Essays*, 1928, 423–4

McCurrich, H J 1929. *The Treatment of the Sick Poor of this Country*

McInnes, E M 1963. *St Thomas's Hospital*

Mackenzie, E 1827. *A Descriptive and Historical Account of ... Newcastle upon Tyne*, 2 vols

Mackenzie, W C 1917. 'Military orthopaedic hospitals'. *BMJ*, 26 May 1917, 669–78

Mackintosh, D J 1909. *Construction, Equipment, and Management of a General Hospital*

McLoughlin, G 1978. *A Short History of the First Liverpool Infirmary 1749–1824*

McMenemey, W H 1947. *A History of Worcester Royal Infirmary*

McNee, T and Angus, D 1985. *Seaham Harbour. The First 100 years. 1828–1928*

Manningham, R 1744. *An Abstract of Midwifry, for the Use of the Lying-in Infirmary* ...

Marland, H 1987. *Medicine and Society in Wakefield 1780–1870*

Marshall, J 1878. *On a Circular System of Hospital Wards*

Marshall, J D 1961. 'The Nottinghamshire reformers and their contribution to the New Poor Law'. Econ Hist Rev, 2 ser **13**, 382–96

Melton, B L 1969. *One Hundred and Fifty Years at the Lawn.* (Privately printed)

Menzies, J 1961. *The Heritage of Oswestry*

Milburn, W 1913. 'A comparative study of modern English, Continental, and American hospital construction'. *Journal of the Royal Institute of British Architects*, 3 ser **20**, 8 Mar 1913, 281–305

Ministry of Health 1945–6. *Hospital Survey*, 10 vols

Minney, R J 1967. *The Two Pillars of Charing Cross*

Morris, E W 1910. *A History of the London Hospital*

Morrison, K A 1997. 'The New Poor Law Workhouses of George Gilbert Scott and William Bonython Moffat'. *Architectural History* **40**, 184–203

Mouat, F J and Snell, H S 1883. *Hospital Construction and Management*

Murphy, C C S 1989. 'From Friedenheim to hospice: a century of cancer hospitals'. In Granshaw and Porter 1989, 221–41

Napper, A 1864. *On the Advantages Derivable by the Medical Profession and the Public from Village Hospitals*

Neate, A 1967. *St Marylebone Workhouse and Institution*

Nicholls, G 1898. *History of the English Poor Law*

Nicholls, T B 1940. *Organisation, Strategy and Tactics of the Army Medical Services in War*, 2nd edn

Nightingale, F 1859a. *Notes on Hospitals*
  1859b. *A Contribution to the Sanitary History of the British Army During the Late War with Russia, Illustrated with Tables and Diagrams*
  1860. *Notes on Hospitals*, 2nd edn
  1863. *Notes on Hospitals*, 3rd edn
  1871. *Introductory Notes on Lying-in Institutions*

O'Donoghue, E G 1914. *The Story of Bethlehem Hospital from its Foundation in 1247*

Oppert, F 1883. *Hospitals, Infirmaries, and Dispensaries: Their Construction, Interior Arrangement, and Management...*, 2nd edn

Orange, J 1840. *History and Antiquities of Nottingham*. Vol II

Orme, N and Webster, M 1995. *The English Hospital 1070–1570*

Osler, Sir W 1917. 'The campaign against Venereal Disease'. *BMJ*, 26 May 1917, 694–6

Oswald, A 1961. 'Gibbs's Great Hall at Bart's'. *Country Life*, 25 May 1961, 1198–1200

Parkes, E A 1857. *Report on the Formation and General Management of Renkioi Hospital, Turkey* (with appendix by I K Brunel, 'Hospital Buildings for the East')

PP 1807 (39), II.69, *Report from the Select Committee appointed to enquire into the State of Lunatics*, 15 July 1807

PP 1814–15 (296), IV.801, *Report from the Committee on Madhouses in England*, 11 July 1815

PP 1834 (44), XXVII.1, *Report of the Royal Commission of Inquiry into the Administration and Practical Operation of the Poor Laws*, 1834

PP 1835 (500), XXXV.107, *First Annual Report of the Poor Law Commissioners ...*, 10 Aug 1835

PP 1836 (595), XXIX.Pt.I.1, *Second Annual Report of the Poor Law Commissioners ...*, 19 Aug 1836

PP 1854–5 (405), XXXII.37, *Report ... on Barrack Accommodation for the Army ...*, 17 Jul 1855

PP 1857–8 (2318), XVIII.1, *Report ... into the Regulations Affecting the Sanitary Condition of the Army, the Organisation of Military Hospitals, and the Treatment of the Sick and Wounded*, 1858

PP 1857–8 (2318), XVIII.1, *Memorandum Relating to the Hospitals of Government which at present exist in Chatham and its Vicinity*, 12 Jun 1843

PP 1857–8 (2401), XIX.325, *Report on the Site, &c. of the Royal Victoria Hospital, Near Netley Abbey*, 1858

PP 1857–8 (361), XXXVII.101, *Report ... upon the Plans of a Proposed Hospital for Aldershot ...*, 24 Jun 1858

PP 1859 (228), IX.1, *Supplement to the Twelfth Report of the Commissioners in Lunacy*, 1859

PP 1861 (2839), XVI.1, *General Report of the Commission appointed for Improving the Sanitary Condition of Barracks and Hospitals*, 1861

PP 1863 (3084), XIII.117, *Appendix to the Report of the Commission for Improving the Sanitary Condition of Barracks and Hospitals (Interim Reports)*, 1863

PP 1864 (3416), XXVIII.1, *Sixth Report of the Medical Officer of the Privy Council*, 1863

PP 1866 (372), LXI.171, *Report of Dr Edward Smith ... on the Metropolitan Workhouse Infirmaries and Sick Wards*, 26 Jun 1866

PP 1866 (387), LXI.389, *Report of H. B. Farnall ... on the Infirmary Wards of the several Metropolitan Workhouses ...*, 2 Jul 1866

PP 1867 (18), LX.119, *Report of U. Corbett ... and W. O. Markham ... relative to the Metropolitan Workhouses*, 8 Feb 1867

PP 1867 (3786), LX.185, *Report of the Committee Appointed to Consider the Cubic Space of Metropolitan Workhouses ...*, 7 Feb 1867

PP 1867–8 (4), LX.325, *Report of Dr Edward Smith ... after Visiting Forty-Eight Workhouses Situate in Various Parts of England and Wales*, 28 Nov 1867

PP 1868–9 (4197), XXVIII.1, *Twenty-First Annual Report of the Poor Law Board, 1868–69*, 1869

PP 1871 (349), XXXI.763, *Thirteenth Report of the Medical Officer of the Privy Council ... 1870*, 1871

PP 1882 (3290), XXX.Pt.II.1, *Second Supplement to Tenth Report of the Local Government Board, Containing Report ... on the Use and Influence of Hospitals for Infectious Diseases*, 1882

PP 1895 (7906), LI.391, *Supplement to the Twenty-Fourth Annual Report of the Local Government Board, 1894–5 ...*, 1895

PP 1907 (3657), XXVII.1, *Annual Report of the Local Government Board 1905–06, Supplement ... on Sanatoria for Consumption and Certain Other Aspects of the Tuberculosis Question*, 1907

PP 1909 (4499), XXXVII.1, *Report of the Royal Commission on the Poor Laws and Relief of Distress*, 1909

PP 1916 (8189), XVI.1, *Final Report of the Royal Commission on Venereal Diseases*, 1916.

PP 1924 (2218), IX.751, *Fifth Annual Report of the Ministry of Health, 1923–24*, 1924

PP 1924 (2450), XIII.311, *Sixth Annual Report of the Ministry of Health, 1924–25*, 1925

Parry-Jones, W 1972. *The Trade in Lunacy*
  1981. 'The model of the Geel Lunatic Colony and its influence on the nineteenth-century asylum system in Britain'. In Scull 1981, 201–17

Parsons, F G 1932–6. *The History of St Thomas's Hospital*, 3 vols
Parsons, H F 1914. *Isolation Hospitals*
Pass, A J 1988. *Thomas Worthington, Victorian Architecture and Social Purpose*
Pater, J E 1981. *The Making of the National Health Service*
Peachey, G C 1924. 'Note upon the provision for lying-in women in London up to the middle of the eighteenth century'. *Proceedings of the Royal Society of Medicine* **17**, 1924 (Epidemiology Section), 72–6
Pearson, S V 1913. *The State Provision of Sanatoriums* 1913–14. 'Mundesley Sanatorium'. *The Tuberculosis Year Book and Sanatoria Annual* **1**, 1913–14, 241–2
Pevsner, N 1952. *London Except the Cities of London and Westminster* (The *Buildings of England* series)
Pevsner, N and Nairn, I 1971. *Surrey* (The *Buildings of England* series, 2nd edn revised by B Cherry)
Pickstone, J V 1985. *Medicine and Industrial Society: A History of Hospital Development in Manchester and Its Region, 1752–1946*
 (ed) 1992. *Medical Innovations in Historical Perspective*
Pinker, R 1966. *English Hospital Statistics 1861–1938*
Poland, J 1893. *Records of the Miller Hospital and Royal Kent Dispensary*
Powell, A 1930. *The Metropolitan Asylums' Board and its Work 1867–1930*
Poynter, F N L (ed) 1964. T*he Evolution of Hospitals in Britain*
Pringle, J 1752. *Observations on the Diseases of the Army, in Camp and Garrison*
Prochaska, F K 1992. *Philanthropy and the Hospitals of London. The King's Fund, 1897–1900*
Pugh, P D G 1976. 'The planning of Haslar'. *Journal of Royal Naval Medical Service* **62**, 78–94, 207–26

Revell, A L 1984. *Haslar, The Royal Hospital*, 2nd edn
Rhodes, P 1977. *Doctor John Leake's Hospital*
Richardson, A E 1955. *Robert Mylne*
Ripman, H A (ed) 1951. *Guy's Hospital 1725–1948*
Rivett, G 1986. *The Development of the London Hospital System, 1823–1982*
Robb-Smith, A H T 1970. *A Short History of the Radcliffe Infirmary*
Roberton, J 1855–6. 'On the defects, with reference to the plan of construction and ventilation, of most of our hospitals for the reception of the sick and wounded'. *Transactions of the Manchester Statistical Society*, 133–48
Robertson, C Lockhurst 1860. 'A descriptive notice of the Sussex Lunatic Asylum, Hayward's Heath ...'. *Journal of Mental Science* **6**, No. 33 Apr 1860, 247–83
Robinson, W 1934. *The Story of the Royal Infirmary Sunderland* 1936. *The Centenary History of the Durham County and Sunderland Eye Infirmary, 1836–1936*
Rook, A *et al* 1991. T*he History of Addenbrooke's Hospital, Cambridge*
Rose, C 1989. 'Politics and the London Royal Hospitals, 1683–92'. In Granshaw and Porter 1989, 123–48
RCHME 1959. *City of Cambridge*
 1980. *City of Salisbury*. Vol I
Royal Institute of British Architects 1993. *Directory of British Architects 1834–1900*

Saint, A 1976. *Richard Norman Shaw*
 (ed) 1989. *Politics and the People of London: The London County Council 1889–1965*
Saundby, R 1914. 'An open-air military hospital, the First Eastern Military Hospital (T.F.), Cambridge'. *BMJ*, 28 Nov 1914, 942–3
Saunders, H St G 1949. *The Middlesex Hospital 1745–1948*
Scott, G G 1879. *Personal and Professional Recollections*
Scull, A T 1979. *Museums of Madness*
 1993. *The Most Solitary of Afflictions: Madness and Society in Britain 1700–1900*
 (ed) 1981. *Madhouses, Mad-Doctors, and Madmen. A Social History of Psychiatry in the Victorian Era*
Sheldrake, J 1989. 'The LCC hospital service'. In Saint 1989,187–97
Slack, P 1985. *The Impact of Plague in Tudor and Stuart England*
Smith, F B 1988. *The Retreat of Tuberculosis 1850–1950*
Smith, G M 1917. *A History of the Bristol Royal Infirmary*
Smith, J 1990. The Metropolitan Convalescent Institution, Walton on Thames. (Typewritten history, Walton and Weybridge Local History Society, Monograph No. 47)

Smith, J R 1987. *The Speckled Monster: Smallpox in England, 1670–1970 ...*
Snell, A 1905. *Exeter Workhouse Infirmary*
Snell, H S 1881. *Charitable and Parochial Establishments*
Stark, W 1810. *Remarks on the Construction of Public Hospitals for the Cure of Mental Derangement ...*
Stevenson, R S and Guthrie, D 1949. *A History of Oto-Laryngology*
Stow, J 1720. *A Survey of the Cities of London and Westminster*, ed J Strype, 2 vols
Stroud, D 1971. *George Dance, Architect, 1741–1825*
Survey of London XLI, 1983. *Southern Kensington: Brompton* XXV, 1955. *St George the Martyr and St Mary Newington, Southwark* XXIII, 1951. *St Mary, Lambeth*. Part 1
Swete, H 1870. *Handy Book of Cottage Hospitals*

Tait, L 1877. *An Essay on Hospital Mortality ...*
Tait, W 1905. *A History of Haslar Hospital*
Taylor, J R B 1988. 'Circular hospital wards: Professor John Marshall's concept and its exploration by the architectural profession in the 1880s'. *Medical History* **32**, 426–48
 1991. *Hospital and Asylum Architecture in England 1840–1914*
Thompson, J D and Goldin, G 1975. *The Hospital: A Social and Architectural History*
Thompson, K 1980. 'The building of the Leicester Union Workhouse, 1836–1839'. In Daniel Williams (ed) *The Adaptation of Change. Essays upon the History of Nineteenth-century Leicester and Leicestershire*, 58–76
Thomson, N C 1935. *The Story of the Middlesex Hospital Medical School*
Thornes, R 1994. *Images of Industry. Coal*
Thornes, R and Leach, J 1991. 'Buxton Old Hall: the Earl of Shrewsbury's Tower House re-discovered'. *Archaeol J* **148**, 256–68
Tomkins, S M 1993. 'Palmitate or Permanganate: the venereal prophylaxis debate in Britain, 1916–1926'. *Medical History* **37**, 382–98
Trinder, I F 1992. *A History of the Royal Masonic Hospital*
Tuke, S 1813. *Description of The Retreat*
Turner, B C 1986. *A History of the Royal Hampshire County Hospital*
Turner, E S 1967. *Taking the Cure*

VCH 1909. *The Victoria County History of London. Vol I* 1963. *A History of the County of Stafford. Vol VIII*

Waksman, S A 1964. *The Conquest of Tuberculosis*
Walford, E 1897. *Old and New London*, 6 vols
Walters, F R 1899. *Sanatoria for Consumptives*
Ward, R 1949. *The Design and Equipment of Hospitals*
Waring, E J 1867. *Cottage hospitals: Their Objects, Advantages and Management*
Watkin, B 1978. *The National Health Service: The First Phase ...*
Watson, F 1934. *The Life of Sir Robert Jones*
Watson, W and Pritchett, J P 1819. *Plans, Elevations, Sections and Description of the Pauper Lunatic Asylum Lately Erected at Wakefield for the West Riding of Yorkshire ...*
Weatherley, L A 1904–6. 'Boards of guardians and the crusade against consumption'. *Tuberculosis* **3**, 66–85
Welch, S C R 1954. *The Royal Air Force Medical Services. Vol I: Administration*
Westminster Hospital Board nd. *The Shape of Things to Come*
Whyman, J 1981. *Aspects of Holidaymaking and Resort Development within the Isle of Thanet, with Particular Reference to Margate, Circa 1736 to Circa 1840. Vol II*
Wilks, S 1892. *A Biographical History of Guy's Hospital*
Winterton, W R 1961. 'The story of the London gynaecological hospitals'. *Proceedings of the Royal Society of Medicine* **54**, No. 3, Mar 1961, 191–8 (*Section of Obstetrics and Gynaecology*, 1–8)
Woodham-Smith, C 1950. *Florence Nightingale, 1820–1910*
Woodward, J 1974. *To Do the Sick No Harm. A Study of the British Voluntary Hospital System to 1875*
Wright, L 1960. *Clean and Decent: The Fascinating History of the Bathroom and The Water Closet ...*
Wyke, T J 1975. 'The Manchester and Salford Lock Hospital, 1818–1917'. *Medical History* **19**, 73–86

Young, K D 1910. *On the Evolution of Hospital Design*

Appendix: Gazetteer of Sites Recorded

The following is a list of all hospital sites for which files have been created by the Royal Commission on the Historical Monuments of England. The list is arranged alphabetically by county, giving the place and the name by which the hospital is or was most commonly known. Founding or significant names by which sites were known, or present names where buildings survive with different uses are given in brackets. Lastly, the National Grid Reference, and the National Buildings Record Index Number are cited. The files are held in the National Monuments Record Centre at Swindon, except those for sites in Greater London which are in the National Monuments Record's London Public Search Room.

The contents of these files vary. Many have full reports, photographs, plans, extensive notes and documentary material; others contain little more than locational details. Any person interested in a particular site is therefore advised to make a written or telephone enquiry in the first instance.

The following abbreviations are used within the list:

BC	Borough Council
CB	County Borough
CC	County Council
EMS	Emergency Medical Service
JHB	Joint Hospital Board
JHC	Joint Hospital Committee
LCC	London County Council
PAI	Public Assistance Institution
PLI	Poor Law Institution
PSA	Port Sanitary Authority
RAF	Royal Air Force
RDC	Rural District Council
RSA	Rural Sanitary Authority
TC	Town Council
UD	Urban District
UDC	Urban District Council
URD	Urban Rural District

AVON

ALMONDSBURY
Almondsbury Hospital (Almondsbury Memorial Hospital) — ST 607 839 — 101525

BATH
Bath Ear, Nose and Throat Hospital — ST 743 655 — 101256
Bath Eye Infirmary — ST 749 655 — 101155
Bellot's Hospital — ST 750 645 — 101140
City of Bath Technical College (Bath United Hospital; Royal United Hospital) — ST 747 646 — 101141
Claverton Hospital (Bath Statutory Hospital for Infectious Diseases) — ST 779 629 — 101260
Combe Down Convalescent Home — ST 760 620 — 101531
Forbes Fraser Hospital — ST 727 657 — 101262
Lansdown Hospital and Nursing Home — ST 748 657 — 101255
Royal Bath United Hospital, West Site (Bath, Somerset and Wiltshire Central Orthopaedic Hospital) — ST 727 658 — 101599
Royal National Hospital for Rheumatic Diseases (Bath General Hospital; Bath Mineral Water Hospital) — ST 749 648 — 101073
Royal United Hospital — ST 728 657 — 101261
St Martin's Hospital (Bath Union Workhouse; Frome Road PLI) — ST 742 622 — 101257

BRISTOL
Brislington House — ST 633 702 — 101333
Bristol General Hospital — ST 588 722 — 101332
Bristol Homoeopathic Hospital — ST 582 738 — 101327
Bristol Royal Infirmary (Bristol Infirmary) — ST 587 735 — 101329
Cossham Memorial Hospital — ST 642 746 — 101331
Glenside Hospital (City and County of Bristol Mental Hospital; Bristol Mental Hospital) — ST 615 761 — 101585
Manor Park Hospital (Bristol Corporation Workhouse; Stapleton Institution) — ST 629 762 — 101326
Nover's Hill Isolation Hospital — ST 587 687 — 102755

Queen Victoria Jubilee Convalescent Home — ST 560 740 — 101532
Royal Hospital for Sick Children (Royal Hospital for Sick Children and Women; Children's Hospital) — ST 585 735 — 101328
Southmead Hospital (Barton Regis Union Workhouse; Bristol Union Workhouse) — ST 591 777 — 100888
University of Bristol Dental Hospital — ST 586 735 — 101330

CLEVEDON
Clevedon Hospital (Clevedon Cottage Hospital) — ST 413 713 — 101526

EASTON-IN-GORDANO
Ham Green Hospital (Bristol Infectious Diseases Hospital) — ST 532 756 — 102756

FRAMPTON COTTERELL
Northwoods Asylum — ST 638 824 — 101573

FRESHFORD
Queen Victoria Cottage Hospital — ST 780 600 — 101527

KEWSTOKE
Birmingham Hospital Saturday Fund Convalescent Home for Women — ST 333 634 — 101529

KEYNSHAM
Keynsham Fever and Smallpox Hospital — ST 653 677 — 102752

MANGOTSFIELD RURAL
Warmley RDC Fever Hospital — ST 666 766 — 102751

PAULTON
Paulton Hospital (Paulton Isolation Hospital) — ST 657 557 — 101335
Paulton Hospital (Paulton Memorial Hospital) — ST 655 557 — 101334

STOKE GIFFORD
Stoke Park Hospital (Stoke Park Colony) — ST 623 775 — 101574

WESTON SUPER MARE
Cannock Chase and Pelsall Miners' Convalescent Home — ST 320 610 — 100769
Drove Road Hospital (WestonsuperMare UDC Infectious Diseases Hospital) — ST 323 616 — 102754
Queen Alexandra Memorial Hospital (Weston-super-Mare Hospital) — ST 323 616 — 101528
The Royal Hospital (The Royal West of England Sanatorium) — ST 316 599 — 102753

WINTERBOURNE
Frenchay Hospital (Frenchay Park Sanatorium and Children's Orthopaedic Home) — ST 636 777 — 102784

YATE
Chipping Sodbury War Memorial Hospital — ST 720 824 — 101530

BEDFORDSHIRE

ASPLEY HEATH
Daneswood Jewish Convalescent Home — SP 930 350 — 102803

BEDFORD
Bedford General Hospital, North Wing (Bedford Workhouse) — TL 055 503 — 100234
Bedford General Hospital, South Wing (Bedford County Hospital) — TL 046 489 — 100222
Bedford Isolation Hospital — TL 057 482 — 100281
Bedford School Sanatorium — TL 027 510 — 100282
Bedford Smallpox Hospital — TL 054 486 — 100280

BIGGLESWADE
Biggleswade Hospital (Biggleswade UDC and RDC Isolation Hospital) — TL 201 459 — 100235
Biggleswade JHB Smallpox Hospital — TL 191 428 — 100220

BROMHAM
Bromham Hospital (Bromham Colony for Mental Defectives) — SP 993 513 — 100299

CLAPHAM
Clapham Hospital (Bedford RDC Isolation Hospital) — TL 024 535 — 100251

DUNSTABLE
Priory Hospital (Dunstable and District Joint Isolation Hospital) — TL 031 204 — 100236

HENLOW
RAF Station Hospital Henlow — TL 167 355 — 100720

LUTON
Bute Hospital — TL 085 213 — 100250
Children's Sick and Convalescent Home — TL 080 210 — 101576
Luton and Dunstable Hospital (Bute Hospital) — TL 050 228 — 100269
Luton and Dunstable Hospital (Luton Maternity Hospital) — TL 051 228 — 100268
St Mary's Hospital (Luton Union Workhouse) — TL 085 214 — 100249
Spittlesea Hospital (Luton Corporation Isolation Hospital) — TL 114 210 — 100270

MOGERHANGER
Park Hospital (Mogerhanger House) — TL 135 487 — 100230

STEPPINGLEY
Ampthill RDC and UDC Smallpox Hospital — TL 018 363 — 100225
Steppingley Hospital (Ampthill RDC and UDC Isolation Hospital) — TL 021 358 — 100226

STOTFOLD
Fairfield Hospital (Three Counties Asylum for Bedfordshire, Hertfordshire and Huntingdonshire; Three Counties Hospital) — TL 204 352 — 100223

WOBURN
Woburn Cottage Hospital (now Maryland College) — SP 942 329 — 100228
Woburn Cottage Hospital (Brewery House) — SP 948 331 — 100227

BERKSHIRE

BRACKNELL
Church Hill House Hospital (Easthampstead Union Workhouse) — SU 864 675 — 100389

BRADFIELD
Wayland Hospital (Bradfield Union Workhouse) — SU 606 717 — 100536

COLD ASH
Home for Sick Children — SU 606 717 — 100611

CROWTHORNE
Wellington College Sanatorium — SU 828 635 — 102759

HUNGERFORD
Hungerford Hospital (Hungerford Union Workhouse) — SU 340 682 — 100569

MAIDENHEAD
Maidenhead Cottage Hospital — SU 880 810 — 101577
St Mark's Hospital (Maidenhead Municipal Borough Infectious Diseases Hospital) — SU 871 813 — 100349
St Mark's Hospital (Maidenhead Union Workhouse) — SU 872 815 — 100387

NEWBURY
Newbury District Hospital — SU 468 663 — 100447
Sandleford Hospital (Newbury Union Workhouse) — SU 473 655 — 100513

OLD WINDSOR
King Edward VII Hospital, Old Windsor Unit (Windsor Union Workhouse) — SU 977 737 — 100237
Windsor Smallpox Hospital — SU 996 754 — 100238

READING
Battle Hospital (Reading Union Workhouse) — SU 697 738 — 100398
Dellwood Maternity Hospital — SU 710 730 — 101591
Prospect Hospital (The Park Isolation Hospital) — SU 685 727 — 100566
Royal Berkshire Hospital — SU 722 728 — 100412

SLOUGH
Upton Hospital (Eton Union Workhouse) — SU 096 794 — 100346

SPEEN
Speen Convalescent Home (Speen Cottage Hospital) — SU 456 680 — 100514

SUNNINGHIL
Heatherwood Hospital — SU 914 687 — 100348

WINDSOR
Combermere Barracks (Windsor Cavalry and Infantry Barracks) — SU 962 757 — 100141
King Edward VII Hospital — SU 964 758 — 100388
St Andrew's Hospital — SU 950 764 — 101534

WOKINGHAM
Wokingham Hospital (Wokingham Union Workhouse) — SU 803 685 — 100347

WOKINGHAM WITHOUT
Pinewood Sanatorium (London Open Air Sanatorium) — SU 835 659 — 100342

BUCKINGHAMSHIRE

AMERSHAM
Amersham Hospital (Amersham Union Workhouse) — SU 955 970 — 100254
Amersham Isolation Hospital — SU 955 968 — 100450

AYLESBURY
Royal Buckinghamshire Hospital (Buckinghamshire County Infirmary) — SU 817 142 — 100257
Stoke Mandeville Hospital (Aylesbury Isolation Hospital; Aylesbury Joint Isolation Hospital) — SU 826 117 — 100259

Stoke Mandeville Hospital (Ministry of
Pensions Hospital) — SU 825 119 — 100258
Tindal Centre (Aylesbury Union Workhouse) SP 825 146 — 100290

BUCKINGHAM
Buckingham Hospital (Buckingham Hospital
and Nursing Home) — SP 696 341 — 100350

CHALFONT ST PETER
Chalfont Centre (Chalfont Colony for
Epileptics) — TQ 004 926 — 100291
The Chalfonts and Gerrards Cross Hospital — SU 996 909 — 100288

CHESHAM
Chesham Hospital (Chesham Cottage Hospital) SP 963 012 — 100287

HALTON
Princess Mary's RAF Hospital — SP 876 086 — 100298

HIGH WYCOMBE
Booker Hospital (Wycombe RDC Isolation
Hospital; Wycombe and District Joint
Isolation Hospital) — SU 836 911 — 100253
Chepping Wycombe Corporation Isolation
Hospital — SU 841 915 — 100285
High Wycombe and Earl of Beaconsfield
Memorial Cottage Hospital (High
Wycombe Cottage Hospital) — SU 869 934 — 100284
Wycombe General Hospital (High Wycombe
and District War Memorial Hospital) — SU 864 926 — 100377

IVER
Iver, Denham and Langley Cottage Hospital — TQ 031 812 — 100340

MARLOW
Marlow Community Hospital (Marlow
Cottage Hospital) — SU 853 867 — 100345

NEWPORT PAGNELL
Newport Pagnell Union Workhouse — SP 886 432 — 100252

SLAPTON
The Grove Hospital (Linslade RDC Infectious
Diseases Hospital; Linslade UDC and Wing
RDC Infectious Diseases Hospital) — SP 911 232 — 100248

STONE WITH BISHOPSTONE AND HARTWELL
Saint John's Hospital (Buckinghamshire
County Asylum) — SP 770 720 — 100256

TAPLOW
Canadian Red Cross Hospital (Duchess of
Connaught's Red Cross Hospital) — SU 913 843 — 100104

CAMBRIDGESHIRE

CAMBRIDGE
Addenbrooke's Hospital — TL 451 579 — 88551
Brookfields Hospital (Borough Hospital for
Infectious Diseases) — TL 473 576 — 100240
Cambridge Smallpox Hospital — TL 477 581 — 100165
Chesterton Hospital (Chesterton Union
Workhouse) — TL 460 599 — 100187
Mill Road Maternity Hospital (Cambridge
Union Workhouse; now Ditchburn Place) TL 461 579 — 100186
First Eastern Military Hospital — TL 442 584 — 100097
Strangeways Research Laboratory (Research
Hospital for the Study of Special Diseases) — TL 470 550 — 100239

ELY
Princess of Wales RAF Hospital (RAF
General Hospital) — TL 547 818 — 100216
St John's Hospital (Ely UDC and RDC
Isolation Hospital) — TL 531 799 — 100162
Tower Hospital (Ely Union Workhouse) — TL 533 799 — 100157

FULBOURN
Fulbourn Hospital (Cambridgeshire County
Asylum) — TL 500 564 — 100241

HEMINGFORD GREY
St Ives Union Workhouse (now The Limes) — TL 307 703 — 100067

HUNTINGDON
Huntingdon County Hospital — TL 235 716 — 100082
Primrose Lane Maternity Hospital
(Huntingdon Municipal Borough Isolation
Hospital; now Huntingdon District Health
Authority Headquarters) — TL 242 720 — 100076
Petersfield Hospital (Huntingdon Union
Workhouse) — TL 234 723 — 100079

PAPWORTH EVERARD
Papworth Hospital (Cambridge Tuberculosis
Colony; Papworth Village Settlement
Central Institution) — TL 288 628 — 100215

PETERBOROUGH
The Gables Maternity Home — TL 182 987 — 100267
Peterborough District Hospital
(Peterborough Union Workhouse) — TL 183 987 — 100262

Peterborough District Hospital, Memorial
Wing (Peterborough District War
Memorial Hospital) — TL 184 987 — 100263
Peterborough Infirmary (Peterborough
Infirmary and Dispensary) — TL 189 985 — 100264
Peterborough Smallpox Hospital — TL 217 993 — 100265
St Peter's Hospital (Peterborough Fever
Hospital; City Sanatorium) — TL 200 985 — 100266

ST NEOTS
St Neots Union Workhouse (now The
White House) — TL 173 597 — 100218

WISBECH
Bowthorpe Hall Maternity Hospital
(Bowthorpe Hall) — TF 468 099 — 100181
North Cambridgeshire Hospital (North
Cambridgeshire Cottage Hospital) — TF 464 096 — 100242
Wisbech Smallpox Hospital — TF 463 109 — 100114

CHESHIRE

ALDERLEY EDGE
Alderley Edge Cottage Hospital — SJ 845 787 — 102122

ALDFORD
Aldford Dispensary (now Brook View) — SJ 410 590 — 102501

ARCLID
Arclid Hospital (Congleton Union Workhouse) SJ 788 624 — 102127
Arclid Infectious Diseases Hospital — SJ 788 626 — 102165

BARROW
East Lancashires Tuberculosis Colony and
Sanatorium — SJ 475 691 — 102718

CHESTER
Chester Royal Infirmary — SJ 401 664 — 102132
Countess of Chester Hospital (Cheshire
County Lunatic Asylum; Deva Hospital) — SJ 401 687 — 102131
St James's Hospital (Chester Union
Workhouse; St James's House) — SJ 420 670 — 100155
Sealand Isolation Hospital (Chester Isolation
Hospital) — SJ 383 668 — 102133

CONGLETON
Congleton Cottage Hospital — SJ 861 629 — 102125
Congleton War Memorial Hospital — SJ 866 624 — 102126
West Heath Isolation Hospital (Congleton
Joint Isolation Hospital; West Heath
Sanatorium) — SJ 837 635 — 102124

CRANAGE
Cranage Hall Hospital (Cranage Hall Colony) SJ 752 682 — 102135

CREWE
Crewe Isolation Hospital — SJ 708 566 — 102167
Crewe Memorial Cottage Hospital — SJ 685 558 — 102166
Railway Hospital — SJ 706 554 — 102169

DAVENHAM
Davenham Day Centre (Northwich, Middlewich
and Winsford Joint Isolation Hospital;
Davenham Isolation Hospital) — SJ 653 713 — 102137

ELLESMERE PORT
Ellesmere Port Hospital (Ellesmere Port
Cottage Hospital) — SJ 393 749 — 102504

GREAT WARFORD
High Grove Nursing Home (Ancoats Hospital
Convalescent Home; Ancoats Children's
Unit) — SJ 805 775 — 102120
Mary Dendy Hospital (Sandlebridge Boarding
Schools) — SJ 809 773 — 102119
Warford Hall (Mary Dendy Hospital) — SJ 817 767 — 102121

KNUTSFORD
Cranford Lodge Hospital (Altrincham Union
Workhouse; Bucklow Union Workhouse) SJ 748 784 — 102116
Knutsford War Memorial Cottage Hospital
(Knutsford and District War Memorial
Cottage Hospital) — SJ 743 786 — 102117

LITTLE WARFORD
The David Lewis Centre (The David Lewis
Manchester Epileptic Colony) — SJ 810 767 — 102134

MACCLESFIELD
Fence Hospital (now Fence House) — SJ 921 736 — 102008
Macclesfield Infirmary — SJ 913 740 — 102000
Moss Lane Smallpox Hospital (Macclesfield
Smallpox Hospital) — SJ 908 718 — 102005
Parkside Hospital (Cheshire County Lunatic
Asylum) — SJ 900 739 — 102006
West Park Hospital (Macclesfield Union
Workhouse) — SJ 909 739 — 102007
Weston Park Nursing Home (Macclesfield
Infectious Diseases Hospital; Moss Lane
Hospital) — SJ 907 720 — 102004

MANLEY
Crossley East Hospital (The Manchester
(Crossley) Sanatorium; Crossley
Sanatorium for Consumptives) — SJ 528 734 — 102140
Delamere Manor Private Nursing Home
(Liverpool Sanatorium, Frodsham;
Crossley Hospital West) — SJ 522 735 — 102141

NANTWICH
Alvaston Isolation Hospital (Nantwich Joint
Infectious Diseases Hospital; now Alvaston
Business Park) — SJ 657 537 — 102714
Barony Hospital (Nantwich Workhouse;
Nantwich Union Infirmary) — SJ 654 533 — 102128

NETHER ALDERLEY
Soss Moss Hospital — SJ 823 766 — 102118

NORTHWICH
Northwich Union Workhouse (now Salt
Museum) — SJ 658 731 — 102136
Victoria Infirmary (Verdin Park) — SJ 654 740 — 102130

RUNCORN
Victoria Memorial Cottage Hospital
(Runcorn Cottage Hospital) — SJ 510 790 — 102505

TARPORLEY
Tarporley War Memorial Hospital — SJ 555 626 — 102139

WARRINGTON
Warrington District General Hospital
(Warrington Infectious Diseases Hospital) SJ 595 886 — 102715
Warrington Infirmary and Dispensary — SJ 604 885 — 102502

WEAVERHAM
The Grange Hospital (Hefferston Grange
Sanatorium) — SJ 604 734 — 102138

WIDNES
Crow Wood Hospital (Widnes Isolation
Hospital) — SJ 527 867 — 102716
West Bank Hospital (Widnes Accident Hospital) SJ 510 850 — 102503

WILMSLOW
Styal Cottage Homes — SJ 844 828 — 102123

WINSFORD
Albert Infirmary — SJ 668 659 — 102168

WINWICK
Winwick Hospital (Lancashire County
Lunatic Asylum) — SJ 600 925 — 102598

WRENBURY CUM FRITH
Wrenbury Private Nursing Home (Wrenbury
Hall Tuberculosis Colony) — SJ 600 486 — 102129

CLEVELAND

ESTON
Eston Hospital — NZ 553 186 — 102190
Eston UD Fever Hospital (Eston Sanatorium) NZ 549 195 — 102664
Normanby Hospital (Eston UD Infectious
Diseases Hospital) — NZ 549 178 — 102191
River Tees PSA Floating Hospital — NZ 536 233 — 102662

GUISBOROUGH
Admiral Chaloner Hospital (Guisborough
Miners' Accident Hospital) — NZ 616 158 — 102193
Graceland Nursing Home (Guisborough
JHB Infectious Diseases Hospital) — NZ 619 151 — 102665
Guisborough General Hospital
(Guisborough Union Workhouse) — NZ 614 163 — 102177
Hutton Cottage Hospital — NZ 590 150 — 102528

HARTLEPOOL
Brierton Hospital — NZ 498 302 — 102182
Cameron Hospital — NZ 494 331 — 102185
Hartlepool General Hospital (Hartlepool
Union Workhouse; Howbeck Infirmary) — NZ 500 345 — 102181
Hartlepool Port Sanitary Hospital — NZ 509 351 — 102187
St Hilda's Hospital (Hartlepool's Hospital) — NZ 530 338 — 102186

LOFTUS
Skinningrove Miners' Accident Hospital — NZ 710 190 — 102529

MIDDLESBROUGH
Carter Bequest Hospital — NZ 487 179 — 102175
Hemlington Hospital (Middlesbrough
Smallpox Hospital) — NZ 499 136 — 102174
Middlesbrough General Hospital
(Middlesbrough Union Workhouse;
Holgate Institution and Municipal
Hospital) — NZ 485 190 — 102171
Middlesbrough Maternity Hospital
(Middlesbrough Maternity Hospital and
Children's Home) — NZ 496 194 — 102188
North Ormesby Hospital (North Ormesby
Cottage Hospital; North Ormesby
General Hospital) — NZ 507 199 — 102189
North Riding Infirmary — NZ 490 202 — 102172

North Riding Infirmary Nurses' Homes — NZ 498 193 — 102297
Poole Hospital (Poole Joint Sanatorium) — NZ 536 134 — 102192
St Luke's Hospital (Cleveland Asylum; Middlesbrough Mental Hospital) — NZ 508 179 — 102173
West Lane Hospital (West Lane Sanatorium) — NZ 481 187 — 102176

REDCAR
Coatham Convalescent Home and Children's Hospital (Home of the Good Samaritan Convalescent Home; Redcar Convalescent Home) — NZ 593 249 — 102527
Redcar UD Fever Hospital (Neasham's Hind House) — NZ 587 248 — 102663
Stead Memorial Hospital — NZ 596 249 — 102179

SALTBURN, MARSKE AND NEW MARSKE
Club House Convalescent Home (Saltburn Convalescent Home) — NZ 661 215 — 102426
Guisborough RDC Isolation Hospital — NZ 618 201 — 102661
Saltburn by the Sea UDC Infectious Diseases Hospital (now Marske End Poultry Farm) — NZ 648 212 — 102365

SKELTON AND BROTTON
Cleveland Cottage Hospital — NZ 694 199 — 102178
Skelton Green Miners' Accident Hospital — NZ 657 181 — 102475

STOCKTON ON TEES
Children's Hospital (Stockton Fever Hospital) — NZ 434 203 — 102180
Portrack Lane Hospital (Stockton Union Workhouse) — NZ 451 196 — 102184
Stockton and Thornaby Hospital (Stockton Surgical Hospital) — NZ 442 183 — 102183

CORNWALL

BODMIN
Bodmin Union Workhouse — SX 074 673 — 100260
East Cornwall Hospital — SX 072 672 — 100300
St Lawrence's Hospital (Cornwall County Lunatic Asylum) — SX 055 669 — 100359

BUDE-STRATTON
Stratton and Bude UDC Isolation Hospital — SS 240 064 — 100314
Stratton Hospital (Stratton Cottage Hospital) — SS 228 064 — 100351

BUDOCK
Falmouth and Truro Port Health Authority Hospital — SW 782 333 — 100293

CAMELFORD
Camelford Union Workhouse — SX 101 834 — 100301

CARN BREA
Barncoose Hospital (Redruth Union Workhouse) — SW 685 416 — 100357

FALMOUTH
Falmouth Hospital and Dispensary (Falmouth Hospital) — SW 802 324 — 100302
Budock Hospital (Falmouth Union Workhouse) — SW 788 333 — 100313
Falmouth and District Hospital (Falmouth Hospital) — SW 796 329 — 100354
Royal Cornwall Sailors' Home and Hospital — SW 811 324 — 100292

FOWEY
Fowey Hospital — SX 123 520 — 100296

HAYLE
St Michael's Hospital — SW 556 367 — 100294

HELSTON
Helston and District Hospital (Helston and District War Memorial Cottage Hospital) — SW 665 264 — 100303
Meneage Hospital (Helston Union Workhouse) — SW 662 272 — 100356

ILLOGAN
Tehidy Sanatorium — SW 647 433 — 100311

LAUNCESTON
Launceston Hospital — SX 328 837 — 100304
Launceston Infirmary and Rowe Dispensary (Rowe Dispensary) — SX 328 844 — 100297
Launceston Union Workhouse — SX 335 838 — 100352

LISKEARD
Lamellion Hospital (Liskeard Union Workhouse) — SX 247 640 — 100295
Passmore Edwards Hospital (Passmore Edwards Cottage Hospital; Liskeard Cottage Hospital) — SX 250 648 — 100305

MADRON
Penzance Union Workhouse — SW 450 324 — 100306

NEWQUAY
Newquay and District Hospital — SW 836 613 — 100307

PENZANCE
West Cornwall Hospital (West Cornwall Infirmary and Dispensary) — SW 467 307 — 100355

REDRUTH
Camborne and Redruth Hospital (West Cornwall Hospital for Convalescent Miners; West Cornwall Miners' and Women's Hospital) — SW 692 417 — 100309

ST COLUMB MAJOR
St Columb Union Workhouse — SW 916 637 — 100358

ST IVES
Edward Hain Hospital (Edward Hain Memorial Cottage Hospital) — SW 518 399 — 100360

ST AUSTELL
St Austell and District Hospital (St Austell Cottage Hospital) — SX 004 525 — 100310

SALTASH
St Barnabas Hospital (St Barnabas Cottage Hospital and Convalescent Home) — SX 427 586 — 100380

TRURO
Royal Cornwall Hospital — SW 823 446 — 100353
St Clement's Hospital (Truro Union Workhouse) — SW 838 456 — 100312

CUMBRIA

ALSTON MOOR
Ruth Lancaster James Cottage Hospital — NY 718 462 — 102534

ARTHURET
Longtown and Border Joint Isolation Hospital (Longtown Isolation Hospital) — NY 392 684 — 102283

BARROW-IN-FURNESS
Devonshire Road Hospital (Barrow-in-Furness Infectious Diseases Hospital) — SD 210 708 — 102088
North Lonsdale Hospital — SD 203 688 — 102085
Rakesmoor Hospital (Barrow-in-Furness Smallpox Hospital) — SD 205 725 — 102089
Risedale Nursing Home (Risedale Maternity Hospital) — SD 206 704 — 102086
Roose Hospital (Barrow-in-Furness Workhouse) — SD 221 689 — 102084

BEAUMONT
Carlisle Infectious Diseases Hospital (Carlisle Smallpox Hospital) — NY 357 562 — 102282

BRAMPTON
Brampton War Memorial Hospital (Brampton and District War Memorial Hospital) — NY 535 607 — 102274

BRIDEKIRK
Dovenby Hall Hospital (Dovenby Hall Colony for the Mentally Defective) — NY 094 331 — 102292

CARLISLE
Carlisle Dispensary — NY 402 560 — 102281
City General Hospital (Carlisle Union Workhouse; City Maternity Hospital) — NY 409 556 — 102279
Cumberland Infirmary — NY 388 561 — 102277
Fever Hospital (now part of Cumberland Infirmary) — NY 386 561 — 102278
Home for Incurables of the Border Counties — NY 387 554 — 102276

COCKERMOUTH
Cockermouth Cottage Hospital — NY 125 310 — 102293
Cockermouth Union Workhouse — NY 118 304 — 100170

GRANGE-OVER-SANDS
North-Eastern Counties Friendly Societies' Convalescent Home — SD 417 789 — 102533
Risedale Convalescent Home — SD 398 768 — 102532

KENDAL
Kendal Borough Sanatorium — SD 520 918 — 102690
Kendal Green Hospital (Kendal Workhouse; Windermere Road Institution) — SD 512 932 — 102082
Kendal Memorial Hospital — SD 511 923 — 102081
Westmorland County Hospital — SD 511 923 — 102080

KESWICK
Mary Hewetson Cottage Hospital — NY 265 241 — 102294

MARYPORT
Maryport Isolation Hospital — NY 039 357 — 102291
Victoria Cottage Hospital — NY 038 357 — 102290

MEATHOP AND ULPHA
Meathop Hospital (North Eastern Counties Friendly Societies' Convalescent Home; Westmorland Sanatorium) — SD 436 801 — 102079

MILLOM
Hodbarrow Hospital — SD 171 789 — 102486

MILNTHORPE
Kitching Memorial Hospital — SD 490 810 — 102531

ORMSIDE
Ormside Hospital (Ormside Fever Hospital) — NY 697 165 — 102689

PENNINGTON
High Carley Hospital, East Site (Lancashire County Sanatorium for Tuberculosis; High Carley Sanatorium) — SD 270 760 — 102395
High Carley Hospital, West Site (Ulverston Union Infectious Diseases Hospital; High Carley Isolation Hospital for Infectious Diseases) — SD 268 760 — 102087

PENRITH
Fairhill Hospital (Penrith UD Isolation Hospital; Fairhill Fever Hospital) — NY 513 313 — 102688
Jubilee Cottage Hospital — NY 519 341 — 102487

ST CUTHBERT WITHOUT
Garlands Hospital (Cumberland and Westmorland Lunatic Asylum) — NY 432 538 — 102284

SILLOTH-ON-SOLWAY
Silloth Nursing Home (Silloth Convalescent Institution; Cumberland and Westmorland Convalescent Institution) — NY 104 531 — 102286

THRELKELD
Blencathra Hospital (Blencathra Sanatorium) — NY 303 256 — 102295

ULVERSTON
Ulverston Cottage Hospital (Ulverston and District Cottage Hospital) — SD 291 784 — 102083
Ulverston Hospital (Ulverston Union Workhouse; Stanley Hospital) — SD 284 786 — 102090

WEDDICAR
Galemire Hospital (Galemire Joint Hospital for Infectious Diseases; subsequently Galemire Veterinary Hospital) — NY 003 153 — 102287

WHITEHAVEN
Meadow View Hospital (Whitehaven Union Workhouse) — NX 975 163 — 100168
Whitehaven and West Cumberland Infirmary (Whitehaven Castle) — NX 977 178 — 82302
Whitehaven and West Cumberland Infirmary — NX 972 178 — 102530

WIGTON
Wigton Hospital (Wigton Union Workhouse) — NY 248 490 — 102285

WORKINGTON
Ellerbeck Hospital (Workington Poor House; Workington Corporation Infectious Diseases Hospital) — NY 006 270 — 102289
Workington Infirmary — NY 001 279 — 102288

DERBYSHIRE

ASHBOURNE
Ashbourne Cottage Hospital (Victoria Cottage Hospital; now Victoria Court) — SK 180 469 — 102410
St Oswald's Hospital (Ashbourne Union Workhouse) — SK 174 464 — 102411

ASTON-ON-TRENT
Aston Hall Mental Hospital (Aston Hall Colony for Mental Defectives) — SK 415 291 — 61425

BAKEWELL
Bakewell Cottage Hospital (Bakewell and District War Memorial Cottage Hospital) — SK 216 683 — 102068
Newholme Hospital (Bakewell Union Workhouse) — SK 220 691 — 102069

BELPER
Babington Hospital (Belper Union Workhouse) — SK 346 470 — 102413

BRETBY
Bretby Hall Orthopaedic Hospital — SK 300 226 — 102604

BURNASTON
Pastures Hospital (Derby County Lunatic Asylum) — SK 297 331 — 102238

BUXTON
Buxton Hospital (Buxton Cottage Hospital) — SK 062 724 — 102419
Devonshire Royal Hospital (Devonshire Hospital and Buxton Bath Charity) — SK 055 737 — 102420

CHESTERFIELD
Chesterfield and North Derbyshire Royal Hospital (Chesterfield and North Derbyshire Hospital) — SK 381 715 — 102235
Scarsdale Hospital (Chesterfield Union Workhouse) — SK 381 715 — 100617
Walton Hospital (Derbyshire Sanatorium; Walton Sanatorium) — SK 374 696 — 102421

DARLEY DALE
Whitworth Hospital — SK 285 615 — 102422

DERBY
City Hospital (Derby City Hospital) — SK 327 350 — 102415
Derbyshire Children's Hospital (Derbyshire Hospital for Sick Children) — SK 349 370 — 102236
Derbyshire Royal Infirmary (Derbyshire General Hospital) — SK 350 355 — 102237
Kingsway Hospital (Derby Borough Lunatic Asylum; Derby Borough Mental Hospital) — SK 328 356 — 102407
Manor Hospital (Derby Union Workhouse; Boundary House Institution) — SK 327 353 — 102408
Nightingale Nursing Home — SK 358 356 — 102409

GLOSSOP
Partington Convalescent Home — SK 030 930 — 102537

Wood's Continuation Hospital (Wood's Hospital) — SK 030 930 102536

HEANOR AND LOSCOE
Heanor and District Memorial Hospital (Heanor, Langley Mill and District Memorial Hospital) — SK 438 460 102417

HOLBROOK
Edith Adela Strutt Memorial Convalescent Home (Derbyshire Infirmary Convalescent Home) — SK 360 450 102538

HOLMESFIELD
Sheffield Poor Children's Holiday and Convalescent Home — SK 320 770 102535

ILKESTON
Ilkeston Hospital (now Apricot Nursing Home) — SK 461 430 102416

PARWICH
Florence Ada Monica Rathborne Convalescent Home (Rathborne Convalescent Home; now Parwich Care Centre for the Elderly) — SK 189 547 102418

RIPLEY
Ripley Hospital (Ripley Cottage Hospital) — SK 396 502 102414

SHIREBROOK
Langwith District Isolation Hospital — SK 517 682 102719

STAVELEY
Chesterfield RDC Isolation Hospital (Mastin Moor Hospital; now Castle View Nursing Home) — SK 460 757 102423

DEVON

ASHBURTON
Ashburton and Buckfastleigh Hospital (Ashburton and Buckfastleigh Cottage Hospital) — SX 761 703 100700

AXMINSTER
Axminster Cottage Hospital (Axminster Carpet Factory) — SY 297 986 100793
Axminster Hospital (Axminster Cottage Hospital) — SY 298 987 100794

BARNSTAPLE
North Devon Infirmary — SS 561 327 100556

BEAWORTHY
Winsford Hospital — SX 445 999 100335

BIDEFORD
Bideford and District Hospital — SS 448 265 100433
The Grenville Nursing Home (Bideford and District Dispensary and Infirmary; Bideford and District Hospital) — SS 451 263 100498
Torridge Hospital (Bideford Union Workhouse) — SS 449 263 100499

BOVEY TRACEY
Bovey Tracey and District Hospital — SX 815 789 100320
Hawkmoor Sanatorium (Devon CC Sanatorium for Tuberculosis) — SX 802 808 100322

CHAGFORD
Dartmoor Sanatorium (now Torr House Hotel) — SX 684 868 100702

CREDITON
Crediton Hospital (Crediton Union Workhouse) — SS 005 820 100368

DARTMOUTH
Dartmouth and Kingswear Hospital (Dartmouth Cottage Hospital) — SX 878 513 100706

DAWLISH
Dawlish Cottage Hospital — SX 958 769 100361

ERMINGTON
Lee Mill Hospital (Plympton St Mary RDC Isolation Hospital; Plymouth Isolation Hospital) — SX 606 563 100379

EXETER
Digby Hospital (City of Exeter Lunatic Asylum) — SS 770 880 60100
Ellen Tinkham School (Heavitree Isolation Hospital; Exeter Corporation Tuberculosis Sanatorium) — SX 962 934 100364
Exeter Dispensary (now Exeter College of Art and Design) — SX 918 928 100321
Exe Vale Hospital (Wonford House Lunatic Asylum; Wonford House Hospital) — SX 937 917 100362
Institution for Trained Nurses and Home Hospital — SX 923 923 100383
Princess Elizabeth Orthopaedic Hospital (Devonian Cripples' Hospital) — SX 930 920 100317
Redhills Hospital (St Thomas Union Workhouse) — SX 907 924 100367
Royal Devon and Exeter Hospital (Devon and Exeter Hospital; now Dean Clarke House) — SX 923 923 100365
Royal Devon and Exeter Hospital (Exeter Incorporation Workhouse; Exeter City Hospital) — SX 932 927 100366
West of England Eye Infirmary — SX 923 922 100318
Whipton Hospital (Exeter City Isolation Hospital) — SX 954 934 100319

EXMOUTH
Exmouth Cottage Hospital — SY 009 810 100363

GREAT TORRINGTON
Torrington Cottage Hospital — SS 490 190 100798

HOLSWORTHY
Holsworthy Hospital (Holsworthy Union Workhouse) — SS 340 042 100370

HONITON
Marlpits Hospital (Honiton Union Workhouse) — ST 164 002 100316

KENTON
Western Counties' Hospital (Western Counties Idiots' Asylum; Royal Western Counties' Hospital) — SX 976 816 100334

KINGSBRIDGE
South Hams Hospital (South Hams, Kingsbridge, Salcombe and District Cottage Hospital) — SX 731 447 100705

LYNTON AND LYNMOUTH
Lynton Cottage Hospital — SS 710 490 100797

MORETONHAMPSTEAD
Moretonhampstead Hospital (Moreton-hampstead Cottage Hospital) — SX 752 862 100701

NEWTON ABBOT
Newton Abbot Hospital (Newton Abbot Cottage Hospital and Dispensary) — SX 860 710 100371
Newton Abbot Hospital (Newton Abbot Union Workhouse) — SX 861 710 100372
Newton Abbot Joint Isolation Hospital — SX 852 702 100323

OKEHAMPTON
Okehampton and District War Memorial Cottage Hospital — SX 591 951 100333

OTTERY ST MARY
Ottery St Mary District Cottage Hospital — SY 100 956 100315

PLYMOUTH
Central Hospital (Devon and Cornwall Homoeopathic Hospital and Three Towns Dispensary) — SX 476 543 100384
Military Families' Hospital (subsequently Cumberland House Residential Unit) — SX 458 544 100332
Mount Gould Hospital (Plymouth Borough Fever Hospital) — SX 498 552 100328
Plymouth General Hospital (South Devon and East Cornwall Hospital; Prince of Wales Hospital) — SX 485 553 100385
Plymouth General Hospital, Freedom Fields (Plymouth Incorporation Workhouse) — SX 487 567 100329
Royal Albert Hospital and Eye Infirmary (Devonport, Stonehouse and Cornwall Hospital) — SX 453 549 100327
Royal Eye Infirmary (Plymouth Eye Dispensary; Plymouth Eye Infirmary) — SX 480 556 100375
Royal Military Hospital (now Devonport High School for Boys) — SX 463 549 100376
Royal Naval Hospital — SX 466 547 100373
Scott Hospital (Devonport Borough Isolation Hospital; Swilly Isolation Hospital) — SX 464 567 100326
Stoke Damerell Workhouse — SX 460 565 100374

SEATON
Seaton and District Community Hospital (Seaton and Beer Cottage Hospital) — SY 240 900 100795

SIDMOUTH
Victoria Cottage Hospital — SY 125 876 100796

SOUTH BRENT
Didworthy Chest Hospital (Devon and Cornwall Sanatorium for Consumptives) — SX 685 622 100331

TAVISTOCK
Tavistock Hospital (Tavistock Cottage Hospital and Dispensary) — SX 474 742 100382

TEIGNMOUTH
Teignmouth, Dawlish and Newton Infirmary and Convalescent Home (Teignmouth Dispensary; Teignmouth and Dawlish Dispensary and Marine Infirmary) — SX 940 730 100799
Teignmouth Hospital — SX 940 730 100800

TIVERTON
Belmont Hospital (Tiverton Union Workhouse) — SS 958 130 38934
Blundell's School Sanatorium — SS 975 130 100434
Post Hill Hospital (Tiverton and District Hospital for Infectious Diseases) — SS 986 013 100503
Tiverton and District Hospital (Tiverton Hospital and Dispensary) — SS 956 008 100500

TORBAY
Brixham Hospital (Brixham Cottage Hospital and District Nursing Institution) — SX 925 554 100707
Erith House Home of Rest (Erith House Residence for Gentlewomen with Chest Disease) — SX 929 638 100703
Kings Ash Hospital (Paignton Isolation Hospital) — SX 874 608 100709
Paignton and District Hospital (Paignton Cottage Hospital) — SX 887 608 100708
Rosehill Children's Hospital — SX 900 650 100817
Torbay Hospital — SX 898 659 100647
Torbay Hospital, Provident Dispensary and Eye Infirmary (Torquay Dispensary; now Castle Chambers) — SX 911 645 100704
Torquay Isolation Hospital — SX 897 662 100648

TOTNES
Broomborough Hospital (Totnes Union Workhouse) — SX 795 603 100325
Totnes and District Hospital (Totnes and District Cottage Hospital; Totnes Cottage Hospital) — SX 810 604 100324

UGBOROUGH
Moorhaven Hospital (Plymouth Borough Lunatic Asylum) — SX 667 577 100330

DORSET

ALLINGTON
Bridport Isolation Hospital — SY 456 939 100478

BLANDFORD FORUM
Blandford Community Hospital (Blandford Cottage Hospital) — ST 884 069 100466

BOURNEMOUTH
Herbert Hospital (Herbert Memorial Convalescent Home) — SZ 066 908 100462
Kings Park Community Hospital (Bournemouth Sanitary Hospital; Bournemouth Municipal Hospital) — SZ 118 924 100403
Royal National Hospital (Royal National Sanatorium for Consumption) — SZ 083 914 100243
Royal Victoria and West Hampshire Hospital, Shelley Road Branch (Boscombe Hospital; Royal Boscombe and West Hampshire Hospital) — SZ 149 939 100401
Royal Victoria and West Hampshire Hospital, Victoria Branch (Royal Victoria Hospital) — SZ 076 915 100402

BRIDPORT
Bridport General Hospital — SY 459 932 100419
Port Bredy Hospital (Bridport Union Workhouse) — SY 469 931 100477

CHARMINSTER
Herrison Hospital (Dorset County Asylum) — SY 678 947 100244

CHRISTCHURCH
Christchurch Hospital (Christchurch Union Workhouse) — SZ 150 939 100461

CORFE CASTLE
Wareham Council Smallpox Hospital — SY 941 843 100670

DORCHESTER
Damers Hospital (Dorchester Union Workhouse) — SY 687 903 100475
Dorchester Isolation Hospital — SY 689 891 100418
Dorset County Hospital — SY 691 906 100417
Royal Horse Artillery Barracks Hospital — SY 686 909 100476

LYME REGIS
Lyme Regis Hospital — SY 336 921 100422

POOLE
Alderney Hospital (Poole BC Isolation Hospital; Alderney Isolation Hospital) — SZ 042 943 100465
Poole General Hospital (Cornelia Hospital; Cornelia and East Dorset Hospital) — SZ 020 913 100464
Poole Hospital (Poole Union Workhouse) — SZ 018 914 100404
St Anne's Hospital (St Anne's Sanatorium) — SZ 052 888 100463

PORTLAND
Portland Hospital (Royal Naval Hospital) — SY 685 741 100481

SHAFTESBURY
Westminster Memorial Hospital (Westminster Memorial and Cottage Hospital) — ST 860 228 100487

SHERBORNE
Coldharbour Hospital — ST 643 176 100066

Sherborne Isolation Hospital	ST 622 173	100425
Sherborne School Sanatorium	ST 635 166	100424
Yeatman Memorial Hospital (Yeatman Hospital)	ST 636 167	100483
St Leonards and St Ives: St Leonard's Hospital (104th US General Hospital)	SU 102 020	100468

STURMINSTER NEWTON

Sturminster Union Workhouse	ST 787 148	100426

SWANAGE

Dorset Red Cross War Memorial Children's Hospital	SZ 033 782	100467
Swanage Cottage Hospital	SZ 128 784	100406

WAREHAM TOWN

Christmas Close Hospital (Wareham and Purbeck Union Workhouse)	SY 918 874	100407

WEYMOUTH

Portway Hospital (Weymouth Union Workhouse)	SY 675 785	100479
Westhaven Hospital (Weymouth Corporation Isolation Hospital)	SY 660 795	100421
Weymouth and District Hospital (Princess Christian Hospital and Sanatorium)	SY 682 803	100480
Weymouth and Dorset County Royal Eye Infirmary	SY 683 803	100423
Weymouth PSA Hospital	SY 666 762	100420
Wimborne Minster: Victoria Hospital (Victoria Cottage Hospital)	SU 004 002	100405

DURHAM

BARNARD CASTLE

Richardson Hospital (Robert Richardson Convalescent Home)	NZ 054 168	102197
Teesdale Union Workhouse	NZ 054 169	102200
Witham Hall (Witham Testimonial)	NZ 050 165	102199

BISHOP AUCKLAND

Binchester Whins Hospital (Auckland, Shildon and Willington JHB Smallpox Hospital; Binchester Whins Smallpox Hospital)	NZ 218 328	102219
Bishop Auckland General Hospital (Bishop Auckland Union Workhouse; Oaklands PLI)	NZ 208 290	102207
Homelands Hospital (Auckland, Shildon and Willington Joint Isolation Hospital; Helmington Row Fever Hospital)	NZ 178 349	102210
Lady Eden Day Unit (Lady Eden Cottage Hospital; Bishop Auckland Cottage Hospital)	NZ 210 290	102208
Tindale Crescent Hospital (Auckland, Shildon and Willington JHB Infectious Diseases Hospital)	NZ 199 276	102209

BRANDON AND BYSHOTTLES

Brandon and Byshottles Urban District Fever Hospital	NZ 235 400	102672

CHESTER-LE-STREET

Chester-le-Street Hospital (Chester-le-Street Union Workhouse)	NZ 274 508	102216
Highfield Hospital (Chester-le-Street Hospital for Infectious Diseases)	NZ 273 524	102217

CHILTON

Chilton Health Centre	NZ 280 290	102491

CONSETT

Consett Infirmary	NZ 090 510	102489
Richard Murray Hospital	NZ 090 500	102490
Shotley Bridge General Hospital (Shotley Bridge Sanatorium; Shotley Bridge Ministry of Pensions Hospital)	NZ 103 527	102213

DARLINGTON

Darlington Memorial Hospital (Darlington War Memorial Hospital)	NZ 283 152	102194
East Haven Hospital (Darlington Union Workhouse; Feetham Infirmary)	NZ 301 142	102201
Greenbank Hospital (Darlington Hospital and Dispensary; Darlington Hospital)	NZ 285 152	102195
Hundents Day Unit (Darlington Infectious Diseases Hospital; Darlington Municipal Borough Fever Hospital)	NZ 301 145	102203
Russell Street Hospital (Darlington Hospital and Dispensary)	NZ 291 148	102202

DURHAM

Dryburn Hospital	NZ 263 437	102223
Durham County Hospital	NZ 267 427	102220
St Margaret's Hospital (Durham Union Workhouse; Crossgate Hospital)	NZ 268 424	102221

EASINGTON

Thorpe Hospital (Easington Rural District Infectious Diseases Hospital; Thorpe Isolation Hospital)	NZ 418 426	102339

GREENCROFT

Maiden Law Hospital (Lanchester Joint Isolation Hospital)	NZ 166 487	102214

HEIGHINGTON

Aycliffe Hospital (School Aycliffe Mental Colony)	NZ 261 234	102196

LANCHESTER

Lanchester Sanatorium	NZ 177 498	102364
Lanchester Union Workhouse	NZ 164 475	102218
Langley: Langley Park Hospital (Lanchester JHB Infectious Diseases Hospital)	NZ 208 445	102671

LOW DINSDALE

Dinsdale Park Retreat	NZ 342 121	102412

MARWOOD

Barnard Castle Fever Hospital (Barnard Castle Infectious Diseases Hospital)	NZ 052 182	102198

MIDDLETON ST GEORGE

Felix House Private Sanatorium	NZ 345 131	102300
Middleton Hall Mental Hospital (now Middleton Hall Nursing Home)	NZ 358 132	102299
Ropner Convalescent Home	NZ 340 130	102526

SEAHAM

Seaham Hall Sanatorium (now Seaham Hall Nursing Home)	NZ 410 505	102369
Seaham Infirmary	NZ 429 496	102425

SEDGEFIELD

Sedgefield Community Hospital (Winterton EMS Hospital; Sedgefield General Hospital)	NZ 360 311	102212
Sedgefield Institution (Sedgefield Union Workhouse)	NZ 353 286	102205
Winterton Hospital (Durham County Lunatic Asylum; Winterton Mental Hospital)	NZ 356 306	102204
Winterton Hospital, South View (Sedgefield RDC Isolation Hospital)	NZ 355 298	102234
Winterton Hospital, Ward 40 (Sedgefield RDC Isolation Hospital)	NZ 360 313	102233

SHINCLIFFE

Sherburn Hospital (Christ's Hospital)	NZ 308 416	102239
Spennymoor: Spennymoor UDC Isolation Hospital (now The Gables)	NZ 251 327	102206

STANHOPE

Horn Hall Hospital (Durham County Consumption Sanatorium; Stanhope Sanatorium)	NY 989 392	102211

STANLEY

South Moor Hospital (South Moor and Craghead Welfare Fund Hospital; Holmside and South Moor Hospital)	NZ 200 515	102215

WITTON GILBERT

Earl's House Hospital (Earl's House Sanatorium)	NZ 251 451	102222

WOLSINGHAM

Holywood Hospital (Durham County Sanatorium; Holywood Hall Sanatorium)	NZ 073 383	102670
Leazes House Sanatorium	NZ 069 374	102669

EAST SUSSEX see under SUSSEX (EAST SUSSEX)

ESSEX

BASILDON

Mayflower Hospital (Billericay RDC Hospital)	TQ 666 955	102798
St Andrew's Hospital (Billericay Union Workhouse)	TL 678 952	100679

BLACK NOTLEY

Black Notley Hospital (Black Notley Sanatorium)	TL 766 201	102796

BRAINTREE

Braintree and Bocking Cottage Hospital	TL 764 246	101419
St Michael's Hospital (Braintree Union Workhouse)	TL 751 231	100680
William Julien Courtauld Hospital (Braintree and Bocking Cottage Hospital)	TL 753 227	101418

BRENTWOOD

Brentwood Community Hospital (Brentwood District Hospital)	TQ 604 942	101278
High Wood Hospital (Highwood School)	TQ 589 946	101277
St Faith's Hospital (Shoreditch Industrial School)	TQ 587 936	101279
Warley Hospital (Essex County Lunatic Asylum)	TQ 588 923	101251

BURNHAM-ON-CROUCH

Burnham-on-Crouch Cottage Hospital	TQ 951 961	101422

CHELMSFORD

Chelmsford and Essex Hospital (Chelmsford Infirmary and Dispensary)	TL 707 065	101245
St John's Hospital (Chelmsford Union Workhouse)	TL 699 049	101244

CLACTON-ON-SEA

Clacton and District Hospital (Clacton and District Cottage Hospital)	TM 172 144	101420
Middlesex Hospital Convalescent Home	TM 184 157	101423
Reckitt Convalescent Home	TM 187 157	101424

COLCHESTER

Essex County Hospital (Essex and Colchester General Infirmary)	TL 989 248	101417
Essex Hall Hospital (Eastern Counties' Asylum for Idiots)	TL 992 263	101600
Medical Reception Station (Colchester Military Hospital)	TL 995 237	100719
Severalls Hospital (Second Essex County Asylum; Severalls County Asylum)	TL 993 283	101579
Turner Village Hospital (Royal Eastern Counties' Institution)	TL 996 273	101578

EPPING

St Margaret's Hospital (Epping Union Workhouse)	TL 469 028	101344

GREAT BADDOW

Baddow Road Hospital (Chelmsford Joint Isolation Hospital)	TL 718 055	101246

HALSTEAD

Halstead Hospital (Halstead Cottage Hospital)	TL 814 310	101413
Halstead UDC Infectious Diseases Hospital	TL 809 300	102797

HARWICH

Harwich and District Hospital (Rosebank House; Harwich and District Cottage Hospital and Fryatt Memorial)	TM 243 312	101421

LOUGHTON

Forest Place Nursing Home (Foresthill Hospital)	TQ 415 944	101336

MALDON

St Peter's Hospital (Maldon Union Workhouse)	TL 845 068	101243

ONGAR

Ongar and District Cottage Hospital	TL 553 042	101414
Ongar War Memorial Hospital (Ongar and District War Memorial Hospital)	TL 552 044	101415

ROCHFORD

Rochford Hospital (Rochford Union Workhouse)	TQ 873 908	101250

RUNWELL

Runwell Hospital (Runwell Mental Hospital)	TQ 760 960	101247

SAFFRON WALDEN

Saffron Walden Community Hospital (Saffron Walden Union Workhouse)	TL 550 386	101342
Saffron Walden District Infirmary	TL 540 360	102800
Saffron Walden General Hospital (Saffron Walden Hospital; now Uttlesford District Council Offices)	TL 536 379	101341

SOUTHEND-ON-SEA

Southend Hospital (Southend General Hospital)	TQ 864 873	101249
Southend Victoria Hospital (Southend Victoria Hospital and District Nursing Institution)	TQ 885 857	101416
Westcliffe Hospital (Southend Borough Sanatorium)	TQ 873 862	101248

STANFORD RIVERS

Ongar Union Workhouse (Ongar Hundred Workhouse; now Piggott Brothers & Co. Ltd)	TL 541 002	100725

THURROCK

South Ockendon Hospital (South Ockendon Colony for Mental Defectives)	TQ 597 824	101370
Thurrock Hospital (Orsett JHB Isolation Hospital; Orsett JHB Isolation Hospital and Sanatorium)	TQ 622 801	102799
Tilbury Cottage Hospital	TQ 639 759	101369

WALTHAM ABBEY

High Beech Convalescent Home	TQ 410 980	101425
Waltham Abbey Isolation Hospital (Waltham Joint Hospital for Infectious Diseases)	TL 401 001	101337

WITHAM

Bridge Hospital (Witham Union Workhouse)	TL 815 140	101242

GLOUCESTERSHIRE

BOURTON-ON-THE-WATER

Moore Cottage Hospital	SP 169 210	100586

CHELTENHAM
Cheltenham General Hospital — SP 953 215 — 78352
Children's Hospital — SO 965 223 — 100587
Cotswold Sanatorium for Tuberculosis — SO 907 132 — 102750
Delancey Hospital — SO 949 201 — 100591
St Paul's Hospital (Cheltenham Union Workhouse) — SP 945 231 — 100618

CIRENCESTER
Cirencester Hospital — SP 017 014 — 100644
Cirencester Memorial Hospital (Cirencester Cottage Hospital) — SP 021 017 — 85070
Watermoor Hospital (Cirencester Union Workhouse) — SP 024 013 — 100641

COBERLEY
Salterley Grange Sanatorium — SO 948 175 — 100589

ELMSTONE HARDWICKE
Tewkesbury RDC Isolation Hospital — SO 897 296 — 100596

FAIRFORD
Fairford Cottage Hospital — SP 154 010 — 100660

GLOUCESTER
Barnwood House Lunatic Asylum — SO 861 180 — 100621
Coney Hill Hospital (Second Gloucestershire County Lunatic Asylum) — SO 859 168 — 100593
Gloucestershire Royal Hospital (Gloucester Union Workhouse; Gloucester City General Hospital) — SO 838 186 — 100594
Gloucester Royal Infirmary (Gloucester Infirmary; Gloucester Royal Infirmary and Eye Institution) — SO 829 183 — 100620
Horton Road Hospital (Gloucestershire County Lunatic Asylum; Gloucestershire First County Mental Hospital) — SO 844 186 — 100619
St Lucy's Children's Hospital and Dispensary (Gloucester Free Hospital for Children of the Poor) — SO 830 180 — 100809

HIGHNAM
Over Isolation Hospital — SO 815 197 — 100592

INNSWORTH
Gloucester Corporation Smallpox Hospital — SO 847 206 — 100624

LYDNEY
Lydney and District Hospital (Lydney and District Cottage Hospital) — SO 629 304 — 101537

MORETON-IN-MARSH
Moreton-in-Marsh District Hospital (Moreton-in-Marsh Cottage Hospital) — SP 204 369 — 101533

STANDISH
Standish Hospital (Gloucester CC Tuberculosis Hospital; Standish House Sanatorium) — SO 816 067 — 100590

STOW-ON-THE-WOLD
Stow-on-the-Wold Union Workhouse — SP 195 257 — 100915

STROUD
Cashes Green Hospital (Stroud JHB Infectious Diseases Hospital) — SO 829 055 — 100623
Stroud General Hospital — SO 857 049 — 100652
Stroud Union Workhouse — SO 863 049 — 100622

TETBURY
Cotswold Hospital (Tetbury Union Workhouse) — ST 892 931 — 100642
Tetbury Hospital (Tetbury Cottage Hospital) — ST 894 929 — 100643

TEWKESBURY
Holme Hospital (Tewkesbury Workhouse) — SO 889 321 — 100625
Tewkesbury Cottage Hospital — SO 895 336 — 100655

WINCHCOMBE
Winchcombe and District Hospital (Winchcombe Cottage Hospital) — SP 017 278 — 101536

GREATER LONDON

BARKING AND DAGENHAM
Barking Hospital (Barking Town Infectious Diseases Hospital; Upney Hospital for Infectious Diseases) — TQ 456 844 — 102766
Dagenham Hospital (West Ham Corporation Smallpox Hospital) — TQ 504 837 — 102765

BARNET
Colindale Hospital (Central London Sick Asylum) — TQ 211 901 — 100890
Edgware General Hospital (Redhill Hospital; Redhill County Hospital) — TQ 198 912 — 101398
Finchley Memorial Hospital (Finchley Cottage Hospital) — TQ 264 914 — 101312
Friern Hospital (Second Middlesex County Pauper Lunatic Asylum; Colney Hatch Mental Hospital) — TQ 285 920 — 101281
Manor House Hospital — TQ 260 871 — 101104

National Hospital Rehabilitation Unit (National Hospital Convalescent Home) — TQ 271 891 — 101397
St Stephen's Hospital (Barnet Joint Isolation Hospital) — TQ 240 956 — 102767
Victoria Hospital — TQ 237 963 — 101541

BEXLEY
Bexley Cottage Hospital and Provident Dispensary (now Upton Social Education Centre) — TQ 481 753 — 101556
Bexley Maternity Hospital — TQ 496 763 — 101594
Cray Valley Hospital (Chislehurst, Sidcup and Cray Valley Cottage Hospital; Chislehurst, Orpington and Cray Valley Hospital) — TQ 460 690 — 101554
Erith and District Hospital (Erith, Crayford, Belvedere and Abbey Wood Cottage Hospital) — TQ 506 776 — 101549
Sidcup Cottage Hospital — TQ 406 710 — 101566

BRENT
Central Middlesex Hospital (Willesden Parish Workhouse; Central Middlesex County Hospital) — TQ 202 828 — 100834
Neasden Hospital (Willesden UDC Isolation Hospital) — TQ 208 850 — 102787
St Andrew's Hospital — TQ 220 860 — 101553
Willesden Cottage Hospital (Passmore Edwards Cottage Hospital) — TQ 225 841 — 101557
Wembley Hospital (Wembley and District Hospital) — TQ 176 849 — 101562

BROMLEY
Beckenham Hospital (Beckenham Cottage Hospital) — TQ 369 692 — 101551
Bromley and District Hospital (Bromley Cottage Hospital) — TQ 406 684 — 101552
Phillips Memorial Homoeopathic Hospital and Dispensary — TQ 307 820 — 101558
West Kent JHB Isolation Hospital (Bromley and Beckenham JHB Infectious Diseases Hospital) — TQ 429 661 — 102768

CAMDEN
Alexandra Hospital (Alexandra Hospital for Children with Hip Disease) — TQ 302 820 — 101066
Eastman Dental Clinic (Royal Free Hospital) — TQ 307 825 — 101084
Elizabeth Garrett Anderson Hospital (New Hospital for Women) — TQ 298 827 — 101082
Great Ormond Street Hospital (London Hospital for Sick Children) — TQ 304 820 — 101062
Hampstead General and North West London Hospital, Out-Patients' Department — TQ 289 838 — 101076
Hampstead General and North West London Hospital (Hampstead General Hospital) — TQ 272 854 — 101100
Institute of Ophthalmology (Central London Ophthalmic Hospital) — TQ 302 824 — 101081
Italian Hospital — TQ 304 819 — 101063
National Hospital for Nervous Diseases (National Hospital for the Paralysed and Epileptic) — TQ 304 821 — 101065
National Institute for Medical Research (North London Hospital for Consumption; Mount Vernon Hospital) — TQ 262 849 — 101101
National Temperance Hospital — TQ 292 827 — 101098
New End Hospital (Hampstead Union Workhouse) — TQ 264 860 — 101089
North Western Fever Hospital (Hampstead Smallpox Hospital) — TQ 273 854 — 101099
Ophthalmic Hospital — TQ 288 827 — 101412
Royal London Homoeopathic Hospital (Homoeopathic Hospital; London Homoeopathic Hospital) — TQ 304 819 — 101064
Royal National Throat, Nose and Ear Hospital (Central London Throat and Ear Hospital) — TQ 306 825 — 101083
Royal Westminster Ophthalmic Hospital (Moorfields Eye Hospital) — TQ 302 813 — 87883
St Luke's Hospital for the Clergy — TQ 292 821 — 101077
St Margaret's Hospital (St Margaret's Home) — TQ 291 852 — 101105
St Pancras Hospital (St Pancras Union Workhouse) — TQ 297 836 — 101106
St Paul's Hospital (British Lying-In Hospital; St Paul's Hospital for Skin and Genito-Urinary Disease) — TQ 320 810 — 101071
Smallpox and Fever Hospital (Smallpox Hospital) — TQ 302 833 — 101093
University College Hospital (North London Hospital) — TQ 295 822 — 101078
Whittington Hospital, Highgate Wing (St Pancras Union Infirmary; Highgate Hospital) — TQ 288 869 — 101069

CITY OF LONDON
Bethlehem Hospital (Bedlam) — TQ 328 816 — 101992
Royal London Ophthalmic Hospital (Moorfields Eye Hospital) — TQ 329 817 — 101102
St Bartholomew's Hospital — TQ 319 815 — 101315

CROYDON
Cane Hill Hospital (Third Surrey County Pauper Lunatic Asylum) — TQ 290 587 — 101293
Croydon General Hospital (Oakfield Lodge) — TQ 321 663 — 101353
Mayday University Hospital (Croydon Union Workhouse Infirmary; Mayday Hospital), Croydon — TQ 321 675 — 101352
Norwood Hospital (now Cambridge House) — TQ 327 708 — 101350
Purley and District Cottage Hospital — TQ 314 618 — 101296
Queens Road Hospital (Croydon Union Workhouse) — TQ 316 674 — 101351
Waddon Hospital (Croydon Borough Hospital) — TQ 304 666 — 102769

EALING
Acton Hospital (Jubilee Cottage Hospital; Passmore Edwards Cottage Hospital) — TQ 195 800 — 101274
Clayponds Hospital (Chiswick UDC Isolation Hospital; Chiswick and Ealing Isolation Hospital) — TQ 181 788 — 102770
Ealing Cottage Hospital and Provident Dispensary — TQ 170 800 — 101546
Ealing Hospital, St Bernard's Wing (Middlesex County Lunatic Asylum; Hanwell Asylum) — TQ 117 180 — 38801
King Edward Memorial Hospital — TQ 170 800 — 101547
Leamington Park Hospital (Acton Isolation Hospital) — TQ 207 815 — 101113
Queen Victoria and War Memorial Hospital (Hanwell Cottage Hospital) — TQ 152 798 — 101185

ENFIELD
Chase Farm Hospital (Chase Farm Schools) — TQ 312 980 — 101252
Enfield War Memorial Hospital (Enfield Cottage Hospital) — TQ 324 976 — 101314
Highlands Hospital (Northern Convalescent Fever Hospital and South Lodge Hospital) — TQ 306 957 — 101254
North Middlesex Hospital (Edmonton Union Workhouse; Strand Union Workhouse) — TQ 335 923 — 100891
St Michael's Hospital (Enfield Union Workhouse) — TQ 326 976 — 101253

GREENWICH
British Hospital for Mothers and Babies — TQ 390 770 — 101593
Brook General Hospital (Brook Fever Hospital) — TQ 423 766 — 101091
Castlewood Day Hospital (Woolwich and Plumstead Cottage Hospital) — TQ 431 767 — 101092
Dreadnought Seamen's Hospital (Royal Naval Hospital Infirmary) — TQ 384 777 — 101280
Eltham and Mottingham Cottage Hospital (now Woodlands) — TQ 428 743 — 101543
Goldie Leigh Hospital (Goldie Leigh Homes) — TQ 470 776 — 102771
Greenwich District Hospital (Greenwich Union Workhouse; St Alfege's Hospital) — TQ 396 782 — 100826
Miller Memorial Hospital (Royal Kent Dispensary) — TQ 376 769 — 101555
Memorial Hospital (Woolwich War Memorial Hospital) — TQ 435 764 — 101090
Royal Herbert Hospital (Herbert Military Hospital; now Royal Herbert Pavilions) — TQ 427 766 — 84673
Royal Naval Hospital (now Royal Naval College) — TQ 385 779 — 100918
Woolwich Naval Hospital (Royal Marines Hospital) — TQ 427 788 — 100721

HACKNEY
German Hospital — TQ 342 849 — 101156
Hackney Hospital (Hackney Union Workhouse) — TQ 361 851 — 101997
Homerton Hospital (Eastern Fever Hospital and Smallpox Hospital) — TQ 356 853 — 102772
Metropolitan Hospital (Metropolitan Free Hospital; Metropolitan Provident Hospital) — TQ 334 842 — 101226
Royal Infirmary for Diseases of the Chest — TQ 323 829 — 102773
St Leonard's Hospital (St Leonard's, Shoreditch, Workhouse) — TQ 335 834 — 101225
St Matthew's Hospital (St Luke's, Middlesex, Workhouse; Holborn Union Workhouse) — TQ 323 829 — 100921
Salvation Army Hospital for Women — TQ 340 840 — 101592

HAMMERSMITH AND FULHAM
Fulham Hospital (Fulham Union Workhouse) — TQ 236 779 — 100827
Hammersmith Hospital (Hammersmith Workhouse) — TQ 225 813 — 101275
Queen Charlotte's Hospital for Women (Queen Charlotte's Hospital; Queen Charlotte's Maternity Hospital) — TQ 221 790 — 101273
Royal Masonic Hospital — TQ 222 789 — 101272
West London Hospital (Elm Tree House; West of London Hospital and Dispensary) — TQ 235 786 — 101276
Western (Fever) Hospital (Fulham Hospital) — TQ 257 775 — 101128

HARINGEY
Coppetts Wood Hospital (Hornsey Isolation Hospital; Hornsey, Finchley and Wood Green Joint Isolation Hospital) — TQ 279 908 — 101311

Hornsey Central Hospital (Hornsey
   Cottage Hospital)   TQ 296 889   101542
Prince of Wales General Hospital
   (Evangelical Protestant Deaconesses'
   Institute and Training Hospital)   TQ 339 893   101109
St Ann's General Hospital (Metropolitan
   Asylums Board North Eastern Fever
   Hospital)   TQ 325 885   102782
St Luke's Woodside Hospital   TQ 284 893   101313
Wood Green and Southgate Hospital
   (Wood Green Cottage Hospital;
   Passmore Edwards Cottage Hospital)   TQ 299 915   101563

HARROW
Edgware General Hospital, Geriatric Unit
   (Stanmore Cottage Hospital)   TQ 170 917   101565
Harrow Cottage Hospital   TQ 140 880   101544
Harrow Hospital (Harrow and District
   Hospital)   TQ 150 868   101545
Royal National Orthopaedic Hospital   TQ 172 939   101108

HAVERING
Old Church Hospital (Romford Union
   Workhouse)   TQ 510 881   100675
Rush Green Hospital (Romford JHB
   Isolation Hospital)   TQ 511 867   102785
Victoria Cottage Hospital   TQ 517 895   101535

HILLINGDON
Harefield Hospital (Harefield County
   Sanatorium)   TQ 052 909   101190
Mount Vernon Hospital   TQ 076 918   101191
Northwood and Pinner Community
   Hospital (Northwood, Pinner and District
   Hospital and Northwood War Memorial)   TQ 100 907   101364
Harlington, Harmondsworth and Cranford
   Cottage Hospital (now Sant Nirankari
   Mandal International Nirankari Bharan)   TQ 077 778   101362

HOUNSLOW
Hounslow Cottage Hospital   TQ 136 755   101103
Hounslow Cavalry Barracks Hospital (now
   Hounslow Cavalry Barracks, Medical
   Centre and Sergeants' Mess)   SU 121 756   100718
Hounslow Hospital   TQ 132 755   101183
South West Middlesex Hospital (Richmond,
   Heston and Isleworth Joint Isolation
   Hospital; South Middlesex and
   Richmond Joint Isolation Hospital)   TQ 156 746   101182
West Middlesex Hospital (Brentford Union
   Workhouse)   TQ 165 763   101184

ISLINGTON
City of London Lying-In Hospital   TQ 327 825   101119
Coldbath Fields Smallpox Hospital   TQ 312 823   101112
Moorfields Eye Hospital (Royal London
   Ophthalmic Hospital)   TQ 326 827   101120
Royal Free Hospital, Liverpool Road Branch
   (London Fever Hospital; now Royal
   Free Place)   TQ 314 837   101122
Royal Northern Hospital (Great Northern
   Hospital; Great Northern Central
   Hospital)   TQ 302 863   101379
St Luke's Hospital   TQ 326 825   101117
St Mark's Hospital (St Mark's Hospital for
   Fistula and Diseases of the Rectum)   TQ 319 829   101121
Whittington Hospital, Archway Wing
   (Holborn Union Infirmary; Archway
   Hospital)   TQ 293 870   101067
Whittington Hospital, St Mary's Wing
   (Islington Workhouse; St Mary's Hospital)   TQ 290 869   101068

KENSINGTON AND CHELSEA
Brompton Hospital (Hospital for
   Consumption and Diseases of the Chest)   TQ 269 784   101058
Chelsea and Westminster Hospital
   (St George's Union Workhouse;
   St Stephen's Hospital)   TQ 263 777   101096
Chelsea Hospital for Women   TQ 271 783   101059
Cheyne Centre for Spastic Children
   (Cheyne Hospital for Children)   TQ 271 776   101095
Princess Beatrice Hospital (Kensington,
   Chelsea and Fulham Hospital)   TQ 256 782   101127
Princess Louise Kensington Hospital for
   Children   TQ 235 816   101111
Royal Cancer Hospital (Free) Institute of
   Cancer Research (Chelsea Hospital for
   Women)   TQ 268 783   101060
The Royal Hospital, Chelsea   TQ 279 779   101123
Royal Marsden Hospital (Free Cancer Hospital) TQ 269 784   101097
St Charles's Hospital (St Marylebone
   Infirmary; St Marylebone Hospital)   TQ 237 818   101110
St Luke's, Chelsea, Workhouse   TQ 271 782   101061
St Luke's Hospital (St Luke's, Chelsea,
   Workhouse Infirmary; Chelsea Infirmary)   TQ 271 783   101130
St Mary Abbots Hospital (Kensington Union
   Workhouse; St Mary Abbots Workhouse)   TQ 256 793   101126

Victoria Hospital for Sick Children (Gough
   House)   TQ 278 779   101094

KINGSTON UPON THAMES
Claremont Hospital (Surbiton Cottage
   Hospital)   TQ 179 674   101115
Surbiton Hospital   TQ 184 671   101118
Tolworth Hospital (Kingston upon Thames Infectious
   Hospital; Tolworth Isolation Hospital)   TQ 192 659   101348

LAMBETH
Belgrave Hospital for Children   TQ 312 775   55401
British Home and Hospital for Incurables   TQ 317 711   101349
King George V Military Hospital (HMSO
   Works Store; now Cornwall House)   TQ 311 803   101173
General Lying-In Hospital   TQ 308 798   101171
Lambeth Hospital (St Mary, Lambeth,
   Workhouse)   TQ 316 788   101038
Royal Waterloo Hospital (Universal
   Dispensary for Children; now Schiller
   International University)   TQ 311 802   101172
St Thomas's Hospital   TQ 307 794   101079
South London Hospital for Women   TQ 289 744   101135
South Western Hospital (South Western
   Fever and Smallpox Hospital)   TQ 305 756   102775
Weir Cottage Hospital   TQ 292 735   101550

LEWISHAM
Grove Park Hospital (Greenwich Union
   Workhouse)   TQ 410 727   101088
Hither Green Hospital (Park Hospital)   TQ 387 741   101399
New Cross Hospital (South Eastern Fever
   Hospital)   TQ 354 774   102776

MERTON
Atkinson Morley's Hospital (Atkinson Morley
   (or Morley's) Convalescent Hospital)   TQ 223 701   101345
Durnsford Lodge Hospital (Wimbledon
   Hospital for Infectious Diseases)   SU 258 716   102783
Nelson Hospital   TQ 247 695   101347
North Wimbledon Hospital   TQ 227 704   101346
Wilson Hospital (Wilson Cottage Hospital)   TQ 278 680   101396

NEWHAM
Albert Dock Hospital (Seamen's Hospital,
   Royal Victoria and Albert Dock)   TQ 416 812   101561
East Ham Isolation Hospital   TQ 418 824   102777
East Ham Memorial Hospital   TQ 418 842   101571
East Ham Memorial Hospital, Children's and
   Out-Patients' Unit (East Ham Cottage
   Hospital; Passmore Edwards Hospital)   TQ 430 830   101572
Newham Maternity Hospital (Whitechapel
   Industrial School; Forest Gate Hospital)   TQ 399 852   101271
Plaistow Hospital (West Ham Fever Hospital) TQ 411 832   102778
St Mary's Hospital for Women and Children   TQ 404 827   101596
West Ham and Eastern General Hospital   TQ 391 842   101570

REDBRIDGE
Chadwell Heath Hospital (Ilford UDC
   Isolation Hospital)   TQ 469 886   102780
Claybury Hospital (Fourth Middlesex
   County Pauper Lunatic Asylum)   TQ 435 915   101107
Goodmayes Hospital (Chadwell Lunatic
   Asylum; West Ham Asylum)   TQ 463 887   101582
Harts Hospital (Hart House; Harts Sanatorium) TQ 404 922   102779
Jubilee Hospital   TQ 400 915   101569
Wanstead Hospital (Merchant Seamen's
   Orphan Asylum; Convent of the Good
   Shepherd)   TQ 405 892   101160

RICHMOND UPON THAMES
Normansfield Hospital   TQ 173 702   101325
Royal Hospital (Richmond Infirmary;
   Richmond Hospital)   TQ 189 742   101568
St John's Hospital   TQ 164 736   101295
Teddington Memorial Hospital (Teddington,
   Hampton Wick and District Memorial
   Hospital)   TQ 155 710   101560

SOUTHWARK
Blackfriars Skin Hospital (Blackfriars
   Hospital for Diseases of the Skin)   TQ 316 801   101174
Dulwich Hospital, North Wing (Camberwell
   Union Workhouse; St Francis' Hospital)   TQ 333 752   101153
Dulwich Hospital (St Saviour's Union
   Infirmary)   TQ 334 751   101154
Evelina Hospital for Sick Children   TQ 320 794   101159
Guy's Hospital   TQ 328 801   101151
Bethlem Hospital (now Imperial War Museum) TQ 314 792   10 1994
King's College Hospital   TQ 325 760   101080
Maudsley Hospital   TQ 327 762   101152
Royal Eye Hospital (Royal South London
   Ophthalmic Hospital)   TQ 316 795   101175
St Giles's Hospital (Camberwell Union
   Infirmary)   TQ 332 769   101170
St Olave's Hospital (Rotherhithe Parish
   Workhouse; St Olave's Union Workhouse;
   Bermondsey and Rotherhithe Infirmary)   TQ 351 793   100832
St Thomas's Hospital   TQ 327 802   101158

SUTTON
Carshalton War Memorial Hospital
   (Carshalton, Beddington and Wallington
   War Memorial Hospital)   TQ 278 639   101394
Cheam Hospital (Croydon and Wimbledon
   Joint Smallpox Hospital)   TQ 234 659   102781
Cuddington Isolation Hospital (Epsom,
   Sutton, Carshalton and Leatherhead
   JHB Isolation Hospital)   TQ 246 609   102764
Queen Mary's Hospital (The Southern
   Hospital; Queen Mary's Hospital for
   Sick Children)   TQ 278 625   101395
St Helier Hospital   TQ 265 662   101393
Sutton Hospital (Sutton and Cheam
   General Hospital)   TQ 250 640   101524
Sutton Hospital (Passmore Edwards Cottage
   Hospital)   TQ 259 642   101548
Wandle Valley Hospital (Wandle Valley
   Isolation Hospital)   TQ 277 667   102786

TOWER HAMLETS
Bethnal Green Hospital (Bethnal Green
   Union Infirmary)   TQ 350 832   101229
East London Hospital for Children   TQ 354 808   101595
London Chest Hospital (City of London
   Hospital for Diseases of the Chest)   TQ 354 833   101116
Mildmay Mission Hospital (Mildmay
   Medical Mission Hospital)   TQ 336 826   101227
Mile End Road Accident and Emergency
   Hospital (Mile End Old Town
   Workhouse; Mile End Hospital)   TQ 359 825   101167
Poplar Hospital (Poplar Hospital for
   Accidents)   TQ 384 811   101213
Poplar Institution (Poplar Union Workhouse) TQ 377 807   101212
Poplar Union Infirmary   TQ 375 812   101211
Queen Elizabeth Hospital for Children
   (East London Hospital for Children)   TQ 343 832   101228
Royal London Hospital (London Hospital)   TQ 347 816   101164
St Andrew's Hospital (Poplar and Stepney
   Sick Asylum)   TQ 379 824   101387
St Clement's Hospital (City of London
   Union Workhouse)   TQ 368 826   101169
St Peter's Hospital (Whitechapel Union Work-
   house; Whitechapel Union Infirmary)   TQ 345 820   101165
South Grove Institution (Whitechapel
   Union Workhouse)   TQ 367 825   101168

WALTHAM FOREST
Connaught Hospital (Holmcroft; Leyton,
   Walthamstow and Wanstead Hospital)   TQ 381 898   101564
Langthorne Hospital (West Ham Union
   Workhouse)   TQ 390 860   101162
Thorpe Coombe Hospital (Northbank House) TQ 382 898   101157
Whipps Cross Hospital (West Ham Union
   Infirmary)   TQ 389 886   101163

WANDSWORTH
Battersea General Hospital (National Anti-
   Vivisection Hospital)   TQ 276 767   101559
Bolingbroke Hospital   TQ 273 746   101086
Brocklebank LCC Institution (Wandsworth
   and Clapham Union Workhouse)   TQ 260 737   101189
Fountain Hospital (Fountain Temporary
   Fever Hospital)   TQ 271 714   101133
Grove Fever Hospital   TQ 268 713   101134
Putney Hospital   TQ 232 759   101567
Queen Mary's Hospital   TQ 223 743   101188
Royal Hospital and Home (Royal Hospital
   for Incurables)   TQ 242 741   101114
Royal Victoria Patriotic Building (Royal
   Victoria Patriotic Asylum; Third
   London General Hospital)   TQ 269 743   101224
St James's Hospital (Wandsworth and
   Clapham Union Infirmary)   TQ 277 732   101074
St John's Hospital (Wandsworth and
   Clapham Union Workhouse; Wandsworth
   and Clapham Union Infirmary)   TQ 265 751   101085
Springfield Hospital (Surrey County
   Pauper Lunatic Asylum)   TQ 271 725   101087
Tooting Bec Hospital (Tooting Bec Asylum)   TQ 269 712   101131

WESTMINSTER, CITY OF
Charing Cross Hospital   TQ 302 806   101011
Charter Nightingale Hospital (Institution
   for Sick Governesses; Florence
   Nightingale Hospital)   TQ 274 819   101043
Coldstream Guards Military Hospital   TQ 295 788   101023
Bessborough Street Clinic (Maternity and
   Child Welfare Centre)   TQ 297 783   101026
Dental Hospital of London   TQ 298 807   101032
Ear, Nose and Throat Department of
   University College (Royal Ear Hospital)   TQ 297 812   101004
Empire Hospital for Paying Patients   TQ 295 789   101021
Gordon Hospital (Western Hospital for
   Fistula and Diseases of the Rectum)   TQ 296 787   101020
Grenadier Guards' Military Hospital   TQ 294 789   101024

Grosvenor Hospital for Women (Pimlico and Westminster Institute; Grosvenor Hospital for Women and Children) TQ 297 787 101019
Harley Street Clinic TQ 286 818 101051
Home and Hospital for Crippled Boys TQ 293 814 101056
Hôpital et Dispensaire Français (French Hospital) TQ 298 808 101031
Hospital for Consumption (Infirmary for Consumption and Diseases of the Chest and Throat; now West End Blood Donor Centre) TQ 290 814 101055
Hospital for Women (Hospital for Diseases of Women) TQ 297 811 101006
Hospital of St John and St Elizabeth TQ 266 832 101045
King Edward VII's Hospital for Officers TQ 284 818 101050
King's College Hospital TQ 309 812 101014
Lister Hospital (British Institute of Preventive Medicine; Lister Institute of Preventive Medicine) TQ 286 781 101027
Lock Hospital TQ 286 796 101028
London Clinic TQ 284 821 101125
Middlesex Hospital TQ 293 817 101181
National Heart Hospital (National Hospital for Diseases of the Heart) TQ 284 817 101049
National Hospital for Neurology and Neurosurgery (London Infirmary for Epilepsy and Paralysis) TQ 265 824 101039
Nature Cure and Anti-Vivisection Hospital (Nature Cure Clinic) TQ 282 820 101048
Paddington Green Children's Hospital TQ 268 818 101034
Paddington Hospital (Paddington Union Workhouse) TQ 253 819 101035
Paddington Hospital (Lock Hospital; Female Lock Hospital) TQ 253 819 101036
Queen Alexandra Military Hospital TQ 301 787 101018
Queen Charlotte's Maternity Hospital (General Lying-In Hospital; Queen Charlotte's Lying-In Hospital) TQ 274 817 101044
Radium Institute TQ 290 816 101052
Royal Dental Hospital of London (Dental Hospital of London) TQ 299 807 101009
Royal National Orthopaedic Hospital (National Orthopaedic Hospital) TQ 289 821 101054
Royal National Throat Nose and Ear Hospital (Free Dispensary for Throat Diseases; Hospital for Diseases of the Throat) TQ 293 804 101002
Royal Orthopaedic Hospital (Institution for the Cure of Club Feet and Other Contractions) TQ 288 811 101000
St Anne's Workhouse TQ 298 812 101007
St George's Hospital (now Lanesborough Hotel) TQ 283 797 101029
St John's Hospital for Diseases of the Skin, Lisle Street TQ 298 808 101008
St John's Hospital for Diseases of the Skin, Leicester Square TQ 298 807 101030
St Luke's Hospital (St Luke's Hospital for Advanced Cases) TQ 254 807 101037
St Mary's Hospital TQ 268 813 101042
St Marylebone Workhouse TQ 281 819 101046
St Peter's Hospital (Hospital for Stone) TQ 303 808 101012
St Philip's Hospital (Strand Union Workhouse; Sheffield Street Hospital) TQ 307 812 101013
Samaritan Free Hospital for Women (Gynaepathic Institute Free Hospital) TQ 275 818 101040
Scots Fusilier Guards' Military Hospital TQ 294 787 101025
Shaftesbury Hospital (L'Hôpital et Dispensaire Français; French Hospital), Holborn TQ 300 812 101070
Temporary Iron Smallpox Hospital TQ 297 794 101033
University College Dental Hospital (National Dental Hospital) TQ 288 820 101053
West End Hospital (West End Hospital for Nervous Diseases, Paralysis and Epilepsy) TQ 285 813 101047
West End Hospital for Neurology and Neurosurgery (Male Lock Hospital) TQ 296 813 101005
Western Ophthalmic Hospital TQ 276 818 101041
Westminster Children's Hospital (Infants' Hospital) TQ 294 787 101022
Westminster Hospital, Broad Sanctuary TQ 299 795 101015
Westminster Hospital, Page Street TQ 301 789 101016
Westminster Union Workhouse (St James's, Westminster, Workhouse) TQ 293 812 101003

GREATER MANCHESTER

ALTRINCHAM
Altrincham General Hospital (Altrincham Hospital and Provident Dispensary) SJ 767 878 102506

ASHTON-IN-MAKERFIELD
Haydock Lodge Private Lunatic Asylum SJ 570 990 102617

ASHTON-UNDER-LYNE
Tameside General Hospital, West Site (Ashton-Under-Lyne District Infirmary; Ashton-Under-Lyne District Infirmary and Children's Hospital) SJ 952 995 102488

BOLTON
Blair Hospital (Blair Convalescent Hospital) SD 710 140 102512
Bolton General Hospital (Bolton Union Workhouse; Townleys Hospital and Fishpool Institution) SD 718 064 100697
Bolton Infirmary and Dispensary (Bolton Dispensary) SD 718 092 102469
Bolton Royal Infirmary (Bolton Infirmary; The New Bolton Infirmary) SD 709 094 102464
Hulton Hospital (Bolton Borough Fever Hospital) SD 692 074 102697
Newlands Nursing Home SD 693 093 102519

BURY
Bealey Hospital (Bealey Memorial Convalescent Hospital) SD 796 077 102511
Bury General Hospital (Bury Dispensary Hospital) SD 809 125 102507
Florence Nightingale Hospital (Florence Nightingale Infectious Diseases Hospital) SD 791 100 102698
Ramsbottom Cottage Hospital (Aitken Memorial and Jubilee Cottage Hospital) SD 789 161 102514

CHEADLE AND GATLEY
Barnes Hospital (Barnes Convalescent Home; Barnes Convalescent Hospital) SJ 852 889 102067
St Anne's Hospital (Cheadle Royal Asylum Children's Convalescent Hospital) SD 850 866 102513

ECCLES
Bridgewater Hospital (Barton Union Workhouse) SJ 763 985 102074
Eccles and Patricroft Hospital (Eccles and Patricroft Dispensary) SJ 770 980 102588
Ladywell Hospital (Ladywell Sanatorium) SJ 782 985 102699
Royal Manchester Children's Hospital (General Hospital and Dispensary for Sick Children) SD 791 012 102602

HALE
St Anne's Hospital (Manchester Hospital for Consumption and Diseases of the Throat and Chest) SJ 762 874 102696

HORWICH
Fall Birch Hospital (Horwich, Westhoughton and Blackrod Infectious Diseases Hospital; Fall Birch Isolation Hospital) SD 660 100 102706

LEIGH
Leigh Infirmary SD 661 009 102463

MANCHESTER
Ancoats Hospital (Ancoats Hospital and Ardwick and Ancoats Dispensary) SJ 854 984 102465
Booth Hall Hospital (Booth Hall Infirmary; Prestwich Union Infirmary) SD 865 031 100747
Chorlton and Manchester Joint Workhouse SJ 856 981 100744
Christie Hospital and Holt Radium Institute SJ 849 925 102600
Duchess of York Hospital for Babies SJ 830 980 102618
Manchester and Salford Hospital for Skin Diseases SJ 830 980 102243
Manchester and Salford Lock Hospital SJ 831 978 102599
Manchester Dental Hospital SJ 830 980 102587
Manchester House of Recovery (now Grand Hotel) SJ 845 981 102701
Manchester Northern Hospital (Manchester Northern Hospital for Women and Children) SD 843 011 102603
Manchester Royal Infirmary, Oxford Road SJ 850 961 102011
Manchester Royal Infirmary, Piccadilly (Manchester Infirmary; Manchester Infirmary and Lunatic Asylum) SJ 843 982 102063
Manchester Royal Infirmary, Central Branch SJ 844 983 102170
Manchester Victoria Memorial Jewish Hospital (Manchester Jewish Hospital) SD 841 004 102241
Monsall Hospital (Barnes House of Recovery) SD 864 008 102702
Nicholls Hospital SJ 857 960 102518
North Manchester General Hospital (Manchester Township Workhouse; Crumpsall Institution) SD 849 023 100743
Royal Eye Hospital SJ 849 961 102066
St Mary's Hospital, Oxford Road SJ 850 959 102064
St Mary's Hospital, Whitworth Street SJ 840 976 102065
St Mary's Hospital, Quay Street SJ 830 980 102266
Withington Hospital (Chorlton Union Workhouse) SD 836 924 102142
Wythenshawe Hospital (Withington UDC Sanatorium for Infectious Diseases; Baguley Sanatorium for Infectious Diseases; Baguley Hospital) SJ 806 876 102695

OLDHAM
Oldham Royal Infirmary (Oldham Infirmary) SD 919 047 102462

ROCHDALE
Birch Hill Hospital (Rochdale Union Workhouse) SD 921 161 100693
Memorial Home for Crippled Children SD 890 130 102520
Rochdale Infirmary SD 895 141 102466

ROYTON
Westhulme Hospital (Westhulme Fever Hospital) SD 915 061 102700

SALFORD
Greengate Hospital (Greengate Dispensary and Open Air School) SJ 820 980 102601
Hope Hospital (Salford Union Infirmary) SJ 786 991 100740
Manchester Hospital for Consumption and Diseases of Throat and Chest SJ 835 980 102705
Salford Royal Hospital SJ 826 986 102467

STOCKPORT
Stepping Hill Infirmary (Stockport Union Infirmary) SJ 912 875 100164
Stockport Infirmary SJ 894 899 102468

STRETFORD
Stretford Memorial Hospital (Basford House Red Cross Hospital) SD 818 951 102515
Urmston Cottage Hospital SJ 767 948 102516

TYLDESLEY
Astley Hospital (Leigh JHB Sanatorium; Astley Sanatorium) SD 698 009 102704

URMSTON
Trafford General Hospital (Davyhulme Hospital; Park Hospital) SJ 755 953 100698

WIGAN
Royal Albert Edward Infirmary SD 584 069 102461
Whelley Hospital (Wigan Borough Sanatorium) SD 591 066 102703

HAMPSHIRE

ALTON
Alton Infirmary (Alton Union Workhouse) SU 725 400 39258
Alton Isolation Hospital SU 726 386 100087
Inwood Cottage Hospital SU 719 394 100085
Lord Mayor Treloar Hospital (Princess Louise Military Hospital; Lord Mayor Treloar Cripples' Hospital and College) SU 707 383 100101

AMPORT
Andover RDC Isolation Hospital SU 309 459 100088

ANDOVER
Andover Cottage Hospital SU 361 456 100089
Andover Infectious Diseases Hospital (Andover Sanatorium) SU 371 461 100091
Andover War Memorial Community Hospital (Andover War Memorial Hospital) SU 354 463 100090
St John's Hospital (Andover Union Workhouse) SU 360 457 100092

ASHURST AND COLBURY
Ashurst Hospital (New Forest Union Workhouse) SU 336 102 100093

BASINGSTOKE
Basingstoke Hospital SU 639 517 100094
Basingstoke UDC Isolation Hospital SU 619 532 100095

BISHOPS WALTHAM
Royal Albert Infirmary SU 550 170 100801

BRAMSHOTT AND LIPHOOK
King George's Hospital (Bramshott Place Sanatorium) SU 844 322 100100

CRONDALL
Leipzig Barracks Hospital SU 818 508 100103

EASTLEIGH
Eastleigh and Bishopstoke UDC Isolation Hospital SU 440 200 100105
Leigh House Hospital (Hursley Union Workhouse; Hampshire CC Sanatorium) SU 430 128 100106
Mount Hospital (The Mount Sanatorium) SU 466 200 100098

ECCHINSWELL AND SYDMONTON
Kingsclere Union Isolation Hospital SU 503 592 100107

FAREHAM
Coldeast Hospital (Coldeast Mental Deficiency Colony) SU 507 082 100102
Fareham RDC Isolation Hospital SU 562 072 100108
St Christopher's Hospital (Fareham Union Workhouse) SU 582 070 100109

FLEET
Fleet Hospital (Fleet Cottage Hospital) SU 800 540 100110
Fordingbridge: Fordingbridge Cottage Hospital SU 146 140 100111
Fordingbridge Hospital (Fordingbridge Union Workhouse) SU 146 143 100112

GOSPORT
Alverstoke House of Industry SZ 609 992 100021
Blake Maternity Hospital (Gosport Borough Isolation Hospital) SU 604 022 100115

Forton Hospital (Fortune Hospital)   SU 610 000   100120
Forton Marine Infirmary   SU 609 004   100121
Gosport and Alverstoke Smallpox Hospital
  (now Don Styler Physical Training Centre)   SU 604 025   100113
Gosport War Memorial Hospital   SZ 601 996   100116
Haslar Royal Naval Hospital   SZ 618 988   100117
Haslar Zymotic Hospital   SZ 617 985   100118
Military Hospital   SZ 616 984   100119

HAVANT
Havant and Waterloo UDC Isolation Hospital   SU 714 066   100124
Havant War Memorial Hospital   SU 713 066   100123
Victoria Cottage Hospital   SU 749 059   100122

HOUND
Royal Victoria Hospital, D Block (Military
  Lunatic Asylum)   SU 468 078   100130
Royal Victoria Military Hospital (Victoria
  Military Hospital)   SU 465 077   100128
Welsh War Hospital   SU 468 079   100129

HYTHE AND DIBDEN
Hythe and Dibden War Memorial Cottage
  Hospital (The White House)   SU 420 067   100131
Hythe and Dibden War Memorial Cottage
  Hospital, Atheling Road   SU 423 076   100212

LYMINGTON AND PENNINGTON
Lymington Day Hospital and Infirmary
  (Lymington Union Workhouse)   SZ 322 959   100136
Lymington Cottage Convalescent Home   SZ 330 947   100134
Lymington Hospital
  (Lymington Cottage Hospital)   SZ 317 958   100133
Lymington Isolation Hospital   SZ 322 961   100135
Lyndhurst: Fenwick Hospital (Fenwick
  Cottage Hospital)   SU 293 089   100137

MEDSTEAD
Broadlands Sanatorium   SU 637 353   100138

MILFORD ON SEA
Milford Cottage Hospital   SZ 292 918   100139
Milford on Sea War Memorial Cottage Hospital   SZ 288 914   100140

NETLEY MARSH
Tatchbury Mount Hospital   SU 333 147   100408

NEW ALRESFORD
Titchborne Down House Hospital
  (Alresford Union Workhouse)   SU 587 315   76971

NURSLING AND ROWNHAMS
St John's Convalescent Home (Village
  Convalescent Home)   SU 380 170   100819

ODIHAM
Odiham Hospital (Odiham Cottage Hospital)   SU 740 508   100143

PETERSFIELD
Heathside Hospital (Petersfield Isolation
  Hospital)   SU 760 232   100145
Petersfield Hospital (Petersfield Cottage
  Hospital)   SU 743 232   100144
Petersfield Pest House   SU 721 235   100146
Petersfield Union Workhouse   SU 751 233   100147

PORTSMOUTH
Hilsea Venereal Hospital (Hilsea Military
  Families' Hospital; Hilsea Artillery
  Barracks Hospital)   SU 655 035   100153
Military Families' Hospital (Female Hospital)   SU 636 005   100152
Military Fever Hospital   SU 636 005   100151
Military Station Hospital (Garrison Hospital)   SU 636 005   100150
Municipal Maternity Hospital   SZ 646 993   100163
Portsmouth and District Foot Hospital   SU 650 013   100166
Portsmouth and Southern Counties' Eye
  and Ear Hospital (Portsmouth and
  South Hampshire Eye and Ear Hospital)   SZ 630 990   100337
Portsmouth Borough Isolation Hospital
  for Smallpox   SU 678 000   100160
Queen Alexandra Hospital (Queen
  Alexandra Military Hospital)   SU 655 059   100099
Royal Marines' Infirmary (Eastney Barracks
  Hospital)   SZ 670 980   100339
Royal Portsmouth Hospital (Royal Ports-
  mouth, Portsea and Gosport Hospital)   SU 643 009   100149
South Coast Medical Surgical and
  Convalescent Home for Women   SZ 647 985   100161
St James's Hospital (Portsmouth Borough
  Lunatic Asylum)   SU 670 001   100167
St Mary's Hospital, East Wing (Portsmouth
  City Hospital for Infectious Diseases;
  Priorsdean Hospital)   SU 662 006   100159
St Mary's Hospital, West Wing (Portsea
  Island Incorporation Workhouse;
  Portsmouth Union Workhouse)   SU 660 005   76977

ROMSEY
Romsey and District Hospital (Romsey
  Cottage Hospital)   SU 364 214   100171
Romsey Nursing Home and Cottage Hospital   SU 353 217   100232
Romsey Union Workhouse   SU 362 214   100172

RUSHMOOR
22 Field Hospital (Thornhill Military
  Isolation Hospital)   SU 878 517   100180
Aldershot Hospital   SU 865 500   100173
Aldershot UDC Smallpox Hospital   SU 880 505   100176
Cambridge Military Hospital   SU 868 512   100177
Connaught Military Hospital   SU 877 529   100178
Farnborough Cottage Hospital (Farnborough
  and Cove War Memorial Hospital)   SU 875 546   100182
Louise Margaret Hospital   SU 869 512   100179
Northfield Hospital (Aldershot Isolation
  Hospital)   SU 877 509   100175

SHEDFIELD
Shedfield Cottage Hospital (Shedfield
  Cottage Hospital and Convalescent Home)   SU 573 144   100183

SHERBORNE ST JOHN
Park Prewett Hospital (Second Hampshire
  County Lunatic Asylum)   SU 615 538   100511

SOUTHAMPTON
Isolation Hospital (Southampton Smallpox
  Hospital)   SU 380 120   100194
Outbathing and Disinfecting Station for
  Infectious Diseases (Urban Sanitary
  Hospital for Infectious Diseases)   SU 413 116   100195
Royal South Hampshire Hospital (South
  Hampshire Infirmary; Royal South
  Hampshire and Southampton Infirmary)   SU 425 127   100190
Southampton Children's Hospital   SU 400 410   100233
Southampton Eye Hospital (Southampton
  Free Eye Hospital)   SU 417 128   100188
Southampton General Hospital
  (Southampton Union Infirmary;
  Southampton Borough Hospital)   SU 150 399   100191
Southampton Workhouse   SU 426 417   100192
St Mary's Cottage Hospital   SU 420 120   100189
Western Hospital (Southampton Isolation
  Hospital)   SU 389 140   100193

WEST END
Moorgreen Hospital (South Stoneham
  Union Workhouse)   SU 474 145   100031

WHITCHURCH
Whitchurch Union Workhouse   SU 473 481   100201

WICKHAM
Knowle Hospital (Hampshire County
  Lunatic Asylum)   SU 561 095   100202

WINCHESTER
County Hospital   SU 470 290   100551
Peninsula Barracks Hospital   SU 477 285   100444
Royal Hampshire County Hospital   SU 471 292   100446
St Paul's Hospital (New Winchester Union
  Workhouse)   SU 476 298   100512
Victoria Hospital for Infectious Diseases   SU 503 294   100204
Winchester College Sanatorium   SU 481 287   100445
Winchester Girls' School Sanatorium   SU 503 293   100213

WINCHFIELD
Hartley Wintney Union Workhouse   SU 781 541   100210

YATELEY
Yateley Cottage Hospital   SU 822 598   100211

HEREFORD AND WORCESTER

BROMSGROVE
All Saints' Hospital (Bromsgrove Union
  Workhouse)   SO 965 716   100597
Barnsley Hall Hospital (Second
  Worcestershire County Lunatic Asylum)   SO 961 726   100631
Blackwell Convalescent Home, Birmingham
  and Midland Counties   SO 980 720   100767
Bromsgrove Cottage Hospital   SO 969 706   100637
Hill Top Hospital (Bromsgrove, Droitwich
  and Redditch JHB Isolation Hospital)   SO 948 698   100630

BROMYARD AND WINSLOW
Bromyard Cottage Hospital   SO 655 548   100520

BURGHILL
St Mary's Hospital (Hereford County and
  City Lunatic Asylum)   SO 482 432   100207

DODDENHAM
Knightwick Sanatorium (Worcestershire
  King Edward VII Sanatorium)   SO 734 566   100662

DROITWICH SPA
Highfield Hospital   SO 899 629   100657
St John's Nursing Home (Droitwich Cottage
  Hospital; St John's Brine Baths Hospital)   SO 903 631   100628

EVESHAM
Evesham Community Hospital (Evesham
  Union Workhouse)   SP 037 430   100661
Evesham Hospital (Evesham Cottage Hospital)   SP 037 430   100802

GREAT MALVERN
Malvern Community Hospital (Malvern
  Hospital)   SO 781 460   100261

HEREFORD
Hereford County Hospital (Hereford Union
  Workhouse)   SO 515 402   100205
Hereford General Hospital (Hereford
  General Infirmary)   SO 514 394   100203
Tupsley Hospital (Hereford Infectious
  Diseases Hospital)   SO 534 395   100209
Victoria Eye Hospital (Victoria Eye and
  Ear Hospital)   SO 505 400   100206

KIDDERMINSTER
Kidderminster General Hospital (Kidderminster Infirmary; Kidderminster
  and District General Hospital)   SO 825 769   100633
Kidderminster General Hospital (Kidderminster Union Workhouse)   SO 822 764   100627

KINGTON
Kington Cottage Hospital (Victoria Cottage
  Hospital)   SO 300 569   100516
Kington Union Workhouse   SO 298 558   100515

LEDBURY
Ledbury Cottage Hospital   SO 708 379   100286

LEOMINSTER
Leominster Community Hospital
  (Leominster Cottage Hospital)   SO 496 585   100518
Old Priory Hospital (Leominster Union
  Workhouse)   SO 499 593   100517

MALVERN WELLS
St Wulstan's Hospital (Great Malvern
  Emergency Hospital)   SO 783 413   100763

PERSHORE
Pershore Cottage Hospital   SO 949 453   100626

POWICK
Powick Hospital (County and City of
  Worcester Lunatic Asylum)   SO 820 507   100247

REDDITCH
Avondale Day Hospital (Smallwood Hospital)   SP 041 678   100629

ROSS-ON-WYE
Dean Hill Hospital (Ross Union Workhouse)   SO 600 239   100521
Ross-on-Wye Cottage Hospital   SO 605 241   100184

STRETTON SUGWAS
Stretton Sugwas Nursing Home (Hereford
  and Weobley RDC Isolation Hospital)   SO 471 438   100208

UPTON UPON SEVERN
Upton upon Severn Union Workhouse   SO 855 400   100522
Wolverley and Cookley: Lea Castle Hospital   SO 852 792   100658

WORCESTER
Ophthalmic Institution (Ophthalmic Hospital)   SO 848 553   100635
Worcester Eye Hospital (Worcester City and
  County Eye Hospital)   SO 846 561   100636
Worcester Royal Infirmary, Castle Street
  Branch (Worcester Infirmary; Worcester
  General Infirmary)   SO 846 562   100656
Worcester Royal Infirmary, Newtown Branch
  (Worcester Hospital for Infectious
  Diseases)   SO 876 549   100651
Worcester Royal Infirmary, Ronkswood
  Branch   SO 871 552   100632
Worcester Union Workhouse   SO 857 550   100646

HERTFORDSHIRE

ABBOTS LANGLEY
Abbots Langley Hospital and Leavesden
  Hospital Annexe (St Pancras Industrial
  School)   TL 102 012   101187
Leavesden Hospital (Metropolitan Asylum
  for Imbeciles; Leavesden Mental Hospital)   TL 103 017   101186

BISHOP'S STORTFORD
Bishop's Stortford and District Hospital
  (Bishop's Stortford Cottage Hospital)   TL 488 222   101514
Herts and Essex Hospital (Bishop's Stortford
  Union Workhouse; Haymeads Institution)   TL 500 209   101343

BUSHEY
Bushey and District Hospital (Bushey Heath
  Cottage Hospital)   TQ 151 945   101516

CHESHUNT
Cheshunt Cottage Hospital   TQ 355 029   101338

COLNEY HEATH
Hill End Hospital (Hertfordshire County
  Asylum)   TL 176 067   101236

HARPENDEN
Harpenden Memorial Hospital (Harpenden
  Auxiliary Hospital and Memorial
  Nursing Centre)   TQ 136 147   101238

Sanatorium for Consumptive Children
(National Children's Home and
Orphanage Sanatorium) TL 132 151 101998
Hemel Hempstead: Bennet's End Hospital
(Hemel Hempstead Joint Isolation
Hospital) TL 068 064 101233
Hemel Hempstead Union Workhouse TL 061 079 101075
King's College Hospital Convalescent Home
(West Hertfordshire Infirmary) TL 060 079 101519
West Hertfordshire Hospital (West
Hertfordshire Infirmary) TL 061 079 101520
West Hertfordshire Infirmary TL 050 090 101518
HERTFORD
East Herts Hospital (Hertford and Ware
Isolation Hospital) TL 350 130 101340
Hertford County Hospital (Hertford
General Infirmary) TL 319 126 101339
Hertford Union Workhouse TL 344 131 100920
HITCHIN
North Hertfordshire and South Bedford-
shire Hospital (North Hertfordshire
and South Bedfordshire Infirmary) TL 182 293 101513
LETCHWORTH
Letchworth Hospital TL 225 323 101512
Rosehill Hospital (Letchworth and Hitchin
Isolation Hospital) TL 208 309 101999
LONDON COLNEY
Cell Barnes Hospital (Cell Barnes Mental
Colony) TL 174 061 101237
Napsbury Hospital (Middlesex County Asylum) TQ 165 038 101222
POTTERS BAR
Potters Bar Hospital TL 258 010 101057
ROYSTON
Royston and District Hospital TL 350 410 101523
Royston Cottage Hospital TL 350 410 101517
Royston Isolation Hospital TL 364 413 102802
SHENLEY
Shenley Hospital (Middlesex County Mental
Hospital) TQ 184 007 101239
ST ALBANS
St Albans and Mid-Hertfordshire Hospital
and Dispensary (St Albans Dispensary) TL 147 069 101515
St Albans and Mid-Herts Hospital (St Albans
Dispensary; St Albans and Mid-Herts
Hospital and Dispensary) TL 144 076 101235
St Albans City Hospital (Sisters' Hospital) TL 144 080 101234
St Albans City Hospital (St Albans Union
Workhouse) TL 144 080 100683
ST STEPHEN
Harperbury Hospital (Middlesex Colony for
Mental Defectives) TL 174 017 101240
WATFORD
Holywell Hospital (Watford Joint Isolation
Hospital) TQ 093 949 101230
Watford and District Peace Memorial Hospital TQ 105 968 101231
Watford Cottage Hospital TQ 109 962 101144
Watford General Hospital (Watford Union
Workhouse; Shrodells Hospital) TQ 105 957 101232
WELWYN
Queen Victoria Memorial Hospital TL 225 159 101511
Victoria Cottage Hospital, Codicote Road TL 220 160 101521
Victoria Cottage Hospital, Elm Gardens TL 220 160 101522

HUMBERSIDE

BEVERLEY
Beverley Cottage Hospital (Beverley Cottage
Hospital and Dispensary) TA 037 398 102033
Westwood Hospital (Beverley Union
Workhouse) TA 027 395 102108
BRANDESBURTON
Brandesburton Hospital (Brandesburton
Hall Institution for the Mentally
Defective; Brandesburton Hall Hospital) TA 112 478 102109
BRIDLINGTON
Avenue Hospital TA 170 678 102114
Bempton Lane Hospital (Bridlington
Municipal Sanatorium) TA 180 691 102678
Lloyd Hospital (Lloyd Cottage Hospital
and Dispensary) TA 177 671 102115
COTTINGHAM
Castle Hill Hospital (Cottingham
Tuberculosis Sanatorium; Castle Hill
Sanatorium) TA 029 325 102106
Castle Hill Hospital (Hull City Hospital for
Infectious Diseases) TA 026 324 102107
De La Pole Hospital (Hull Borough Asylum;
Hull City Mental Hospital) TA 025 316 102105

DRIFFIELD
Alfred Bean Hospital TA 034 585 102111
Driffield Cottage Hospital (now Ten Gables
Nursing Home) TA 031 583 102112
East Riding General Hospital (Driffield
Union Workhouse) TA 033 585 102110
Northfield Hospital (East Riding County
Isolation Hospital; now Northfield Manor
Nursing Home) TA 022 880 102113
GOOLE
Bartholomew Hospital SE 739 231 102034
Holland House Nursing and Residental
Home (Goole Joint Isolation Hospital) SE 749 255 102675
St John's Hospital (Goole Union Workhouse) SE 742 239 102224
GRIMSBY
Grimsby and District Hospital TA 265 097 102485
Grimsby Corporation Isolation Hospital for
Infectious Diseases (Scartho Sanatorium) TA 256 056 102680
Grimsby Maternity Hospital TA 270 090 102570
Laceby Smallpox Hospital TA 220 056 102679
HORNSEA
Hornsea Children's Convalescent Home TA 205 487 102104
Hornsea Cottage Hospital (Hornsea and
District War Memorial Hospital) TA 204 481 102103
HOWDEN
Howden RDC Isolation Hospital SE 755 285 102676
IMMINGHAM
Immingham Hospital (Immingham
Isolation Hospital) TA 192 150 102677
KINGSTON UPON HULL
Citadel Hospital (Garrison Hospital) TA 100 280 102674
Community Mental Health Centre (Hull and
Sculcoates Dispensary) TA 093 292 102093
Evan Fraser Hospital TA 098 330 102673
Hull Borough Lunatic Asylum (Hull and
East Riding Refuge) TA 280 280 102577
Hull Maternity Hospital (Hull Sanatorium;
Hull City Hospital) TA 130 295 102094
Hull Royal Infirmary (Hull General Infirmary) TA 093 290 102424
Hull Royal Infirmary (Hull Workhouse;
Western General Hospital) TA 084 289 102092
Kingston General Hospital (Sculcoates
Union Workhouse; Beverley Road
Institution) TA 091 301 102097
Newland Homes (Port of Hull Sailors'
Orphan Cottage Homes) TA 082 317 102098
Princess Royal Hospital (Hull Royal
Infirmary, Sutton Annexe) TA 135 326 102096
Tilworth Grange Hospital TA 130 323 102095
Townend Maternity Home (Hull Hospital
for Women) TA 070 317 102099
Victoria Hospital for Sick Children TA 087 291 102091
PATRINGTON
Patrington Union Workhouse TA 310 227 102101
Winestead Hall Hospital (Winestead Colony) TA 297 259 102100
SCUNTHORPE
Brumby Hospital (Brumby Isolation
Hospital) SE 900 097 102666
Scunthorpe General Hospital (Scunthorpe
War Memorial Hospital) SE 890 100 102576
Scunthorpe Maternity Hospital
(Scunthorpe Council Maternity Home) SE 900 097 102605
WALKINGTON
Broadgate Hospital (East Riding Lunatic
Asylum; East Riding Mental Hospital) TA 016 379 102032
WITHERNSEA
Withernsea Hospital and Withernsea Health
Centre (Hull and East Riding
Convalescent Home and Sanatorium) TA 342 277 102102

ISLE OF WIGHT

MEDINA
Frank James Memorial Hospital (Cowes
Cottage Hospital) SZ 500 950 100808
NEWPORT
Whitecroft Hospital SZ 490 880 100810
RYDE
Royal Isle of Wight County Hospital SZ 590 920 100750
VENTNOR
Royal National Hospital for Consumption
and Diseases of the Chest SZ 547 769 102758

KENT

ASHFORD
Ashford Cottage Hospital TR 012 431 101322
Ashford Hospital TR 002 431 101323

Ashford Isolation Hospital TR 003 440 101132
Willesborough Hospital (East Ashford
Union Workhouse) TR 034 423 101321
AYLESFORD
Preston Hall Hospital (Preston Hall
Sanatorium) TQ 728 581 102795
BENENDEN
Benenden Hospital (Benenden Sanatorium) TQ 834 352 102793
BIRCHINGTON
St Mary's Convalescent Home TR 300 690 101430
BOBBING
Keycol Hill Hospital (Sittingbourne and
Milton Joint Hospital for Infectious
Diseases) TQ 873 645 102790
BROADSTAIRS AND ST PETERS
Yarrow Home for Convalescent Children
(now Thanet Technical College) TR 393 673 101148
CANTERBURY
Kent and Canterbury Hospital, Ethelbert Road TR 155 563 101137
Kent and Canterbury Hospital, Longport
Street (General Kent and Canterbury
Hospital) TR 154 576 101139
Mount Hospital (Canterbury City Sanatorium) TR 178 582 101178
Nunnery Fields Hospital (Canterbury Union
Workhouse) TR 150 567 101136
St Martin's Hospital (Canterbury Borough
Lunatic Asylum; Stone House Asylum) TR 167 577 101177
CHARTHAM
St Augustine's Hospital (Second Kent
County Lunatic Asylum) TR 116 542 101176
CHATHAM
All Saints' Hospital (Medway Union
Workhouse; Medway Hospital) TQ 763 670 100687
Chatham Convalescent Home TQ 750 640 101431
Melville Hospital TQ 759 687 101410
COXHEATH
Linton Hospital (Maidstone Union Workhouse) TQ 744 509 101221
CRANBROOK
Passmore Edwards Convalescent Home for
the Metropolitan Hospital TQ 770 360 101432
DARENTH
Darenth Park Hospital (Darenth Asylum for
Imbeciles and Schools for Imbecile
Children; Darenth Park Colony) TQ 571 730 101217
Southern Hospital (Gore Farm Smallpox
Camp; Southern Convalescent Hospital) TQ 568 723 101218
DARTFORD
Bexley Hospital (First LCC Asylum; Bexley
Heath Asylum) TQ 515 727 101206
Bow Arrow Hospital (Dartford and District
Infectious Diseases Hospital) TQ 556 743 101215
Joyce Green Hospital TQ 546 760 101208
Livingstone Hospital TQ 548 738 101207
Long Reach Hospital TQ 550 773 101210
Orchard Hospital TQ 543 768 101209
West Hill Hospital (Dartford Union
Workhouse; King Edward Hospital) TQ 538 743 101216
DEAL
North Barracks Hospital (Royal Military
Hospital) TR 375 517 90875
Royal Marines School of Music, East Barracks
(Royal Naval Hospital) TR 376 513 101317
Victoria Hospital (Deal and Walmer War
Memorial Hospital) TR 368 522 101316
DOVER
Dover Infectious Diseases Hospital TR 306 419 102792
Royal Victoria Hospital (Dover Hospital) TR 314 418 101318
DOWNSWOOD
West Kent General Hospital TQ 764 559 101437
EASTRY
Betteshanger Cottage Hospital TR 308 545 101426
EDENBRIDGE
Edenbridge and District Cottage Hospital TQ 440 460 101428
Edenbridge and District War Memorial
Hospital TQ 445 454 101427
FAVERSHAM
Faversham Cottage Hospital TR 015 613 101433
FOLKESTONE
Alfred Bevan Memorial Convalescent Home
(Beach Rocks Hospital) TR 200 350 101438
Folkestone Borough Sanatorium for
Infectious Diseases TR 230 300 102794
Royal Victoria Hospital (Victoria Hospital) TR 222 366 101319
GILLINGHAM
Medway Hospital (Royal Naval Hospital) TQ 770 676 101366

GRAVESEND
Gravesend and North Kent Hospital
(Gravesend Hospital) — TQ 644 743 — 101368
St James's Hospital (Gravesend and Milton
Union Workhouse) — TQ 644 736 — 100686

HAWKHURST
Hawkhurst Cottage Hospital (Hawkhurst
Village Hospital) — TQ 745 307 — 101429

HERNE BAY
Herne Hospital (Blean Union Workhouse) — TR 176 652 — 101179
Passmore Edwards Convalescent Home for
Friendly Societies — TR 170 670 — 101435
Passmore Edwards Convalescent Home for
Railwaymen — TR 190 680 — 101434
Queen Victoria Memorial Hospital (Queen
Victoria Memorial Cottage Hospital) — TR 188 679 — 101436

HOTHFIELD
Lakeside Court Nursing Home (West
Ashford Union Workhouse) — TQ 968 464 — 101324

LENHAM
Kent County Sanatorium — TQ 924 523 — 101325

LEYBOURNE
Leybourne Grange (Leybourne Grange
Colony for Mental Defectives) — TQ 677 594 — 101223

LYMINGE
St Mary's Hospital (Elham Union Workhouse) — TR 167 393 — 101320

MAIDSTONE
Kent County Ophthalmic and Aural Hospital
(Kent County Ophthalmic Hospital) — TQ 764 558 — 101220

MARGATE
Danepark Nursing Home (Princess Mary's
Hospital for Children; Princess Mary's
Convalescent Home) — TR 361 709 — 101143
Margate Cottage Hospital — TR 356 704 — 101145
Royal Sea Bathing Hospital (Margate
Infirmary for the Relief of the Poor;
Royal Sea Bathing Infirmary) — TR 343 705 — 101142
Thanet District Hospital (Margate and
District General Hospital) — TR 360 698 — 101146
Westbrook Day Centre (Westgate Day
Hospital and Victoria House) — TR 337 702 — 101138

PEMBURY
Pembury Hospital (Tonbridge Union
Workhouse; Kent County Hospital) — TQ 615 413 — 100689

RAMSGATE
Haine Hospital (Isle of Thanet JHB
Isolation Hospital) — TR 362 677 — 101147
Ramsgate Hospital (Seamen's Infirmary;
Ramsgate Seamen's Infirmary and
General Hospital) — TR 377 646 — 101149

ROCHESTER
Fort Pitt Military Hospital — TQ 750 675 — 100722
St Bartholomew's Hospital — TQ 752 678 — 101365
St William's Hospital (Chatham and Roch-
ester Joint Infectious Diseases Hospital) — TQ 748 666 — 101367

ROYAL TUNBRIDGE WELLS
Kent and Sussex Hospital — TQ 582 399 — 101357
Tunbridge Wells General Hospital — TQ 584 398 — 101538
Tunbridge Wells Homoeopathic Hospital
(Tunbridge Wells Homoeopathic
Hospital and Dispensary) — TQ 583 394 — 101358

SEVENOAKS
Emily Jackson Hospital (Children's Hospital
for the Treatment of Hip Disease) — TQ 526 552 — 101356
Sevenoaks Hospital (Holmesdale Cottage
Hospital) — TQ 531 566 — 101354
Sevenoaks Isolation Hospital — TQ 519 529 — 101355

SHEERNESS
Sheerness Military Hospital — TQ 916 749 — 100919

SITTINGBOURNE
Sittingbourne Memorial Hospital — TQ 907 631 — 101439

STONE
Stone House Hospital (City of London
Lunatic Asylum) — TQ 561 741 — 101214

SWANLEY
Hospital Convalescent Home (Parkwood
Convalescent Home) — TQ 530 680 — 101440
White Oak Hospital (White Oak School) — TQ 525 685 — 101597

TONBRIDGE
Tonbridge Cottage Hospital (Tonbridge UD
Infectious Diseases Hospital) — TQ 592 447 — 102791
Queen Victoria Cottage Hospital — TQ 584 452 — 101442

WHITSTABLE
Whitstable and Tankerton Hospital
(Whitstable and Tankerton Cottage
and Convalescent Hospital) — TR 125 668 — 101180

WILMINGTON
Kettlewell Convalescent Home — TQ 530 730 — 101441

WROTHAM
Cecil Cragg Cottage Hospital — TQ 620 590 — 101443

LANCASHIRE

ACCRINGTON
Accrington Victoria Hospital (Accrington
Cottage Hospital) — SD 769 293 — 102447

BILLINGTON
Brockhall Hospital (Brockhall Certified
Institution for Mental Defectives;
Brockhall Inebriates Reformatory) — SD 700 365 — 102619

BLACKBURN
Blackburn and East Lancashire Royal
Infirmary (Blackburn General Infirmary) — SD 679 267 — 102429
Park Lee Hospital (Blackburn Fever
Hospital; Blackburn Hospital) — SD 685 265 — 102720

BLACKPOOL
Blackpool Health Centre (Blackpool
Hospital; Blackpool Victoria Hospital) — SD 321 356 — 102552
Blackpool Victoria Hospital — SD 333 364 — 102545
Devonshire Road Hospital (Blackpool
Sanatorium) — SD 316 370 — 102722

BURNLEY
Burnley Victoria Hospital — SD 851 342 — 102444
Marsden Hospital (Burnley JHB Sanatorium;
Burnley JHB Infectious Diseases Hospital) — SD 854 352 — 102721

CHORLEY
Chorley and District Hospital (Chorley
Dispensary; Chorley Cottage Hospital
and Dispensary) — SD 593 178 — 102551

CLITHEROE
Clitheroe Hospital (Clitheroe Union
Workhouse) — SD 755 430 — 100732

ELSWICK
Elswick Hospital (Fylde, Preston and
Garstang Joint Smallpox Hospital;
Lancaster CC Sanatorium) — SD 430 381 — 102723

FLEETWOOD
Fleetwood Hospital (Fleetwood Cottage
Hospital) — SD 328 482 — 102540

FYLDE
Lytham Hospital (Lytham Cottage Hospital;
Lytham East Beach Hospital) — SD 376 274 — 102446
St Anne's Hospital (St Anne's War Memorial
Hospital) — SD 333 299 — 102445

HASLINGDEN
Rossendale General Hospital (Haslingden
Union Workhouse; Moorland House PLI) — SD 797 225 — 100731

HEATH CHARNOCK
Heath Charnock Hospital (Chorley JHB
Infectious Diseases Hospitals; Chorley
JHB Infectious Diseases Hospital and
Sanatorium) — SD 609 156 — 102724

LANCASTER
Beaumont Hospital (Lancaster and District
JHB Central Isolation Hospital) — SD 474 636 — 102693
Lancaster Moor Hospital (Lancashire
County Lunatic Asylum) — SD 494 614 — 102622
Royal Albert Hospital (Asylum for Idiots
and Imbeciles of the Northern
Counties; Royal Albert Asylum) — SD 476 600 — 102624
Royal Lancaster Infirmary — SD 477 610 — 102442

LYTHAM ST ANNE'S
Manchester Children's Hospital
Convalescent Home — SD 312 297 — 102541

MORECAMBE AND HEYSHAM
Queen Victoria Hospital (Queen Victoria
Cottage Hospital) — SD 439 644 — 102544

NELSON
Reedyford War Memorial Hospital
(Reedyford Hall Auxiliary Military
Hospital) — SD 857 387 — 102543

ORMSKIRK
Brandreth Hospital (Ormskirk Dispensary
and Cottage Hospital) — SD 413 089 — 102539
Ormskirk and District General Hospital
(Ormskirk Union Workhouse) — SD 421 080 — 100736

PENDLE
Christiana Hartley Maternity Home (Colne
Jubilee Cottage Hospital; Colne
Maternity Home) — SD 874 401 — 102448
The Hartley Hospital — SD 916 409 — 102449

PRESTON
Bushell's Hospital (Bushell's House) — SD 550 360 — 102542
Deepdale Isolation Hospital (Preston Urban
and Port Sanitary District Isolation
Hospital) — SD 547 311 — 102694
Preston Royal Infirmary (Preston House
of Recovery; Preston and County of
Lancaster Queen Victoria Royal Infirmary) — SD 545 302 — 102443
Sharoe Green Hospital (Preston Union
Workhouse) — SD 539 318 — 100737

RUFFORD
Rufford Hospital (Rufford New Hall;
Rufford Sanatorium) — SD 455 164 — 92181

SCARISBRICK
New Hall Hospital (New Hall Isolation
Hospital) — SD 373 144 — 102383

WESTBY-WITH-PLUMPTONS
Fylde JHB Infectious Diseases Hospital — SD 386 305 — 102692

WHALLEY
Calderstones Hospital (Calderstones
Certified Institution for Mental Defectives) — SD 723 375 — 102620

WHITTINGHAM
Whittingham Hospital (Fourth Lancashire
County Lunatic Asylum) — SD 568 358 — 102623

WILPSHIRE
Langho Centre (Langho Epileptic Colony) — SD 690 339 — 102621

WRIGHTINGTON
Wrightington Hospital (Wrightington Hall) — SD 530 105 — 102691

LEICESTERSHIRE

ASHBY-DE-LA-ZOUCH
Ashby-de-la-Zouch and District Hospital
(Ashby-de-la-Zouch and District Cottage
Hospital) — SK 386 168 — 100785

DESFORD
Desford Hall Convalescent Home — SK 470 030 — 100787

HINCKLEY
Hinckley and District Hospital (Hinckley
Cottage Hospital) — SK 429 937 — 100788

KIBWORTH HARCOURT
Kibworth Hall Hospital (Kibworth Hall) — SP 680 950 — 83762

KIRBY MUXLOE
Roundhill Maternity Hospital — SK 525 040 — 100196

LEICESTER
Faire Hospital — SK 586 048 — 100789
Fielding Johnson Hospital (Leicester Private
Hospital) — SK 591 037 — 102001
Groby Road Hospital (Leicester Isolation
Hospital) — SK 565 063 — 100665
Leicester Frith Hospital (Leicester Frith
Institution; Glenfrith Hospital) — SK 555 068 — 100818
Leicester General Hospital (Leicester Union
Infirmary; North Evington Infirmary) — SK 622 039 — 100885
Leicester Royal Infirmary (Leicester Infirmary) — SK 586 035 — 100289
Towers Hospital (Leicester Borough Asylum) — SK 618 061 — 100792
Westcotes Maternity Hospital (Westcotes
Grange) — SK 573 039 — 100790

LOUGHBOROUGH
Loughborough General Hospital
(Loughborough and District General
Hospital and Dispensary) — SK 538 197 — 100784
Regent Hospital (Loughborough Union
Workhouse) — SK 525 204 — 100714

LUTTERWORTH
Lutterworth Cottage Hospital (Fielding
Palmer Cottage Hospital) — SP 547 847 — 100711

MARKET BOSWORTH
Bosworth Park Infirmary (Bosworth Park) — SK 408 033 — 100775

MARKET HARBOROUGH
Market Harborough and District Hospital
(Market Harborough Cottage Hospital
and Nursing Association) — SP 727 882 — 100779

MARKFIELD
Markfield Sanatorium (Leicestershire
Sanatorium and Isolation Hospital;
now Markfield Islamic Foundation and
Markfield Court) — SK 493 088 — 100659

MELTON MOWBRAY
Framland Nursing Home (Melton and
Belvoir Joint Isolation Hospital;
Framland Hospital) — TF 854 089 — 100666
Melton and District War Memorial Hospital
(Wyndham Lodge) — SK 752 185 — 100780
St Mary's Hospital (Melton Mowbray Union
Workhouse) — SK 759 193 — 100713

MOUNTSORREL
Mountsorrel Cottage Hospital and Convalescent Home — SK 586 142 — 100781

NARBOROUGH
Carlton Hayes Hospital (Leicestershire and Rutland County Asylum; Narborough Asylum) — SK 537 984 — 100791

OAKHAM
Catmose Vale Hospital (Oakham Union Workhouse) — SK 862 093 — 100712
Rutland Cottage Hospital (Rutland Memorial Cottage Hospital) — TF 854 089 — 100668

WOODHOUSE
Empitts Convalescent Home — SK 520 140 — 100786
Swithlands Convalescent Home — SK 520 140 — 100782
Zachary Merton Convalescent Home — SK 520 140 — 100783

LINCOLNSHIRE

BOSTON
Boston General Hospital (Boston Cottage Hospital; Boston Hospital) — TF 329 434 — 102555

BOURNE
Bourne Hospital (Bourne Rural District Isolation Hospital) — TF 102 189 — 102728

BRACEBRIDGE HEATH
St John's Hospital (Lincolnshire County Asylum; Bracebridge Asylum) — SK 981 676 — 102247

CAISTOR
Caistor Hospital (Caistor House of Industry; Caistor Union Workhouse) — TA 012 013 — 100837

GAINSBOROUGH
Foxby Hill Hospital (Gainsborough Infectious Diseases Hospital) — SK 821 885 — 102729
Gainsborough Union Workhouse (subsequently Oakdene) — SK 819 885 — 100838
John Coupland Hospital — SK 808 913 — 102433

GRANTHAM
Grantham Hospital — SK 914 368 — 102554

GRIMSBY
Grimsby District General Hospital (Grimsby Union Workhouse; Scartho Road Institution) — TA 263 073 — 100841

HORNCASTLE
Horncastle Cottage Hospital — TF 266 703 — 102434
Horncastle War Memorial Hospital (Horncastle Public Dispensary; Horncastle War Memorial Cottage Hospital) — TF 261 698 — 102435

HUNDLEBY
Swan Memorial Cottage Hospital — TF 392 662 — 102559

LINCOLN
Lincoln County Hospital (The New Lincoln County Hospital) — SK 987 718 — 102431
Lincoln County Hospital (now Lincoln Theological College) — SK 976 718 — 102430
Lincoln General Dispensary — SK 970 710 — 102558
St George's Hospital (Lincoln City Hospital; Lincoln City Hospital and Dawber Sanatorium) — SK 964 730 — 102730

LOUTH
Louth Hospital (Louth and District Hospital and Dispensary) — TF 320 800 — 102556

MABLETHORPE AND SUTTON
Lincolnshire Seaside Convalescent Home — TF 513 845 — 102590

SKEGNESS
Derbyshire Miners' Convalescent Home — TF 658 574 — 91077
Skegness and District Hospital (Skegness Cottage Hospital) — TF 561 634 — 102436
National Deposit Friendly Society Convalescent Home (now Skegness Town Hall) — TF 560 630 — 102589

SLEAFORD
Rauceby Hospital (Kesteven County Asylum; Rauceby Mental Hospital) — TF 041 440 — 102553

SPALDING
The Johnson Hospital — TF 246 224 — 102437

STAMFORD
Stamford and Rutland Hospital (Stamford and Rutland General Infirmary) — TF 037 075 — 15576

WILLINGHAM
Reynard Hospital (Willingham Hospital) — SE 872 844 — 102557

WOODHALL SPA
Alexandra Hospital (Alexandra Cottage Hospital) — TF 198 632 — 102438

MERSEYSIDE

BEBINGTON
Clatterbridge Hospital, North Site (Wirral Joint Fever Hospital) — SJ 321 823 — 102402
Clatterbridge Hospital, South Site (Wirral Union Workhouse) — SJ 320 821 — 102401
Port Sunlight Cottage Hospital (now Sunlight Lodge Nursing Home) — SJ 338 848 — 102482

BIRKENHEAD
Birkenhead and Wirral Children's Hospital (Wirral Hospital and Dispensary for Sick Children) — SJ 312 881 — 102609
Birkenhead General Hospital (Birkenhead Borough Hospital) — SJ 313 893 — 102510
Birkenhead Maternity Hospital — SJ 320 880 — 102594
St Catherine's Hospital (Birkenhead Union Workhouse) — SJ 318 875 — 102406
St James's Hospital (Birkenhead CB Infectious Diseases Hospital) — SJ 293 897 — 102711

FORMBY
Shaftesbury House — SD 298 064 — 102389

HAYDOCK
Haydock Cottage Hospital — SJ 560 960 — 102524

HESWALL
Royal Liverpool Children's Hospital (Royal Liverpool Country Hospital for Children) — SJ 260 820 — 102593

HOYLAKE
Hoylake Cottage Hospital Trust (Hoylake and West Kirby Queen Victoria Memorial Cottage Hospital) — SJ 223 897 — 102483

LIVERPOOL
Bootle Royal Borough Hospital (Bootle Borough Hospital) — SJ 336 948 — 102388
Broadgreen Hospital (Highfield Infirmary; Highfield Sanatorium) — SJ 404 909 — 102382
Brownlow Hill Infirmary (Liverpool Parish Workhouse) — SJ 357 902 — 100746
City Hospital North (Netherfield Institution for Infectious Diseases; Netherfield Road Hospital) — SJ 353 924 — 102707
David Lewis Northern Hospital — SJ 339 911 — 102478
Dental Hospital, Pembroke Place — SJ 340 900 — 102591
Fazakerley Hospital, North Site (City Hospital) — SJ 380 972 — 102379
Fazakerley Hospital, South Site (Fazakerley Sanatorium; Aintree Hospital) — SJ 380 969 — 102380
Hahnemann Hospital (now Hahnemann Building) — SJ 355 897 — 102397
Hospital for Cancer and Skin Diseases (The Liverpool Radium Institute; now Josephine Butler House, North Site) — SJ 356 898 — 102398
Hospital for Cancer and Skin Diseases (Lying-In Hospital and Dispensary; now Josephine Butler House, South Site) — SJ 356 898 — 102252
Hospital for Consumption — SJ 354 900 — 102396
Liverpool Central Home for District Nurses — SJ 358 892 — 102399
Liverpool Convalescent Institution — SJ 422 863 — 102525
Liverpool Dental Hospital, Mount Pleasant (Liverpool Dispensary for Diseases of the Teeth) — SJ 352 901 — 102390
Liverpool Eye and Ear and Throat Infirmary (Liverpool Eye and Ear Infirmary) — SJ 356 898 — 102248
Liverpool Fever Hospital — SJ 357 902 — 102708
Liverpool Hospital for Women — SJ 340 900 — 102608
Liverpool Infirmary — SJ 357 904 — 102377
Liverpool Lock Hospital — SJ 340 900 — 102606
Liverpool Lunatic Asylum — SJ 340 900 — 102616
Liverpool Maternity Hospital — SJ 357 900 — 102378
Liverpool Northern Hospital, Great Howard Street — SJ 338 912 — 102479
Liverpool Northern Hospital, Leeds Street — SJ 337 916 — 102480
Liverpool Royal Infirmary — SJ 358 905 — 35826
Liverpool Royal Lunatic Asylum — SJ 340 900 — 102615
Lying-In Hospital — SJ 357 903 — 102366
Mill Road Maternity Hospital (West Derby Union Workhouse) — SJ 363 915 — 102391
Mossley Hill Hospital (Mossley Hill Ministry of Pensions Hospital) — SJ 385 875 — 102517
Olive Mount Hospital (Olive Mount Children's Convalescent Hospital; Olive Mount Children's Hospital) — SJ 395 898 — 102522
Park Hill Hospital (Park Hill House; Liverpool Temporary Infectious Diseases Hospital) — SJ 359 872 — 102712
Rathbone Hospital (City Hospital East) — SJ 393 905 — 102392
Royal Liverpool Children's Hospital, Eaton Road — SJ 404 919 — 102387
Royal Liverpool Children's Hospital, Myrtle Street (Liverpool Infirmary for Children; Royal Liverpool Children's Hospital, City Branch) — SJ 357 898 — 102249
Royal Southern Hospital (Southern Hospital) — SJ 350 888 — 102476
St Paul's Eye Hospital — SJ 338 909 — 102250
Seaforth Barracks Hospital — SJ 327 973 — 102384
Sefton General Hospital (Toxteth Park Union Workhouse) — SJ 378 888 — 102393
Sir Alfred Jones Memorial Hospital — SJ 404 845 — 102394
Slater Street Infirmary (now Liverpool Palace) — SJ 349 900 — 69328
Southern Hospital (Southern and Toxteth Hospital) — SJ 349 392 — 102477
Stanley Park Hospital (Stanley Park Hospital for the Diseases of the Chest and Women) — SJ 347 933 — 102607
Tuebrook Villa Mental Hospital (Tuebrook Villa) — SJ 380 910 — 102595
Women's Hospital (Liverpool Samaritan Hospital for Women) — SJ 358 897 — 102253
Walton Hospital (West Derby Union Workhouse) — SJ 358 954 — 102381

MAGHULL
Maghull Homes — SD 369 011 — 102400

SOUTHPORT
North of England Children's Sanatorium — SD 347 174 — 102523
Promenade Hospital — SD 338 179 — 102251
Fleetwood Road Hospital (Homoeopathic Cottage Hospital) — SD 353 192 — 102521
Southport General Infirmary — SD 349 162 — 102385
Southport General Infirmary, North-East Site (Christiana Hartley Maternity Hospital) — SD 349 163 — 102386

ST HELENS
Cowley Hill Hospital (The Hollies) — SJ 510 950 — 102592
Rainhill Hospital (Third Lancashire County Lunatic Asylum; West Derby Lunatic Asylum) — SJ 493 928 — 102009
St Helens Hospital (St Helens Cottage Hospital) — SJ 522 940 — 102481

WALLASEY
Leasowe Hospital (Leasowe Hospital for Crippled Children) — SJ 262 915 — 102710
Manor House Hospital (Liverpool Homes for Aged Mariners and Widows of Seamen; John Davies Memorial Infirmary for Aged Mariners) — SJ 315 927 — 102508
Victoria Central Hospital — SJ 309 917 — 102405
Victoria Central Hospital, North-East Site (Highfield; Highfield Maternity Hospital) — SJ 306 916 — 102404
Victoria Central Hospital, South-West Site (Mill Lane Hospital) — SJ 306 915 — 102403
Victoria Cottage Hospital (Seacombe Cottage Hospital) — SJ 320 880 — 102596
Wallasey Cottage Hospital — SJ 296 925 — 102484

WHISTON
Whiston Hospital (Prescot Union Workhouse; Whiston PLI) — SJ 479 919 — 100741

WIRRAL
Heswall Sanatorium (West Derby Union, Liverpool Parish and Toxteth Park Township Joint Sanatorium; Cleaver Sanatorium) — SJ 257 824 — 102709

NORFOLK

ATTLEBOROUGH
Wayland Union Infirmary (Wayland Union Infirmary) — TM 030 961 — 100528

AYLSHAM
St Michael's Hospital (Aylsham Union Workhouse) — TG 184 266 — 100554

CROMER
Cromer and District Hospital — TG 225 414 — 100469
Fletcher Hospital (Fletcher Convalescent Home) — TG 219 414 — 100410

DITCHINGHAM
All Hallows Country Hospital — TM 330 910 — 100804

EAST DEREHAM
Dereham Hospital (Central Isolation Hospital) — TF 992 143 — 100559

GIMINGHAM
Mundesley Hospital (Mundesley Sanatorium) — TG 297 365 — 100409

GREAT AND LITTLE PLUMSTEAD
Little Plumstead Hospital (Little Plumstead Mental Deficiency Colony) — TG 309 108 — 100544

GREAT YARMOUTH
Estcourt Hospital (Yarmouth Isolation Hospital) — TG 527 086 — 100448
Gorleston Cottage Hospital — TM 525 039 — 100443
Gorleston Isolation Hospital — TG 515 032 — 100449
Northgate Hospital (Great Yarmouth Union Workhouse) — TG 524 084 — 100126

Royal Artillery Barracks Hospital TG 527 059 100214
Royal Hospital (Yarmouth Hospital) TG 526 073 100200
St Nicholas's Hospital (Royal Naval Hospital) TG 527 064 36915

GRESSENHALL
Gressenhall House of Industry (now Museum
of Rural Life) TF 974 169 100532

HELLESDON
Hellesdon Hospital (Norwich City Asylum) TG 199 119 100570

HIGH KELLING
Bramblewood Sanatorium Chapel (now All
Saints' District Church) TG 104 398 100563
Kelling Hospital (Kelling Sanatorium) TG 097 397 100560
Pine Heath Hospital (Children's Sanatorium
for the Treatment of Phthisis) TG 105 397 100561
Thornfield Hall Care Home for the Elderly
(Voewood; Kelling Place) TG 098 398 100562

KING'S LYNN
King's Lynn Union Workhouse (now North-
West Norfolk Health Authority Offices) TF 627 196 100530
West Norfolk and King's Lynn Hospital
(West Norfolk and Lynn Hospital) TF 624 196 100557

MORLEY
Wymondham College (77th USAAF Station
Hospital; 231st USAAF Station Hospital) TM 075 984 100529

NORTH WALSHAM
North Walsham and District War Memorial
Cottage Hospital TG 285 294 100805

NORWICH
Bethel Hospital TG 227 084 100336
Colman Hospital (Jenny Lind Hospital) TG 213 075 100552
Norfolk and Norwich Eye Infirmary TG 226 077 100555
Norfolk and Norwich Hospital TM 225 079 100525
West Norfolk Hospital (Norwich Isolation
Hospital) TG 209 088 100553
West Norwich Hospital, North (Norwich
Workhouse) TM 209 090 100526

SHOTESHAM
Shotesham Infirmary TM 239 991 100571

SWAFFHAM
Swaffham Cottage Hospital TF 821 093 100558

SWAINSTHORPE
Vale Hospital (Henstead Union Workhouse) TG 212 012 100545

THETFORD
Thetford Cottage Hospital TL 872 832 100527

THORPE ST ANDREW
St Andrew's Hospital (Norfolk County
Lunatic Asylum) TG 279 086 100458

WELLS-NEXT-THE-SEA
Wells and District Cottage Hospital (Wells
Cottage Hospital) TF 890 430 100803

NORTH YORKSHIRE, see under YORKSHIRE
(NORTH YORKSHIRE)

NORTHAMPTONSHIRE

BRACKLEY
Brackley Cottage Hospital SP 588 373 100344

DAVENTRY
Danetre Hospital (Daventry Union
Workhouse) SP 574 619 100507

HOLCOT
Brixworth RDC Isolation Hospital SP 787 691 100415

KETTERING
Kettering and District General Hospital
(Kettering General Hospital) SP 858 789 100457
Kettering Hospital for Infectious Diseases
(now Rockingham Paddocks) SP 866 808 100416
St Mary's Hospital (Kettering Union
Workhouse) SP 870 780 100456

NORTHAMPTON
Kingsthorpe Grange Nursing Home
(Northampton Borough Infectious
Diseases Hospital) SP 749 644 100459
Northampton Borough Tuberculosis Hospital
(Kingsthorpe UDC Infectious Diseases
Hospital) SP 737 645 100460
Northampton General Hospital
(Northampton General Infirmary) SP 762 604 100411
Royal Victoria Dispensary SP 757 603 100506
St Andrew's Hospital (Northampton General
Lunatic Asylum) SP 770 605 100470
St Edmund's Hospital (Northampton Union
Workhouse) SP 764 610 100471

OUNDLE
Oundle Infectious Diseases Hospital TL 129 878 100414

Oundle School Sanatorium TL 037 887 100413
Oundle Union Workhouse TL 036 887 83285

RUSHDEN
Rushden Hospital (Rushden House
Sanatorium) SP 959 659 100399

STAVERTON
Daventry Rural District Isolation Hospital SP 548 610 100437

THRAPSTON
Thrapston Union Workhouse SP 995 782 100473

UPTON
St Crispin's Hospital (Northamptonshire
County Asylum; Berry Wood Asylum) SP 712 611 100438

WELLINGBOROUGH
Isebrook Hospital (Wellingborough Union
Workhouse; Park Hospital) SP 898 675 100452
Southwood House (Wellingborough Cottage
Hospital) SP 891 671 100451
Wellingborough Infectious Diseases Hospital SP 898 687 100453

NORTHUMBERLAND

ALNWICK
Alnwick Infirmary NU 192 130 102318
Alnwick Union Workhouse NU 190 128 102319

ASHINGTON
Ashington Hospital (Ashington Hospital and
Infirmary) NZ 275 874 102309
North Seaton Hospital (Ashington UDC
Infectious Diseases Hospital) NZ 279 859 102310

BERWICK-UPON-TWEED
Berwick Infirmary NU 998 534 102316
Berwick-upon-Tweed Union Workhouse NU 997 534 102317
Berwick-upon-Tweed Barracks Hospital NU 001 530 102254

BLYTH
Blyth PSA Infectious Diseases Hospital NZ 300 825 102311
Thomas Knight Memorial Hospital (now
Thomas Knight Nursing Home) NZ 315 815 102312

CHOLLERTON
Barrasford Sanatorium (Newcastle upon
Tyne and Northumberland Sanatorium) NY 923 767 102687

CORBRIDGE
Bridge End Maternity Hospital NY 989 640 102270
Charlotte Straker Cottage Hospital (now
Charlotte Straker House) NY 988 647 102269

HALTWHISTLE
Haltwhistle War Memorial Hospital
(Haltwhistle and District War Memorial
Hospital) NY 705 641 102273

HEBRON
Northgate Hospital (St Andrew's Colony;
Northgate and District Hospital) NZ 186 878 102302

HEXHAM
Hexham General Hospital (Hexham Union
Workhouse; Hexham Emergency Hospital) NY 941 640 102271
Hexham War Memorial Hospital (St
Wilfrid's; Hexham and District War
Memorial Hospital) NY 936 635 102272
Lough Lane Hospital (Hexham
Convalescent Home) NY 930 640 102597

MORPETH
Morpeth Cottage Hospital (Loansdean
Cottage Hospital) NZ 198 849 102308
Morpeth Cottage Hospital (now Wansbeck
House) NZ 194 863 102305
Morpeth Isolation Hospital NZ 187 848 102307
Morpeth Union Workhouse NZ 196 862 102306
St George's Hospital (Northumberland
Pauper Lunatic Asylum; Northum-
berland County Mental Hospital) NZ 202 870 102304

PONTELAND
Ponteland Hospital (Castle Ward Union
Workhouse; Ponteland PLI) NZ 165 733 102357

PRUDHOE
Prudhoe Hospital (Prudhoe Hall Colony) NZ 106 619 102267

ROTHBURY
Coquetdale Cottage Hospital (Coquet
House) NU 054 016 102313
Rothbury Union Workhouse (now
Silverton House and Lodge) NU 063 012 102314

SLALEY
Wooley Hospital (Wooley Sanatorium) NY 966 596 102268

STANNINGTON
St Mary's Hospital (Gateshead Borough
Lunatic Asylum; Stannington Hospital) NZ 181 811 102631
Stannington Children's Hospital
(Stannington Sanatorium) NZ 188 819 102303

NOTTINGHAMSHIRE

BALDERTON
Newark Municipal Isolation Hospital (now
The Firs) SK 823 532 102727

EAST RETFORD
East Retford Cottage Hospital (East Retford
Dispensary; now Whitehall Youth Centre) SK 700 800 38240
Retford Hospital (Retford and District
Hospital) SK 700 800 102583

MANSFIELD
Forest Hospital (Mansfield Corporation
Forest Fever Hospital) SK 557 602 102726
Harlow Wood Orthopaedic Hospital SK 550 572 102614
Mansfield and District Hospital (Mansfield
and Mansfield Woodhouse District
Hospital; Mansfield General Hospital) SK 538 614 102451
Ransom Hospital (Nottinghamshire CC
Ransom Sanatorium) SK 575 596 102725

NEWARK
Newark Dispensary SK 800 530 102453
Newark Hospital (Newark Town and District
Hospital and Dispensary) SK 801 535 102452

NEWSTEAD
Newstead Hospital (Newstead Sanatorium) SK 543 551 100669

NOTTINGHAM
Basford Hospital (Basford RDC Infectious
Diseases Hospital) SK 556 441 102078
City Hospital SK 567 440 102072
City Hospital, West Site (Nottingham
Epidemic Hospital; Heathfield Hospital) SK 563 440 102073
Free Hospital for Sick Children (Russell
House) SK 570 400 102582
Mapperley Hospital (Nottingham Borough
Lunatic Asylum; Nottingham City Mental
Hospital) SK 588 427 102635
Nottingham and Midland Eye Infirmary
(now Nottingham Family Health Services
Authority) SK 567 398 102077
Nottingham General Dispensary SK 570 400 102584
Nottingham General Hospital SK 568 397 102075
Nottingham General Hospital (Children's
Hospital) SK 568 398 102076
Nottingham Women's Hospital SK 570 400 102610

SOUTHWELL
Southwell Parish Workhouse (now Baptist
Chapel) SK 699 535 100717

UPTON
Southwell Union Workhouse (Thurgarton
Incorporation Workhouse; subseqeuntly
Greet House) SK 711 542 100716

WORKSOP
Kilton Hospital (Worksop Union Infirmary) SK 594 803 100897
Worksop Victoria Hospital (Worksop Jubilee
Cottage Hospital) SK 593 803 102450

OXFORDSHIRE

ABINGDON
Abingdon Cottage Hospital SU 495 974 100396
Abingdon Hospital (Abingdon Joint
Isolation Hospital) SU 484 970 100395

BANBURY
Horton General Hospital (Horton Infirmary;
Horton Infirmary and Peace Memorial
Hospital) SP 456 396 100343
Niethrop Hospital (Banbury Union
Workhouse) SP 447 411 100386

BICESTER
Bicester Community Hospital (Bicester
Cottage Hospital) SP 580 223 100454

BIX AND ASSENDON
Smith Hospital (Henley and Hambledon
Rural Districts Isolation Hospital; now
Smith School) SU 746 843 100585

BURFORD
Burford Community Hospital (Burford
Cottage Hospital) SP 249 122 100547

CHIPPING NORTON
Chipping Norton and District War Memorial
Hospital SP 314 274 100616
Cotshill Hospital (Chipping Norton Union
Workhouse) SP 317 275 83991

CHOLSEY
Fairmile Hospital (Berkshire, Reading and
Newbury Lunatic Asylum) SU 598 860 100397

DIDCOT
Didcot Hospital (Didcot and District Hospital) SU 513 897 100392

GARSINGTON
Oxford Corporation Isolation Hospital — SP 563 023 — 100439

GREAT FARINGDON
Faringdon Health Centre (Faringdon Cottage Hospital) — SU 283 946 — 100394

HENLEY-ON-THAMES
Townlands Hospital (Henley Workhouse) — SU 756 828 — 100615

LITTLEMORE
Littlemore Hospital (Oxford County and City Pauper Lunatic Asylum) — SP 536 023 — 100523

OXFORD
Churchill Hospital — SU 544 058 — 100583
East Oxford Health Centre (Oxford Incorporation Workhouse; Cowley Hospital) — SP 532 058 — 100455
John Radcliffe Hospital (Manor House; Osler Pavilion) — SP 542 075 — 100510
Nuffield Orthopaedic Centre (Wingfield Convalescent Home; Wingfield Morris Orthopaedic Hospital) — SU 547 065 — 100508
Radcliffe Infirmary (Radcliffe Infirmary and Oxford Eye Hospital) — SU 509 071 — 100612
Rivermead Rehabilitation Centre (Oxford Isolation Hospital) — SP 520 039 — 100440
Slade Hospital (Oxford Corporation Hospital for Infectious Diseases) — SP 554 052 — 100441
Warneford Hospital (Warneford Asylum; Radcliffe Asylum) — SP 542 062 — 100584

THAME
Thame Community Hospital (Victoria Nursing Home; Victoria Cottage Hospital) — SU 712 056 — 100442
Thame Union Workhouse (now Rycotewood College) — SP 701 064 — 100509

WALLINGFORD
Wallingford Hospital (Herbert Morrell Cottage Hospital; Morrell Memorial Hospital) — SU 605 888 — 100390

WANTAGE
Wantage Hospital (Wantage Cottage Hospital) — SU 403 880 — 100393

WATLINGTON
Watlington Community Hospital (Watlington Farm; Watlington and District Hospital) — SU 695 940 — 100614
Watlington Cottage Hospital — SU 690 945 — 100613

SHROPSHIRE

BARROW
King Edward VII Memorial Sanatorium — SO 654 979 — 102737

BASCHURCH
Baschurch Convalescent Home (Florence House; Baschurch Cripples' Home) — SJ 420 210 — 101539

BERRINGTON
Berrington War Hospital (Atcham Union Workhouse; now Shropshire Health Authority Offices) — SJ 539 076 — 101298

BRIDGNORTH
Bridgnorth and South Shropshire Infirmary — SO 715 934 — 101391

BROSELEY
Lady Forester Memorial Hospital (Broseley Cottage Hospital) — SJ 679 014 — 101389

ELLESMERE URBAN
Ellesmere Community Care Centre (Ellesmere Cottage Hospital) — SJ 398 349 — 101305

GOBOWEN
Shropshire Orthopaedic Hospital (Baschurch Home; Robert Jones and Agnes Hunt Orthopaedic Hospital) — SJ 305 323 — 101303

MARKET DRAYTON
Market Drayton Cottage Hospital — SJ 673 337 — 101307

MUCH WENLOCK
Lady Forester Community Hospital (Lady Forester Memorial Hospital) — SJ 622 007 — 101390

NEWPORT
Annabella, Lady Boughey Cottage Hospital — SJ 740 190 — 101540

OSWESTRY
Oswestry Cottage Hospital (Oswestry and Ellesmere Cottage Hospital; now Holbache House) — SJ 287 297 — 101302

OSWESTRY RURAL
Oswestry Union Workhouse (Oswestry Incorporation Workhouse) — SJ 289 279 — 101304

PREES
Prees Higher Heath Isolation Hospital (now Chesmere Boarding Kennels and Cattery) — SJ 563 365 — 101306

SHIFNAL
Shifnal Hospital (Shifnal Union Workhouse; now Park Court) — SJ 748 072 — 37504

SHREWSBURY
Monkmoor Isolation Hospital (Shrewsbury and Atcham Joint Isolation Hospital) — SJ 514 139 — 101310
Royal Salop Infirmary (Salop Infirmary; now Parade Shopping Centre) — SJ 494 126 — 101300
Shrewsbury School Sanatorium — SJ 482 123 — 101297
Shropshire Eye, Ear and Throat Hospital — SJ 491 123 — 101301
Royal Shrewsbury Hospital (Salop and Montgomery Counties Pauper Lunatic Asylum; Bicton Asylum) — SJ 461 130 — 101299

WELLINGTON
Wellington Cottage Hospital (The Bowring Memorial Cottage Hospital) — SJ 644 111 — 101388

WHITCHURCH URBAN
Whitchurch Cottage Hospital — SJ 545 419 — 101308
Whitchurch Hospital (Whitchurch Union Workhouse; Deermoss Hospital) — SJ 545 420 — 101309

SOMERSET

AXBRIDGE
St John's Hospital (Axbridge Union Workhouse; subsequently St John's Court) — ST 428 545 — 100605
St Michael's Cheshire Home (St Michael's Free Home for Consumptives) — ST 440 548 — 100653

BISHOPS LYDEARD
Sandhill Park Hospital — ST 156 298 — 100497
Tone Vale Hospital (Somerset County Asylum) — ST 168 273 — 100255

BRIDGWATER
Blake Hospital (Bridgwater Union Workhouse) — ST 297 373 — 100432
Bridgwater and District General Hospital (Bridgwater Infirmary) — ST 302 370 — 100496

BURNHAM-ON-SEA AND HIGHBRIDGE
Burnham-on-Sea War Memorial Hospital — ST 307 493 — 100770

BUTLEIGH
Butleigh Hospital (Sir George Bowles Hospital; Butleigh Cottage Hospital) — ST 520 331 — 100774

CHARD TOWN
Chard and District Cottage Hospital — ST 320 080 — 100771
Chard and District Hospital (Chard Union Workhouse) — ST 331 087 — 100429

COSSINGTON
Somerset CC Isolation Hospital — ST 350 400 — 102757

CREWKERNE
Crewkerne Hospital — ST 438 094 — 100491

DUNSTER
Dunster Cottage Hospital (Dunster Village Hospital) — SO 989 436 — 100772

EDINGTON
Edington Cottage Hospital — ST 382 394 — 100495

FROME
Selwood Hospital (Frome Union Workhouse; now Ecos Court) — ST 770 475 — 100573
Victoria Hospital (Victoria Hospital and Nursing Home) — ST 773 477 — 100603

MINEHEAD
Minehead and West Somerset Hospital — SS 970 463 — 100493

SELWORTHY
Minehead and Williton Isolation Hospital — SS 931 458 — 100428

SHEPTON MALLET
Norah Fry Hospital (Shepton Mallet Union Workhouse) — ST 612 434 — 100606
Shepton Mallet District Hospital — ST 620 630 — 100604
St Peter's Hospital (Shepton Mallet Isolation Hospital) — ST 606 436 — 100574

ST CUTHBERT OUT
Mendip Hospital (Somerset County Lunatic Asylum; Somerset and Bath Lunatic Asylum) — ST 571 465 — 100158

TAUNTON
Cheddon Road Hospital (Taunton Borough Isolation Hospital) — ST 228 264 — 100427
Musgrove Park Hospital — ST 314 243 — 100435
Taunton and Somerset Hospital — ST 235 245 — 100431
Trinity Hospital (Taunton Union Workhouse) — ST 236 244 — 100492

WELLINGTON
Wellington and District Hospital (Wellington and District Cottage Hospital) — ST 139 203 — 100773

WELLS
Priory Hospital (Wells Union Workhouse) — ST 540 455 — 100575
Wells and District Hospital (Wells Cottage Hospital) — ST 557 461 — 100768

WINCANTON
Verrington Hospital (Wincanton Rural District Isolation Hospital) — ST 704 289 — 100430

Wincanton and East Somerset Memorial Hospital — ST 715 285 — 100778
Wincanton and East Somerset Memorial Hospital (old) — ST 710 280 — 100777
Wincanton Cottage Hospital — ST 710 280 — 100776

YEOVIL
Summerlands Hospital (Yeovil Union Workhouse) — ST 545 165 — 100488
Yeovil District Hospital — ST 555 163 — 100490
Yeovil Municipal Maternity Home (Yeovil General Dispensary) — ST 552 165 — 100489

SOUTH YORKSHIRE, see under YORKSHIRE (SOUTH YORKSHIRE)

STAFFORDSHIRE

BAGNALL
Highlands Hospital (North Staffordshire Joint Smallpox Hospital; Bagnall Isolation Hospital) — SJ 925 505 — 102732

BARTON-UNDER-NEEDWOOD
Barton-under-Needwood Cottage Hospital — SK 187 182 — 101472

BERKSWICH
Sister Dora Convalescent Hospital — SJ 960 210 — 101475

BIDDULPH
Biddulph Grange Orthopaedic Hospital (now Biddulph Grange) — SJ 892 592 — 92178

BRERETON AND RAVENHILL
Rugeley Hospital (Rugeley District Hospital and Dispensary) — SK 048 173 — 102042

BURNTWOOD
St Matthew's Hospital (Second Staffordshire County Asylum; Burntwood Asylum) — SK 077 095 — 101405

BURTON UPON TRENT
Burton District Hospital (Burton upon Trent Union Workhouse) — SK 234 244 — 101407
Burton on Trent General Hospital (Burton General Infirmary) — SK 246 228 — 101408

CANNOCK CHASE
White Lodge Community Unit (White Lodge) — SJ 970 100 — 102043

CHEDDLETON
St Edward's Psychiatric Hospital (Staffordshire County Asylum; Cheddleton Hospital) — SJ 974 535 — 101575

HAMMERWICH
Hammerwich Hospital (Hammerwich Cottage Hospital) — SK 058 081 — 101476

KINVER
Prestwood Chest Hopital (Prestwood House; Prestwood House Sanatorium) — SO 864 862 — 102736

LEEK
Alsop Memorial Cottage Hospital — SJ 986 566 — 102255
Moorlands Hospital (Leek Union Workhouse) — SJ 995 562 — 100879

LICHFIELD
Lichfield Victoria Hospital — SK 112 088 — 101474
Lichfield Victoria Nursing Home and Cottage Hospital (Lichfield Victoria Nursing Home) — SK 112 088 — 101473
St Michael's Hospital (Lichfield Union Workhouse) — SK 126 098 — 100877

LOGGERHEADS
Cheshire Joint Sanatorium — SJ 735 355 — 102733

LONGTON
Longton Cottage Hospital — SJ 900 430 — 101580

NEWCASTLE-UNDER-LYME
Newcastle-under-Lyme Borough Infectious Diseases Hospital — SJ 847 454 — 102734

RUGELEY
Rugeley Home and Cottage Hospital — SK 040 180 — 101471

STAFFORD
Coton Hill Hospital (Coton Hill Institution for the Insane) — SJ 934 237 — 101598
Staffordshire General Infirmary (Stafford General Infirmary) — SJ 919 237 — 101409
St George's Hospital (Staffordshire County Asylum) — SJ 924 238 — 101583

STOKE-ON-TRENT
Bucknall Hospital (Hanley, Stoke and Fenton Joint Infectious Diseases Hospital) — SJ 910 480 — 101124
Burslem, Haywood and Tunstall War Memorial Hospital — SJ 874 511 — 101478
City General Hospital (Stoke upon Trent Union Workhouse; Wolstanton and Burslem Union Workhouse) — SJ 858 452 — 101402
Hartshill Orthopaedic Hospital (Longfield House; North Staffordshire Cripples' Aid Society Orthopaedic Hospital) — SJ 863 456 — 101403

Haywood Hospital (now Burslem Technical College Annexe)	SJ 876 499	101477
Longton Cottage Hospital	SJ 900 430	101581
Longton Cottage Hospital (now Mount Pleasant Mission Chapel)	SJ 900 430	101580
North Staffordshire Infirmary, Etruria	SJ 874 473	101444
North Staffordshire Infirmary, Hartshill (The Dispensary and House of Recovery; North Staffordshire Infirmary and Eye Hospital)	SJ 876 454	101404
Stanfield Hospital (Stanfield Isolation Hospital; Stanfield Sanatorium)	SJ 873 511	102731
Wolstanton and Burslem Union Workhouse	SJ 867 531	100861

STONE

Trent Hospital (Stone Union Workhouse)	SJ 899 338	102044

SWYNNERTON

Stone JHB Infectious Diseases Hospital	SJ 872 333	102735

TAMWORTH

Tamworth General Hospital (Tamworth Cottage Hospital)	SK 208 052	101406

YOXALL

Meynell Ingram Cottage Hospital	SK 145 188	101479

SUFFOLK

ALDEBURGH

Aldeburgh Cottage Hospital, High Street	TM 466 566	100000
Aldeburgh Cottage Hospital, Park Road	TM 460 565	100001

BARHAM

Barham Isolation Hospital	TM 122 510	100004
Bosmere and Claydon Road Infectious Diseases Hospital	TM 122 510	100003
Bosmere and Claydon Union Workhouse (Barham House of Industry)	TM 122 512	100002

BECCLES

Beccles and District War Memorial Hospital	TM 421 899	100006
Beccles Cottage Hospital	TM 424 904	100005
Beccles Isolation Hospital	TM 428 902	100007
Beccles Fever Hospital (now The Manse)	TM 426 896	100046

BLYTHBURGH

Blythburgh and District Hospital (Bulcamp House of Industry)	TM 440 762	100008

BURY ST EDMUNDS

Isolation Hospital	TL 859 625	100012
Isolation Hospital (now Laurel House)	TL 864 629	100011
Pest House (now Holywell Cottage)	TL 852 631	100014
St Mary's Hospital (Thingoe Union Workhouse)	TL 847 638	100009
West Suffolk CC Emergency Hospital for Infectious Diseases (now Highbury House)	TL 850 640	100015
West Suffolk CC Sanatorium	TL 869 634	100013
West Suffolk General Hospital (Ordnance Depot; Suffolk General Hospital)	TL 850 638	100010

CARLTON COLVILLE

Lowestoft BC Smallpox Hospital (The Sanatorium)	TM 504 892	100045

CLARE

Clare and Bumpstead JHB Infectious Diseases Hospital (later Knights Farm)	TL 754 450	100016

EYE

Hartismere Hospital (Hartismere Union Infirmary)	TM 143 739	100017

FELIXSTOWE

Bartlet Hospital (Bartlet Convalescent Home)	TM 310 347	100019
Felixstowe General Hospital (Croydon Cottage Hospital for Felixstowe and Walton)	TM 307 348	100018
Suffolk Convalescent Home (Suffolk Convalescent Home and Sea Bathing Infirmary)	TM 290 342	100020

FOXHALL

Ipswich CB Sanatorium for Pulmonary Tuberculosis	TM 215 437	100033

FRAMLINGHAM

Framlingham Infirmary for Infectious Diseases	TM 289 629	100080

HADLEIGH

Hadleigh and District Cottage Hospital	TM 027 422	100022

HALESWORTH

Patrick Stead Hospital	TM 390 780	100023
Town Farmhouse (Isolation Hospital; Pesthouse Farm)	TM 393 780	100024

HAVERHILL

Haverhill UD Infectious Diseases Hospital	TL 667 448	100026

HOLBROOK

Royal Hospital School (Royal Hospital School Infirmary)	TM 165 352	102801

IPSWICH

Christchurch Park Hospital (Suffolk Victoria Nursing Institute; Ipswich Nursing Home)	TL 162 450	100034
Ipswich and East Suffolk Hospital, Heath Road Wing (Ipswich Union Workhouse)	TM 192 450	100029
Ipswich Barracks Hospital	TM 159 453	100035
Ipswich Hospital, Anglesea Road Wing (East Suffolk and Ipswich Hospital and Dispensary; East Suffolk and Ipswich Hospital)	TM 150 452	100028
St Clement's Hospital (Ipswich Borough Lunatic Asylum)	TM 190 439	100036
St Helen's Hospital (Ipswich Borough Infectious Diseases Hospital)	TM 192 442	100030
Suffolk Victoria Nursing Home (Ipswich Maternity Home)	TM 165 445	100081

KEDINGTON

Risbridge Hospital (Risbridge Union Workhouse)	TL 702 470	100038

KESGRAVE

Ipswich Smallpox Hospital	TM 229 445	100032

LEISTON

Isolation Hospital	TM 453 620	100039

LOWESTOFT

Lowestoft and North Suffolk General Hospital (Lowestoft Hospital)	TM 549 934	100041
Lowestoft BC Isolation Hospital (Lowestoft Smallpox and Fever Hospital)	TM 538 935	100043
Mutford and Lothingland General Dispensary and Infirmary	TM 500 900	100084
Normanston Hospital	TM 527 933	100061
St Luke's Hospital (Empire Hotel)	TM 542 914	100044

MELTON

Phyllis Memorial Home	TM 286 511	100048
St Audry's Hospital (Melton House of Industry; Suffolk County Lunatic Asylum)	TM 283 519	100047

MILDENHALL

Mildenhall Cottage Hospital	TL 713 747	100049

NAYLAND-WITH-WISSINGTON

British Legion Sanatorium (Maltings Farm Sanatorium; now Maltings Farm)	TL 952 338	100051
Jane Walker Hospital (East of England Sanatorium; British Legion Sanatorium)	TL 950 343	100052
Pest House (now The Old Pest House)	TL 971 348	100053

NEWMARKET

Newmarket and Moulton JHB Infectious Diseases Hospital (Exning Fever Hospital)	TL 632 665	100055
Newmarket General Hospital (Newmarket Union Workhouse)	TL 639 642	100054
Rous Memorial Hospital	TL 648 634	100056

ONEHOUSE

Stow Lodge Hospital (Onehouse House of Industry)	TM 032 591	100058

OULTON

Lothingland Hospital (Oulton House of Industry)	TM 523 954	100060
Mutford and Lothingland Road Isolation Hospital (Oulton Smallpox Hospital)	TM 523 942	100059

REYDON

Southwold URD Infectious Diseases Hospital	TM 509 778	100063

SEMER

Cosford Union Workhouse (Semer House of Industry)	TM 008 452	100064

SHIPMEADOW

Shipmeadow House of Industry (now The Viewpoint)	TM 378 898	100065

SHOTLEY

HMS Ganges Royal Naval Hospital	TM 250 338	100057

SOTHERTON

Pest House (now Pest House Cottages)	TM 447 795	100068

SOUTHWOLD

Southwold Cottage Hospital (Victoria Memorial Hospital)	TM 507 764	100069

STOWMARKET

Hill House Isolation Hospital (Stowmarket UDC Infectious Diseases Hospital)	TM 042 598	100070

STRADBROKE

Hoxne Union Workhouse (now The Red House)	TM 250 732	100062

SUDBURY

St Leonard's Hospital	TL 877 414	100071

Sudbury Borough Isolation Hospital	TL 876 418	100083
Sudbury Hospital	TL 878 417	100072
Walnut Tree Hospital (Sudbury Union Workhouse)	TL 870 414	100073

TATTINGSTONE

Isolation Hospital	TM 134 374	100075
St Mary's Hospital (Tattingstone House of Industry)	TM 135 373	100074

WICKHAM MARKET

Plomesgate Union Workhouse (now Deben Court)	TM 304 556	100077

WOODBRIDGE

Infectious Diseases Hospital	TM 256 494	100078

SURREY

BANSTEAD

Netherne Hospital (Third Surrey County Lunatic Asylum; Netherne Mental Hospital)	TQ 296 563	101294

CAMBERLEY

Frimley and District Hospital (Frimley and Camberley District Hospital)	SU 880 580	101460
Ridgewood Centre (Brompton Hospital Sanatorium; Frimley Sanatorium)	SU 905 592	101401

CAPEL

Capel Cottage Hospital (Capel Village Hospital; now Broadwood)	TQ 170 400	101452

CATERHAM

Caterham and Dene Hospital (Caterham and District Hospital)	TQ 336 556	101453
Caterham Guards Depot Hospital	TQ 300 500	100916
St Lawrence's Hospital (Metropolitan Asylum for Imbeciles)	TQ 326 558	101292

CHARLWOOD

Charlwood and Horley Cottage Hospital	TQ 283 437	101462

CHELSEA AND FARLEIGH

Warlingham Hospital (Croydon Borough Lunatic Asylum; Croydon Mental Hospital)	TQ 370 590	101587

CHERTSEY

Botleys Park Hospital (Botleys Park; Botleys Park Colony for Mental Defectives)	TQ 023 651	101380

CRANLEIGH

Cranleigh Village Hospital	TQ 060 390	36301

DORKING

Dorking General Hospital (Dorking Union Workhouse)	TQ 165 487	101288

EGHAM

Royal Holloway Sanatorium	TQ 002 583	101601

ELMBRIDGE

Locke King Clinic (Weybridge Cottage Hospital)	TQ 080 640	101467
Thames Ditton Hospital (Thames Ditton Cottage Hospital)	TQ 155 673	101469
Walton-on-Thames Hospital (Walton, Hersham and Oatlands Cottage Hospital)	TQ 100 660	101470
Weybridge Hospital	TQ 073 649	101464

EPSOM AND EWELL

Epsom and Ewell Cottage Hospital	TQ 217 609	101457
Epsom College (Epsom College Sanatorium)	TQ 220 600	102760
Horton Hospital (Seventh LCC Asylum; Horton Asylum)	TQ 197 617	101283
Long Grove Hospital (Tenth LCC Asylum; Long Grove Asylum)	TQ 194 625	101284
Manor Hospital (Sixth LCC Asylum; Horton Manor Asylum)	TQ 192 615	101285
St Ebba's Hospital (LCC Epileptic Colony; Ewell Epileptic Colony)	TQ 204 626	101286
West Park Hospital (Eleventh LCC Asylum; West Park Asylum)	TQ 185 613	101282

ESHER

Cobham and District Cottage Hospital	TQ 110 607	101454
Princess Frederica's Convalescent Home	TQ 140 670	101447

FARNHAM

Black Lake Convalescent Maternity Home	SU 870 430	101448
Hale Sanatorium (Hale Convalescent Home)	SU 840 480	101445
Trimmer's Cottage Hospital	SU 840 460	101459

GUILDFORD

Royal Surrey County Hospital (Surrey County Hospital)	TQ 989 494	101458
Woodbridge Hospital (Guildford RSA Isolation Hospital; Guildford, Godalming and Woking JHB Isolation Hospital)	SU 999 505	102763
Worthing Hospital Convalescent Home	SU 990 490	101446

HAMBLEDON
King George V Hospital and Hydestile
  Hospital (Highdown Sanatorium; King
  George V Sanatorium; St Thomas's
  Hospital, Hydestile branch) SU 972 402 102761

HASLEMERE
Haslemere and District Hospital (Haslemere
  and District Cottage Hospital) SU 900 320 101461

LEATHERHEAD
Great Bookham Cottage Hospital TQ 130 540 101468
Victoria Memorial Cottage Hospital (now
  Victoria House) TQ 172 567 101287

LIMPSFIELD
Caxton Convalescent Home (now Caxton
  House) TQ 435 512 101291

MOLE VALLEY
Dorking Cottage Hospital TQ 160 480 101455

OXTED
Oxted General Hospital TQ 389 535 101290

REIGATE
Banstead Hospital (Third Middlesex County
  Lunatic Asylum) TQ 263 613 101258
East Surrey Hospital (Reigate and Redhill
  Cottage Hospital) TQ 271 502 101463
Queen Elizabeth Hospital (Queen Elizabeth
  Hospital for Sick Children) TQ 263 581 101602
Royal Earlswood Hospital (Royal Earlswood
  Asylum for Idiots) TQ 280 486 101289
Zachary Merton Convalescent Home TQ 250 590 101451

RUNNYMEDE
Chertsey Cottage Hospital TQ 040 660 101466
Egham Cottage Hospital SU 990 710 101456

STAINES
Ashford Hospital (Staines Union Workhouse) TQ 062 724 101360
Ashford Hospital, Holloway Unit (Staines
  Isolation Hospital) TQ 065 731 101361
Staines Hospital TQ 048 710 101259

WALTON AND WEYBRIDGE
Ellesmere Hospital (Metropolitan
  Convalescent Institution) TQ 093 644 101400

WITLEY
Bethlehem Convalescent Home SU 940 390 101450

WOKING
Brookwood Hospital (Second Surrey County
  Lunatic Asylum; Knaphill Asylum) SU 961 581 101586
Ottershaw Hospital (Bagshot, Chertsey,
  Walton and Weybridge Joint Isolation
  Hospital; Ottershaw Hospital for
  Infectious Diseases) TQ 028 639 102762
St Nicholas's and St Martin's Orthopaedic
  Hospital (St Nicholas Home for Crippled
  Children; Pyrford Orthopaedic Hospital) TQ 043 590 101590
St Peter's Convalescent Home TQ 019 589 101449
Victoria Cottage Hospital TQ 000 580 101465

SUSSEX (EAST SUSSEX)

BATTLE
Battle Hospital (Battle Union Workhouse) TQ 732 159 100905

BEXHILL
Bexhill Hospital TQ 743 084 101484
Metropolitan Convalescent Institution
  Home for Men TQ 730 080 101486
Metropolitan Convalescent Institution Home
  for Women TQ 730 080 101485

BRIGHTON
Bevendean Hospital (Brighton Borough
  Sanatorium) TQ 331 060 101199
Brighton Dispensary TQ 310 060 101483
Brighton General Hospital (Brighton
  Workhouse; Brighton Municipal Hospital) TV 328 052 101198
French Convalescent Home TQ 334 034 101480
John Howard Convalescent Home TQ 334 034 101482
London and Brighton Female Convalescent
  Home TQ 310 060 101481
Royal Alexandra Hospital for Sick Children
  (Hospital for Sick Children) TQ 306 048 101193
Royal Sussex County Hospital (Sussex
  County Hospital and General Sea
  Bathing Infirmary) TQ 327 039 101197
Sussex Eye Hospital TQ 327 038 101196
Sussex Throat and Ear Hospital (Brighton,
  Hove and Sussex Throat and Ear
  Dispensary) TQ 308 045 101192

EAST CHILTINGTON
Pouchlands Hospital (Chailey Union
  Workhouse) TQ 383 173 101205

EASTBOURNE
All Saints' Hospital (All Saints' Convalescent
  Hospital) TV 601 974 101489
Leaf Homoeopathic Cottage Hospital TV 619 992 101487
Princess Alice Memorial Hospital (Princess
  Alice Memorial Cottage Hospital) TV 611 997 101488
St Luke's Hospital (All Saints' Memorial
  Convalescent Hospital for Children) TV 601 972 101490
St Mary's Hospital (Eastbourne Union
  Workhouse) TV 596 994 100906

HASTINGS
Buchanan Hospital (Buchanan Cottage
  Hospital) TQ 800 101 101494
Eversfield Hospital (Eversfield Chest Hospital) TQ 791 089 102789
Hastings, St Leonard's and East Sussex
  Hospital (Hastings Infirmary; East Sussex,
  Hastings and St Leonard's Infirmary) TQ 811 091 101411
Hertfordshire Convalescent Home TQ 790 090 101491
Mount Pleasant Hospital (Hastings Borough
  Sanatorium; Mount Pleasant Sanatorium) TQ 831 110 102788
Railway Mission Convalescent Home TQ 790 090 101492
Royal East Sussex Hospital (East Sussex
  Hospital) TQ 811 094 101166
St Helen's Hospital (Hastings Union
  Workhouse) TQ 831 114 100907

HELLINGLY
Hellingly Hospital (East Sussex Asylum) TQ 598 125 101584

HOVE
Convalescent Police Seaside Home TQ 280 050 101493
Foredown Hospital (Hove Sanatorium) TQ 258 071 101201
Hove General Hospital (Brighthelmstone
  Dispensary) TQ 280 050 101202
New Sussex Hospital (New Sussex Hospital
  for Women) TQ 310 040 101203

LEWES
Victoria Hospital (Lewes Victoria Hospital
  and Dispensary) TQ 404 103 101204

NEWHAVEN
Newhaven Downs Hospital (Newhaven
  Union Workhouse) TQ 440 011 101195
Newhaven Valley Hospital (Newhaven UD
  Isolation Hospital) TQ 435 019 101194

SEAFORD
Surrey Convalescent Home for Men TV 480 990 101495
Seaside Convalescent Hospital TV 486 989 101496

SUSSEX (WEST SUSSEX)

ARUNDEL
Arundel and District Hospital TQ 011 071 101266

BOGNOR REGIS
Bailey Convalescent Home SZ 930 990 101505
Bognor Regis War Memorial Hospital SU 935 002 101263
Children's Convalescent Home for Surrey SZ 939 991 101504
Merchant Taylors' Company Convalescent
  Home for Men SZ 930 990 101506
Victorian Convalescent Home for Surrey
  Women SZ 939 989 101503
Victoria Wellesley Home for Convalescent
  Women and Girls SZ 939 991 101502

BURGESS HILL
Jewish Convalescent Home for Ladies TQ 310 190 101508

CHICHESTER
Graylingwell Hospital (West Sussex County
  Lunatic Asylum) SU 866 064 101269
Royal West Sussex Hospital (West Sussex,
  East Hampshire and Chichester Infirmary
  and Dispensary) SU 859 056 101268

CRAWLEY
Crawley and Isfield Cottage Hospital TQ 270 360 101500

CUCKFIELD
Cuckfield Hospital (Cuckfield Union
  Workhouse) TQ 308 257 101375

EASEBOURNE
King Edward VII Hospital (King Edward VII
  Sanatorium) SU 880 249 101270

EAST GRINSTEAD
Queen Victoria Hospital (Queen Victoria
  Cottage Hospital; East Grinstead Hospital) TQ 308 257 101371
Queen Victoria Hospital (Queen Victoria
  Cottage Hospital) TQ 399 392 101499

HAYWARDS HEATH
Haywards Heath Hospital (King Edward VII
  Memorial Eliot Hospital) TQ 323 240 101498
St Francis' Hospital (Sussex County Lunatic
  Asylum) TQ 336 228 101376

HORSHAM
Horsham Hospital (Horsham Cottage
  Hospital) SU 175 314 101372
Horsham Union Workhouse TQ 189 317 101373

HURSTPIERPOINT
Goddards Green Hospital (Cuckfield
  Isolation Hospital; now The Dene) TQ 289 202 101374

LITTLEHAMPTON
Littlehampton and District Hospital TQ 031 020 101267

PETWORTH
Petworth Cottage Hospital SU 970 210 101501

RUSTINGTON
Rustington Convalescent Home TQ 044 013 101264
Zachary Merton Community Hospital
  (Zachary Merton Convalescent Home) TQ 057 020 101265

STEYNING
Southlands Hospital (Steyning Union
  Workhouse) TQ 227 060 101378

WORTHING
Catherine Marsh Convalescent Home TQ 130 030 101509
Surrey County Hospital Convalescent Home TQ 130 030 101507
Worthing Hospital (Worthing Infirmary) TQ 153 031 101497

TYNE AND WEAR

BOLDON
Boldon Sanatorium (East Boldon Hospital;
  now Thorncliffe) NZ 380 605 102338
Whiteleas Hospital (Whiteleas Smallpox
  Hospital) NZ 364 630 102329

GATESHEAD
Bensham General Hospital (Gateshead
  Union Workhouse) NZ 247 612 102343
Dryden Road Hospital (Jubilee Children's
  Hospital; Gateshead Children's
  Hospital) NZ 259 615 102342
Gateshead Dispensary NZ 256 633 102497
Gateshead Nursing Association Nurses'
  Home NZ 620 260 102494
Norman's Riding Hospital (Blaydon, Ryton
  and Wickham JHC Isolation Hospital) NZ 166 608 102684
Queen Elizabeth Hospital, East Site NZ 270 606 102340
Queen Elizabeth Hospital, West Site
  (Sheriff Hill Hospital) NZ 268 604 102427
Whinney House Hospital (Whinney House) NZ 255 604 102682
Windy Nook Hospital (Felling UDC
  Isolation Hospital; now Windy Nook
  Preliminary Training School) NZ 271 606 102341

GOSFORTH
Sanderson Hospital (Home for Destitute
  Crippled Children; Sanderson
  Orthopaedic Hospital School for
  Children) NZ 233 679 102353

HEBBURN
Ellison Hall Masonic Club (Hebburn Hall;
  Hebburn Hall Accident Infirmary) NZ 311 641 102321
Hebburn Hospital (Hebburn Fever
  Hospital) NZ 307 636 102322

JARROW
Danesfield Maternity Hospital NZ 336 642 102324
Monkton Hall Hospital (Monkton Hall;
  Monkton Hall Psychiatric Hospital) NZ 319 636 37536
Palmer Memorial Hospital NZ 325 652 102320
Primrose Hill Hospital (Jarrow Fever
  Hospital) NZ 331 638 102325
River Tyne PSA Floating Hospital NZ 330 650 102328

LONGBENTON
Scaffold Hill Hospital (now Rising Sun
  Country Park, Resource Centre) NZ 302 695 102683

NEWBURN
Lemington Hospital (Newburn Isolation
  Hospital) NZ 178 654 102356

NEWCASTLE UPON TYNE
Fenham Barracks (Royal Artillery Cavalry
  and Infantry Barracks) NZ 238 652 102359
Fleming Memorial Hospital for Sick
  Children (now Fleming Business
  Centre) NZ 250 658 102256
Hospital for Sick Children, Out-Patients'
  Department NZ 252 641 102367
House of Recovery NZ 243 642 102368
Hunters Moor Hospital (Home for
  Incurables; St Mary Magdalene Home) NZ 236 657 102358
Lying-In Hospital (now Broadcasting House) NZ 251 644 102257
Newcastle Dispensary, Nelson Street NZ 243 641 102495
Newcastle Dispensary, New Bridge Street NZ 253 643 102499

Newcastle Dispensary (St John's Lodge) NZ 250 640 102500
Newcastle General Hospital (Newcastle
  upon Tyne Union Workhouse) NZ 228 645 102355
Newcastle Throat and Ear Hospital (now
  Newcastle College, Rye Hill Building) NZ 238 638 102586
Northumberland, Durham and Newcastle
  Eye Infirmary NZ 240 640 102630
Princess Mary Maternity Hospital
  (Northern Counties' Orphanage) NZ 249 660 102354
Royal Victoria Infirmary NZ 244 650 102352
St Nicholas's Hospital (Newcastle upon
  Tyne City Asylum; Coxlodge Asylum) NZ 240 680 102585
Walker Park Hospital (Walker Accident
  Hospital) NZ 291 642 102492
Walkergate Hospital (City Hospital) NZ 282 659 102301

NORTH SHIELDS
Balkwell Isolation Hospital NZ 334 687 102685
Moor Park Hospital (Moor Park Isolation
  Hospital; now Moor Park) NZ 332 693 102363
Tynemouth Victoria Jubilee Infirmary NZ 348 686 102361

SOUTH SHIELDS
Cleadon Park Sanatorium (Cleadon Park
  Infectious Diseases Hospital) NZ 382 637 102681
Deans Hospital (South Shields Fever
  Hospital) NZ 361 655 102326
Ingham Infirmary NZ 370 661 102330
South Tyneside District Hospital (South
  Shields Union Workhouse; Harton
  Institution and General Hospital) NZ 366 643 102327

SUNDERLAND
Cherry Knowle Hospital (Sunderland
  Borough Asylum) NZ 402 520 102629
Children's Centre (Children's Hospital) NZ 382 555 102335
Durham County and Sunderland Eye
  Infirmary (Sunderland and North
  Durham Eye Infirmary) NZ 395 564 102332
Grindon Hall Community Unit (Grindon
  Hall; Grindon Hall Sanatorium) NZ 362 558 102336
Hammerton House Hospital (Hammerton
  House; now Hammerton Hall) NZ 399 559 102347
Havelock Hospital, East Site (Sunderland
  Borough Infectious Diseases Hospital) NZ 365 563 102348
Havelock Hospital, West Site (Sunderland
  RDC Infectious Diseases Hospital) NZ 364 564 102349
High Barnes Home for the Aged
  (Institution for the Little Sisters of the
  Poor) NZ 375 559 102498
Monkwearmouth Hospital (Monkwearmouth
  and Southwick Hospital) NZ 394 590 102350
Ryhope General Hospital (Cherry Knowle
  Colony Emergency Hospital) NZ 405 524 102351
Sunderland Barracks Hospital NZ 407 577 102346
Sunderland District General Hospital
  (Sunderland Union Workhouse;
  Highfield Institution) NZ 480 566 102337
Sunderland Emergency Hospital
  (Sunderland Central Library) NZ 399 564 102496
Sunderland Eye Infirmary (Sir John
  Priestman Durham County and
  Sunderland Eye Infirmary) NZ 398 551 102333
Sunderland Infirmary (St Mary's School;
  now Sunderland University) NZ 391 568 102334
Sunderland Royal Infirmary (Sunderland
  Infirmary) NZ 390 565 102331

TYNEMOUTH
Preston Hospital (Tynemouth Union
  Workhouse; Tynemouth Corporation
  PAI) NZ 354 689 102362

WALLSEND
Sir G B Hunter Memorial Hospital
  (Wallsend Infirmary) NZ 301 669 102360
Willington Quay Maternity Hospital NZ 319 669 102611

WHICKHAM
Dunston Hill Hospital (Dunston Hill
  Ministry of Pensions Hospital;
  Whickham and District Hospital) NZ 220 613 102344
Whickham Cottage Nursery (Whickham
  Rectory; Whickham War Memorial
  Cottage Hospital) NZ 207 612 102345

WHITLEY BAY
Prudhoe Memorial Convalescent Home NZ 350 732 102493

WARWICKSHIRE

ALCESTER
Alcester and Feckenham RDC Infectious
  Diseases Hospital (Hertford Memorial
  Hospital and Sanatorium) SP 092 579 100277
Alcester Hospital (Alcester Union Workhouse) SP 095 577 100245

BUDBROOKE
Budbrooke Barracks Hospital SP 262 651 100278

COLESHILL
St Gerard's Children's Hospital (Warwickshire
  Orthopaedic Hospital for Children) SP 190 890 100811

HATTON
Central Hospital (Warwickshire County
  Pauper Lunatic Asylum) SP 252 670 100821
King Edward VII Memorial Sanatorium SP 255 669 100246

NUNEATON AND BEDWORTH
Manor Hospital (Nuneaton Cottage Hospital) SO354 923 100761
Nuneaton Union Workhouse SP 350 900 100908

ROYAL LEAMINGTON SPA
Royal Midlands Counties Home for
  Incurables (Midlands Counties Home
  for Incurables) SP 310 650 100820
Warneford General Hospital (Warneford
  Hospital; Warneford Leamington and
  South Warwickshire Hospital) SP 324 651 100654

RUGBY
Hospital of St Cross SP 506 744 100760
Rugby School Sanatorium SP 505 747 102749

SHIPSTON-ON-STOUR
Ellen Badger Hospital (Ellen Badger
  Memorial Hospital) SP 260 410 100762

STRATFORD-UPON-AVON
Bellevue Smallpox Hospital SP 189 555 100275
Children's Hospital (Nursing Home and
  Children's Hospital) SP 199 549 100276
Stratford-upon-Avon Hospital SP 197 552 100272
Stratford-upon-Avon Hospital (Stratford-
  upon-Avon Union Workhouse) SP 196 553 100273
Stratford-upon-Avon JHB Infectious Diseases
  Hospital SP 192 559 100274

WARWICK
Heathcote Hospital SP 314 635 100650
School Sanatorium SP 291 645 100283
South Warwickshire Hospital (Warwick
  Union Workhouse) SP 285 659 100634
Warwick Provident Dispensary and Cottage
  Hospital (Warwick Dispensary; now The
  Old Dispensary) SP 283 649 100279

WEST MIDLANDS

BIRMINGHAM
All Saints' Hospital (Birmingham Borough
  Fever Hospital) SP 049 883 102745
All Saints' Hospital (City of Birmingham
  Pauper Lunatic Asylum) SK 044 884 100824
Birmingham Accident Hospital and
  Rehabilitation Centre (Queen's Hospital) SK 062 861 100754
Birmingham and Midland Ear and Throat
  Hospital SP 090 870 100815
Birmingham and Midland Eye Hospital SP 090 870 100816
Birmingham and Midland Homoeopathic
  Hospital SP 090 870 100806
Birmingham and Midland Hospital for
  Women SP 091 835 101588
Birmingham Children's Hospital, Broad
  Street SP 065 865 100814
Birmingham Children's Hospital, Ladywood
  Road SP 055 863 101589
Birmingham Dental Hospital SP 090 870 100812
Birmingham General Hospital (The New
  Birmingham General Hospital) SK 073 874 100752
Birmingham General Hospital SK 072 877 100751
Birmingham Maternity Hospital SP 090 870 100813
Dudley Road Hospital (Birmingham Union
  Workhouse) SP 047 878 100400
East Birmingham Hospital (Birmingham
  Corporation Infectious Diseases Hospital) SP 117 867 102743
East Birmingham Hospital, Chest
  Department (Birmingham Corporation
  Infectious Diseases Hospital;
  Birmingham City Sanatorium, Yardley
  Green Hospital) SP 113 864 102742
Hollymoor Hospital (Third City of
  Birmingham Lunatic Asylum) SP 003 784 100823
Jaffray Hospital (Jaffray Suburban Hospital) SK 108 912 100766
Moseley Hall Hospital (Moseley Hall; Moseley
  Hall Convalescent Home for Children) SP 074 831 100765
Queen Elizabeth Medical Centre
  (Birmingham United Hospitals; Queen
  Elizabeth Hospital) SK 043 839 100753
Rubery Hill Hospital (Second City of
  Birmingham Lunatic Asylum) SO 992 778 100825
St Chad's Hospital SP 045 860 100025

West Heath Hospital (Kings Norton RSA
  Infectious Diseases Hospital; West
  Heath Sanatorium) SP 033 777 102744

COVENTRY
Coventry and Warwickshire Hospital SP 336 796 100667
Coventry Fever Hospital SP 336 797 100663
Gulson Road Hospital (Coventry Union
  Workhouse) SP 342 787 100715
Paybody Hospital (The Elms; Coventry and
  District Crippled Children's Guild
  Convalescent Home) SP 303 805 100755
Whitely Hospital (Coventry Isolation Hospital) SP 351 771 100664

DUDLEY
Corbett Hospital (Hill House) SO 900 852 100759
Guest Hospital (Blind Asylum) SJ 951 914 100757
Stourbridge Dispensary SO 898 842 100758

HALESOWEN
Hayley Green Hospital (Stourbridge and
  Halesowen Isolation Hospital) SO 946 819 102738

KNOWLE
Middlefield Hospital (Midland Counties
  Idiot Asylum) SP 176 756 100822

SANDWELL
Moxley Hospital (South Staffordshire Joint
  Smallpox Hospital) SO 968 950 102740

SUTTON COLDFIELD
Sutton Coldfield Hospital (Sutton Coldfield
  Cottage Hospital) SK 129 967 100764

WALSALL
Ambulance Training Centre (Pelsall Hall;
  Pelsall Hall Sanatorium, Nurse Training
  School) SK 016 033 102748
Goscote Hospital (Walsall Isolation Hospital) SK 015 018 101386
Manor Hospital (Walsall Union Workhouse) SP 003 984 101385
St Margaret's Hospital (Great Barr Hall;
  Great Barr Colony for Mental Defectives) SP 057 953 101384
Walsall and District Hospital (Walsall General
  Hospital) SP 011 980 100807
Walsall General (Sister Dora) Hospital
  (Walsall Cottage Hospital; Walsall and
  District Hospital) SP 011 980 102045
Walsall General Hospital (Walsall Borough
  Epidemic Hospital) SP 008 997 102746

WEDNESFIELD
New Cross Hospital (Wolverhampton Union
  Workhouse) SJ 935 004 101381
Wolverhampton Union Workhouse SO 925 980 101200

WEST BROMWICH
West Bromwich District Hospital SJ 001 912 100756

WOLVERHAMPTON
Bilston UD Fever Hospital SO 950 971 102741
Heath Town Isolation Hospital SO 936 994 102747
Pond Lane Community Handicap Unit
  (Wolverhampton Borough Hospital for
  Infectious Diseases) SJ 909 972 102739
Royal Hospital (South Staffordshire Hospital
  and Wolverhampton Dispensary;
  Wolverhampton and Staffordshire
  General Hospital) SO 919 982 101392
West Park Hospital (Wolverhampton
  Hospital for Women) SO 905 989 101383
Wolverhampton and Midland Counties Eye
  Infirmary (Wolverhampton Eye Infirmary) SO 906 987 101382

WEST SUSSEX, see under SUSSEX (WEST SUSSEX)

WEST YORKSHIRE, see under YORKSHIRE (WEST
YORKSHIRE)

WILTSHIRE

BRITFORD
Odstock Hospital SU 148 273 100567

CHIPPENHAM
Chippenham Hospital (Chippenham
  Cottage Hospital; Chippenham and
  District Hospital) ST 925 728 100579
Frogwell Hospital (Chippenham and
  Malmesbury Joint Isolation Hospital) ST 902 737 100581
St Andrew's Hospital (Chippenham Union
  Workhouse) ST 913 727 100607

DEVIZES
Devizes and District Hospital SU 005 617 100576
St James's Hospital (Devizes Union
  Workhouse) SU 007 616 100600

LAVERSTOCK
Salisbury and District Joint Isolation Hospital SU 146 334 100538

MALMESBURY
Malmesbury Hospital (Old Manor House;
   Malmesbury and District Hospital)   ST 935 865   100710

MARLBOROUGH
Marlborough Children's Hospital
   (Marlborough Union Workhouse;
   Children's Convalescent Home)   SU 184 695   100565
Savernake Cottage Hospital   SU 205 686   100535
Marlborough Isolation Hospital   SU 184 696   100564

MELKSHAM
Melksham Cottage Hospital   ST 908 632   100609
Melksham Cottage Hospital   ST 905 639   100608

PEWSEY
Pewsey Hospital (Pewsey Union Workhouse;
   Wiltshire CC Mental Deficiency Colony)   SU 157 603   100539

PURTON
Northview Hospital (Cricklade and Wootton
   Bassett Union Workhouse)   SU 085 874   83102

ROUNDWAY
Roundway Hospital (Wiltshire County Pauper
   Lunatic Asylum)   SU 009 599   100610

SALISBURY
Harvard Common Cold Research Centre
   (American Red Cross Field Hospital Unit;
   First General Medical Field Laboratory)   SU 139 280   100543
Old Manor Hospital (Fisherton House;
   Fisherton House Lunatic Asylum)   SU 133 303   100537
Salisbury General Infirmary   SU 141 299   100568
Tower House PLI (Alderbury Union
   Workhouse; Salisbury Union Workhouse)   SU 143 283   100542

SOUTH TIDWORTH
Tidworth Military Barracks Isolation Hospital   SU 227 484   100198
Delhi Military Hospital   SU 228 481   100197

STRATTON ST MARGARET
St Margaret's Hospital (Swindon and
   Highworth Union Workhouse)   SU 175 876   100231

SWINDON
Great Western Railway Medical Fund Hospital   SU 145 846   100341
Hawthorn Centre (Swindon Isolation
   Hospital)   SU 153 595   100595
Seymour Clinic (Swindon Corporation
   Maternity Hospital; Kingshill House)   SU 138 837   100598
Swindon Smallpox Hospital   SU 149 868   100027
Victoria Hospital (Swindon and North
   Wiltshire Victoria Cottage Hospital)   SU 138 836   100599

TROWBRIDGE
St John's Hospital (Trowbridge and District
   Joint Isolation Hospital)   ST 852 567   100577
Trowbridge Community Hospital (Adcroft
   House; Trowbridge and District Hospital)   ST 854 584   100582

WARMINSTER
Beckford Lodge Hospital   ST 878 445   100578
Warminster Community Hospital
   (Warminster Cottage Hospital)   ST 874 452   100549

WESTBURY
Prideaux Voluntary Hospital   ST 871 512   100548
Westbury and District Cottage Hospital,
   Hospital Road   ST 872 506   100601
Westbury and District Cottage Hospital,
   Westbourne Road   ST 872 512   100602

WINSLEY
Winsley Chest Hospital (Royal Victoria
   Memorial Sanatorium; Winsley
   Sanatorium)   ST 792 609   100580

WROUGHTON
Princess Alexandra's RAF Hospital (RAF
   General Hospital; Princess Alexandra
   Hospital)   SU 162 792   100640

YORKSHIRE, NORTH YORKSHIRE

AUSTWICK
Harden Bridge Hospital (Settle Rural District
   Infectious Diseases Hospital)   SD 762 676   102071

BEDALE
Mowbray Grange Hospital (Bedale Union
   Workhouse; Mowbray Grange Sanatorium)   SE 269 879   102053

CLIFTON (WITHOUT)
Clifton Hospital (North and East Riding
   Pauper Lunatic Asylum)   SE 585 525   92384

EASINGWOLD
Claypenny Hospital (Easingwold Union
   Workhouse)   SE 534 704   100863
St Monica's Hospital (St Monica's Cottage
   Hospital)   SE 520 690   102560

EMBSAY WITH EASTBY
Eastby Sanatorium and Sanatorium School
   (Bradford Union Sanatorium)   SE 025 550   102376

FULFORD
Fulford Hospital   SE 606 479   102246
Naburn Hospital (City of York Asylum)   SE 606 477   102260

GIGGLESWICK
Castleberg Hospital (Settle Union
   Workhouse; Giggleswick Institution)   SD 810 638   100864

GRASSINGTON
Grassington Hospital (Grassington
   Sanatorium)   SE 016 635   102041

HARROGATE
Harrogate and District General Hospital
   (Harrogate Infirmary)   SE 323 558   102474
Harrogate Infirmary (Harrogate Cottage
   Hospital; Harrogate Infirmary and
   Dispensary)   SE 300 550   102564
Heatherdene Convalescent Home
   (Sunderland Infirmary Convalescent
   Home)   SE 300 550   102571
Royal Bath Hospital and Rawson
   Convalescent Home   SE 294 551   102567
St Andrew's Police Convalescent Home
   (Northern Police Convalescent Home)   SE 318 553   102259

HINDERWELL
Palmer Memorial Hospital (Palmer Memorial
   Miners' Accident Hospital)   NZ 780 181   102471

KIRKBYMOORSIDE
Adela Shaw Orthopaedic Hospital (Crippled
   Children's Hospital; Yorkshire Children's
   Orthopaedic Hospital)   SE 693 865   102612

KNARESBOROUGH
Knaresborough Hospital (Harrogate and
   Knaresborough Joint Isolation Hospital;
   Harrogate, Knaresborough and
   Wetherby Joint Isolation Hospital)   SE 349 555   102655
Knaresborough Hospital (Knaresborough
   Union Workhouse)   SE 351 573   100865
Scotton Banks Hospital (Scotton Banks
   Sanatorium)   SE 335 582   102002

MALTON
Malton, Norton and District Hospital
   (Malton, Norton and District Cottage
   Hospital)   SE 781 719   102562

MOULTON
Morris Grange Nursing Home (Morris
   Grange; Morris Grange Sanatorium)   NZ 223 042   102049

NEWBY AND SCALBY
Cross Lane Hospital (Scarborough Hospital
   for Infectious Diseases; Scarborough
   Sanatorium)   TA 026 902   102058
Smallpox Hospital (Scarborough Smallpox
   Hospital; Scarborough Corporation
   Sanatorium)   TA 033 910   102059

NORTHALLERTON
Friarage Hospital (Northallerton Union
   Workhouse; Northallerton EMS Hospital)   SE 371 942   102052
Northallerton Maternity Hospital (Mount
   Pleasant Emergency Maternity Home)   SE 362 947   102566
Rutson Hospital (Northallerton Cottage
   Hospital)   SE 368 942   102051
Sandy Bank Nurses' Home (Northallerton
   Isolation Hospital)   SE 378 933   102054

RICHMOND
Richmond Cottage Hospital   NZ 173 015   102657
Richmond Victoria Hospital (Richmond
   and District Victoria Hospital)   NZ 172 013   102048

RIPON
Ripon and District Hospital (Ripon
   Dispensary; Ripon Dispensary and
   Cottage Hospital)   SE 309 712   102561
St Wilfred's Hospital (Ripon and Wath
   Rural Districts Fever Hospital)   SE 314 715   102686

SCARBOROUGH
Scarborough Cottage Hospital and
   Convalescent Home (Scarborough
   Cottage Hospital)   TA 043 889   102056
Scarborough Hospital   TA 020 885   102047
Scarborough Hospital and Dispensary   TA 031 876   102057
St Mary's Hospital (Scarborough Union
   Workhouse)   TA 039 888   102055
St Thomas's Hospital (Royal Northern Sea
   Bathing Infirmary; Royal Northern Sea
   Bathing Infirmary and Convalescent
   Home)   TA 045 885   102046

SELBY
Selby Cottage Hospital   SE 613 322   102563
Selby War Memorial Hospital   SE 607 316   102568

SHERBURN IN ELMET
Sherburn Smallpox Hospital   SE 490 330   102660

SKELTON
Fairfield Hospital (Fairfield House; Fairfield
   Sanatorium; now Fairfield Manor Hotel)   SE 570 556   102656

SKIPTON
Raikeswood Hospital (Skipton Union
   Workhouse)   SD 985 520   102070
Skipton Cottage Hospital (Skipton and
   District Cottage Hospital; Skipton and
   District Hospital)   SD 986 517   102375
Skipton General Hospital (Skipton and
   District Hospital)   SD 989 511   102374

THIRSK
Lambert Memorial Hospital   NY 429 820   102050

WHITBY
Eskdale Hospital (Whitby Urban District
   Infectious Diseases Hospital; now
   Dalewood House)   NZ 908 094   102060
St Hilda's Hospital (Whitby Workhouse)   NZ 902 105   102061
Whitby Cottage Hospital (now Whitby
   Area Health Office and Clinic)   NZ 901 121   102472
Whitby Hospital (Whitby War Memorial
   Cottage Hospital; Whitby War Memorial
   Hospital)   NZ 897 107   102473

WHIXLEY
Whixley Hospital (Whixley Inebriate Colony;
   Mid-Yorkshire Institution for the
   Mentally Defective)   SE 444 568   102370

YORK
Bootham Park Hospital (York Lunatic Asylum)   SE 610 520   60268
Bungalow Hospital (Bungalow Isolation
   Hospital)   SE 614 554   102658
City Hospital (City of York General Hospital)   SE 608 532   102296
County Hospital (subsequently Divisional
   Head Office, Yorkshire Water)   SE 608 523   102439
The Retreat   SE 620 520   60269
St Mary's Hospital (York Union Workhouse;
   The Grange Hospital)   SE 608 530   60266
Yearsley Bridge Hospital (York Fever
   Hospital)   SE 616 535   102659
York Dispensary (Gray's Dispensary)   SE 600 510   102565
York Military Hospital (Fulford Military
   Hospital)   SE 608 504   100917

YORKSHIRE (SOUTH YORKSHIRE)

ASTON CUM AUGHTON
Swallownest Hospital (South Rotherham,
   Handsworth and Kiveton Park District
   Isolation Hospital)   SK 454 860   102668

BARNSLEY
Barnsley General Hospital (Barnsley Union
   Workhouse; St Helen Hospital)   SE 332 070   102161
Beckett Hospital (Beckett Dispensary)   SE 342 067   102159
Kendray Hospital (Kendray Hospital for
   Infectious Diseases; Kendray Fever
   Hospital)   SE 361 056   102157
Lundwood Hospital (Barnsley Smallpox
   Hospital; Lundwood Smallpox Hospital)   SE 380 071   102158
Mount Vernon Hospital (Barnsley and
   Wakefield Sanatorium)   SE 349 048   102160

BRIERLEY
Brierley Common Isolation Hospital
   (Hemsworth Infectious Diseases
   Hospital; now Burntwood Sports and
   Leisure Centre)   SE 424 107   102162

CONISBROUGH
Conisbrough Hospital (Doncaster and
   Mexbrough Isolation Hospital;
   Conisbrough Isolation Hospital)   SK 523 986   102148
Denaby Main Hospital (Fullerton Hospital;
   now Fullerton House School)   SK 498 993   102147

DONCASTER
Doncaster Royal Infirmary   SE 591 041   102143
Doncaster Royal Infirmary and Dispensary
   (Doncaster Infirmary and Dispensary;
   now Doncaster Metropolitan Borough
   Council Offices)   SE 576 031   102163
St Catherine's Hospital (St Catherine's
   Institution)   SE 568 002   102145
Tickhill Road Hospital (Doncaster Isolation
   Hospital; Tickhill Road Infectious
   Diseases Hospital)   SE 566 004   102146
Western Hospital (Doncaster Union
   Workhouse)   SE 556 005   102164

ECCLESFIELD
Grenoside Grange Hospital (Wortley RDC
  Infectious Diseases Hospital) SK 334 935 102713

MEXBOROUGH
Montagu Hospital SE 475 006 102144

PENISTONE
Penistone Union Workhouse SE 244 039 100850

RAWMARSH
Rose Hill Hospital (Rawmarsh UDC Isolation
  Hospital; Rose Hill Isolation Hospital) SK 437 971 102154

ROTHERHAM
Badsley Moor Lane Hospital (Rotherham
  Isolation Hospital; Badsley Moor Lane
  Infectious Diseases Hospital) SK 444 928 102152
Badsley Moor Lane Sanatorium (Rotherham
  Smallpox Hospital; Badsley Moor Lane
  Fever Hospital) SK 447 928 102156
Doncaster Gate Hospital (Rotherham
  Hospital and Dispensary; Rotherham
  Hospital) SK 431 928 102151
Moorgate General Hospital (Rotherham
  Union Workhouse; Alma Road
  Institution) SK 430 922 102150
Rotherham District General Hospital
  (Oakwood Hall; Oakwood Hall Hospital;
  Oakwood Hall Sanatorium) SK 436 909 102149

SHEFFIELD
Children's Hospital SK 340 872 102226
Crimcar Lane Hospital SK 296 861 102667
Jessop Hospital for Women SK 345 873 102228
King Edward VII Orthopaedic Hospital
  (King Edward VII Memorial
  Institution for Crippled Children) SK 296 875 102224
Lodge Moor Hospital (Borough Smallpox
  Hospital) SK 287 860 102227
Middlewood Hospital (South Yorkshire
  Lunatic Asylum; Wadsley Hospital) SK 320 914 102230
Nether Edge Hospital (Eccleshall Bierlow
  Union Workhouse; Eccleshall Institution) SK 337 849 102229
Northern General Hospital (Sheffield Union
  Workhouse) SK 362 907 102225
Royal Hallamshire Hospital (Royal Sheffield
  Infirmary and Hospital) SK 338 870 102470
St George's Hospital (Borough Hospital for
  Infectious Diseases; City Hospital) SK 341 876 102231
Sheffield Royal Hospital (Sheffield Public
  Dispensary; Sheffield Public Hospital and
  Dispensary) SK 349 871 102441
Sheffield Royal Infirmary (Sheffield
  General Infirmary) SK 347 882 102440
Whiteley Wood Clinic (Woofindin
  Convalescent Home; Whiteley Wood
  Hospital) SK 307 852 102232

THORNE
Thorne Union Workhouse SE 682 132 102155

WATH UPON DEARNE
Wathwood Hospital (Wath, Swinton and
  District Infectious Diseases Hospital;
  Wath Wood Hospital) SK 436 993 102153

YORKSHIRE (WEST YORKSHIRE)

AIREBOROUGH
High Royds Hospital (Second West Riding
  Lunatic Asylum; Menston Asylum) SE 175 430 102627

BATLEY
Carlinghow Nursing Home (Batley and
  District Cottage Hospital; Batley and
  District Hospital) SE 237 251 102549
Oakwell Hospital (Oakwell JHB Infectious
  Diseases Hospital) SE 221 277 102637
Oakwell Smallpox Hospital SE 226 275 102636

BINGLEY
Bingley Hospital (Bingley Cottage Hospital) SE 114 393 102373

BRADFORD
Bierley Hall Hospital (Bierley Hall
  Sanatorium) SE 176 295 102642
Bradford Children's Hospital SE 152 347 102613
Bradford Royal Infirmary (Bradford
  Infirmary) SE 163 331 102457
Bradford Royal Infirmary (New Royal
  Infirmary) SE 136 345 102456
Calverley Hospital (Pudsey, Farsley,
  Calverley, Eccleshill and Idle Hospital
  for Infectious Diseases) SE 194 344 102652
Leeds Road Hospital (Bradford Fever
  Hospital; Bradford Fever and
  Smallpox Hospital; City Hospital) SE 774 330 102641

North Bierley Hospital (North Bierley Joint
  Hospital for Infectious Diseases) SE 178 270 102643
Royal Eye and Ear Hospital (Bradford Eye
  and Ear Hospital) SE 161 334 102628
St Catherine's Home (St Catherine's Home
  for Cancer and Incurables) SE 151 348 102572
St Luke's Hospital (Bradford Union
  Workhouse) SE 158 320 102316
Westwood Hospital (Westwood Institution
  for Mental Defectives) SE 123 303 102547

BRIGHOUSE
Brighouse JHB Infectious Diseases Hospital SE 151 235 102645

CASTLEFORD
Castleford, Normanton and District
  Hospital (Castleford, Normanton and
  District Cottage Hospital) SE 417 249 102550

DEWSBURY
Dewsbury and District General Infirmary SE 242 223 102455
Dewsbury General Hospital SE 238 221 102454
Mitchell Laithes Isolation Hospital
  (Dewsbury and District Joint Infectious
  Diseases Hospital) SE 259 204 102653
Staincliffe General Hospital (Dewsbury
  Union Workhouse) SE 233 228 100852
Whitley Sanatorium (Thornhill Hospital;
  Whitley Hospital) SE 229 182 102639

HALIFAX
Green Lane Hall Hospital (Green Lane
  Hall Sanatorium) SE 129 284 102040
Halifax General Hospital (Halifax Union
  Infirmary) SE 096 232 100859
Halifax Infirmary (Halifax Infirmary and
  Dispensary) SE 090 250 102263
Halifax Royal Infirmary (Halifax General
  Infirmary) SE 089 241 102458
Northowram Hospital (Northowram Hall
  Isolation Hospital) SE 110 277 102649

HEBDEN ROYD
Stoney Royd Isolation Hospital (Halifax
  Borough Fever Hospital) SE 099 241 102650

HOLME VALLEY
Holme Valley Memorial Hospital SE 144 092 102569

HUDDERSFIELD
Huddersfield Royal Infirmary (Huddersfield
  and Upper Agbrigg Infirmary) SE 141 169 102460
Mill Hill Hospital (Huddersfield
  Sanatorium for Infectious Diseases) SE 172 171 102638
St Luke's Hospital (Huddersfield Union
  Workhouse; Crosland Moor Workhouse) SE 126 154 100853

ILKLEY
Coronation Hospital (Ilkley Coronation
  Cottage Hospital; Ilkley Coronation
  Hospital) SE 123 475 102372
Grove Convalescent Hospital (Ilkley Bath
  Charity Hospital; Ilkley Hospital and
  Convalescent Home) SE 116 475 102371
Middleton Hospital (Middleton Sanatorium) SE 131 492 102025
Scalebor Park Hospital (Third West Riding
  Lunatic Asylum) SE 169 458 102626
Wharfedale Children's Hospital (Wharfedale
  Joint Isolation Hospital) SE 175 445 102035

KEIGHLEY
County Hospital (Keighley Union Infirmary) SE 049 406 100858
Keighley and District Victoria Hospital
  (Keighley Cottage Hospital) SE 060 410 102578
Keighley, Bingley and Shipley JHB Fever
  Hospital and Sanatorium (Keighley and
  Bingley JHB Infectious Diseases Hospital;
  Morton Banks War Hospital) SE 084 422 102640
Keighley Union Workhouse SE 055 408 100857

KIRKBURTON
Storthes Hall Hospital (Fourth West Riding
  Lunatic Asylum) SE 179 123 102003

LEEDS
Chapel Allerton Hospital SE 311 366 102019
Cookridge Hospital (Cookridge
  Convalescent Hospital) SE 254 390 102014
Crooked Acres Hospital SE 260 364 102026
Holbeck Union Workhouse SE 295 319 102029
Hospital for Women (Hospital for Women
  and Children) SE 294 341 102022
Hunslet Union Workhouse SE 306 317 102298
Ida and Robert Arthington Hospital (Ida
  Hospital) SE 255 389 102013
Jewish Herzl Moser Hospital (Theodor
  Herzl Memorial Home) SE 309 352 102038
Killingbeck Hospital (Killingbeck Smallpox
  Hospital; Killingbeck Sanatorium) SE 344 349 102017
Leeds Dispensary (Leeds Public Dispensary) SE 290 330 102574

Leeds General Infirmary (Leeds Infirmary) SE 297 341 102031
Leeds House of Recovery SE 315 343 102644
Leeds Infirmary SE 297 336 102062
Leeds Maternity Hospital SE 291 344 102021
Leeds School of Medicine SE 295 340 102039
Meanwood Park Hospital (Meanwood Hall
  Colony for Defectives; Meanwood Park
  Colony) SE 286 382 102020
Seacroft Hospital (Manston Smallpox Hospital;
  Manston Infectious Diseases Hospital) SE 350 345 102010
St James's University Hospital (Leeds Union
  Workhouse) SE 317 347 102018
St Mary's Hospital (Bramley Union
  Workhouse; St Mary's Infirmary) SE 256 338 102028
Wyther Infants' Hospital SE 259 347 102027

MELTHAM
Colne and Holme Valleys Joint Isolation
  Hospital SE 091 124 102651

MIRFIELD
Mirfield Memorial Hospital (Mirfield
  Memorial Cottage Hospital) SE 206 203 102548

MORLEY
Churwell Grange Isolation Hospital (Grange
  Isolation Hospital) SE 278 292 102012

OTLEY
Wharfedale General Hospital (Wharfedale
  Union Workhouse; Otley Institution) SE 198 465 102024

PONTEFRACT
Northgate Lodge Hospital (Pontefract Union
  Workhouse; Headlands Hospital) SE 456 223 102264
Pontefract General Infirmary (Pontefract
  Dispensary and Cottage Hospital) SE 458 218 102575

PUDSEY
Woodlands Convalescent Home SE 200 390 102573

ROTHWELL
Haigh Hospital (Rothwell Isolation Hospital;
  Rothwell, Methley and Hunslet Joint
  Isolation Hospital) SE 345 288 102016
Hunslet Smallpox Hospital (Rothwell Methley
  and Hunslet Joint Smallpox Hospital) SE 345 302 102030
St George's Hospital (Hunslet Union
  Workhouse; Rothwell PLI) SE 330 289 102015

SHIPLEY
Heaton Royds Hospital (Shipley and Wind-
  hill Joint Infectious Diseases Hospital) SE 138 364 102648
Sir Titus Salt's Hospital SE 140 370 102579

SOUTH ELMSALL
Warde Aldham Hospital (Warde Aldham
  Cottage Hospital) SE 466 102 102580

TODMORDEN
Fielden Hospital (Fielden Hospital for
  Infectious Diseases) SD 965 244 102037
Stansfield View Hospital (Todmorden
  Union Workhouse) SD 962 238 102265
Todmorden Hospital (Sourhall Smallpox
  Hospital; now Sourhall Road Cottages) SD 918 246 102036

WAKEFIELD
Ackton Hospital (Normanton, Castleford,
  Featherstone, Whitwood and Altofts
  Joint Isolation Hospital) SE 414 221 102654
Carr Gate Hospital (Wakefield and District
  Smallpox Isolation Hospital; Carr Gate
  Isolation Hospital) SE 314 240 102647
Clayton Hospital (Clayton Hospital and
  Wakefield Dispensary) SE 329 214 102459
Snapethorpe Hospital SE 302 198 102646
Stanley Royd Hospital (West Riding
  Pauper Lunatic Asylum) SE 337 217 102625
Wakefield Western County Hospital
  (Wakefield Union Workhouse) SE 343 207 100856

WETHERBY
Wharfe Grange Hospital (Wetherby Union
  Workhouse) SE 398 484 102023

INDEX